Interpreting the Gospels

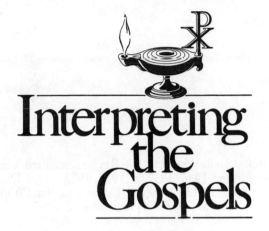

Interpreting the Gospels

Edited by

James Luther Mays

FORTRESS PRESS   Philadelphia

Library of Congress Cataloging in Publication Data

Main entry under title:

Interpreting the gospels.

"The essays . . . collected in this volume appeared originally in . . . the periodical Interpretation: a journal of Bible and theology."
1. Bible. N.T. Gospels—Criticism, interpretation, etc.—Addresses, essays, lectures. I. Mays, James Luther. II. Interpretation.
BS2555.2.I53   225.6   80–8057
ISBN 0–8006–1439–9

8287G80   Printed in the United States of America   1–1439

Contents

Foreword

Much of the cultural heritage of the civilization of which we are a part has been influenced significantly by the figure of Jesus of Nazareth. Convinced that in Jesus Christ God had visited his people in a unique and unrepeatable way, his early followers proclaimed him as crucified and risen Lord to the borders of the world they knew. That influence has continued in Western culture through the church, as well as in art, poetry, and literature. It has exerted an equal, if more subtle, influence on the political history of our world. Marxism, as has often been observed, is a secular expression of a utopian form of Christian apocalypticism. Similarly, Jesus' concern for the outcast and the needy has been given institutional expression in the programs of social welfare which have played so prominent a part in Western democracies. An understanding of Jesus of Nazareth is thus helpful, if not indispensable, for any who would understand the cultural and political tides that continue to flow in our common lives. It is to a study of the literary expression of the career of that Jesus, contained in the New Testament Gospels, that this book is devoted.

The essays on the Gospels collected in this volume appeared originally in the pages of the periodical *Interpretation: A Journal of Bible and Theology*. In accordance with the purpose of that quarterly, the essays intend to point more to the theological than to the historical dimensions of the Gospels. That the methods and results of a critically rigorous approach to Scripture are necessary for such discussion is assumed by all the authors represented in this volume. Yet all share a concern for the ongoing life of the community of faith, and the essays reveal both perspectives.

Continuing requests for copies of the five issues in which these essays appeared have made it clear that pastors have found in their pages a resource of continuing value for the task of proclaiming the gospel. Inquiries from bookstores for sets of the issues have made it plain that they are being used as textbooks and as collateral reading in colleges and universities, as well as in seminaries, where the Gospels are being seriously investigated. That evidence has convinced the editors of *Interpretation* and the directors of Fortress Press that there is a need for a volume which makes readily available to gospel students this collection of essays.

The first set of essays poses the problem inherent in the fact that there are four canonical Gospels, rather than simply one narrative. It is also evident that before there were Gospels in the sense we know them there was the gospel, the proclamation of which commanded the considerable talents and energy of early Christian missionaries like the apostle Paul. The first four essays confront the historical and theological problems posed by the gospel in four Gospels and explore some avenues of approach which promise significant theological results.

Each of the four Gospels, considered here in canonical order, is then explored from four perspectives. One article serves as guide to understanding the Gospel through reviewing recent research and through pointing to contemporary trends in the recognition of both significant problems and emerging consensus. A second essay sets for itself the task of inviting the reader to a serious consideration of the respective Gospel, pointing to the distinctive contribution the Gospel has to make to the theological enrichment of faith in Jesus of Nazareth. A third essay focuses directly on the key figure of the Gospel and sketches the christological dimensions apparent from a careful study of the Gospel's narrative. A fourth essay directs our attention to some key aspect in the Gospel's theological purview, whether that be the church, Jesus' relation to the disciples, or the Gospel's relation to its readers. A key element necessary for understanding the unique contribution of each Gospel to our total theological understanding is thus highlighted.

Such a collection of essays by some of the leading gospel scholars of our time puts into the hands of its readers a unique resource for renewing acquaintance with those stories that lie at the heart of our faith. Useful for preachers, especially those who follow a lectionary cycle, the essays will open new vistas and summon from their memories perspectives since dimmed by the passing of time. Students will find the essays a valuable resource for becoming acquainted with methods used by serious contemporary biblical scholarship and with some of the results those methods yield. Serious inquirers will find here resources to broaden and deepen their appropriation of these ancient documents whose contemporaneity to their readers has amazed and comforted Christians for centuries.

However the essays may be used, they will give to the reader a perspective on the meaning and significance modern scholars have found in the four Gospels, and that provides the major reason for their reissuance in this one volume.

—PAUL J. ACHTEMEIER

Abbreviations

AB	Anchor Bible
AnBib	Analecta biblica
ANQ	*Andover Newton Quarterly*
ATANT	Abhandlungen zur Theologie des Alten und Neuen Testaments
ATR	*Anglican Theological Review*
BETL	Bibliotheca ephemeridum theologicarum lovaniensium
BEvT	Beiträge zur evangelischen Theologie
Bib	*Biblica*
BR	*Biblical Research*
BTB	*Biblical Theology Bulletin*
BZ	*Biblische Zeitschrift*
BZNW	Beihefte zur ZNW
CBQ	*Catholic Biblical Quarterly*
CBQMS	Catholic Biblical Quarterly—Monograph Series
CNT	Commentaire du Nouveau Testament
ConNT	*Coniectanea neotestamentica*
CSEL	Corpus scriptorum ecclesiasticorum latinorum
CTM	*Concordia Theological Monthly*
ETL	*Ephemerides theologicae lovanienses*
EvT	*Evangelische Theologie*
ExpTim	*Expository Times*
FRLANT	Forschungen zur Religion und Literatur des Alten und Neuen Testaments
HTKNT	Herders theologischer Kommentar zum Neuen Testament
HTR	*Harvard Theological Review*
IDB	G. A. Buttrick, ed., *Interpreter's Dictionary of the Bible*
IDBSup	Supplementary volume to *IDB*
Int	*Interpretation*
JAAR	*Journal of the American Academy of Religion*
JBL	*Journal of Biblical Literature*
JR	*Journal of Religion*
JTS	*Journal of Theological Studies*
NEB	New English Bible
NICNT	New International Commentary on the New Testament

NovT	*Novum Testamentum*
NovTSup	Novum Testamentum, Supplements
NTA	*New Testament Abstracts*
NTD	Das Neue Testament Deutsch
NTS	*New Testament Studies*
PSTJ	*Perkins (School of Theology) Journal*
RelSRev	*Religious Studies Review*
RevExp	*Review and Expositor*
RSV	Revised Standard Version
SANT	Studien zum Alten und Neuen Testament
SBLDS	Society of Biblical Literature (SBL) Dissertation Series
SBM	Stuttgarter biblische Monographien
SBT	Studies in Biblical Theology
SE	*Studia Evangelica* I, II, III (= TU 73 [1959], 87 [1964], 88 [1964], etc.)
SNT	Studien zum Neuen Testament
SNTSMS	Society for New Testament Studies Monograph Series
TDNT	G. Kittel and G. Friedrich, eds., *Theological Dictionary of the New Testament*
THKNT	Theologischer Handkommentar zum Neuen Testament
TS	*Theological Studies*
TT	*Teologisk Tidsskrift*
TU	Texte und Untersuchungen
TWNT	G. Kittel and G. Friedrich, eds., *Theologisches Wörterbuch zum Neuen Testament*
UNT	Untersuchungen zum Neuen Testament
WMANT	Wissenschaftliche Monographien zum Alten und Neuen Testament
WUNT	Wissenschaftliche Untersuchungen zum Neuen Testament
ZNW	*Zeitschrift für die neutestamentliche Wissenschaft*
ZTK	*Zeitschrift für Theologie und Kirche*

1.
The Gospel in the Theology of Paul

Joseph A. Fitzmyer, S.J.

"Gospel" is Paul's personal way of expressing the significance of the Christ-event, the meaning that the person, life, ministry, passion, death, resurrection, and lordship of Jesus of Nazareth had and still has for human history and existence.

It is widely admitted today that long before the four canonical Gospels took shape there existed a growing tradition in the early church about what Jesus did and said, about who and what he was. Why that came to be regarded as a "gospel" tradition is not immediately clear. Nor is it perfectly evident why the literary narrative accounts about him eventually composed came to be called "Gospels." Indeed, the word *euangelion* is neither used very often in the Gospels themselves nor in the New Testament outside of the Pauline corpus (see I Pet. 4:17; Rev. 14:6). This situation stands in contrast to the abundant Pauline use of the term. It raises, moreover, a question about the relationship of the Pauline *euangelion* not only to the use of it elsewhere in the New Testament but to the literary form that came to be known as a "gospel."

It seems rather obvious, however, that *euangelion* in the first verse of the earliest Gospel was a factor in the development of the title for the four canonical accounts: "The beginning of the good news of Jesus Christ, the Son of God" (Mark 1:1). *Euangelion* is not used there as a title of the literary form being introduced, as the noun came to be used later on; hence the translation "good news." But within the synoptic tradition neither Matthew nor Luke follows Mark in so introducing their accounts: Matthew uses *biblos*, "a book," and Luke, *diēgēsis*, "a narrative account." (If one were to look for a comparable designation in the Fourth Gospel, it would have to be *martyria*, "testimony," 1:19.) The sense of *euangelion* in Mark 1:1, however, is found elsewhere in this early Gospel (see 1:14, 15;

1

8:35; 10:29; 13:10; 14:9 [also 16:15]): the message about God's new mode of salvific activity on behalf of human beings made present in Jesus Christ, his Son.

One detects at least a Matthean reluctance to use *euangelion* as often as did Mark, but much more significant is the avoidance of the term by Luke in his Gospel (see, however, Acts 15:7; 20:24) and by John. The contrast is intensified when one considers the related verb *euangelizesthai*; Mark never uses it, neither does John, and Matthew has it only once (11:5). Luke, however, uses it frequently in both the Gospel (10 times) and Acts (15 times) but almost always merely in the generic sense of "preaching" (like *kēryssein* or *lalein*).[1]

By way of contrast, both the noun and the verb appear frequently in the Pauline corpus. This is significant not only because of the abundant use of the terms in these earliest New Testament writings, but also because of their role in Pauline teaching. Are they factors in the use of *euangelion* in Mark or in the apparent hesitancy of the other evangelists to pick it up? If, as is usually held, the Marcan Gospel came into being only about A.D. 65,[2] most of the Pauline corpus was already in existence—certainly at least those uncontested Pauline writings, in which the noun occurs most frequently.[3] To try to show what the relation of the Pauline use of *euangelion*/ *euangelizesthai* to the gospel tradition might have been, one has to consider various aspects of "gospel" in Pauline theology. My discussion of the Pauline notion of gospel, therefore, will fall into three parts: (I) the Pauline use of *euangelion*/*euangelizesthai*; (II) the main characteristics of the Pauline gospel; (III) the origin and background of the Pauline gospel.

I. THE PAULINE USE OF
EUANGELION/EUANGELIZESTHAI

Paul uses the noun *euangelion* 56 times in his letters (and it occurs four times in the pastorals); the verb *euangelizesthai* appears 21 times (and

---

1. An exception would have to be made for the etymological sense of the verb in Luke 4:18, where he so uses it in a quotation from Isa. 61:1.

2. It should be recalled, however, that some interpreters would date Mark after A.D. 70. Yet if one were to prefer to go along with J. A. T. Robinson (*Redating the New Testament* [Philadelphia: Westminster Press, 1976], p. 352) and date all the New Testament writings before A.D. 70, one should note that even for him the *entire* Pauline corpus antedates Mark. See my review, *Int* 32 (1978): 309–13.

3. Since the use of *euangelion* in II Thess., Col., and Eph. is so similar to that of the uncontested Pauline letters, I shall include data from them in this survey, considering only the pastorals as Deutero-Pauline.

never in the pastorals).[4] In general, *euangelion* serves as a label to express in summary fashion the message that Paul, "a servant of Jesus Christ, called to be an apostle" (Rom. 1:1, RSV), announced to the world of his day—and, through his letters, to human beings of all ages since then.

Paul sometimes used the noun *euangelion* to express his activity of evangelization (Gal. 2:7; Phil. 4:3, 15; I Cor. 9:14b, 18b; II Cor. 2:12; 8:18). In this sense he often used the verb.*euangelizesthai* absolutely (Gal. 1:8f., 16; 4:13; I Cor. 1:17; 9:16a,b, 18; 15:2; II Cor. 10:16; Rom. 1:15; 15:20). But in the vast majority of passages *euangelion* denotes the content of his apostolic message—what he preached, proclaimed, announced, or talked about.[5] That content, succinctly stated, is "the gospel of Christ" (I Thess. 3:2; Gal. 1:7; Phil. 1:27; I Cor. 9:12; II Cor. 2:12; 9:13; 10:14; Rom. 15:19), "the gospel of our Lord Jesus" (II Thess. 1:8), or "the gospel of his Son" (Rom. 1:9), wherein the genitive is normally understood as objective, that is, the good news about Christ. In some of these instances, however, one can also detect the nuance of Christ as the originator of the gospel (e.g., Rom. 15:18f.). More specifically, the gospel is "the good news of the *glory* of Christ" (II Cor. 1:1), that is, a message about the risen Christ: "It is not ourselves that we preach, but Christ Jesus as Lord" (II Cor. 4:5). Here Paul uses of Christ the title *par excellence* for his risen status. At times, however, the content of the gospel can also be expressed as "the faith" (Gal. 1:23, in a content-sense) or as "the unfathomable riches of Christ" (Eph. 3:8).

Another synonym for the gospel in the Pauline letters is "the word" (I Thess. 1:6) or "the word of God" (II Cor. 2:17). Often enough, when he is discussing the gospel, he refers to it by these synonyms (see II Cor. 4:2; Phil. 1:12–14; I Thess. 2:13). What is implied in "God's gospel" thus finds expression in a more traditional term, borrowed from the Old Testament itself (I Chron. 17:3 [Heb.]).[6]

---

4. See Robert Morgenthaler, *Statistik des neutestamentlichen Worschatzes* (Zurich: Gotthelf-Verlag, 1958), p. 101; Kurt Aland, *Vollständige Konkordanz zum griechischen Neuen Testament* (Berlin: Walter de Gruyter, 1978), II, 118–19.

5. With the noun *euangelion*, Paul uses various verbs: *euangelizesthai* (Gal. 1:11; I Cor. 15:1; II Cor. 11:7); *lalein* (I Thess. 2:2); *kēryssein* (I Thess. 2:9; Gal. 2:2); *katangellein* (I Cor. 9:14); *gnōrizein* (Eph. 6:19). See further Einar Molland, *Das paulinische Euangelion: Das Wort und die Sache*, Avhandlinger utgitt av Det Norske Videnskaps-Akademie i Oslo, II, Hist.-Filos. Klasse, 1934, no. 3 (Oslo: J. Dybwad, 1934), pp. 11f., 41f.

6. See further Col. 1:5, "the word of truth, the gospel"; Eph. 1:13, "the word of truth, the gospel of your salvation" (RSV). Cf. II Cor. 6:7. See Rudolf Bultmann, *Theology of the New Testament*, 2 vols. (London: SCM Press, 1952), I, 88f.

But "gospel" is *par excellence* Paul's *personal* way of summing up the significance of the Christ-event, the meaning that the person, life, ministry, passion, death, resurrection, and lordship of Jesus of Nazareth had and still has for human history and existence. "Christ did not send me to baptize but to preach the gospel" (I Cor. 1:17, RSV). This is why Paul speaks at times of "my gospel" (Rom. 2:16; 16:25), "the gospel that I preach" (Gal. 2:2; cf. 1–8, 11), or "our gospel" (I Thess. 1:5; II Thess. 2:14; II Cor. 4:3; cf. I Cor. 15:1).

Though "my gospel" emphasized Paul's personal awareness about the special nature of the commission given to him by God to preach his Son among the Gentiles (Gal. 1:16), he did not mean thereby that he was announcing a message wholly peculiar to himself or different from that preached by others "who were apostles before me" (Gal. 1:17). For he insisted, "Whether it was I or they, so we preach and so you came to belief" (I Cor. 15:11). He knew of only one gospel (Gal. 1:6) and called down an anathema on anyone who would seek to proclaim a different one (Gal. 1:8). Involved in this mode of speaking about the gospel was Paul's own struggle to be recognized in the early Christian church as an apostle and as an authentic preacher of "the gospel," as the first part of Galatians (1:1—2:10) and isolated passages in his letters (e.g., I Cor. 9:1–2; II Cor. 11:4–6) make clear. He was only too keenly conscious of the special grace of apostolate that had been given to him and that enabled him to announce the good news of Christ Jesus.

Paul realized, of course, that he was preaching a message which had its origin in God himself, "God's gospel" (I Thess. 2:2, 8f.; II Cor. 11:7; Rom. 1:1; 15:16). Just as Christ in his person and ministry brought God's salvific bounty to human beings in a new way, so now, as object of the gospel that is preached, his work is carried on, and the gospel brings that salvific bounty in its way. In it God accosts human beings, soliciting from them a response of "faith working through love" (Gal. 5:6, RSV). Because of its origin in God himself, it manifests its character as "gift" and "grace" (cf. II Cor. 9:14f.).

Obviously, what Paul preached about Christ was phrased by him at times in other ways. Synonyms for "the gospel" reveal some aspects of that notion. They are found in such affirmations as "we preach Christ crucified" (I Cor. 1:23, RSV; cf. 15:12; II Cor. 1:19; Phil. 1:15, 17) or in phrases like "the story of the cross" (I Cor. 1:18), "the word of faith" (Rom. 10:8), or simply "Jesus" (II Cor. 11:4). Indeed, the last cited passage clearly implies an identity of "the gospel" and "Jesus." In all of these formulations, however, Paul plays on nuances of the Christ-event itself.

That one essential in his thinking he viewed in various ways and expressed the effects thereof under various images.[7] In all, however, he sought to proclaim a message about "Jesus our Lord, who was handed over for our transgressions and raised for our justification" (Rom. 4:24–25), about him who became "the source of life" for human beings, "Christ Jesus, whom God made our wisdom, our uprightness, sanctification, and redemption" (I Cor. 1:30). Paul never told his "story of the cross" in the form of stories about what Jesus did and said. Yet even before those stories took final shape he had presented his "gospel," his interpretation of the Christ-event.

II. THE MAIN CHARACTERISTICS OF THE PAULINE GOSPEL

The above survey reveals in a superficial way the various modes in which Paul spoke of the "gospel," but it is now necessary to probe a little more deeply into the characteristics or aspects of that gospel. We may single out six of them.

(1) The first characteristic that we should consider is the *revelatory* or *apocalyptic* nature of the gospel, for it is the means whereby God's salvific activity toward human beings is manifested in a new way, involving specifically the lordship of Jesus Christ. The thesis of Romans makes this immediately clear, since that aspect of God, which is at the root of that salvific activity, namely, "the righteousness of God," is revealed in the gospel (1:17). This is why it is "good news," because it makes known the reality of the new age, the reality of the *eschaton* (cf. Eph. 3:3–6).

(2) A very important characteristic of the gospel for Paul is its *dynamic* character. Though the evangelists' stories about what Jesus did and said may be a more vivid and less abstract way of presenting the Christ-event and its effects, Paul's use of abstractions, such as we have quoted above— including "the gospel"—should not obscure this very important aspect of it. In announcing the thesis of Romans, Paul begins by insisting that he is not ashamed of the gospel, because it is "the power of God [*dynamis theou*] for the salvation of everyone who has faith, for the Jew first and also the Greek" (1:16). In other words, he views the gospel not merely as an abstract message of salvation nor as a series of propositions about Christ (e.g., "Jesus is Lord") which human beings are expected to apprehend and

---

7. For further discussion of these effects of the Christ-event, see my article "Reconciliation in Pauline Theology," in J. W. Flanagan and A. W. Robinson, eds., *No Famine in the Land: Studies in Honor of John L. McKenzie* (Missoula: Scholars Press, 1975), pp. 155–77, esp. 155–57.

give assent to, but rather as a salvific force unleashed by God himself in human history through the person, ministry, passion, death, and resurrection of Jesus, bringing with it effects that human beings can appropriate by faith in him. That is why it is "God's gospel," though in the human words of Paul.[8] That is why Paul could maintain that he proclaims a Son whom God has raised from the dead, Jesus, who "*is delivering* us from the coming wrath" (author's italics; I Thess. 1:10) and that his gospel came to the Thessalonians "not in words only, but with power [*en dynamei*] and the Holy Spirit, and with much conviction" (I Thess. 1:5). In his earliest letter Paul thus hints that the power associated with the gospel is somehow related to the Spirit of God himself (see further Eph. 1:13). That is why he can speak of "the word of God, which is at work [*energeitai*] among you who believe" (I Thess. 2:13).

(3) Another characteristic of the Pauline gospel is its *kerygmatic* relationship. This is expressed not only by the verbs associated with it, mentioned above in part I, which emphasize its proclamatory character, but also in the association of the gospel with a pre-Pauline tradition. For Paul has embedded elements of a primitive proclamation in I Corinthians 15: 1–7; indeed, he makes use of language that implies dependence on a prior tradition ("the gospel, which you received . . . ; I passed on to you above all what I received," 15:1–3). To be noted in this passage is his reference to the "form" or "terms" (*tini logō*) in which he "evangelized" them (15:2). This seems even to suggest that the primitive kerygma or gospel had already taken a somewhat fixed shape in the pre-written tradition. Moreover, what appears in that embedded fragment is merely another way of formulating what Paul calls his "gospel": "that Christ died for our sins according to the Scriptures, that he was raised on the third day according to the scriptures, and that he appeared to Cephas, then to the twelve, and then he appeared to more than five hundred at one time. Then he appeared to James, then to all the apostles. . . . Last . . . he appeared to me."[9] This relation of the Pauline gospel to the primitive kerygma is what enabled Paul to affirm, "Whether it was I or they, so we preach and so you came to belief" (I Cor. 15:11).

---

8. See Heinrich Schlier, "*Euangelion* im Römerbrief," in H. Feld and J. Nolte, eds., *Wort Gottes in der Zeit: Festschrift Karl Hermann Schelkle zum 65. Geburtstag dargebracht* (Düsseldorf: Patmos, 1973), pp. 127–42.

9. The last phrase in v. 7 is a Pauline addition to the kerygmatic fragment. For further discussion of this passage, see R. E. Brown et al., eds., *Peter in the New Testament* (New York: Paulist Press; Minneapolis: Augsburg Publishing House, 1973), pp. 33–36. Paul has also embedded further fragments of the kerygma into other parts of his letters (e.g., Rom. 1:3–4; I Thess. 1:9–10).

In the New Testament *kērygma* can denote either (a) the content of Christian preaching (Rom. 16:25; I Cor. 1:21), as in I Corinthians 15:1–7, cited above, or (b) the activity of proclaiming (I Cor. 2:4; 15:14), or (c) the role or task given to a preacher or herald (Titus 1:3). Martin Kähler, in a reaction against exaggerated efforts of the *Leben-Jesu-Forschung* of the last century, insisted that "the real Jesus is the preached Jesus."[10] This is truly part of the kerygmatic aspect (*Botschaftscharakter*) of the Pauline gospel, since its purpose is to re-present Jesus to human beings of all ages, ever since he first appeared in human history, as one who confronts them with God's new mode of salvific activity to be appropriated by faith working itself out through love. This kerygmatic aspect is not independent of the gospel's dynamic character discussed above; it merely presents it in a different light. But it needs to be emphasized, even though one cannot divest either the kerygma or the gospel in Pauline thinking of a content sense, as C. H. Dodd saw years ago.[11] For an essential part of the Pauline gospel is its backward glance—what Christ Jesus *did* "once and for all" (Rom. 6:10) for human beings. That immediately says "content," even though the effort to re present that "what" is equally important. Both of the aspects constitute the proclamatory or kerygmatic character of the gospel.[12]

Yet another aspect of the kerygmatic character of the gospel has to be considered, namely, the implication that the gospel (as content) and evangelization (as activity) are related to an emergent official process in the Christian community. As the structures of the church begin to appear in the Pauline letters, one detects an awareness of those who are official gospel-heralds (*euangelistai* [not to be confused, of course, with "evangelists" in the modern sense of Gospel-authors]). This provision in church structure is born of the corporate appreciation of Easter faith: To say "Jesus is Lord," there have to be gospel-preachers as well as gospel-hearers (Rom. 10:8–17). The gifts and services listed in I Corinthians 12:8–12, 28–30 or Romans

10. See *Der sogenannte historische Jesus und der geschichtliche, biblische Christus* Leipzig: A. Deichert, 1892), p. 22 (new edition by Ernst Wolf [Munich: Chr. Kaiser Verlag, 1953], p. 44).

11. *The Apostolic Preaching and Its Developments* (London: Hodder and Stoughton, 944), pp. 7–17; *The Gospel and the Law of Christ* (London: Longmans, Green, 947), p. 5; *History and the Gospel* (New York: Scribner's, 1938), p. 7.

12. For further discussion of the kerygmatic character of the gospel, see my article "The Kerygmatic and Normative Character of the Gospel," in *Evangelium—Welt—Kirche: Schlussbericht und Referate der römisch-katholisch/evangelisch-lutherischen Studienkommission "Das Evangelium und die Kirche," 1967–1971, Auf Veranlassung des Lutherischen Weltbundes und des Sekretariats für die Einheit der Christen,* ed. H. Meyer (Frankfurt am M.: O. Lembeck; J. Knecht, 1975), pp. 111–28, esp. 118–21.

12:6–8 eventually come to include the *euangelistai* (Eph. 4:11).[13] But, if this implication is truly present, it must be rightly understood and in two ways: (1) Hidden in it is the logical priority of the gospel over the structured community (or "church"); it is the gospel that calls the church into being, as it were. (2) The kerygmatic character of the gospel relates the communal faith-reaction to it only because of a Spirit-guided process of tradition: No one, individual or community, can react to the proclaimed gospel and identify himself/herself/itself with other Christians in confessing that "Jesus is Lord" unless empowered by the Spirit (I Cor. 12:3). That, ultimately, is why Paul reminded the Christian community of the "form" or "terms" in which he had originally "evangelized" them. He appeared among them as *euangelistēs*, a gospel-herald with a Spirit-empowered challenge, accosting them from an already existent tradition and representing an emerging, structured community.

These diverse, yet related, aspects of the kerygmatic character of the gospel lead to yet another characteristic of it.

(4) A significant characteristic of the gospel in Pauline thinking is its *normative* role. For there is a sense in which the gospel stands critically over Christian conduct, church officials, ecclesiastical teaching, and even the written Scriptures themselves. This role emerges from various ways in which Paul treats of "the gospel."

In Galatians 1:6–9 Paul makes it clear that the gospel he has preached to the Galatian churches tolerates no rival. There is simply no "other gospel" (1:7). This was said in a context of the Judaizing problem in the early church in which certain Jewish practices were being imposed on Gentile Christians (circumcision, dietary regulations, and the celebration of certain feasts in a Jewish calendar). Though Paul was anxious to "share" his gospel with others (I Thess. 2:8), he never tolerated its adulteration or contamination, because he recognized its sovereignty and unmanipulability.

In preaching the gospel, Paul insisted that human beings were expected to listen to it (Eph. 1:13), welcome it (II Cor. 11:4), even obey it (II Thess. 1:8; Rom. 10:16). In short, they were to "believe" or "put faith" in the Christ Jesus preached in it (Rom. 1:5, 17; 10:16). Their hearing of it (*akoē*) was not to stop short of a personal commitment to it (*hypakoē*, Rom. 10:16–17; 1:5; 16:26). Thus, the gospel is understood to exercise a certain authority over human beings, playing a normative role linked to its kerygmatic character: It accosts them, challenging them to conform to its proclamation.

---

13. See also Acts 21:8; II Tim. 4:5.

With regard to Christian conduct, Paul sees the gospel as an inspiration and guide for it: "Let your manner of life be worthy of Christ's gospel: whether I come and see you or am absent, may I hear such things about you, that you stand firm in one spirit and strive with one mind side by side for the faith of the gospel" (Phil. 1:27). Here Paul sees the united testimony of Christians governed by the gospel itself and not by any allegiance to him.

Though we may look in vain in the Pauline letters for a passage in which he discusses explicitly the relationship of the church to the gospel, we can detect some of his thinking about this relationship when we recall the famous Antioch incident (Gal. 2:11–14). There he rebuked Cephas, "one of the pillars of the church" (2:9), when he saw that he was not "walking straight according to the truth of the gospel" (2:14). Regardless of how one interprets the respective roles of Cephas and Paul in the early chapters of Galatians,[14] it is clear that Paul considered the gospel as a norm: its "truth" was the gauge of the conduct even of a church official. And the implication is that the gospel is above him.

But "norm," almost by definition, seems to imply restriction, boundary, or limit. Yet the gospel, especially as it has been historically understood ever since Marcion, who sought to separate law and gospel as two antitheses,[15] has seemed rather to be liberating or open. This idea seems to be founded in yet another place in Galatians itself; in 2:5 Paul speaks of "the truth of the gospel," mentioning it in a context of "the freedom that we have in Christ Jesus" (2:4, RSV), which has to be preserved in the face of the "false brothers" who were seeking to undermine it. The freedom of which Paul speaks there was being endangered in the Judaizing problem, when Christians, who should have understood the role of the liberating gospel in Christian life, were seeking to impose forms of a man-made legalism on other Christians. One may see a dialectic here in the Pauline notion of gospel, which is normative but liberating. It plays a *liberating* role vis-à-vis the restrictions of man-made legalism, whereas it plays a *normative* role because of its God-based origin. If one wants to accept the new mode of salvation offered to humanity in Christ Jesus, one has to accept its demands. But in the long run the irony exists in that the very "truth of the gospel" according to which Paul was asking Cephas to walk was itself a liberation of him from a man-made contamination of the gospel itself.

---

14. For various possibilities of interpretation, see *Peter in the New Testament* (n. 9 above), pp. 27–32.
15. Tertullian (*Adv. Marc.* 1.19) wrote of him: "Separatio legis et evangelii proprium et principale opus est Marcionis" (see also 1.21; 4.1 [CSEL 47:314, 318, 423]).

But the gospel can also be understood as an entity that even plays a normative role over the Scriptures themselves. All through this discussion of the Pauline notion of gospel, we have been regarding it as "the good news of Jesus Christ," dealing with it as the "word" (I Thess. 1:6) in a pregnant sense, as "the word of God" (II Cor. 2:17), as a reality that existed prior to the written Gospels and even prior to Paul's preaching of Christ. But the Scriptures—those of the New Testament—came into being only several decades after the gospel or the word of God had already been dynamically and kerygmatically at work. The New Testament writings, in all their diversity, record a distillation of that dynamism and kerygma—in a privileged form, to boot, that no subsequent church teaching or dogmatic formulation can rival—but they still remain a reflection, an inspired reflection, of the gospel reality. And as such the gospel acts as a norm even for the written Scriptures.[16] Herein one would find at least one aspect of the relation of the gospel (in the Pauline sense) to the written Gospels.[17]

(5) Still another characteristic of the Pauline gospel is its *promissory* nature. In the very opening formula of the Letter to the Romans, Paul speaks of God's gospel, "which he promised aforetime through his prophets in the sacred scriptures" (1:2). The gospel, then, is looked on as a concrete realization of God's promises of old. This is, however, the only place in Romans where Paul brings "the gospel" into close relationship to "the promise." This may seem strange in view of his explicit quotation of the prophetic words of Isaiah 52:7, about the beautiful feet of those who announce good news, quoted in 10:15 in the context of the need of Christian heralds so that human beings may come to faith. Though the notion of God's promise of old plays an important role in Paul's treatment of Abraham in Romans 4:13–21, 9:4–13, and in Galatians 3:14–29, 4:21–31, where it is pitted against "the law," in none of these passages is the gospel explicitly introduced or brought into relationship with the promise. However, in the Epistle to the Ephesians the two ideas are closely joined (cf. 1:13; and esp. 3:6).[18]

---

16. The normative role of the gospel vis-à-vis the Old Testament is seen in Paul's attitude toward it, viewing some of its essential teachings in the light of the Christ-event (see Rom. 4:23–24; 15:4).

17. For some comments on the gospel as a canon-critical principle (discussed by Käsemann), see my "Kerygmatic and Normative Character," p. 124.

18. It may cause some surprise that it is only in the Epistle to the Ephesians that gospel and promise are really brought into explicit relationship. For those who regard Ephesians as Deutero-Pauline it may create something of a difficulty, but it should be kept in mind in view of the emphasis put on these notions over against law at the time of the Reformation.

(6) The preceding characteristic, especially as it is presented in Ephesians 3:6, introduces yet another: the *universal* character of the gospel in
Pauline thinking. This aspect of the gospel is proposed in the thesis of
Romans, where it is described as the power of God for salvation "for everyone who believes, for the Jew first and for the Greek" (1:16). Indeed, the
word that is preached and that seeks to elicit faith in view of salvation is
announced to all, "for there is no distinction between Jew and Greek; the
same Lord is Lord of all" (Rom. 10:12, RSV). Paul recognized that he
had been entrusted with the gospel for the uncircumcised, just as Peter
had been entrusted with it for the circumcised (Gal. 2:7). If Paul admitted a priority in the matter to the Jews, as he did in Romans 1:16 (cf.
2:10), that is simply because of the relation of the gospel to the promise
mentioned above and because of the prerogatives that he, even as a Christian apostle, always admitted about his former co-religionists (see Rom.
3:1–2); "to them belong . . . the promises" (Rom. 9:4, RSV). But, he
insisted, "God shows no partiality" (Rom. 2:11). Thus the salvific bounty
made available to human beings in the Christ-event was destined for Jew
and Gentile.

III. THE ORIGIN AND BACKGROUND OF "GOSPEL"

The foregoing survey of the use of *euangelion/euangelizesthai* and of its
various characteristics in Pauline theology reveals that it was a notion of no
little importance to the apostle. How did he come to express his interpretation of the Christ-event in terms of it?

The initial survey of the use of *euangelion/euangelizesthia* in the Gospels and Acts in the introduction to this essay revealed how rarely these
terms were used by the evangelists in contrast to Paul. Though one may
want to debate the question, the data in Mark and Matthew are such that
one cannot conclude with certainty that Jesus himself made much use of
the terms or of the Aramaic counterpart of *euangelion*. The Greek noun
appears on his lips in Mark 1:15; 8:35; 10:29; 13:10; 14:9; [16:15].[19] But
in the Matthean parallels to the first three of these sayings it is absent.
Moreover, though the great commission of the risen Christ in the Marcan
appendix (16:15) is phrased in terms of it (in keeping, as it were, with a
theme in the Gospel itself), the commission in Matthew avoids all reference to it (28:18–20). Hence the question is raised whether the use of it
in Mark 13:10 and 14:9 (on which Matt. 24:14 and 26:13 depend) is to
be attributed to Marcan formulation or not. If it were to be, then further

---

19. In Mark 1:1, 14 it occurs in a remark of the evangelist.

questions arise. Willi Marxsen is of the opinion that Mark introduced the term *euangelion* into the material of the synoptic tradition and that Paul's understanding of "gospel" is the presupposition of the Marcan usage, even though one may not assume direct dependence.[20] This may be an acceptable interpretation of the evidence,[21] but it raises the further question about how Paul came to use the term so frequently and significantly.

The noun *euangelion* had already been in use in Greek literature and inscriptions long before Paul. In Homer's *Odyssey* it denotes a "reward given to a herald of good news" (14.152, 166). In the sense of "good news" or even simply of "news" it is often found in Hellenistic writings.[22] A religious connotation was associated with the word when it came to designate a "sacrifice" offered to gods "for good news."[23] A still more significant use of the word is found on the Calendar Inscription from Priene (in Asia Minor), first published in 1899. It had been set up as part of the introduction of the use of the Julian Calendar into the Roman province of Asia, making New Year's Day coincide with the emperor Augustus' birthday, 23 September: "And [the birthday] of the god (= Augustus, the *divi filius*) was for the world the beginning of the good tidings due to him" (*ērxen de tō kosmō tōn di' autou euangeli [ōn hē genethlios] tou theou*).[24] Here a beneficial, even sacral, connotation of the plural *euangelia* is recognized to be present.

Yet despite this considerable Greek evidence of the use of *euangelion* in the contemporary world, recent students and commentators have been reluctant to ascribe the Pauline use of *euangelion* solely to this background, because *euangelizesthai* occurs in the Greek Old Testament in a far closer

---

20. Willi Marxsen, *Mark the Evangelist: Studies on the Redaction History of the Gospel* (Nashville: Abingdon Press, 1969), p. 146.

21. Marxsen seeks to explain further differences that Mark introduced beyond the Pauline conception (e.g., a certain identification of Jesus with the gospel [see 8:35; 10:29, "for my sake and that of the gospel"] with the result that in the Marcan usage Jesus is both the subject and the object of the gospel; see *ibid.*, pp. 126–50). On this explanation, see Georg Strecker, "Literarkritische Überlegungen zum *euangelion*-Begriff im Markusevangelium," in *Neues Testament und Geschichte: Historisches Geschehn und Deutung im Neuen Testament: Oscar Cullmann zum 70. Geburtstag* (Zurich: Theologischer Verlag; Tübingen, J. C. B. Mohr [Paul Siebeck], 1972), pp. 91–104.

22. E.g., Plutarch *Sertor.* 11.4; Appian *Bell. civ.* 3.93 §384; 4.20 §78; Josephus *J. W.* 2.17, 4 §420; 4.10, 6 §618. The profane use of *euangelion/euangelia* can also be found in the Greek Old Testament: II Sam. 4:10; 18:20, 22, 25, 27; II Kings 7:9; Jer. 20:15.

23. E.g., Diodorus Siculus 15.74, 2; Plutarch *Sertor.* 26.3.

24. See Wilhelm Dittenberger, *Orientis graeci inscriptiones selectae*, 2 vols. (Leipzig: S. Hirzel, 1903–5; reprinted, Hildesheim: G. Olms, 1970), sec. 458, pp. 40f. Cf. Wilhelm Schneemelcher, "1. Gospel," in Hennecke and Schneemelcher, eds., *New Testament Apocrypha*, trans. R. M. Wilson, 2 vols. (London: Lutterworth Press, 1963, 1965), I, 71–75.

religious sense (e.g., Ps. 68:12; 96:2; Nah. 2:1; Isa. 52:7; cf. Ps. Sol. 11:1).[25] It is often the translation of the Hebrew noun *bĕśôrāh*, "good news [announced by a herald]." The dependence of the Pauline usage on that in the contemporary emperor cult is, indeed, simply not that evident. There exists a notable difference between the eschatological connotation of Pauline *euangelion* and its beneficial connotation in that cult. Moreover, the fact that Paul deliberately quotes Isaiah 52:7 in Romans 10:15, precisely in a context in which he is speaking of the preaching of "the gospel" (10:16), shows that his notion of *euangelion* is heavily dependent on the Old Testament idea of God's herald and his message.

It is, of course, not impossible that the Christian kerygma was already cast in terms of *euangelion* prior to Paul—I Corinthians 15:1-2 may even suggest that—but we cannot be sure. Yet, in any case, it seems as though the Christian use of *euangelion* as the good news about the risen Jesus as Lord and the new mode of salvation available to human beings in him may have emerged quite independently of the so-called sacral or beneficial use of *euangelion* in the contemporary emperor cult in the eastern Mediterranean lands.

If we are right in relating the Pauline use of *euangelion* to that in the Old Testament writings of the post-exilic period, then we can appreciate better the nuance of Paul's reference to the "gospel promised aforetime through his prophets" (Rom. 1:2) and the promissory character of the gospel that Paul himself preached.

That Paul's use of *euangelion* is related to the New Testament Gospels is thus rather likely, even though he never uses the word in the sense of a literary composition. We have seen above that his use of the term may have been the presupposition of the Marcan introduction of the term into his account of what Jesus did and said. From there it would have spread as a Christian word to designate the other "Gospels" (canonical and apocryphal). The distinctive Christian use of the term is seen when one considers that Greek *euangelion* was not translated into Latin as *nuntius bonus* (as it might have been), but was rather simply transcribed as *evangelium* because of the distinctive content-sense that it carried. Having entered Latin as *evangelium*, it spread to the romance languages as *évangile, vangelo, evangelio.*

---

25. The background of the Pauline usage has been well worked out by Peter Stuhlmacher, *Das paulinische Evangelium: I. Vorgeschichte*, FRLANT 95 (Göttingen: Vandenhoeck & Ruprecht, 1968).

2.
The Gospel and the Gospels

Charles H. Talbert

The canonical gospels are attempts to compose an inclusive and balanced presentation of the presence of God in Jesus and of the discipleship that presence evokes.

In literary terms, what is a gospel? How are our Gospel books—Matthew, Mark, Luke, and John—related to the gospel or oral preaching of the early church? Though final answers are lacking,[1] this century has witnessed both the rise of a critical consensus about how such questions should be answered and a challenge to that consensus that offers an alternate set of answers. This essay will attempt to describe both.

The critical consensus that emerged early in this century is closely connected with the name of Rudolf Bultmann.[2] This position can be clarified if we observe how Bultmann answers two questions. In the first place, how did the gospel or oral preaching contribute to the individuality of the canonical gospels? For Bultmann the gospel was set forth in I Corinthians 15:3–5, the kerygma of the cross and resurrection. Here the apostle Paul says he is giving the preaching of the apostles (vv. 1–2, 11, RSV): ". . . Christ died for our sins in accordance with the scriptures, . . . he was buried, . . . he was raised on the third day in accordance with the scriptures, . . . he appeared to Cephas, then to the twelve." From this text Bultmann draws the conclusion that the gospel is the proclamation of the death and resurrection of Jesus as a fulfillment of Scripture.

---

1. L. E. Keck, "Oral Traditional Literature and the Gospels: The Seminar," in W. O. Walker, Jr., ed., *The Relationships among the Gospels* (San Antonio: Trinity University Press, 1978), pp. 103–4.

2. "Evangelien," in H. Gunkel et al., eds., *Die Religion in Geschichte und Gegenwart* (Tübingen: J. C. B. Mohr [Paul Siebeck], 1928²), II, 418–22; Eng. trans. in J. Pelikan, ed., *Twentieth Century Theology in the Making* (New York: Harper & Row, 1971), I, 86–92; *The History of the Synoptic Tradition*, trans. J. Marsh (New York: Harper & Row, 1963), pp. 373f.; *Theology of the New Testament*, trans. K. Grobel (New York: Scribner's, 1951), I, 86.

The canonical gospels, according to Bultmann, are the result of a gradual expansion of this kerygma of Jesus' death and resurrection. (a) The account of the Baptist and the proofs of fulfilled predictions were included to give fuller visualization of the kerygma and to assign it to a place in the divine plan of salvation. (b) Other material was included because the Christian sacraments had to be accounted for in the life of Jesus, the cultically worshiped Lord. (c) Miracle stories were incorporated into the scheme since Jesus' life, considered divine, served as proof of his authority. (d) Apophthegms came into the collection also as visualizations of Jesus' authority. They in turn occasioned the inclusion of other sayings. (e) The sayings of Jesus were included because, for Christian congregations, Jesus in his role as teacher was important. (f) Current exhortations and congregational regulations in force were taken up because such regulations had to be accounted for in the life of Jesus. This means that, for Bultmann, the Gospel of Mark, the earliest gospel, was simply the end product of a traditio-historical development or evolution unrelated to the generic forms which existed independently of the milieu in which the Jesus tradition moved.[3] In the critical consensus, a gospel is an expansion of the cross-resurrection kerygma. As such, it is as unique literarily as the Christian kerygma is in terms of its content.

The apocryphal gospels, moreover, are regarded within the critical consensus as deviations from the pattern of the canonical gospels.[4] After Mark had created the gospel genre by this process of assimilation, the other canonical gospels followed suit. The apocryphal gospels, however, deviated much further from the Marcan pattern than did Matthew, Luke, and John. With this view of the distinctive character of the apocryphal gospels, Bultmann had arrived at an explanation of the development of the gospel from its earliest oral form through the canonical gospel books into the period of corruption represented by the apocryphal gospels.

In the second place, we may observe how Bultmann answers a second question: What is the theological significance of the uniqueness of the canonical gospel form? The unique genre, he thinks, corresponds to and protects the unique content of the Christian gospel. John Drury writes: "A religion which likes to think of itself as uniquely true amongst religions,

---

3. Norman Petersen, "So-called Gnostic Type Gospels and the Question of Gospel Genre," paper prepared for the Task Force on the Gospel Genre, Society of Biblical Literature, October 1970, pp. 40, 45, 53.

4. Helmut Koester, "One Jesus and Four Primitive Gospels," in *Trajectories through Early Christianity*, by J. M. Robinson and H. Koester (Philadelphia: Fortress Press, 1971), pp. 158f.

and deduces that conviction from the unique status of its founder amongst the world's holy men, or projects such a status upon him, will naturally be enthusiastic about the discovery that the primary sources for knowing him are singular phenomena."[5] In a period dominated by the theology of the Word in which the distinctiveness of the Christian proclamation was being asserted, the claim that the gospel form was also unique was felt to be a buttress for Christian uniqueness.

Problems with Bultmann's synthesis are sensed today at every level of his explanation. (1) No longer can one assume that there was only one form of Christian kerygma, the cross-resurrection one of I Corinthians 15: 3-5. The diversity of early Christian proclamation was first brought to light by H. E. Tödt's study of the theological perspective of the Q material, in which Jesus' death is not "for our sins" but is rather Israel's No to God's messenger and the resurrection is God's Yes or validation of Jesus' message of repentance.[6] If there was originally no one form of proclamation of Jesus as Savior, then problems arise in the Bultmannian schema. How are the gospel books then to be seen as related to the different forms of proclamation?

(2) To assume that genres are formed merely as end products of an evolutionary development would run counter to the best thinking about genre by today's literary critics. A genre comes into being initially as a conscious creation of a specific time and place, prompted by a specific occasion.[7] Furthermore, to argue that the gospel genre is unique raises the question of the possibility of effective communication, since all human communication is genre-bound.[8]

(3) It seems inappropriate to regard the apocryphal gospels as deviations from the model of the canonical gospels, since prototypes of the varieties of apocryphal gospels can be found already in the first century, earlier in some cases than the canonical gospels. For example, Q seems to belong to the same type of sayings-collection genre as does the apocryphal Coptic Gospel of Thomas. Thomas could, then, be regarded as a continuation of the literary form, collections of logia, which we find represented in

---

5. John Drury, *Tradition and Design in Luke's Gospel* (Atlanta: John Knox Press, 1977), p. 26.

6. *The Son of Man in the Synoptic Tradition*, trans. D. M. Barton (London: SCM Press, 1965). The significance of Tödt's study for the issue of the diversity of the kerygma was recognized immediately by R. H. Fuller, *The New Testament in Current Study* (London: SCM Press, 1963), pp. 151–53.

7. B. E. Perry, *The Ancient Romances* (Berkeley: University of California Press, 1967), chap. 1.

8. E. D. Hirsch, *Validity in Interpretation* (New Haven: Yale University Press, 1967), p. 76.

Q. This seems much more accurate as an explanation than to regard Thomas as a departure from the form of the canonical gospel.[9]

(4) The questions of content and genre are separable. A distinctive religious content does not demand a distinct literary genre to communicate it. Genesis 1, for example, belongs to the genre of ancient Near Eastern creation story and actually corresponds very closely in many ways to the Babylonian myth of creation. This in no way detracts, however, from its distinctive Israelite theological content. The letter form, furthermore, was a common cultural mode of expression and yet Paul could communicate his uniquely Christian gospel by means of a non-Christian genre. If one wishes to communicate a uniquely Christian message, this does not demand a distinctive literary genre as its vehicle.[10] Problems at these four levels have undermined the critical consensus at its crucial points. The Bultmannian synthesis that developed in the first part of this century to explain the emergence of our canonical gospels has crumbled. An alternative explanation has arisen to fill the void. It is to a description of this alternative that we now turn.[11]

The alternative to the critical consensus crystallized in the work of Bultmann agrees that in the New Testament the term "gospel" refers to oral preaching. The basic meaning of *euangelion* is the preached word, the glad tidings communicated orally.[12] The content of the preached word is the good news that the divine presence is manifest in Jesus for our salvation. To put it in Pauline terms, God was in Christ reconciling the world to himself (II Cor. 5:18f.).

Since the preaching bears witness to Christ, the writings which contain the tradition about Jesus—his words and deeds—came, at least by the end of the second century A.D., to be called gospels.[13] Again, this is common ground for Bultmann and the alternative to his thought. Disagreement begins to emerge when we focus on the recent recognition of the different types of collections of Jesus material in early Christianity.[14] *One type* of

---

9. Koester, "One Jesus and Four Primitive Gospels," pp. 158–204.

10. Charles H. Talbert, *What Is a Gospel?* (Philadelphia: Fortress Press, 1977). pp. 117f.

11. The basic material from which the following description has been drawn may be found in Charles H. Talbert, *Literary Patterns, Theological Themes and the Genre of Luke-Acts* (Missoula: Scholars Press, 1974), chap. 8, and *What Is a Gospel?*

12. Gerhard Friedrich, *"Euangelion,"* in *TDNT* 2:735; Wilhelm Schneemelcher in Edgar Hennecke, ed., *New Testament Apocrypha*, trans. R. McL. Wilson (Philadelphia: Westminster Press, 1963), I, 71. Such sources furnish data for both camps.

13. E.g., Clement of Alexander *Stromateis* I.136.1.

14. I am indebted to the seminal work of Koester, "One Jesus and Four Primitive Gospels," for what follows.

collection consists of _miracle_ matter. The Childhood Gospel of Thomas, for example, tells the story of Jesus as a boy in which Jesus is depicted as a god walking around in a little boy's body, performing one miracle after another, some of which are not particularly moral. This apocryphal gospel should not be thought of as a departure from the canonical gospel type because already in the first century we find a prototype. Although scholars disagree about the sources used by the fourth evangelist, there is a consensus that one source behind the Gospel of John was a Signs Source composed of seven or eight miracles and climaxed by the statement "Now Jesus did many other signs in the presence of the disciples, which are not written in this book; but these are written that you may believe that Jesus is the Christ, the Son of God. . . ." (John 20:30f., RSV). The collection of miracles seems to have been one way of speaking about Jesus in the early church. In doing so, the Christians were appropriating and using for their own purposes the genre "aretalogy," which existed independently in the Mediterranean world.

A _second type_ of collection of Jesus material in the ancient church was that which grouped the _sayings_ of Jesus together. The Coptic Gospel of Thomas is an example from the apocryphal New Testament. Here, after an introduction which says "These are the secret words which the living Jesus spoke," we find a series of sayings of Jesus strung together without any narrative framework. That such a collection should not be regarded as a deviation from the model of the canonical gospels is made clear by the existence of such collections of Jesus' sayings in the first century. The Q source behind Matthew and Luke, according to the two-document hypothesis, fits into this type very easily. It consists almost exclusively of sayings of Jesus without a narrative framework. In speaking of Jesus in this way, the church was appropriating the genre "words of the wise" from its Mediterranean milieu.[15]

A _third type_ of collection of Jesus material found in early Christianity was one which portrayed Christ as a _revealer_, as one who makes a revelation to some disciple or disciples. The Apocryphon of John is representative of most of the apocryphal gospels which have Gnostic links. It presents the risen Christ who appears to John to give him a mystery which he could pass on to his fellow disciples. In the first century, the Revelation to John resembles this type of collection. In the Book of Revelation the risen Lord appears to the prophet John to give him a prophecy of the last days.

---

15. J. M. Robinson, "On the Gattung of Q," in _Trajectories through Early Christianity_, pp. 71–113.

If, moreover, there was a pre-Marcan Christian source behind Mark 13, then even earlier we find evidence of a Christian portrayal of Jesus as a revealer of the End. In depicting Jesus in this way, the early Christians were making use of the genre "apocalypse" for their own purposes.

A *fourth type* of collection of Jesus material found in the ancient church is a composite which includes miracles, sayings, and revelation matter, and in addition has a passion narrative. The four canonical gospels, of course, belong to this variety. Since the other kinds of collections of Jesus material have their parallels in the genres of non-Christian antiquity, it would seem probable that this Christian type would also. Exactly what the parallel is will be discussed further on in this essay.

What is the significance of the early Christians' speaking about Jesus in these different ways? The importance of these collections lies in the fact that they point to distinctive understandings of the *divine presence* made manifest in Jesus and to the views of *discipleship* associated with those particular ways of seeing God's acts in Jesus.[16] If, for example, a Christian presented Jesus in terms of a collection of miracle stories, how would he understand the nature of God's presence in Jesus? The presence of God would be regarded as manifest in an extraordinary display of power. Furthermore, a disciple's response of faith would then be understood as receiving the benefits of the power for himself and subsequently becoming a channel of this power to others. If, however, one presented Jesus in terms of a collection of sayings which gave instructions about how to live and reasons for living that way, the implicit view of God's nature would be different. Such a collection would say that God's presence is manifest in moral guidance for living. A disciple, moreover, would be understood as one who followed the moral guidance set forth. If, furthermore, one depicted Jesus as a revealer making a disclosure of divine secrets, there would be yet another view of God's presence operative. In a revelation collection, God's presence is assumed to be manifest where there is the disclosure of the secrets of one's ultimate origin or destiny. In such a structure, discipleship would mean to receive the disclosed secrets, to repent, and to be ready for the ultimate outcome of history.[17]

---

16. I am still indebted to the inspiration of Koester, though my treatment of the canonical gospels is my own.

17. These types of proclamation still exist in the church today. For example, Kathryn Kuhlman's *I Believe in Miracles* (Old Tappan, N.J.: Fleming H. Revell, 1969) is a collection of twenty-one miracle stories which are intended to evoke faith in Jesus who lives. Any presentation of Jesus as a moral teacher and example, as in liberal theology, is in direct line from the sayings-gospels. Hal Lindsey in *The Late Great Planet Earth* (Grand Rapids: Zondervan, 1970) represents a proclamation of Jesus in terms of prophecy, in this case interpreted in an eccentric way.

The composite gospel with a passion narrative added would also point to a particular understanding of the divine presence and to a distinctive view of discipleship. In three of the four canonical gospels, the passion narrative has soteriological significance. Matthew, Mark, and John all view Jesus' death as in some sense connected with the forgiveness of sins: (a) Matthew 26:28 has Jesus say over the cup at the last supper, "This is my blood of the covenant, which is poured out for many for the forgiveness of sins" (RSV). The words "for the forgiveness of sins" are peculiar to Matthew and indicate something of the evangelist's view of Jesus' death. (b) Mark 10:45 has Jesus say that the Son of man "came not to be served but to serve, and to give his life as a ransom for many" (RSV). Mark 15:38 speaks of the curtain of the temple being torn in two, from top to bottom, when Jesus died. This means that as a result of Jesus' death the presence of God formerly confined to the Holy of Holies and available to the high priest only one day a year is now made available to all people in all times and places. This applies even to those who crucified Jesus, like the centurion who makes the confession "Truly this man was the Son of God" (15:39, RSV). That God gives his presence to those who rejected his Son is the equivalent to saying that God forgives sinners. (c) In John 19:14ff. Jesus is crucified on the day of preparation for the Passover, in the afternoon when the Passover lambs were slain (Exod. 12:6). This, of course, is tied to the fourth evangelist's picture of Jesus as the lamb of God who takes away the sins of the world (John 1:29, 36). In these three Gospels, then, the passion narrative functions to say that God is present where sins are forgiven and that faith is receiving God's acceptance. The dominance of the passion narrative in all three Gospels says that this understanding of the divine presence in Jesus is central and that this view of discipleship is the core of the reality. Neither Matthew, Mark, nor John, however, tells his story of Jesus as just a passion narrative and nothing more. Each one has, in addition to the passion narrative which is central, miracles, sayings, and a revelation section. This, in effect, says that God's presence in Jesus is manifest centrally in the forgiveness of sins but that it also involves power, moral guidance, and the disclosure of our ultimate destiny. These three Gospels also agree that discipleship involves not only the central experience of God's forgiveness but also the experience of power, the following of moral guidance, and the hope and readiness that a disclosure of one's ultimate destiny evokes. The apocryphal Gospel of Nicodemus may have told its story of Jesus solely as a passion narrative, but the canonical gospels did not. They are composites to which a passion narrative has been added or passion narratives to which three other types of material have been added. Either way, they can no more be reduced to a passion narrative than to a collection of miracles or sayings or a revelation. They are not straightforward developments of the passion kerygma in I Corinthians 15:3–5.

Only Luke fails to speak of the connection between Jesus' death and the forgiveness of our sins.[18] His passion narrative is mainly a grand rejection story, the prototype for the rejection narratives in Acts connected with Stephen and Paul. The death of Jesus is the human No to God's messenger, and the resurrection is God's Yes which vindicates the martyr. Forgiveness of sins is preached in his name to all the nations (Luke 24:47), but it is not an atonement-centered proclamation. In Luke-Acts forgiveness flows from the one who is exalted (Acts 2:38; 4:11ff.; 5:31). The special emphasis in Luke-Acts is tied to its Sitz im Leben.[19] Confronted by an over-realized eschatology which viewed life in the Spirit as taking one out of the vicissitudes of this life, Luke designed a picture of Jesus that would show him not only in terms of power, morality, and knowledge— all of which emphasize authority over the world—but also in terms of suffering and death. He enters into his glory only after experiencing his suffering (Luke 24:26). The one anointed with the Spirit lived out his life within the structures of this world, as evidenced by the fact that he was rejected, he suffered, and he died. Correspondingly it is through many tribulations that the disciples must enter the kingdom of God (Acts 14:22). For Luke, the significance of the passion narrative was that it said that when God's presence is experienced as power, morality, and knowledge of our ultimate destiny, it is experienced within the world and does not take us immediately out of the world. Our ultimate transcendence over the evil world comes only at our resurrection at the parousia. In this world even the Spirit-empowered ones undergo rejection, suffering, and death. It is significant, however, that Luke, just as the other three canonical evangelists, does not tell his story of Jesus merely as a passion narrative. Rejection, suffering, and death are not the essence of the Christian's life, even though the Christian still experiences them. None of the canonical gospels is merely a dramatization of the type of kerygma in I Corinthians 15:3–5.

The early Christians, then, agreed that the gospel was the good news that God was present in Jesus for our salvation. It has become clear, how-

---

18. Charles H. Talbert, *Luke and the Gnostics* (Nashville: Abingdon Press, 1966), chap. 5.

19. For what follows, cf. Charles H. Talbert, "The Redaction Critical Quest for Luke the Theologian," in D. G. Buttrick, ed., *Jesus and Man's Hope* (Pittsburgh: Pittsburgh Theological Seminary, 1970), I, 171–222.

ever, that there was considerable difference among the believers about
the nature of the divine presence manifest in Jesus. Consequently, the
gospel was both preached and written down in different ways. There were
written collections which focused on miracle, morality, and knowledge of
our ultimate future, as well as the stance represented by our canonical
gospels. Viewed in this light, the canonical gospels appear to be attempts
to avoid the reductionism of seeing the presence of God in Jesus in only
one way and attempts to set forth a comprehensive and balanced understanding of both the divine presence and the discipleship it evokes. The
canonical gospels are not so much kerygma as reflections of the contro-
versies about the legitimacy of the various forms of proclamation in the
ancient church. They come into their present shape not so much as the
result of a gradual attraction of Jesus tradition around the core magnet
of a passion narrative but rather as the result of conscious and deliberate
composition related to a clear-cut theological stance about the nature of
God and the nature of discipleship.

When the four evangelists put together our canonical gospels as they
did, did they have any *precedents* either theological or literary? The alternative to Bultmann answers "yes" on both counts. Let us look first of all at
the theological precedents existing in the early church before our Gospels
were written. Paul's Corinthian correspondence is instructive. In the mid-
fifties the apostle Paul faced two different sets of problems in the church
at Corinth. First Corinthians reflects a set of difficulties related to an over-
realized eschatology among some of the converts.[20] These problem children
believed that with their possession of the Spirit they had already come into
the fullness of the new age. They had already begun to reign (4:8). As a
result, they believed they had transcended their sexuality (chap. 7; 11:
2–16), they possessed knowledge (chaps. 8–10), they spoke a heavenly language (chaps. 12–14), and so they enjoyed in the present everything that
ordinary Christians hoped for in the future. Consequently, they saw no
need for a future resurrection (chap. 15). In response, Paul not only set
forth an eschatological reservation (15:20–28) but also emphasized that
life in the Spirit, such as the apostles lived, did not exempt them from
hardships and suffering (4:9–13). Here in the mid-fifties we find the emphasis that is so prominent in Luke-Acts.

Second Corinthians 10–13 reflects a different set of difficulties created
by a group of wandering Jewish-Christian apostles who claimed superiority

---

20. Anthony C. Thiselton, "Realized Eschatology at Corinth," *NTS* 24 (1978):
510–26, is representative.

over Paul because of their miracles and revelations of the Lord and their authoritative speech.[21] To them Paul responded by affirming that he worked miracles (12:12), received revelations (12:1ff.), and spoke with authority (10:8ff.). It was not these evidences of power to which he attributed the most weight, however. It was his weakness to which he appealed (11:21; 11:23–29, 30; 12:9f.; 13:4, 9), because God's power is made perfect in weakness (12:9). Paul's weakness, as he refers to it here, is composed of his sufferings, hardships, and subjection to the affairs of this age. Here we have a theological precedent for the Gospels now in our New Testament canon. Paul affirms miracles and revelations and authoritative speech but subordinates them all to his emphasis on suffering. Although there is no possibility of showing the direct influence of Paul on the composition of our canonical gospels, the precedents are there. The canonical gospels appear to have incorporated a theological stance similar to that expressed by Paul in his Corinthian correspondence.

If in the struggle over the issue of the legitimate way to preach Jesus some Christians, at least as early as Paul, had concluded that the gospel embraced power, morality, and knowledge but that the passion was central, were there any literary precedents for what the evangelists were wanting to do? The alternative to the critical consensus expressed by Bultmann looks to the biographical writings of the Greco-Roman world for such models.[22]

The starting point is the recognition that a distinction can be drawn between *didactic* "lives," which call for emulation of the hero or avoidance of his example, and *non-didactic* lives, which are unconcerned with moral example. Among the didactic lives in Greco-Roman antiquity two types of subjects were sometimes founders of communities or cults: philosophers and rulers. Among the didactic lives of philosophers and rulers we can distinguish five functional types: Type A—to provide the readers a pattern to copy (e.g., Lucian's *Life of Demonax*, Plutarch's "Cleomenes"); Type B—to dispel a false image and provide a true model (e.g., Philostratus' *Life of Apollonius of Tyana*, Pseudo-Callisthenes' *Life of Alexander the Great*); Type C—to discredit by exposé (e.g., Lucian's *Alexander the False Prophet*, Curtius' *History of Alexander*); Type D—to establish where the

---

21. Dieter Georgi, *Die Gegner des Paulus im 2 Korintherbrief* (Neukirchen-Vluyn: Neukirchener Verlag, 1964), is perhaps the dominant statement of this viewpoint.

22. For what follows, see Talbert, *What Is a Gospel?* chap. 4; also Charles H. Talbert, "Biographies of Philosophers and Rulers as Instruments of Religious Propaganda in Mediterranean Antiquity," in Temporini and Haase, eds., *Aufstieg und Niedergang der Römischen Welt* (Berlin: Walter de Gruyter, 1978), II.16.1, pp. 1619–51.

true tradition of the founder was to be located in the period after his demise (e.g., "Life of Epicurus" in Diogenes Laertius' *Lives of Eminent Philosophers*; this type of biography is not found among the "lives" of rulers of antiquity); Type E—to validate and/or provide the hermeneutical key (e.g., Porphyry's *Life of Plotinus*, Philo's *Life of Moses*). Philo's *Moses* was designed to introduce his *Exposition of the Law*, just as Porphyry's *Life of Plotinus* was intended to introduce Plotinus' *Enneads*.

These five functional types of lives of philosophers and rulers are found over an extensive period of time. All have pre-Christian examples. All have examples from as late as the second, third, and sometimes fourth centuries. In other words, such biographies would have been in circulation before, at the time of, and after the period of Christian origins. Of these five functional types, it is important to note the striking similarity between Type B lives and the canonical gospels. In a very real sense, all four of our canonical gospels are shaped so as to dispel a false image of the Savior and to provide a true one to follow. In New Testament jargon, our Gospels belong to the debates over the legitimacy of the various forms of kerygma in early Christianity, that is, to the arguments over which Jesus is the "true" Jesus and which way of life is the "true" Christian way. Like the Type B biographies, the canonical gospels often include alien traditions and try to neutralize them or reinterpret them by their inclusion in a new whole with a different thrust. Both Type B lives of philosophers and rulers and the four canonical gospels aim to dispel a false image of the hero and to provide a true one to follow.

It is also important to note the similarity between the Type D biographies of founders of philosophical schools and Luke-Acts.[23] Following the life of the founder of the Christian movement, Acts gives us an extensive succession narrative as part of the story of the founder's life. In this, it belongs together with those Greco-Roman biographies of philosophers which also included succession material within the life of the hero. In Luke-Acts, then, we find similarities to both Type B and Type D lives. It would seem that just as aretalogies, words of the wise, and apocalypses served to express certain understandings of the good news as it related to Jesus, so certain forms of Greco-Roman biography proved serviceable in the task of communicating an inclusive and balanced view of God's presence in Christ and of what constitutes discipleship. Again, it is no more possible to show direct influence of such biographies on the canonical

---

23. For a full exploration of this matter, see Talbert, *Literary Patterns*, chap. 8. *The Life of Pachomius*, trans. A. A. Athanassakis (Missoula: Scholars Press, 1975), gives us an example of a life of a Christian saint cast into the Type D biography form.

gospels than it was to provide evidence for Pauline theological influence upon them. At the same time, literary as well as theological precedents or models existed in terms of which the evangelists could express themselves in their culture. In theological terms, the canonical gospels represent attempts at an inclusive and balanced presentation of who the God who acted in Jesus was and what he calls for in us. In literary terms, the canonical gospels are biographies designed to prevent a misunderstanding of Jesus and to depict him in his true form.

It is now time to turn to some of the implications of this alternative to Bultmann's views about the growth of the gospel tradition. Three may be mentioned. In the first place, the canonical gospels warn us against the danger of reductionism, that is, reducing the presence of God to one manifestation only and reducing discipleship to one dimension only. The church by the end of the second century had restricted the "gospel" books to four. Today the church uses these four as the subject of its proclamation. Theologically, the significance of this is that to read and preach from these four Gospels is to confess as normative the inclusive picture of Jesus found therein and the inclusive understanding of the divine presence implied thereby together with the inclusive view of the discipleship that accompanies them. It was no accident that the collections of Jesus tradition included within the New Testament canon were not of one type of material only, whether miracle or sayings or revelation or passion narrative. The inclusiveness of the canonical gospels with the passion narrative playing a central role constitutes a continuing call to modern Christians to resist the temptation to reductionism in understanding the gospel.

In the second place, the canonical gospels offer us a model for dealing with error/heresy. Heresy is usually the result of Christians' absolutizing a part of the truth at the expense of the whole. The way the four Gospels deal with such error is by "inclusive reinterpretation." They take a part or parts and include it/them within a larger whole with a distinctive point of view which causes the part(s) to be read differently.[24] This is in contrast

---

24. See Talbert, *What Is a Gospel?* chap. 5. "Inclusive reinterpretation" is more than a literary technique, though it is that. It is an attitude toward life that characterizes much of the Mediterranean world. I first became aware of it as an attitude toward life when my family and I lived in Rome for a year. (a) On our street was a furniture-making shop. Whereas we had always been accustomed to discarding a broken piece of furniture, these artisans would take a small piece of a leg from a long-lost chest and build a chest around it. (b) The buildings in the city of Rome often had Roman bases around which medieval structures had been built and were now modern in the sense that a modern whole encased the earlier parts. (c) The inner columns of the cathedral in Syracuse are the columns of the earlier temple of Isis around which the Christian basilica has been constructed.

to the procedure of neutralizing alien or differing viewpoints by their exclusion from the gospel (e.g., sayings only; miracles only; revelation only; passion only). The two methods stand out clearly in the second century. Marcion's canon was comprised of only the Gospel of Luke and ten epistles of Paul, all properly edited to rid them of Jewish corruptions. The main-line church rejected not only Marcion's canon but also his method of arriving at "the gospel." Main-line Christianity used the principle of inclusive reinterpretation. The Gospel of Luke was included in its canon as one of four gospels, and Paul's ten letters were also included but along with the pastorals, Acts, and letters of other apostles. In so doing, Marcion's canon was neutralized and Luke and Paul were read in terms of the thrust of the larger whole. To listen to the canonical gospels today means to hear their call for inclusive reinterpretation as a way of dealing with heresy in the church.[25]

In the third place, the canonical gospels teach us something about appropriate Christian communication of the good news. Two things must be held in balance. On the one hand, there is a need for our language about Jesus to reflect accurately the many-faceted experience of the divine presence. On the other hand, there is the necessity for our proclamation about Jesus to be made through a vehicle that not only is experientially accurate but also meshes with the conventions of modern communication. If our Gospels are any indication, there is a compatability between the use of cultural literary convention on the one hand and a distinctive theological stance on the other. When either is lost, proclamation suffers.

---

25. Inclusive reinterpretation is, of course, not the only way that heresy is dealt with in the New Testament. The pastoral Epistles' appeal to authority; and attack on the character of the opposition seems, however, better suited to a setting in which Christian leaders are outclassed by their opponents.

3.

The Gospel in Four Editions

JACK DEAN KINGSBURY

The differences among the four canonical gospels are ultimately
the expression of distinctive Christologies which represent the
refraction of the significance of Jesus for the church.

Why are there four Gospels in the New Testament and not more? Or,
conversely, why is there not just one canonical gospel? The answer to the
first question is that the early church settled on Matthew, Mark, Luke,
and John because it judged them to be "apostolic": They were thought to
date from the apostolic age and to be apostolic in outlook.

The answer to the second question is that the same process that led
the early church to affirm a plurality of gospels also led it to resist con-
certed attempts to reduce the number of generally accepted gospels to
one. Perhaps the most radical such attempt was that of Marcion (ca. A.D.
140), who contended that Luke alone should stand as The Gospel of the
church. Of particular interest, however, is the attempt Tatian made around
A.D. 170 to fashion a diatessaron: by weaving together the texts of the
four traditional gospels, he sought to compile a single gospel that would
supplant the others. At stake in the long controversy surrounding Tatian's
Diatessaron was the distinctiveness of each of the four Gospels.

History shows, therefore, that the early church opted for a plurality of
gospels within limits and that it also set considerable store on preserving
intact the distinctiveness of each one. What this means theologically is
that the early church placed great value on having at its disposal a number
of Gospels which it could regard as authoritative and which, because of
the distinctiveness of each, could bear multifaceted witness to the essentially multifaceted revelation of God in Jesus Christ.

The purpose of this essay is to explore the four Gospels with a view to
capturing something of the distinctiveness of each. Such distinctiveness
is due in large measure to the fact that the respective evangelists treat
some of the same basic topics in quite different ways. Hence, to facilitate

27

the comparison of one Gospel with another, we discuss in our survey of each a handful of selected topics. These topics are such as pertain to the structure of a Gospel and to the evangelist's understanding of salvation-history, Jesus, discipleship, and salvation.

I

The Gospel according to Mark[1] is perhaps best termed a kerygmatic story. As the opening verse indicates, it proclaims the good news of what God has accomplished in Jesus Messiah (Christ), his Son. What distinguishes it most is its strong concentration on the cross of Jesus.

This concentration on the cross comes to the fore in the way Mark shapes his story and develops his view of the history of salvation. In broad terms, Mark's story divides itself into a prologue (1:1–13[15]) and two main parts (1:14—8:26; 8:27—16:8). It tells of the earthly ministry of Jesus, beginning with his baptism (1:9–11) and concluding with his death and resurrection (chaps. 14–16). The culmination of the whole comes at the end in the account of Jesus' suffering and death on the cross. Accordingly, the very contours of Mark's story make it plain that, for him, it is the cross that is the decisive event in the earthly ministry of Jesus.

From the standpoint of salvation-history, Mark makes an even more ambitious claim on behalf of the cross of Jesus. To his way of thinking, the age prior to the appearance of John the Baptist and of Jesus is the time of Old Testament prophecy; the age following their appearance is the time of eschatological fulfillment (1:2–3, 15), or the time of the gospel (1:1, 14–15; 13:10). The time of the gospel extends to the end of time, and it encompasses within it the ministries to Israel of John the Baptist (1:2–8) and of Jesus and his disciples (1:14f.; 3:14f.; 6:7, 12f.) and the ministry to the nations of the post-Easter church (13:10; 14:9).

As Mark thus fills out the time of the gospel with the respective ministries of John, of Jesus and his disciples, and of the post-Easter church, he nevertheless leaves no doubt that the critical figure in this time is Jesus himself: John is his forerunner, and the post-Easter church proclaims a gospel that is about him. Consequently, in Mark's perspective it is Jesus himself who is pivotal to the whole of the history of salvation. Still, we have already learned that what is most important about Jesus for

---

1. For a recent survey of Marcan studies, cf. J. D. Kingsbury, "The Gospel of Mark in Current Research," *RelSRev* 5 (April 1979). For two popular studies of the theology of Mark, cf. Paul J. Achtemeier, *Mark*, Proclamation Commentaries (Philadelphia: Fortress Press, 1975); and Werner H. Kelber, *Mark's Story of Jesus* (Philadelphia: Fortress Press, 1979).

Mark is his cross. In the last analysis, therefore, the claim that Mark advances by means of his scheme of the history of salvation is that the cross of Jesus is pivotal to the entire history of God's dealings with humankind.

Mark's sharp focus on the cross is also evident in other major features of his Gospel. This is the case literarily with the numerous allusions to and predictions of the suffering and death of Jesus, which crop up almost from the beginning of his narrative. For example, Mark portrays John the Baptist as the forerunner of Jesus (1:2–3), and he takes this to mean that John reflects in his ministry and fate the ministry and fate of Jesus. It is, then, with an eye on Jesus that Mark writes as early as 1:14 that John has been handed over, or betrayed, to the authorities. Again, at 2:20 Mark has Jesus himself declare that "the days will come, when the bridegroom is taken away . . . ," and the entire section 2:1—3:6 closes on the somber note that "the Pharisees . . . held counsel . . . against him, how to destroy him" (RSV). Nor is this all, for already at 3:19 Judas is identified as the one "who betrayed him."

In the section 3:20—6:6, Mark alludes more subtly to the impending passion of Jesus by calling attention to his alienation from family and people. Thus, the conflict that erupts (3:20f., 31–35) simply presages his later rejection in the synagogue at Nazareth by family, relatives, and villagers alike (6:1–6). In similar fashion, the Marcan Jesus tells his disciples in chapter 4 that God does not impart his revelation to the crowd and that it is blind, deaf, and without understanding (vv. 1f., 11f.).

With this state of affairs, Mark has set the stage for the second half of his story (8:27—16:8). Here it is Jesus' predictions of his death and resurrection (8:31; 9:31; 10:33f.) and the subsequent statement that the "chief priests and the scribes . . . sought a way to destroy him" (11:18, RSV; cf. 3:6 and 12:12) that guide the flow of the narrative. Add to these the fateful sayings of Jesus that Judas will betray him, Peter will deny him, and all the disciples will be offended at him (14:18–21, 27, 30), and the point has been reached where only the appointed climax itself, the death and resurrection of Jesus (chaps. 15–16), has yet to be told.

Another major feature of Mark's Gospel which accentuates the importance of the cross is the so-called "messianic secret." In general, Mark presents Jesus as the Messiah, the Son of God, and the Son of Man. As the Son of Man, Jesus interacts with his opponents in the course of his ministry (2:6–10, 23–28), suffers and dies at the hands of the Jewish and Roman authorities (8:31; 9:31; 10:33f.), and will return at the end of time with great power and glory to preside over the last judgment and to usher in the consummated kingdom of God (4:26–29, 30–32; 8:38; 9:1; 13:26f.).

The messianic secret, in turn, has to do with the divine sonship of Jesus. As Mark describes it, Jesus is the Son of God in the sense that God has empowered him with his Spirit for messianic ministry (1:9–11). What this means is that Jesus acts during his ministry on the authority of God himself (11:27–33). In his words and deeds people encounter even "now" the end-time kingdom of God (1:22, 27; 4:11, 26–29, 30–32).

Still, the ministry of Jesus does not reach its culmination in Mark's Gospel until the cross. Accordingly, Mark insists that the divine sonship of Jesus cannot be understood aright until it is perceived in faith from the perspective of the cross (and resurrection). To drive this point home, Mark delays any fully valid recognition of Jesus' divine sonship on the part of a human being until the Roman centurion, at the foot of the cross, utters the "Christian confession" that Jesus is the Son of God (15:39).

A final major feature of Mark's Gospel which underlines the centrality of the cross is the theme of the ignorance of the disciples. Although Mark depicts the disciples as summoned by Jesus to be with him (3:13f.), and although they are the recipients of special instruction (4:11, 34; 7:17–23; 8:31—9:1; 9:30–50; 10:23–45; 11:20–25; chap. 13) and of divine revelation (4:11; 9:2–8; 8:29) and are even commissioned to a ministry in Israel like that of Jesus himself (3:15; 6:6b–7, 12f., 30), they nevertheless remain incapable of comprehending what Jesus tells them or who he is or what he is about (cf. 4:13, 40f.; 6:52; 7:18; 8:16–21; 9:32). This is particularly true of his teaching concerning his suffering and death (8:31–33; 9:31–35; 10:33–37). As a result the disciples do not hold to Jesus when his enemies come to take him, despite their firm assurances to the contrary (14:31), and one betrays him (14:45), another denies him (14:72), and all desert him (14:50). Even so, Mark implies that the ignorance of the disciples is only temporary. He intimates that when the disciples shall see the resurrected Jesus, who remains the crucified one (16:6), in Galilee, he will reconcile them to himself and they, too, will see him from the standpoint of the cross and resurrection, comprehending what previously they had not perceived (cf. 9:9f.; 14:27f.; 16:6f.).

As Mark sees things from his vantage point in A.D. 70, the risen Jesus, who is one with the crucified Jesus (16:6), summons people through the proclamation of the gospel (1:1, 14f.; 13:10), and perhaps the rite of baptism as well (1:8), to become his disciples (cf. 1:16–20; 8:34). In becoming a disciple of Jesus, one becomes a member of the end-time people of God, of the temple "not made with hands" (14:58, RSV; cf. 10:29f.; 12:9f.). This community of disciples lives under the sign of the kingdom and of the cross (1:14f.; 8:34f.). As Jesus has given himself for them on the cross (14:22–24), so he enables them to take up their crosses and to give of themselves: in leading lives of service and love (9:35; 10:42–44); in proclaiming the gospel to the nations (13:10); and in remaining faithful to him in the face of both error (13:6, 21f.) and the prospect of being "handed over" to persecution and even to death (8:34–38; 10:30; 13:9, 11–13). Furthermore, as people who live under the sign of the cross, this community looks to the coming of Jesus Son of Man in "great power and glory," for when he comes he will "gather" his elect to himself and bestow on them the bliss that attends the consummated kingdom of God (13:26f.).

II

In times past, the Gospel according to Matthew[2] has often been described as an expanded and revised version of Mark. What is correct about this assessment is that it takes account of the fact that virtually the whole of Mark reappears in Matthew. The upshot is that Matthew, too, has the nature of a kerygmatic story. Nevertheless, when it comes to the matter of distinctiveness, it can hardly be stressed enough that Matthew possesses a character all its own: Theologically, the story it narrates is not controlled by the motif of the cross but by the notion of the abiding presence of God with his people in the person of Jesus Messiah, his Son; and literarily, Matthew is so written that it is more transparent than Mark to the post-Easter time of the church.

Mention was just made of the theological thought that controls Matthew's kerygmatic story. Through the structure of his story, Matthew brings this thought to full expression. The story itself falls into three main parts. These treat of the origins and identity of Jesus (1:1—4:16), of his public ministry in Israel (4:17—16:20), and of his suffering, death, and resurrection (16:21—28:20). Moreover, this story is bracketed by two key passages: "Behold, a virgin shall conceive and bear a son, and his name shall be called Emmanuel (which means, God with us)" (1:23, RSV); and "Lo, I [the risen Son of God] am with you always, to the close of the age" (28:20, RSV; italics mine). In combination these structural features

---

2. On the theology of Matthew, cf. J. D. Kingsbury, *Matthew: Structure, Christology, Kingdom* (Philadelphia: Fortress Press, 1978); and idem, *Matthew*, Proclamation Commentaries (Philadelphia: Fortress Press, 1978).

reveal that what Matthew intends with his kerygmatic story is, again, to proclaim the truth that in the person of Jesus Messiah, God has drawn near with his end-time rule to dwell with his people, the church, until the consummation, thus inaugurating the final age of salvation.

This central thought depicts the church of Jesus Son of God as the end-time people of God. Through his concept of the history of salvation, Matthew elaborates this thought by raising the claim that Jews and Gentiles alike are to believe in Jesus and join his church. Like Mark, Matthew differentiates between the time of Old Testament prophecy and the time of eschatological fulfillment (e.g., cf. 1:22f.; 2:15, 17f., 23; 4:14–16; 8:17; 12:17–21; 13:35; 21:4f.; 27:9f.). But whereas Mark construes the time of fulfillment as the time of the gospel, Matthew construes it simply as the time of Jesus (earthly—exalted). This time of Jesus extends from his birth (1:23) to his parousia (25:31; 28:20). Its characteristic mark is that Jesus is held up as the hope of Israel (1:17) and the nations (28:19). In attributing such exclusivity to Jesus, Matthew dares to assert that, as far as the eternal fate of both Jews and Gentiles is concerned, Jesus is of ultimate significance and they are to become his disciples.

The central theological thought that God abides with his people in the person of Jesus is likewise determinative for Matthew's portrait of Jesus. In Matthew's eyes, Jesus is Emmanuel, the Messiah Son of God in whom God is present among people (1:23), and therefore the one in whom God's end-time rule is a present reality already in this age (14:33; 16:16; 26:63; 4:17; 12:28). By the same token, Jesus is also the Son of Man, that royal figure who, as Matthew particularly stresses, will return at the consummation of the age to judge the nations and to usher in God's splendid kingdom (10:23; 13:41–43; 16:28; 19:28; 24:30f.; 25:31–46, esp. 34, 40).

Matthew combines the theological notion of the presence of God in Jesus with the literary concern to make his story transparent to his own age of the church (A.D. 90) in order to clothe the earthly Son of God in the glory of the risen Son of God his church worships and confesses. Thus, throughout his Gospel, Matthew employs the verb *proserchomai* ("to come to," "to approach") in stereotyped expressions to depict all manner of persons as approaching Jesus with the same reverence that would be due a deity or king. In a similar vein, Matthew employs the verb *proskyneo* ("to do obeisance to") to show that Jesus is the worthy object of worship (e.g., 2:2, 11; 9:18; 14:33; 28:9, 17). Again, the disciples and those who come to Jesus in the attitude of faith do not simply address him as teacher, as in Mark's Gospel, but as Lord (*kyrie*), which is a title that characterizes him as one of exalted station and divine authority (e.g., 8:2,

6, 8, 21, 25; 14:28, 30). On another level, Matthew spiritualizes the person
of Jesus both by dropping Marcan references to his feelings (pity, anger,
wonder, pneumatic frenzy, indignation, and love)[3] and by editing out a
number of queries Jesus poses in Mark which, on the surface, seem to indicate a lack of knowledge or perception on his part.[4] Finally, Matthew
heightens the majesty of Jesus by modifying or omitting Marcan expressions that appear to circumscribe his authority or allude to the fact that
some desire of his went unfulfilled.[5]

In Matthew's sketch of the disciples, this element of transparency is
especially prominent. In Mark the disciples are said to be hard of heart
(6:52; 8:17) and without understanding (6:52; 8:17, 21) and even faith
(4:40). In Matthew, on the other hand, they possess post-Easter insight:
in principle, they know and confess the mystery of Jesus' person (14:33;
16:16); they understand his teaching (13:11, 23, 51; 16:12; 17:13); and
they are aware of his fate (26:2). Also, they are never depicted as being
persons without faith, but merely as being persons of little faith (6:30;
8:26; 14:31; 16:8). They are, in short, like the Christians of Matthew's
church.

The great speeches of Jesus, too, reflect adaptation to post-Easter circumstances. Theologically, the objective Matthew pursues with them is to
assert the integrity of his church's tradition: The position his church takes
under the aegis of the risen Son of God (18:18–20) on such matters as
ethics and eschatology (chaps. 5–7; 13; 23; 24–25), missionary practice
(chap. 10), and church discipline (chap. 18) is shown to have originated
with the earthly Son of God.

To illustrate the relevance of these speeches to the time of Matthew,
consider the missionary discourse of 9:35—10:42. The opening verses describe the implied occasion on which Jesus delivers this speech: Commissioning his disciples to a ministry in Israel patterned after his own, Jesus
instructs the disciples prior to their departure (10:1, 5–8). As one moves
through the speech, however, it soon becomes apparent that the purview
is much broader than indicated and, in fact, embraces even the mission
to the Gentiles (10:18). In other words the missionary discourse of Jesus,
like all of his great discourses, is meant to communicate at two levels: At
the level of the story Matthew tells, it is the earthly Jesus in each speech
who is addressing himself to the disciples or to the Jewish crowds; but at

---

3. Cf., respectively, Mark 1:41; 3:5; 6:6; 8:12; 10:14, 21.
4. Cf., e.g., Mark 5:9, 30; 6:38; 8:23; 9:12, 16, 21, 33; 10:3; 14:14.
5. Cf. Mark 1:45; 6:48; 7:24; 9:30; Mark 6:5 with Matt. 13:58; Mark 11:13 with
Matt. 21:19.

the level of Matthew's own historical situation, it is the resurrected Jesus in each speech who is addressing himself to the Christians of his church.

We stated that the central truth Matthew proclaims is that in the person of Jesus Messiah, his Son, God has drawn near with his end-time rule to dwell to the close of the age with his people, the church. In line with this truth, the locus of salvation for Matthew is not the cross per se but the presence of Jesus, the earthly and exalted Son of God, with his church. The exalted Son of God presides over and resides in his church (16:18; 18:18–20). This is the place, therefore, where God's end-time rule is a present reality (cf. 21:43). People enter into the sphere of God's rule by hearing the gospel of the kingdom (24:14; 26:13) and submitting to baptism (28:19). In this sphere, there is salvation from sin by virtue of the atonement Jesus has achieved through his death on the cross (1:21; 20:28; 26:28; 27:51), and there is access through prayer to the guiding and saving power of the exalted Jesus (chaps. 8–9; 18:18–20). The mission Matthew's church has is that of proclaiming the gospel of the kingdom to all the nations. Accordingly, as it makes its way toward the parousia, it discharges this task under the aegis of the exalted Son of God (28:20).

III

Of the synoptic evangelists, Luke[6] alone provides his Gospel with a prologue in which he states his purpose for writing (1:1–4). Here, and in the opening verses of Acts, he declares that he intends to draw up an orderly account of what Jesus began both to do and to teach until the day of his ascension so that his readers (ca. A.D. 90), such as Theophilus, might know the truth concerning their faith (Luke 1:3f.; Acts 1:1f.). Hence, in consideration of Luke's own words, his work should perhaps be characterized as kerygmatic history, even though this term is not appreciably different in meaning from that of kerygmatic story. The distinctiveness of Luke's orderly account, or kerygmatic history, lies in the emphasis it places on the theme that God, in the person of Jesus, bestows his end-time salvation on Israel.

This distinctive emphasis reflects itself in the structure of Luke's Gospel and in his concept of the history of salvation. To discuss these two features, however, some account must also be taken of the Book of Acts. A glance at these twin writings reveals that Luke, like Mark and Matthew, also distinguishes between the time of Old Testament prophecy and the time of

---

6. For a popular study of the theology of Luke, cf. Frederick W. Danker, *Luke*, Proclamation Commentaries (Philadelphia: Fortress Press, 1976).

eschatological fulfillment (cf., e.g., Luke 4:17–21; Acts 2:16–21). More-over, for Luke, too, the time of fulfillment begins with John[7] and Jesus (Luke 1–2) and will not end until Jesus Son of Man will return in glory for judgment at the close of the age (Luke 12:8f.; 17:26–37; 21:25–28). Yet, in comparison with Mark and Matthew, Luke writes exceed-ingly large the truth that history bows to the purposes of God. In the Gospel and in Acts, for example, frequent mention is made of divine necessity (*dei*) and the Holy Spirit is often depicted as determining the course of events.[8] Salvation-historically, therefore, Luke employs the Gos-pel to show how God keeps his promises of old and through Jesus Messiah, whom he anoints with his Holy Spirit, proffers salvation to his people Israel (Luke 4:1—9:50; 9:51—21:38). And in the Book of Acts, Luke shows how God further realizes his purposes in history as he empowers the apostles and Paul with the Holy Spirit so that they might proclaim salvation in the name of the risen Jesus to all the nations, beginning from Jerusalem (Luke 24:46–49; Acts 1:8).

The structure of Luke's Gospel, as we mentioned, likewise stands in the service of its overall theme of salvation for Israel. The materials Luke uses in composing his Gospel are, according to the two-source hypothesis, Mark, Q, and sources peculiar to himself. The story Luke fashions from these materials begins by presenting Jesus as Israel's royal Messiah (1:5—3:38) and continues with a description of his public ministry of word and deed in Galilee (4:1—9:50). Following this activity in Galilee, Luke por-trays Jesus as undertaking a long journey to Jerusalem (9:51—21:38). In-deed, this journey unfolds in six stages, and at each stage except the last specific reference is made to the circumstance that Jesus is going toward Jerusalem (9:51; 13:22; 17:11; 18:31; 19:28; 20:1). This third section of Luke's Gospel is easily the longest, and in scope and character it is without parallel in either Mark or Matthew. In the final section of his Gospel, Luke, like Mark and Matthew, also tells of the death and resurrection of Jesus (chaps. 22–24). But in contrast to them he locates the appearances of the risen Jesus not in Galilee but in Jerusalem (chap. 24). How is one to explain this tendency on the part of Luke to make Jerusalem the focal point of attention? Clearly, Luke focuses on Jerusalem because it is the

---

7. In contrast to Matthew, however, the time of eschatological fulfillment does not first begin for Luke with events surrounding the birth of Jesus but with those surround-ing the birth of John the Baptist (1:5—2:40).

8. On divine necessity cf. Luke 2:49; 4:43; 9:22; 12:12; 17:25; 21:9; 22:37; 24:7, 26f., 44. On the direct guidance of affairs by the Holy Spirit, cf. Acts 1:8; 10:19f.; 11:12; 13:2, 4; 15:28f.; 16:6f.; 20:23; 21:4, 11.

place of the Temple and the center of Israel. In the visit of Jesus to Jerusalem, God proffers salvation to Israel (19:41–44). By the same token, the rejection of Jesus in Jerusalem is likewise the more grievous.

Luke's descriptions of John the Baptist and of Jesus have also been colored by the theme of salvation for Israel. In the synoptic Gospels, John is pictured as calling Israel to repentance.[9] John does this in Mark and Matthew as the forerunner of Jesus; he does this in Luke as the forerunner of the people of Israel (cf. 7:27 to Exod. 23:20 [LXX]).

As for Jesus, Luke, too, depicts him as the Son of Man who suffers and who will come in glory at the end of history to inaugurate the final judgment (9:22; 12:8f.; 17:26–37; 21:25–28). In addition Luke touches on the Old Testament prophecy of II Samuel 7:8–16 and portrays Jesus as the royal Messiah and Son of God from the house of David in whom the kingdom of God is already a present reality (1:32–35; 11:20; 17:20f.). And because the term *pais* in Greek can mean "son" and "servant," Luke goes beyond Mark and Matthew and develops a rich servant-Christology: Jesus, the royal Messiah, is at once the Son of God and the servant of God (cf. 3:21f. to 4:17–19).

As the Son and servant of God, the Lucan Jesus is powerful in word and deed (24:19). Although Luke in his treatment of miracles is sometimes criticized by scholars for taking excessive delight in them, it is more accurate to say that he utilizes them in his Gospel to portend the great magnitude of the salvation God is disposed to pour out upon Israel in the person of Jesus, Son and servant (cf. 8:39; 9:42f.; 13:12f.; 17:13–15, 18; 18:42f.; 19:37).

But if Luke presents Jesus as the bearer of God's end-time salvation to Israel, he likewise leaves no doubt as to who the recipients of this salvation are. They are not the rulers of Israel, for they oppose Jesus and make themselves responsible for his condemnation and crucifixion (24:20). On the contrary, the recipients of salvation are the lowly and the outcasts of society: the shepherds (2:8–20); women and widows (1:48; 2:36–38; 7:12–15, 36–50; 8:2f., 43–48; 10:38–42; 13:10–13; 24:22–24); children (18:15–17); soldiers (3:14); sinners (5:30, 32; 7:34, 36–50; 15:1f., 7, 10; 18:13; 19:7); tax-collectors (3:12f.; 5:27f.; 7:29, 34; 15:1; 18:10–14; 19:1–10); criminals (23:40–43); the poor, the suffering, and the oppressed (6:20–22); the sick and the afflicted (7:21f.). It is, in short, to the lost in Israel that Jesus brings salvation (19:10), and they receive him in faith (5:20; 7:50; 8:48; 17:19; 18:42).

---

9. Cf., e.g., Mark 1:4; Matt. 3:2; Luke 1:16f.; 3:3, 8.

This brings us to the soteriology of Luke. Nowhere is this delineated better than in the speeches of Acts (cf. 2:14–39; 3:12–26; 4:9–12; 5:30–32; 10:34–43; 13:16–38). For Luke, the locus of salvation is neither the cross nor, owing to the ascension (Acts 1:9–11), the continued presence of Jesus with his followers. Instead, it is the life and resurrection of Jesus which make possible the word of salvation (Acts 13:26). As Luke puts it, the task of the church-as-Israel is to proclaim repentance, the forgiveness of sins, baptism, and the gift of the Holy Spirit to all the nations in the name of Jesus of Nazareth who, though put to death, has been raised by God to be the Lord and Judge of all (cf. Acts 2:23f., 32–40; 10:34–48). Where such proclamation takes place, people come to faith and are added to the number of those who are being saved (cf. Acts 2:41, 44–47; 4:4; 5:14; 6:7; 13:26, 43, 48f.; 14:1; 17:1–4, 10–12).

IV

Like the other evangelists, John,[10] too, tells of the ministry and of the passion and resurrection of Jesus, thus penning a kerygmatic story. What is distinctive about his story is that he casts the earthly Son of God, in whom people are called to believe, in the glory of the pre-existent, divine Word (1:1, 14, 18; 20:31).

Because John identifies Jesus of Nazareth, the Messiah Son of God, with the pre-existent, heavenly Word, the schema he follows in narrating his story about Jesus is completely different from that of the synoptic evangelists. The latter, as we saw, work with the horizontal time-line: there is the time of Old Testament prophecy, and there is the time of the Baptist and of Jesus, the time of eschatological fulfillment. Although John shows that he is familiar with this mode of thinking (12:38–41; 13:18; 15:25; 17:12; 19:24, 36f.), he nevertheless adapts his story to a schema which is vertical and spatial in character and which sets forth the descent and ascent of the cosmic savior (3:17; 4:42; 16:28).

The lines of this schema are clearly visible in the structure of the Gospel. In the prologue (1:1–18), John speaks of the descent of the eternal Word in the sense that he who pre-exists with God and is the agent of creation becomes flesh and so enters the world (1:1–3, 9, 14, 18). In 1:19 through 12:50 of his Gospel, John describes the signs that the Word become flesh, the Son of God, performs as he dwells on earth. In 13:1 through 20:31,

---

10. For two popular studies on the theology of John, cf. D. Moody Smith, *John*, Proclamation Commentaries (Philadelphia: Fortress Press, 1976); and Robert Kysar, *John: The Maverick Gospel* (Atlanta: John Knox Press, 1976).

John describes his passion, which culminates in the cross and resurrection
(chaps. 19–20). In John's eyes, however, the "lifting up" of Jesus on the
cross is symbolic already of his exaltation (3:14f.; 8:28; 12:32f.; 17:1).
Hence, through exaltation by the cross and resurrection, John pictures the
Son of God as ascending to his Father in heaven (1:18; 14:28; 16:5,
28; 20:17).

John portrays Jesus Son of God, who descends from the Father, as showing forth his divine glory in word and deed. Through word and deed, therefore, he reveals himself and consequently the heavenly Father to humans.
The deeds Jesus performs John terms "signs" (*sēmeia*), and in the first
section of his Gospel he tells of seven such signs (2:1–11; 4:46–54; 5:1–9;
6:1–14, 15–25; 9:1–8; 11:1–45; cf. also 21:1–14). These signs are all of the
nature of gigantic, miraculous feats. Yet, to see in them only the element
of the miraculous is to misconstrue them, as the Jews do when they eat
their fill of the loaves of bread and on this account want to make Jesus
their king (6:15, 26). Quite the opposite, the purpose of Jesus' signs is to
reveal to people who he in reality is, namely, the bread of life, the Son
whom God has sent into the world so that "whoever believes in him
should have eternal life" (6:35, 40; 20:30f.).

The words of Jesus in John's Gospel are likewise intended to reveal his
divine glory and true identity. In this connection, the Johannine Jesus
openly declares who he is. For example, the Samaritan woman says, "I
know that Messiah is coming" (4:25, RSV), and in reply to this Jesus
asserts, "I who speak to you am he" (4:26, RSV). This "I am" saying
points to other sayings in which Jesus speaks of himself as the revelation
of God on earth: "I am the bread of life" (6:35); "the light of the world"
(9:5); "the door of the sheep" (10:7); "the good shepherd" (10:11);
"the resurrection and the life" (11:25); "the way, the truth, and the life"
(14:6); and "the vine" (15:5) (RSV). But despite such plain speech,
John makes it clear that people do not as a matter of course comprehend
who Jesus is. Thus, when Jesus says in the presence of the Jews, "Before
Abraham was, I am" (8:58, RSV), they respond by taking up stones to
throw at him (8:59). Accordingly, in the case of the words of Jesus as in
the case of his signs, it is faith that is the critical factor: Apart from faith,
the words of Jesus cannot be heard aright (8:42–47).

This truth, that people must believe in Jesus in order to perceive who
he is and what he is about, which recurs like a refrain throughout John's
Gospel, is intimately related to John's peculiar concept of the final judgment. The synoptic evangelists associate the final judgment with the end
of history and the parousia of the transcendent Son of Man. John does

not follow suit. In his perspective, the Son of Man, whom the synoptists await at the end of time, is the Son of God who has already descended from heaven to earth (5:26f.). With the advent of the Son of God, the final judgment has already begun ("Now is the judgment of this world," 12:31, RSV): People either believe in the Son of God and have "eternal life," or they do not believe in him and stand "condemned already" (3: 16–21). For John, therefore, the final judgment is a present reality and takes place in the attitude of faith or of repudiation which people assume toward Jesus.

Throughout his ministry on earth, the Johannine Jesus steers course toward the hour of his glorification (12:23; 17:1). This hour of glorification is the hour of his death (12:23f., 27, 33), the time when he must depart out of the world to the Father (13:1) and enter upon the glory that was his as the one who is pre-existent with the Father (17:5). Exalted to power through death and resurrection (12:32), Jesus leaves his disciples behind (14:28f.; 16:4b–5, 10, 28). Although he leaves them behind, he does not leave them alone but bestows on them the Holy Spirit (20:22), the Paraclete who will abide with them (14:16f.; 15:26; 16:7, 13). Through the bestowal of the Spirit-Paraclete, the exalted Jesus commissions his disciples to continue his ministry in the world (17:18; 20:22f.). The Paraclete will enable them to do this, for he will teach them all things (14:26) and guide them into all truth (16:13), which is to say that he will enlighten them as to the true significance of all that Jesus has said and all that he has done while on earth (cf. 2:22; 12:16). Hence, enlightened by the Paraclete, the disciples, through their own words and deeds (14:12; 15:20), will themselves become witnesses to the revelation of God that is in Jesus Messiah, his Son (15:27). Of course as the witnesses of Jesus, the disciples can also expect to incur in the world the same manner of hostility and repudiation which Jesus encountered (1:10; 15:18–20; 17:14). Irrespective of this, however, they can be of good cheer, for Jesus has overcome the world (16:33).

John is to be seen as writing his Gospel around A.D. 95. Consequently, what Jesus says in John's Gospel about the Spirit-Paraclete as residing in the community of the disciples is applicable to John's own community. This community, under the guidance of the Paraclete, believes in Jesus as the Messiah, the divine Son of God, and holds that its members, in so doing, have eternal life already in this age (3:15–18; 20:30f.). If, therefore, the question is raised as to the soteriology of John, the answer must be that for him it is the sphere of belief in Jesus as the Messiah, the Son of God, that is the locus of salvation (3:15–18; 20:30–31). Indeed, the reason John ever even took pen in hand was to confirm the members of his community precisely in this belief (20:30f.).

With these brief sketches, we have now dealt with the gospel in four editions. What we have discovered is that the one gospel about God's saving activity in Jesus has, in each of these writings, a strikingly different orientation: in Mark it is the cross; in Matthew it is the continued presence of Jesus with his disciples; in Luke it is the resurrection and the word of salvation; in John it is the Spirit-wrought belief in Jesus as the divine Son of God.

4.

The Hermeneutical Significance
of Four Gospels

ROBERT MORGAN

The fact of four different Gospels can be faced as a theological
opportunity rather than as a merely historical problem by the
hermeneutic of an understanding of Christianity as based upon
the christological dogma.

The plurality of gospels was experienced as a problem in the early church
as soon as the Four were brought together during the second century as
part of a New Testament canon.[1] Four Gospels seemed to constitute an
admission that none of them was perfect and to threaten the unity of their
Christian theological subject-matter at both a theoretical and a practical
level. Conflicting accounts of Jesus could undermine doctrinal affirmations
about him as well as obscure the "picture" of him required by Christian
piety. The exact relationship of Christology and piety and the dependence
of both upon Scripture is neither clear nor uncontested; but if Christians
are to acknowledge Jesus Christ as in some sense the revelation of God,
then they need a coherent account and view of him.

Contradictions between the Gospels and differences between John and
the Synoptics were noted by some of the church fathers.[2] But only the
hostile rationalism of a Celsus, a Porphyry, or the emperor Julian could
adumbrate the modern form of the problem by stripping away the dogmatic belief of the church and contrasting this with the historical man

---

1. See now esp. Helmut Merkel, *Die Pluralität der Evangelien als theologisches und
exegetisches Problem in der Alten Kirche* (Bern: Lang, 1978). Merkel provides the
relevant passages from Irenaeus *Adv. Haer.* 3.1.1–2.1 and 11.8–9. His earlier book,
Widersprüche zwischen den Evangelien (Tübingen: J. C. B. Mohr [Paul Siebeck],
1971), provides detailed discussion. Cf. also Oscar Cullmann, "The Plurality of the
Gospels as a Theological Problem in Antiquity," in A. J. B. Higgins, ed., *The Early
Church* (London: SCM Press, 1956).

2. Most famously, Clement on John as "The Spiritual Gospel"; most incisively,
Theodore of Mopsuestia on its christological teaching. See Merkel, *Pluralität*, pp.
xx, 126f.

from Nazareth. The modern contrast between the Jesus of history and the Christ of faith pales the older problem of the plurality of Gospels into insignificance. Both problems, however, are concerned with Christology; and in an intellectual milieu dominated by historical criticism, they cannot be treated in isolation.

I

The plurality of Gospels is sheer gain for the historian. The existence of different and partly independent sources increases the chances of obtaining secure historical knowledge. Their literary interrelationships help determine their relative antiquity and also enable the historian to clarify the process by which tradition was transmitted prior to and during their composition.

There can be no denying the legitimacy of these questions. A religion based upon particular historical events would today lose all respect and credibility if it did not subject them to critical scrutiny. Historical research now constitutes an important part of the "interface" which theology must always cultivate between Christian faith and the rational endeavors of the day. In addition, the ecumenical significance of different denominations studying the same Scriptures by the same literary and historical methods remains enormous, although different from what was thought by "biblical theologians" a generation ago. In various ways historical study is changing the face of the Christian churches and their theology.

Nevertheless, a reading of the Gospels which sets aside Christian doctrinal presuppositions leads to a purely human Jesus, and a theology which adopts this reading without reservation has already sided against the dogmatic Christology of traditional Christianity, Protestant as well as Catholic and Orthodox. This new anti-dogmatic version of Christianity has seemed to many theologians the only possible way forward in a world grown suspicious of dogma.

That supposition comes naturally to New Testament scholars. It is odd to follow one procedure in historical work and another in one's doctrinal thinking. And yet in practice Christian scholars have long since learned to read the Gospels with bifocal spectacles. They read them "just like any other book" for certain purposes (e.g., historical study) but treat them as Scripture, that is presupposing that they speak of God, in other (e.g., liturgical and devotional) contexts. It is at least worth asking whether Christology should not take this duality seriously instead of starting "from below" with the (in principle if not in fact) cognitively more solid results of historical research.

There is no disputing that Christology must take up with historical study. That is an important part of the theologian's responsibility to "tie knots," as Troeltsch put it, between faith and reason. But it does not follow that historical methods and conclusions must determine the structure of Christology. A rational method which excludes the question of God from its purview can neither be expected to yield theological truth nor be allowed to rule on whether such truth is a possibility. It was a curious reversal of theological method to make Christology depend primarily upon rational investigation rather than upon the believer's apprehension of Jesus. Christology has normally based itself on Christian faith and sought to relate this to the knowledge of the day. It introduces logical considerations and a philosophical conceptuality to make rational sense of the varied symbolic expressions of early Christian faith and experience. But its claim to truth is based primarily on the conviction that Christian faith itself is true. Although it acknowledges the competence of historical research where its theological statements involve historical judgments, its frame of reference is different. It presupposes Christian faith, however provisional particular formulations may be.

The main difference between the fathers and their rationalist critics, ancient and modern, is that the former were committed to the Christian dogmatic evaluation of Jesus as truly God, whereas the latter denied this. Both sides handled the plurality of Gospels in the light of their prior dogmatic or anti-dogmatic interest. The modern complication is that the anti-dogmatic interest has itself dominated much modern Christian theology. What began as a rationalist critique of Christianity in favor of "natural religion" was internalized by liberal Christian theology and has led to new versions of this faith.

It would be premature to declare the option of non-dogmatic forms of Christianity bankrupt. Historical study has so modified the notion of dogma that it is almost misleading to pose the alternative as one between dogmatic and anti-dogmatic versions of Christianity. But, from a traditional Christian standpoint, it was rash of liberal theology to allow itself to be stampeded by modern rationalism into abandoning the christological dogma simply because its cognitive dimension had been challenged. The truth and even the meaning of the dogma are problematical in a culture which has no agreed definition of divinity or acceptance of the "sacred." But there is evidently more to it than cognition. Within some Christian religious systems it functions in relation to their mythic and ritual dimensions, and anyone for whom these are important will hesitate before following rationalistic theologians who are insensitive on these fronts. It may be wiser to claim less for the dogma, reinterpreting it in the light of modern historical study, than to abandon it.

Since the confession of Christ's divinity is separable from the Greek metaphysical terms in which the dogma was once formulated, it can be taken as part of the "given" or self-definition of Christianity to be theologically articulated afresh according to the demands of new intellectual climates, including the claims of modern historical study. It is maintained as part and parcel of confessing Jesus as Lord, and the reasons one holds it are simply the reasons for one's being a Christian. Provided it is not expressed in ways which conflict with the knowledge gained by reason, the truth of the dogma can be assimilated to the wider and less tangible question of the truth of Christianity. This does not reduce the importance of rational argument in defense of Christianity. It does mean that the divinity of Christ is not the point at which the apologist can hope to convince the critic or inquirer. It is Christianity as a whole rather than this particular dogma which he will seek to commend—though he will no doubt have to remove misunderstandings about it. In other words, anyone wishing to understand it before attempting to pass judgment should not isolate the confession of Christ's divinity from the wider religious context in which it is made.

This alternative view of Christianity as based upon the christological dogma interpreted anew is a live option now that the liberal approach is no longer the only one to take radical historical criticism seriously. It is perhaps even attractive now that the idealist metaphysics of history by which the older liberal theology combined its historical conclusions with theological judgments finds little support. Theories of historical development once seemed an acceptable substitute for dogma, providing some sort of rational justification for belief in God and veneration of Jesus. Today these theories are themselves in need of dogmatic support, and theologies which lack this are hard pressed to say anything specifically Christian about Jesus. They sometimes seem reduced to talking about faith without reference to its object.

The divide between a more "traditionalist" and a more "Enlightenment" interpretation of Christianity is rarely clear-cut. Many theologians have a foot in both camps. But it is worth sharpening the alternative to highlight two different approaches to the canon and the problem of four Gospels. The liberal will start from the conclusions reached by historical research; the traditionalist will allow the christological dogma to guide his approach. In each case a prior theological decision is being made, and the choice is genuinely open—contrary to the naïve on either side who think theirs is the only possible approach for a "real" historian or a "real" believer.

Historically, the development of Gospel criticism in the nineteenth and early twentieth centuries was associated in Germany with the liberal types of theological response which were prepared to separate the dogma from the history rather than allow it to interfere with historical study. In fact both D. F. Strauss (*Life of Jesus* [1835]) and F. C. Baur in their different ways wished to reinterpret rather than simply discard the dogma. But they both (following different elements in Hegel) based their Christologies upon the sharp distinction (essential in historical work) between the Jesus of history and the Christ of faith. Both liberal Protestant lives of Jesus and also the later kerygmatic theology continued to make this distinction the basis of their otherwise very different Christologies.

The alternative strategy of integrating one's historical conclusions within a Christology which aims to express the traditional dogma is more novel. It is only quite recently that traditionalists have learned to work with the more radical results of Gospel criticism[3] instead of fighting a rearguard action for conservative positions on the historical questions. The liberal statement of the problem as one of getting from historical judgments about Jesus and the early church to theological evaluations has achieved almost canonical authority in much Protestant New Testament theology. It seems best, then, to concentrate in what follows upon the traditionalist alternative, which starts from the dogmatic evaluation of Jesus and attempts to integrate historical conclusions into a fundamentally Christian framework. This cannot be a matter of "overcoming history by dogma" (in Newman's notorious phrase); the integrity of historical research must be preserved, and this leads modern theologians to understand the dogma in new ways. But neither can it be a matter of surrendering dogma to history (or rather, to the rationalist impulse at work in modern historiography). There are arguably more things in heaven and earth than are dreamt of in that philosophy.

II

The alternative to reading the four Gospels with "purely historical" spectacles and sharply distinguishing between the historical Jesus and the Christologies of the early church is not a return to pre-critical naïveté. It is more like wearing bifocals which allow the Christian to engage in the close detail work of historians and also permit a specifically "Christian" reading of Scripture: a reading which presupposes the community's assumption that these documents speak of God and that God's rule draws near us in Jesus—the assumption epitomized in the christological dogma.

---

3. Good examples are Edward Schillebeeckx, *Jesus, An Experiment in Christology* (London: E. T. Collins, 1979); Walter Kasper, *Jesus the Christ*, trans. V. Green (New York: Paulist Press, 1976); Jürgen Moltmann, *The Crucified God*, trans. Wilson and Bowden (London: SCM Press, 1974).

The analogy with spectacles concedes that this theological reading is the result of a prior dogmatic decision in favor of Christianity. It is not imposed upon the reader by the material itself, though clearly the Gospels invite it (Mark 1:1; John 20:31). It even requires some resistance to the dominant "pull" of contemporary Western culture against reading about one who was a historical figure in any but purely historical categories. A Christian theological reading of the Gospels despises neither the historical facts (unlike Strauss, Kähler, and Bultmann) nor the tradition of Christian evaluation (unlike most liberals). It seeks to hold these together, whereas historical research as such necessarily puts them asunder. It recognizes the distinction without following liberal and kerygmatic theology in making it constitutive for Christology.

History-of-traditions research is an inescapable task of gospel study in a historically conscious age. But the important question is how much is expected of it. For some (e.g., Jeremias) it is all-important, as the only possible route to the historical Jesus. For others its chief importance lies rather in enabling us to understand the methods and message of the evangelists and their predecessors, that is, the proclamation of the early church. Both historical goals are valuable in themselves and may inspire contemporary Christians to imitation. In both cases the historical answers are important for understanding and practicing Christianity. The historians of the New Testament were clearly the arbiters of Christianity on the liberal model, and for all their protests, kerygmatic New Testament theologians (also historians by trade) scarcely claimed less for their work.

On the alternative "traditionalist" model, this history-of-traditions research is taken up, but its importance is relativized; rather less depends upon the accuracy of its results—which is just as well, since these are often highly speculative. The traditionalist seeks to understand the historical development of the tradition, on the assumption that Christians are broadly right about Jesus. He does not expect this assumption to be rationally demonstrated through historical research, but he does expect it to permit an intelligible account of the development.

The crucial aspect of the development of the gospel tradition is the difference between Jesus' mission and message and that of the post-resurrection church. It can be described in different ways, some of which reflect the Enlightenment's impulse to criticize it. Thus Harnack claimed that the gospel as Jesus proclaimed it has to do with the Father only and not the Son.[4] Even if this thesis were historically more convincing than it is

---

4. Adolf Harnack, *What Is Christianity?* (New York: Harper Torch Books, 1957), p. 144. Wellhausen called this *grundfalsch* if taken as a statement of fact rather than a theological postulate (*Einleitung in die drei ersten Evangelien* [Berlin, 1911²], p. 153).

(which is not to deny the grain of truth in it), the traditionalist would wish to avoid such formulations which place Jesus and the early church in an antithetical relationship. Without denying the differences or wishing to force the historical evidence, he will look for formulations which at least permit his assumption that, broadly, the early church was right about Jesus. This does not, of course, preclude the possibility that his historical research may convince him (as it convinced Reimarus) that the development from Jesus to the early church was actually illegitimate—in which case he will cease to be a traditionalist. But assuming the evidence leaves this possibility open, he will avoid formulations which appear to deny it.

Bultmann's question, how the proclaimer became the proclaimed,[5] can also be read in a similar negative light, as can Loisy's statement that Jesus foretold the kingdom and it was the church that came.[6] It is equally possible to describe the change from Jesus to the post-resurrection church in ways which better express the continuity between these. Thus Bultmann himself writes illuminatingly of the shift from implicit to explicit Christology, and Loisy's dictum might be rewritten as "Jesus proclaimed the kingdom; it was the *Christ* that came." It is true that "the church came," but the point at issue is the legitimacy of its christological confession. The development can be understood historically and phenomenologically in ways which allow the believer his conviction that God vindicated Jesus, however this is to be understood.

The Christian assumption that the development was broadly right does not commit the traditionalist to endorsing every aspect of it. Some formulations may be subject to the theological criticism which is always necessary in theological evaluation of a piece of inevitably ambiguous human history. The need for such criticism becomes plainer as the traditionalist traces the further development from Jesus to early catholicism and beyond. The road to Nicaea is itself a history of critical theological judgments. A generally positive view of the doctrinal development does not prevent the modern historically trained theologian from seeing value in what was rejected as heresy or from criticizing aspects of orthodoxy. His general confidence in the tradition, or in God's saving presence and activity in history through the church (if not exclusively there), by no means involves blanket justifications of what is inevitably also a history of human error. The Christian mystery has been preserved despite the weakness and sin of the tradition-bearers.

---

5. E.g., *Faith and Understanding* (London: SCM Press, 1969), p. 284.
6. Alfred Loisy, *The Gospel and the Church* (1903; Philadelphia: Fortress Press, 1976), p. 166.

The Christian tradition, from Jesus himself through the earliest churches, the four Gospels, and the subsequent history of church and doctrine, is open to public inspection. Traditional Christians, liberals, and non-Christians can discuss it rationally on the basis of shared methods of study. Their evaluations of the history will differ, according to their different perspectives, but discussion is possible. The main difference between the traditional and the liberal theologian is how much they need from their historical results. These must provide the fundamental framework for the liberal, whereas the traditionalist brings his framework to the history. He is prepared to have it broken or modified, but if the evidence allows, he will read it in the light of his dogma.

All three types of historian attempt a reconstruction of Jesus and the development of Christology, but only the liberal theologian attempts to base his own Christology directly upon them. The traditionalist is a latecomer in this debate and therefore in a position to trim his dogmatic sails to the historical wind. He can look for a specifically Christian reading of the Gospels—within the limits of historical reason. The result may well be that he gives up the substance of patristic Christology and retains the dogma of the divinity of Christ in a more formal sense, as indicating the christological center of Christianity but requiring articulation in a Christology before it can properly be believed or disbelieved.

That Jesus is truly God, that God vindicated this man and identified himself with his ministry and passion, is dogma because it is sheer assertion, sheer foolishness, which cannot be rationally demonstrated or made probable. Christology attempts to express it coherently and relate it to the rest of our knowledge, only *a posteriori*, reflecting on it as something "given." This struggle for intelligibility and credibility is essential for the life and communication of Christian faith, and what is achieved here will be reflected in a material theological interpretation of the New Testament. But in contrasting a dogma-based approach to the Gospels with the purely historical approach characteristic of New Testament scholarship, the point here is a purely formal one: It is simply a declaration of intent to read the Gospels on the assumption that the development of Christology was in principle correct. This Christian presupposition cannot be rationally legitimated, but the question can be posed whether on this assumption the development of a saying or a parable from Jesus (where this original form of a tradition can be reconstructed), through the early church to the evangelist(s), is intelligible. Is it possible to explain the shift of focus from the implicit Christology of Jesus' message and activity to the explicit Christology of the post-Easter churches? If it were not, the traditionalist's presupposition would be eroded, if not decisively falsified, and would soon be abandoned.

This question can only be satisfactorily posed at the level of individual Gospel traditions whose history can be reconstructed with some probability. Assertions and denials of the "continuity" between the Jesus of history and the Christ of faith at the level of total reconstructions have not carried conviction because these reconstructions are themselves so uncertain. They are of course necessary guidelines for the purpose of tracing the history of individual units of tradition. One cannot make sense of even the small pieces of evidence except in the light of a provisional view of the larger totalities to which they contribute. But these hypothetical total reconstructions of Jesus, the early church and the theology of the evangelists, do not themselves provide the best means of testing the intelligibility of the development and seem to have only an indirect bearing upon a traditionalist Christian's thology.

It is both historically necessary and theologically appropriate that the questions of continuity should be posed at the level of individual units of tradition, rather than through such abstractions as the "historical Jesus" and the "Christ of faith." It is at this level that the Gospels ordinarily function to nourish Christian faith, and it is through this faith that they inform Christology. The questions raised for Christians by historical study of the Gospels need, therefore, to be answered at this level; and it is in this piecemeal tracing of the history of individual traditions[7] that the relatively firm conclusions of historical research can be built into a modern Christology and piety which continues to take its bearings from the christological dogma. The believer needs to be reasonably confident that the gospel tradition which he uses conveys the truth about Jesus. He may not reflect upon the nature of this truth, and may, if pressed, mistakenly identify it with historical accuracy. But even this mistake reflects a correct intuition that if the Lord of his faith is indeed the man from Nazareth, then understanding and responding to him in the context of God's concern for his world must include some understanding of his historical ministry, teaching, and passion.

The dogmatic definition of Jesus as truly God and truly man (however this is spelled out in Christology) provides a framework within which Christian faith may be nourished through hearing a particular pericope or text. Further guidance is provided by the Christian tradition, especially

---

7. A most impressive set of examples is to be found in H. Weder, *Die Gleichnisse Jesu als Metaphern* (Göttingen: Vandenhoeck & Ruprecht, 1978).

Christology; but the dogma gives this its parameters and provides the spectacles with which most Christians read the Gospels. The "truly man" of the dogmatic formula itself invites attention to the historical element necessary in understanding anyone who was truly a man. The "truly God" of itself explains nothing, but it holds open the possibility and asserts the necessity of a religious response to Jesus as he is mediated through Christian witness.

If one accepts the necessity of the christological dogma as structuring the orthodox Christian's reading of the Gospels, a hermeneutical consequence suggests itself. The question of the significance of four Gospels in the canon should not be answered in isolation from the actual character of each and in particular the striking differences between John and the Synoptics. The greatest pioneer of historical theology, Ferdinand Christian Baur, claimed that one's whole view of Christianity

> will be radically and essentially different, according as we on the one hand take it for granted that the four gospels agree with each other throughout, or on the other recognize the divergencies between the Johannine gospel and the Synoptics as amounting to a contradiction which renders a historical unity impossible. If it be assumed that the four gospels agree with each other and are capable of being harmonized, the absolute importance which the gospel of John assigns to the person of Jesus must determine our whole view of the gospel history. We must then regard Christianity as consisting in the fact of the incarnation of the eternal Logos: it is a miracle in the strictest sense, and absolutely. The human is lost in the divine, the natural in the supernatural. Whenever the first three gospels disagree with the fourth, the authority of the latter must be held to be decisive. This, however, amounts to a complete abandonment of all historical treatment of the gospel history. The history is so determined and absorbed by the element of miracle, as nowhere to afford any firm footing for the scientific enquirer. . . .[8]

One may agree with Baur that harmonizing John and the Synoptics to produce a historical unity is impossible and yet continue to contend that there is a theological unity here. Despite the diversity which the historian ascertains, all four Gospels offer more or less adequate Christian interpretations of Jesus. There is therefore a unity of theological meaning in these diverse witnesses. Baur and the liberals after him based their interpretation of Christianity upon the sharp distinction between the history of Jesus, drawn from the Synoptics, and subsequent Christology. For some of the

---

8. *The Church History of the First Three Centuries* (London and Edinburgh: Williams and Norgate, 1878), I, 24f.

liberals this meant virtually setting the witness of John aside. But the procedure which Baur rightly repudiated at the level of historical investigation suggests an alternative theological possibility. "If it be assumed that the four gospels agree with each other" at the fundamental Christian theological level (as is implied by the New Testament canon as such), then "the absolute importance which the gospel of John assigns to the person of Jesus" makes it the hermeneutical key to a specifically Christian reading of them all. It "must determine our whole view" of the Gospels' subject-matter, if we regard Christianity as based upon the historical facts in which Christians see the incarnation of the eternal Logos.

Those who maintain this dogmatic view of Christianity while accepting Baur's "historical treatment of the gospel history" will deny that "the human is lost in the divine, the natural in the supernatural," that "the history is determined and absorbed by the element of miracle." The dogmatic view of Jesus was once fused with a view of miracle which is incompatible with modern historical research. But now that a distinction is made within the Gospel material between historical and theological judgments, it is possible to affirm the mystery of the incarnation without prejudging specific historical issues. A dogmatic view of Christianity, at least in the minimal sense defended here, does not rob the "scientific enquirer" of his footing.

Marcion gave Galatians the key position in his canon, and W. Schulz[9] would place the genuine Pauline Epistles first. The argument here implies that the Fourth Gospel might well come first. But there is no need formally to propose this; it has provided the key to the New Testament for the vast majority of Christians even in its present position.[10]

III

We turn now from the dogmatic framework to the ways in which individual units of gospel tradition, the passage heard or read, the verse expounded or meditated, sustain Christian faith and so assist in producing the raw material of Christology. Faith images of Jesus are composite products which reflect a wide range of rational and imaginative experience. But the canonical gospels have a special place, both as a stimulus and a control. This finite number of Jesus traditions combine in any number of new ways within the mirrors provided by the believer's whole tradition and

---

9. *Die Mitte der Schrift* (Stuttgart: Kreuz Verlag, 1976), p. 433.
10. E.g., Calvin claimed that "this Gospel is the key which opens the door to the understanding of the others."

kaleidoscope of faith

personal experience to produce ever new images of the living Christ in the
kaleidoscope of faith.

The ways in which biblical and other materials combine to illuminate
individual minds and inspire individual hearts are infinite. The plurality of
Gospels has always facilitated this mobility of Christian faith images of
Jesus, and awareness of the history of the tradition behind them heightens
this. Combinations which the historian cannot countenance as representing
the thought of any single biblical author spring naturally to the believer's
mind and move his heart. They cannot and do not appeal to the historian
for validation; such speech and prayer appeal to the demonstration of the
Spirit and of power. The development of faith images, like all religious
insight, is more an art than a science; and theological interpretation of
Scripture should draw bold conclusions from this.

What, then, is the role of historical research? Understanding the witness
of the evangelists and their predecessors can enrich theological interpretation with new suggestions, as well as overcome obscurities in the text. The
astonishing extent to which history-of-traditions work has multiplied the
possibilities of exegetical disagreement, even while solving some problems
and discrediting some solutions, suggests that the exegete's work will never
be completed. But what must seem depressing to problem-solving historians, and disastrous to biblicists who expect ready-made answers from the
biblical text, is a challenge and an opportunity to the theological interpreter. It increases the range of nuances in the biblical paint-box out of
which he draws faith images. Even where these can claim with some plausibility to represent the thought of one evangelist, this settles nothing for
the critical theologian who is not committed to finding everything in the
Bible true or valuable.

However, this possibility of comparing particular interpretations of the
Gospels with the author's meaning, however uncertain this is, does point
to a more important function of historical research. The historian's role
may be rather small in generating faith images of Jesus; its fertility as a
source of suggestions is the result of its failure to achieve assured results
which exclude alternative hypotheses. But historical science is as strong in
criticism as it is weak in constructive impulses, as Nietzsche recognized.
And the Christian community needs critical controls as well as creativity.
It is ultimately a matter of spiritual discernment when one Christian
rightly rejects the faith image of another. But charity demands rational
argument, in which the two sides attempt to persuade one another, and
both share their common search for the Christian truth in a particular
situation. This can be done by clarifying which parts of the tradition (as

well as what in contemporary experience) are providing the basis for the conflicting positions adopted. Sometimes appeal is being made by both sides to the same traditions, and here the author's own meaning provides an ideal norm, even if it is not always accessible. A good deal of German New Testament theology in particular consists of this mode of theological argument.

It is important that this critical role of historical research vis-à-vis faith images should not be too powerful. Unrestrained criticism can destroy any tradition and any religious sensibility. The plurality of Gospels, as well as the uncertainty of most exegetical conclusions, limits their effectiveness in theological criticism by relativizing their witness. In a particular act of finding the Christian thing to say or do the believer might find himself conflicting with Matthew or John, but in tune with the central thrust of Mark or Luke, for example.

That possibility is the consequence of a more fundamental issue illuminated by the plurality of Gospels. As the second-century superscriptions remind us, none of the Gospels is *the* Gospel. They are all fallible human witnesses. Their theological subject-matter lies beyond the text and beyond anything the historian can draw from these sources. The biggest danger of the so-called quest of the historical Jesus is the suggestion that the historian's conclusions might provide not simply one critical norm amongst others but the foundation and substance of Christian faith. This critical reduction to a single norm, like Tatian's solution to the plurality of Gospels, would be in danger of making *the* Gospel into a new law. The variety of witnesses (which include the other New Testament writers) to the one Lord is one way of ensuring that this Lord transcends not only these witnesses but also all subsequent Christian theological and ethical positions and decisions. That need not lead to resignation or skepticism. There is no evading the demands of the moment upon one's concrete obedience. But any act of theological interpretation is a venture and a risk. One might be mistaken and therefore must remain open to the manifold witness of the tradition and the understanding of others within the community.

N B

A normative portrait of Jesus would perhaps facilitate theological criticism of unsatisfactory faith images and judgments. But any simple measuring of these against that would rapidly extinguish the freedom of the Spirit. It would also imply that the Christian gospel could be identified with any one formulation of it. Perhaps Matthew, and certainly later harmonizers, wanted this. One can understand why. The Christian church has always had to exercise some control over the enthusiasms of faith. Perhaps that is why the Gospels were composed. But it seems to have been a higher wisdom which resulted in a plurality of Gospels in the canon. It is no longer necessary to engage in fanciful defenses of the fourfold gospel. By the end of the second century they had become a part of Christianity's self-definition and identity. History-of-traditions study has taught us to use them in new ways and has stimulated new theological thought. But they are the same Gospels, now sometimes read with a greater awareness of the layers of tradition they contain. Through centuries of experience of the Spirit drawing from them the things of Jesus, and leading believers into all truth, the believing community can say: By their fruits do we know them.

5.

Interpreting the Gospel of Matthew

Charles E. Carlston

Matthew should be read as a *traditor*, one who passes along his tradition; as a theologian, one who thinks about what he is doing; and as a churchman, one who knows that a larger circle than his immediate friends will be influenced by his acts.

Perhaps the most important question to ask before beginning the study of Matthew is, For what do I want to study this book? Obviously, one ought not to proceed in preparing six Lenten sermons as he or she would in getting ready for class lectures in a seminary or preparing leadership training materials for adult church school. But the obvious, alas, is by no means universally observed. Anyone who has ever listened to a sermon on *ekklesia* in Matthew or, conversely, been subjected to a sermon on discipleship in a classroom knows exactly what the difficulty is, whether the misplaced sermonizer does or not. Similarly, the goals of one's study will determine not only the method of study but also the kinds of data one will look for and the significance to be attached to those data. And so on.

For our purposes we can probably assume some combination of academic and instructional (rather than private and devotional) intentions. This means that Matthew should be read as a *traditor*, one who passes along his tradition; as a theologian, one who thinks about what he is doing; and as a churchman, one who knows that a larger circle than his immediate friends will be influenced by his acts. To the extent that we can discern his intention and follow him in it, we are performing the same tasks.

While many methods of studying Matthew yield valuable and important insights, perhaps one of the most important is *Redaktionsgeschichte*, the study of his redactional activity on the materials available to him. And this method has the peculiar advantage that it is best done by beginning not with commentaries and learned works but with the text itself. In this brief essay, then, we shall deal primarily with things that the reader can see and check for himself or herself, data often nearly self-evident and sometimes comparatively unambiguous in purpose and significance.

To be sure, some initial assumptions must be made about the kinds of materials with which the author was working. My own assumption, shared by perhaps 80 or 90 percent of those scholars who have given concentrated thought to the matter, is that Matthew had before him as he wrote both his own ecclesiastical traditions and two written documents, Mark and Q. If one is not sure about this or does not remember the argument, some time spent in reviewing the so-called "synoptic problem" in any good New Testament introduction would surely be time well spent. And when this matter is reasonably clear one may, properly armed with a synopsis (a side-by-side listing in columns of the materials in the first three Gospels), begin almost immediately to see what Matthew did with what he had. Obviously, a certain caution is called for here: Even the most probable solution to the synoptic problem is not completely certain; we cannot always know what the source was in any case (some of the material that is now peculiar to Matthew, for example, may have come from Q and been omitted by Luke); and even when we are quite sure of the source and the redaction we may be quite *unsure* of the reasons behind the redaction. Victory is not for the fainthearted, however, and we can reach varying degrees of certainty (or, if one prefers, plausibility) about three types of materials:

I. DISTINCTIVE PASSAGES

Here we are looking for two things, to some extent simultaneously: (1) sayings, incidents, parables that are in Matthew but not in either of the other two synoptic Gospels, and (2) materials whose import seems to be like that of other similar passages elsewhere in the Gospel. In other words, we can readily find materials that occur in Matthew alone, and we can be increasingly sure that we are dealing with a Matthean theme or interest when we see it evidenced in multiple ways.

Consider, for example, the Sermon on the Mount. Some of this material comes from Q, since Luke (chap. 6) cites it as well, often in nearly identical form. And some of it may represent either individual sayings (6:14f., cf. Mark 11:25) or longer liturgical passages (the Lord's Prayer in 6:9–13) that must have been fairly widespread in the oral tradition. But Matthew has clearly not left his sources untouched. The parallels between 5:13 ("You are the salt of the earth," RSV) and 5:14 ("You are the light of the world," RSV) show his hand stylistically, while 5:16 ("Let your light so shine . . . ," RSV) reflects, in its stress on good works as an evangelistic method, Matthew's way of dealing with the perennial Christian problem of faith and works. (The problem in its Pauline form was probably unknown to him.) But he does not leave the matter there. In 5:17–20, partly on the basis of his sources (v. 18 is a revision of the Q-saying in Luke 16:17, while v. 19 must originally have been in a different context, as the peculiar phrase "these commandments" shows), he defines what he means: Christian ethics is a fulfillment, not an abolition, of the Law (probably because he knows of "antinomian" Christians, who reject the Law) and requires a righteousness which goes beyond that of the "scribes and Pharisees." Six antitheses then follow (5:21–47), a series of statements in the form "You have heard it said . . . , but I say unto you . . . ," which indicate a sharpening and interiorizing of the Law. In all of this we may properly speak of an "ethicizing" of the Christian tradition, an emphasis that is developed and elaborated in many ways elsewhere in the Gospel.

What immediately follows is, except for the Lord's Prayer (which may have come to him from the liturgy or Q or both), unique to Matthew; and it all has the same theme: almsgiving, prayer, and fasting are all good, but not if done to demonstrate one's piety. This is surely a point at which the contemporary preacher will look for "relevance," preferably by asking himself Judas' question (26:25). (Experience suggests that he will usually answer in the negative and slyly suggest ways in which his parishioners will be forced to answer differently. College students probably will be unable to relate these verses to anything in their own experience, in which case most instructors may be counted on to show how forcefully they apply to parents or the institutional church.)

Finally, the sermon closes (6:19–7:27) with Q material, modified in various small ways: in 7:6 with the addition of the "pearls before swine" saying, which probably reflects the author's Jewish-Christian background; and in 7:15, 21ff. with a brief discussion about false prophets, which suggests that the Matthean community knew of Jewish-Christian pneumatics who must be opposed in the name of the faith. (In Corinth, where the same problem arises, the pneumatics were probably of Gentile rather than Jewish origin.) Again the preacher, especially in some communities, will have to ask, "How can these things be?"

In these few chapters, in other words, merely pausing over what is peculiarly Matthean will shed a good deal of light on Matthew's special situation and understanding of the Gospel; for those with eyes to see, such pauses may well illuminate much else beside.

The distinctive material is, of course, by no means limited to chapters 5–7. The birth stories are unique, touching at best tangentially the Lucan traditions (Joseph and Mary, the virginal conception, Bethlehem and Nazareth) but generally different from them. They ask essentially two questions: Who is Jesus? (chap. 1) and Where did he come from? (chap. 2). The answers provided for the questions foreshadow much of what follows: Jesus is the Son of David (cf. 12:23 and 15:22); he is "God with us" (cf. 28:20); events happen as they do because Scripture foretold them (cf. the so-called "formula quotations" in 1:23; 2:6, 15, 18, 23; 4:15f.; 8:17; 12:18–21; 13:35; 21:5; 27:9f., which may well come from a formal exegetical "school" with which Matthew was acquainted, as well as the many quotations and allusions taken over or supplied by Matthew himself). Again we may note the care with which the First Gospel is constructed and the way in which even small elements serve the fundamental theological interests of the writer.

Sometimes the material added is a scriptural comment that in its Matthean context slightly shifts the emphasis. Thus, for example, the two-fold use of Hosea 6:6 at Matthew 9:13 and 12:7. In the former passage the contrast "mercy, not sacrifice" (introduced by the rabbinic "Go and learn . . .") elaborates a cultic conflict into an ethical one, rendering more precise the quite different interests of Hosea and Mark. And at 12:7 Matthew has used the same text to show that the ordinary rules can hardly be expected to apply in the presence of the Kingdom (? v. 6) or of Jesus (v. 8) —even while he moves back slightly from the broad abolition of sabbatarianism implied in his Marcan source (Mark 2:27). In 12:16–21, he has appended to Jesus' command of silence (12:16; cf. Mark 3:12) a long quotation from Isaiah 42:1–4, which shows that the Spirit-filled proclaimer of justice and victory need not publicly announce his power and might—a variation on the Marcan messianic secret, but hardly a simple restatement of it.

Similarly, Matthew may add a saying or parable of Jesus to another saying or parable in such a way as to reinterpret it, as, for example, in 22: 11–14. Here a parable (the wedding garment) is appended to another parable (the great feast; cf. Luke 14:16–24) in such a way as to stress at the same time God's readiness to go beyond the usual understanding of the elect people of God and his insistence on reserving the right to demand appropriate conduct of his new people. As a continuous parable this sequence is very awkward—who could be expected to wander the streets in coat and tails on the odd chance that someone might hustle him into a wedding, and what are the chances that everyone *else* present might have done exactly that? But as a moral reminder that God's grace by no means abolishes moral obligation (and chap. 25 makes it clear that this could only be Matthew's intention) it makes perfectly good sense, in our day as in his.

That Matthew uses traditional material for his own special purposes is further attested by at least one of the small pericopes (17:24–27, on the Temple tax) and three of the parables in chapters 17–21 (the unmerciful servant, 18:23–35; the laborers in the vineyard, 20:1–16; and the two sons, 21:28–32). The parable of the Temple tax offers guidance on whether or not Christians are to pay the half-shekel tax once required of Jews for the Temple services but after the destruction of Jerusalem required for the maintenance of the temple of Jupiter Capitolinus. The parable of the unmerciful servant reflects Matthew's *quid pro quo* understanding of forgiveness, also attested in his editorial commentary on the Lord's Prayer in 6:14f. The one about laborers in the vineyard is probably a plea for equality between Jewish Christians and the Johnny-come-latelies in Matthew's own church, Gentile Christians. And the parable of the two sons, originally and primarily no doubt an explanation of God's rejection of the Jews (like the wicked husbandmen, 21:33–46, which immediately follows), almost certainly has paraenetic overtones as well: acts, not words. (This concern is also made clear in the following parable, where his Marcan source speaks only once of "fruit" while Matthew uses the theme three times.) Whether this rather subtle point escaped Matthew's readers we cannot know; our own experience, however, suggests that they probably did. It is easy to believe that God might have rejected others for our sake, almost impossible to believe that he might turn from us to other more obedient and profitable servants.

To be sure, a great deal of the special material in the last two chapters seems to many to be of somewhat limited usefulness today. The great elaboration of the anti-Pharisaic materials behind chapter 23 (themselves an elaboration of Jesus' relationship with Pharisaism) are part of the heavy burden of anti-Semitism that sensitive Christians are trying to get rid of, and (given the difficulty mentioned at the close of the preceding paragraph) few of us have the moral courage to transfer its harsh judgments to the contemporary seat of "Pharisaism," which must be either the Christian church or some state or federal capital in this country. We are by no means persuaded that the wicked always die miserably, as the Judas incident suggests. We hardly know what to make of the rather extreme way the rising of other bodies at Jesus' resurrection implies that the general resurrection has begun. We see Pilate's claim of innocence and the purported innocence of his wife (who becomes a Christian in later legend) as having their closest modern parallels in impenitent felons in high office. We are not especially moved by the "proof" of the resurrection afforded by the story of the Jewish guard and their acceptance of a bribe or, for that matter, by the earthquake's offering of seismic evidence for what our hearts and minds joyfully affirm without it. In all of this, Matthew's Jewish-Christian tradition is reflected. No doubt it will always be of mighty significance for some, but for most of us, it is largely not so.

This is hardly the case, however, with the great commission, 28:16–20, by growing consensus a key passage in determining Matthew's special concerns. Here motifs from both Jewish-Christian and Gentile-Christian tradition are combined, doubtless by Matthew himself, into one single complex, concise, and moving statement of the church's nature, its christological base, its mission, its hope—and much more. Many central Matthean themes are here taken up and brought once more to center stage, forming a spectacular climax which, along with the careful and logical structure of the Gospel as a whole, helps explain why Matthew rather than any of its canonical or noncanonical competitors eventually became the favorite Gospel of the great church.

II. UNIQUE BEGINNINGS AND ENDINGS

A somewhat more difficult way of isolating particular Matthean concerns is to look closely at the way sections begin or end. We have already noted some of this in connection with the birth stories and with the close of the Gospel itself. But it is evident in many other places as well.

Consider, for example, the mission charge of chapter 10. The materials of this highly composite chapter come primarily from Mark and Q, as a glance at a synopsis shows. But various elements of the composition are highly instructive. In Mark the arrangement is fairly casual: Jesus calls four disciples as early as 1:16–20; he calls "the men he wanted" (NEB) in 3:13–19, where the names of the Twelve are given; in chapter 6 he finally gets around to sending them on a mission, with minimal instructions and little detail. In Matthew all is quite different: After the preparation for his ministry (chaps. 3–4), Jesus shows himself as the Messiah of the word (5–7) and the Messiah of the deed (8–9). He then goes around teaching and healing (9:35f.) and urging the disciples to pray that God will send laborers for the harvest (9:37f.). He then *immediately* calls the Twelve (whose names are given) and gives them authority and elaborate instructions for an extended mission. Clearly the mission charge intends to show what the disciples were primarily about and, by extension (as the parallels between v. 7 and 3:2; 4:17 show), what the Christian preacher is *always* primarily about. Even before the general summary of the preaching, however, Matthew tells us that Jesus warned the disciples (10:5f.) to restrict their ministry to Jews and not to preach to Samaritans or Gentiles. This is the *first* thing Jesus tells them. It is true that this saying—and 15:24, which may have been patterned after it—reflects a situation long before Matthew's time, the controversy over the Gentile mission, and represents the views of the "particularists" in the matter. But the great commission at the close of the Gospel (28:16–20) shows that Matthew cannot have envisaged a particularist mission in the church of his own day. While various explanations of the data are possible, the most likely one is that Matthew wants to portray the period of Jesus' earthly ministry as one of a restricted ministry and the post-resurrection mission of the church, resting on the authority of the risen Lord, as universal in scope.

That Matthew's interest lies at least partly in the church's ministry of his own day is also shown by the fact that he includes in this discourse material which in Mark 13 refers to persecution *at the end time* (10:17–25; cf. Mark 13:9–13), thus referring what originally belonged in apocalyptic and eschatological categories to the ongoing life of the church within history. Finally, he closes the whole mission discourse with a thoroughly generalized promise, applicable to all times, to one who loses his life for Jesus' sake and to those who receive the disciples/prophets (10:40f.) or actively aid the disciples (10:42). No other evangelist begins or ends a similar discourse in quite the same way.

Very similar phenomena are evident in Matthew's editorial revision of the Marcan parable chapter (chap. 4 = Matt. 13). The beginning is not essentially modified from Mark, but the ending is completely changed. Mark has closed the chapter with the parables of the seed growing secretly (4:26–29) and the mustard seed (4:30ff.), ending with the statement that all of Jesus' teaching was parabolic and was fully explained to the disciples (4:34). Matthew, on the other hand, has eliminated "the seed" (the tares is a substitute for, not a variant of, the Marcan parable), coupled the parables of the mustard seed (from Mark and Q) and the leaven (from Q), omitted the notion of private explanations and substituted a formula-quotation (13:35), appended an explanation of the tares (13:36–43) and the twin parables of the hidden treasure and the pearl of great price (13:44ff.), added the parable of the net (13:47–50); and finally, when the disciples insist that they have understood all this (13:51), closes the chapter with the saying (parable?) of the householder who brings new and old things from his treasure-room. Some literary phenomena are interesting but perhaps not very important: the use of the parables in pairs (mustard seed/leaven, tares/net, hidden treasure/pearl); the considerable interval between the parable of the tares and its explanation; the question-answer-statement pattern in verses 51f. But the conceptual differences and reem-phases are significant: He is not particularly interested in the motif of non-understanding/explanation, so he contents himself with explaining a single parable, the tares, while omitting the Marcan generalization that Jesus explained "everything" privately. He has no objection to allegory (apparently unlike Luke), so he gives an elaborate allegorical explanation of the tares (13:36–43) and a briefer but similar one for the net (13:49f.). (In the latter case, not entirely happily, since he repeats "the furnace of fire," which makes sense for weeds but not for fish, though it is an appro-priate and well-understood apocalyptic symbol.) These two parables reflect the twin convictions that God will judge the world (or, much more prob-ably, the church) but that men should not do so. And he closes the entire discourse with the observation that the disciples understand, a motif for which he has prepared his readers both by the Q insertion at 13:16f. (the Q reference is to joy over the manifestations of the kingdom, not to dis-cernment) and by the tiny modifications in his Marcan source at 13:19, 23, where "understanding" and "failure to understand" are included among the characteristics of the various soils. Much can be discerned of his special understanding of discipleship by noting just such material, particularly in strategic places at the beginning or end of long speeches.

A final example of the significance of the ending of sections may be found in chapter 24. This is something like a farewell discourse in all three synoptic Gospels. (Jesus' *last* speech to the disciples, at the Lord's Supper, is so firmly fixed in the liturgical tradition that it is not really suitable for those final blessings and exhortations which farewell discourses usually contain. Hence the apocalypse, the last speech but one, must serve this purpose.) And Matthew has considerably diverged from his Marcan source. Mark closes the discourse with the little parable of the waiting servants (13:34–37) and with the universalized exhortation to watch (13:37). But Matthew has substituted Q material as a considerable expansion of the "watch" theme (24:37–51) and then gone on to add three long parables, all cast in an apocalyptic mold and all providing a much longer and more sonorous ending than the brief Marcan exhortation. The ten virgins par-able (25:1–13), peculiar to Matthew, gives a figurative example of some who failed to "watch" and suggests their judgment in the solemn "I never knew you." The parable of the talents (25:14–30), possibly though not

certainly from Q, reminds the readers of the necessity of faithful steward-
ship (under the threat of apocalyptic judgment). And the last great parable, the sheep and the goats (25:31–46), gives a very precise indication
of what Matthew expects the church to be about. For him it is self-evident
that the church includes those who insincerely profess faith, and it is
equally evident that the test of faith is concrete and specific acts of compassion and mercy. We may, if we are so inclined, wish that he had read
more widely in the literature on the faith-works controversy, but he had
not, and he can only suggest what seems to him (and has seemed to most
sensible people, within and outside the church, ever since) the crucial test
of one's profession. Here, as in other passages of the Gospel, his ecclesiastical concerns become obvious.

III. CHANGES IN WORDING AND ORDER

This kind of material in Matthew is at once the most pervasive and the
most elusive. Comparatively little is taken over *verbatim* from his sources,
yet even when we can be reasonably certain that a particular change was
made consciously (which is not always the case) we are often not sure
that his intention is recoverable. It is probably better, therefore, to begin,
as above, with larger blocks of material. The difficulty with more minor
items, however, is not insuperable, and even tentative suggestions (particularly if they may be made for more than one reason or in the case of
more than one passage) have a certain legitimacy.

A complex but interesting example of this phenomenon occurs in the
temptation (chap. 4), where it is evident that Matthew and Luke depend
on Q but uncertain which of the two evangelists has rearranged the order
of the last two temptations. Psychologically, Luke's order is more persuasive: the great temptation comes second, a lesser one last. A spy story
from several wars back perhaps illustrates the point. A particular man was,
as I recall the details (the story is true, my memory fallible), accused of
being a German spy, but he insisted that he was French and knew not a
word of German. No interrogation, no trick, could shake this insistence.
He was called in for final questioning; at the end the interrogator nodded
curtly, shuffled papers on his desk, and said, "Jetzt bin ich zufrieden. Sie
können gehen" ("OK, I'm satisfied. You can go"). His guard down, the
man turned, a fraction; and so, no doubt, temptation often works.

This almost certainly, however, is not the explanation of the text. Quite
possibly Luke, who has a special interest in Jerusalem and Jesus' activity
there, put Jesus at the Temple in Jerusalem for the final temptation be-

cause it is in the Temple, teaching daily, that Jesus ends his public ministry (Luke 21:37). It is also possible, however, that Matthew puts the great and climactic temptation last because it fits more properly there by every literary test. And it is highly probable that whether Matthew follows Q's order or changes it he still intends the scene as anticipating the climax to the whole Gospel, the great commission. At the beginning, as at the end, Jesus' power exceeds that of Satan.

Other examples (chosen more or less at random) may, if pursued carefully, yield equally interesting results. John's objection to baptizing Jesus (3:14f.) is surely intended to eliminate any possible christological misunderstanding. (Luke does not quite say that John baptized Jesus, and neither does John. The *problem* was everywhere recognized; the solutions differ.) The heavenly voice (3:17) now announces publicly to the people (not privately to Jesus) the divine sonship. The requirement of not allowing divorce (Mark 10:11) is slightly modified in a casuistic direction by the addition of the clause "except for unchastity" (RSV; so also at 19:9). Quite evidently the proclamation of the divine ideal and ecclesiastical practice are not easily to be squared—as the sectarians of every generation have found ever since. The strange phrase "sons of the kingdom" is created at 8:12 possibly to make easier the double reference to Jews in Jesus' day and Christians in Matthew's. In 9:11 the Pharisees speak to the disciples about Jesus as "your teacher," and here (as occasionally elsewhere in the Gospel) Jesus' opponents, willy-nilly, speak orthodox Christian truth. In a sense quite different from any of the other Gospels, Matthew's Jesus is indeed a teacher.

The Jonah-saying in 12:40 is elaborated in Matthew to refer to the coming resurrection. (It should be noted that Justin's citation of the passage shows that this could well be a later importation into the Matthean text.) The good seed in the Matthean form of the sower parable (13:8, 23) brings forth not thirty-, sixty-, and hundredfold, but the other way around: hundred-, sixty-, and thirtyfold. Here the point is uncertain. If he had wished to say, like Luke, that the Word is successful, he would have cited only the hundredfold growth, as Luke does. Perhaps he is rather suggesting, as a hoary homiletic tradition long has, that the great days of the church are not in the present but in the past. In many of the details of the things that defile (Matt. 15; cf. Mark 7), Matthew backs away from the antinomianism of his Marcan source; he cannot quite bring himself to say, as Mark does, that Jesus "declared all foods clean." Once more Matthew shows both his Jewish-Christian tradition and his high pastoral sensibilities.

In 15:28 the Syrophoenician woman's faith is specifically described as "great," a deliberate counter to the Matthean concept "of little faith" (cf. *oligopistos/oligopistia* in any Greek concordance). The rewards promised *in this life* for following Jesus are, in 19:29, quietly eliminated; perhaps simply because, like modern novelists, he knows full well how ambiguous the rewards of goodness often are. Finally, Matthew provides a fascinating glimpse into his own mind in 24:20, where the general apocalyptic warning "Pray that it not come about in winter" becomes "Pray that your flight may not be in winter or *on a sabbath!*" (RSV). Anyone with rabbinic training would easily have been able to show that in emergencies (of which presumably the end of the world would be one) the laws about the length of a day's journey could be suspended! Yet no doubt we need a few people of the straightforward legalistic mentality (which Matthew ordinarily is *not*), if only to keep the rest of us from too consistently finding excuses in our special situations for doing exactly what we want.

None of this is definitive, and it certainly is not exhaustive. Nor is it the only way to study Matthew. But pointers of this kind provide small handles by which, with patience and discernment, we may grasp many of the distinctive elements in Matthew's appropriation of the faith. Without such an effort we will fall far short of understanding one of the first and greatest interpreters of Jesus.

6.

The Form and Message of Matthew

While the First Gospel certainly reflects ecclesiological concerns, it is principally the Christology of Matthew that has determined its character.

The objective of this essay is to show how the form and the message of the First Gospel relate to each other. Our thesis is that, taken together, they reveal Matthew to be, above all, the Gospel of the Son of God.

THE FORM OF THE GOSPEL

Attempts to solve the problem of the structure of the First Gospel are legion, but broadly they may be divided into three categories. The first category (which we may safely set aside) comprises topical outlines drafted with no clear indication as to how any given outline enables one to comprehend better the nature or the purpose of the work as a whole.[1]

The second category comprises minor variations of a single outline, but here each proposal does reflect to a large degree the respective commentator's conception of the nature or the purpose of the Gospel. The one responsible for the basic outline countless others have adopted is B. W. Bacon.[2] His position is that the First Gospel contains five "books" which culminate in discourses of Jesus and are supplemented by preamble (chaps. 1–2) and epilogue (chaps. 26–28).[3] The evangelist was a Christian legalist who, as a member of a church threatened by lawlessness, met this heresy

---

1. Unfortunately, most outlines of Matthew fall into this category, as any survey of the commentaries will show.
2. Cf. B. W. Bacon, *Studies in Matthew* (London: Constable, 1930).
3. *Ibid.*, pp. 82, 265–335.

by providing a systematic compend of the commandments of Jesus in five parts, after the fashion of the Mosaic Pentateuch.[4] Structural evidence of Matthew's intention is the fivefold, stereotyped formula found throughout the Gospel, which reads: "And it happened when Jesus finished . . ." (cf. 7:28; 11:1; 13:53; 19:1; 26:1).

Bacon's outline is still strongly advocated today,[5] but with alternative interpretations as to the nature and purpose of the First Gospel. G. D. Kilpatrick, for example, asserts that Matthew has modeled his Gospel after the Pentateuch in such a way as to contrast Jesus and the Law and to shape it to function as a lectionary for his church's services of worship.[6] Krister Stendahl maintains that this fivefold Gospel, the product of a school, presents Jesus as the Wisdom of God and assumes the form of a manual for teaching and administration within the church.[7] Still other scholars, such as Pierre Benoit,[8] Pierre Bonnard,[9] and David Hill,[10] claim Bacon's outline for the First Gospel but view it as underlining the apologetic and especially the didactic character Matthew intended to give it. And Willi Marxsen[11] and Norman Perrin,[12] who follow Bacon to the extent that they, too, find the heart of the First Gospel in the so-called five great discourses, aver that this structural feature shows the document to be a "book" which highlights "sermons" or "verbal revelation" mediated by (the risen) Jesus to the church of Matthew.

It is important to observe that, with the exception of Perrin,[13] all the commentators just cited are of the opinion that the most significant factor in determining the nature of the First Gospel has been the ecclesiology of Matthew. A review of the third category of scholarly attempts to come

---

4. *Ibid.*, pp. 29, 40f., 47, 81f.

5. For a representative list of those who advocate Bacon's outline, although in some cases with variation, cf. J. D. Kingsbury, "The Structure of Matthew's Gospel and His Concept of Salvation-History," *CBQ* 35 (1973): 451 n. 3.

6. *The Origins of the Gospel according to Saint Matthew* (Oxford: Clarendon Press, 1946), pp. 135ff.

7. *The School of St. Matthew* (Philadelphia: Fortress Press, 1968), pp. 24–27, 29, 35.

8. *L'évangile selon Saint Matthieu*, 3d ed. (Paris: Éditions du Cerf, 1961), pp. 7–11.

9. *L'évangile selon Saint Matthieu*, CNT 1 (Neuchâtel: Delachaux et Niestlé, 1963), pp. 7, 10.

10. *The Gospel of Matthew*, New Century Bible (London: Oliphants, 1972), pp. 43–48, 63.

11. *Mark the Evangelist*, trans. R. A. Harrisville (Nashville: Abingdon Press, 1969), pp. 138–42.

12. *The New Testament: An Introduction* (New York: Harcourt Brace Jovanovich, 1974), pp. 173–77.

13. Perrin, in contrast to the other commentators mentioned, appears to attach greater importance to the Christology of Matthew as a prime factor giving shape to the Gospel (cf. *ibid.*, pp. 169–92).

to grips with the structure of the First Gospel reveals that they, too, have been informed by this opinion. What makes this category unique, however, is the fact that the question as to the form of the Gospel receives its answer not in terms of a topical outline but in terms of Matthew's concept of the history of salvation.

Thus, Wolfgang Trilling takes the view that the passages 28:18-20, 21:43, and 27:25 prove that Matthew's overall purpose is to portray the church as the "true Israel" which has replaced the Jews, or the "false Israel," who have forfeited their place in the history of salvation as the chosen people of God.[14] From another perspective Georg Strecker holds that in response to the delay of the parousia, Matthew composed a "life of Jesus" with eschatological relevance and ordered it as the "way of righteousness" in the history of salvation, which spans the "time of the fathers and of the prophets," the "time of Jesus," and the "time of the church."[15] And Rolf Walker, identifying the age of Matthew as the age of the Gentile mission, argues that Matthew writes at once a "life of Jesus" and an "acts of the apostles" in order to set forth in three epochs particularly the more recent history of salvation: the "pre-history of the Messiah," the "history of the call of Israel," and the "call of the Gentiles."[16]

Our discussion thus far is necessary background to current Matthean research. It also gives indication of the questions we must answer if we are to achieve the goal of this essay. Just how viable, for example, is the topical outline of Bacon? Can one offer a more suitable suggestion? Is a scheme of salvation-history the primary way in which Matthew has indeed organized his Gospel? Has either Trilling, Strecker, or Walker correctly delineated Matthew's concept of salvation-history? And is it true that the ecclesiology of Matthew is the factor that has most determined the nature of the First Gospel? These questions call for us to reconsider the problem of the form of the First Gospel.

THE FORM OF THE GOSPEL
RECONSIDERED

By and large, no one contests the idea that Matthew operates with a scheme of salvation-history; the issue under debate is how this is to be

---

14. *Das wahre Israel*, SANT 10 (Munich: Kösel-Verlag, 1964), pp. 95f., 162, 213.
15. *Der Weg der Gerechtigkeit*, FRLANT 82 (Göttingen: Vandenhoeck & Ruprecht, 1962), pp. 45-49, 184-88.
16. *Die Heilsgeschichte im ersten Evangelium*, FRLANT 91 (Göttingen: Vandenhoeck & Ruprecht, 1967), pp. 114f.

defined. Trilling, Strecker, and Walker all ascribe to Matthew a concept of salvation-history in three epochs according to which the lines of demarcation are drawn so as to distinguish sharply between the times of Israel, of Jesus, and of Matthew, or of the church. In emphasizing, respectively, the church as the true Israel, the delay of the parousia, or the influx of the Gentiles into the church, Trilling, Strecker, and Walker reveal that, again, they understand Matthew's scheme of salvation-history to have been molded by his ecclesiology.

Now of course Matthew wrote his Gospel with an eye to his own age. The point is, in what way did he construe this age as being integrated into the history of salvation?

Through his use of the Old Testament, especially the so-called formula quotations, Matthew indicates that the coming of Jesus means that the time of prophecy has been brought to an end and the time of fulfillment inaugurated. In addition, through his use of the eschatological phrase "[in] those days," Matthew shows that he conceives of the time of fulfillment as extending from the days of John and of Jesus to the consummation of the age (cf. 3:1; 24:19, 22a, 22c, 29).[17] If this is correct, then the conclusion is inescapable that the history of salvation divides itself into two epochs, not three, so that Matthew's own age, the time of the church, is to be regarded after the fashion of a subcategory of the time of fulfillment, or better, of the time of Jesus.[18]

Materially, Matthew makes this same point in various ways; for one thing, he brings no narrative of the ascension, shifting the accent instead to the continued presence of Jesus with his disciples to the close of the age (cf. 1:23; 14:27; 18:20; 28:20); for another, he assimilates the missions of John and of the disciples to that of Jesus (cf., e.g., 3:2 and 10:7 to 4:17); and third, he takes care to emphasize continuity between "then" and "now" throughout his Gospel by depicting the earthly Jesus in the effulgence of the resurrected Jesus and by making the earthly disciples the representatives of his church, attributing to them insight that, historically, it appears certain they did not attain until after Easter.[19]

17. Cf. Kingsbury, "Structure of Matthew's Gospel," pp. 468–71.

18. In principle, we see no conflict between our position and that, for example, of W. G. Thompson ("An Historical Perspective in the Gospel of Matthew," *JBL* 93 [1974]: 262), who argues that Matthew took care to distinguish in terms of the experiences of his church between past, present, and future. The only point we would want to make is that, as we see it, Matthew would construe these periods as, again, "subcategories" of the more comprehensive epoch of the "time of Jesus."

19. Kingsbury, "Structure of Matthew's Gospel," pp. 471ff.

We are concerned to press the argument that Matthew basically operates with two epochs in developing his concept of the history of salvation
with the result that the time of the church is to be seen as a "subcategory"
of the time of Jesus, because this, in turn, compels the following observation: contrary to Trilling, Strecker, and Walker, whatever the influence
of Matthew's ecclesiology upon his understanding of the history of salvation, it is the confessional truth of the abiding presence of Jesus with his
disciples (the Christology of Matthew) that, more than any other factor,
has given shape to his concept of the history of salvation.

If this sketch of Matthew's approach to the history of salvation is accurate, it confronts us at once with a question we posed earlier: Is, then,
salvation-history the chief principle according to which Matthew has organized his Gospel? This question can be answered in the affirmative only
should it be established that Matthew provides the reader with no basis
for constructing a topical outline. To ascertain this, however, we must ask
once more about the viability of Bacon's topical outline.

The critique of Bacon's outline is scattered but massive. Of the arguments brought against it, there are two which prove fatal. The most common one focuses on the inappropriateness of designating the infancy narratives of Matthew as a "preamble" and the passion and resurrection narratives as an "epilogue." To do this is to place these narratives outside the
main structure of the Gospel[20] and hence to overlook both the climactic
nature of the cross and resurrection in the gospel-story and the fact that
Matthew is not without a concept of history.[21] The second argument has
to do with the number five relative to the great discourses of Matthew as
well as with their alleged Pentateuchal coloring: Owing to the logia-
character of chapter 11[22] and the complete change of setting between
chapter 23 and chapters 24–25, to be consistent must one not speak more
properly of a "Matthean Hexateuch"[23] or indeed of Matthew as compiling
seven[24] great discourses?

These arguments make it clear that Bacon's outline and the concomitant

---

20. Cf. W. D. Davies, *The Setting of the Sermon on the Mount* (Cambridge: University Press, 1964), p. 25.
21. Cf. Strecker, *Der Weg der Gerechtigkeit*, p. 147 n. 2; Trilling, *Das wahre Israel*,
pp. 217f.
22. Cf. Walker, *Die Heilsgeschichte im ersten Evangelium*, p. 146 n. 112.
23. Cf. Austin Farrer, *St. Matthew and St. Mark* (London: Dacre Press, 1954),
chap. 11.
24. Cf. H. B. Green, "The Structure of St. Matthew's Gospel," in *Studia Evangelica*,
TU 102 (Berlin: Akademie-Verlag, 1968), p. 48.

views as to the nature and purpose of the First Gospel are unable to stand
the test of critical scrutiny. Neither do the several interpretations advocated by others and noted above survive the fall of Bacon's hypothesis.
Whether Matthew's document is described as "liturgical," "apologetic,"
"catechetical," "didactic," a "manual," or even a "book," the term either
tends to be one-sidedly paraenetic in connotation or does not do justice
to the circumstance that Matthew himself summarizes his work as the
"gospel of the kingdom" (RSV; 24:14; 26:13; cf. also 4:23; 9:35).[25]

Consequently, Bacon's outline of the First Gospel will not do. Does
another outline better commend itself?

Thirty years ago, N. B. Stonehouse mentioned almost in passing that the
verses 4:17 and 16:21 mark the broad structure of the First Gospel.[26]
Literarily, the distinctive feature of these verses is that they contain the
formula "From that time on Jesus began . . ." (RSV). As we have argued
elsewhere,[27] our position is that this formula does indeed demarcate the
broadest divisions of Matthew.

A glance at this formula shows that it calls attention to the person of
Jesus in that it cites his name, and it lends historical movement to the
narrative in that it alerts the reader to the beginning of a new phase of his
activity. At the same time, the verses 4:17 and 16:21 reveal themselves to
be well-rounded literary units that stand out from the immediate context.
In announcing programmatically a central theme Matthew proposes to
develop, these verses function within the Gospel much as superscriptions.
Accordingly, if we press these verses thematically, and 1:1 as well, we
discover that Matthew's Gospel divides itself neatly into broad divisions
of a topical nature as follows: (I) The Person of Jesus Messiah (1:1—
4:16); (II) The Proclamation of Jesus Messiah (4:17—16:20); and (III)
The Suffering, Death, and Resurrection of Jesus Messiah (16:21—28:20).

On the assumption that this outline is sound, what insight does it provide into the form and nature of the First Gospel? Concerning the form
of the Gospel, the fact that the material lends itself so well to this outline
proves that the history of salvation is not the chief or indeed sole principle by which Matthew organizes his work. On the contrary, it is plain

---

25. Contrary to Marxsen (*Mark the Evangelist*, p. 141), Julius Schniewind (*Das
Evangelium nach Matthäus*, NTD 2 [Göttingen: Vandenhoeck & Ruprecht, 1936],
p. 241) is correct in making this observation.
26. *The Witness of Matthew and Mark to Christ* (London: Tyndale Press, 1944),
pp. 129ff.
27. Cf. Kingsbury, "Structure of Matthew's Gospel," pp. 453–66.

that Matthew develops his concept of the history of salvation within the framework of a carefully conceived topical outline.

Concerning the nature of the First Gospel, we should not fail to note that this outline is thoroughly christological in tenor. We recall, however, that the same was true of our definition of Matthew's concept of salvation-history. Hence, two independent lines of inquiry can now be seen to support the view that, while the First Gospel certainly reflects ecclesiological concerns, it is principally the Christology of Matthew that has determined its character.

We need pursue our analysis of the form of Matthew's Gospel no further. What we have learned is that, despite the many facets of this Gospel, it is fundamentally a christological document. Our delineation of Matthew's topical outline and definition of his concept of salvation-history demonstrate that even as Matthew narrates his story of the person, ministry, and passion and resurrection of Jesus Messiah, he is at pains to place it within the flow of the history of salvation. But what is the salvation-historical significance of the gospel-story of Jesus Messiah? The form of Matthew's Gospel impels us to ask this question, but only a study of its message can supply the answer.

THE MESSAGE OF THE GOSPEL

Matthew employs "gospel of the kingdom" (24:14; 26:13; cf. also 4:23; 9:35) to summarize his writing. Unfortunately, he nowhere explicitly defines this. How, then, does he understand it?

At this juncture our probe of the structure of the Gospel proves its worth, for the first main part (1:1—4:16) provides the key. This part, as we saw, focuses on the person of Jesus Messiah (1:1). Specifically, he is said to be the "Son of David" and the "Son of Abraham." He is the "Son of David" because Joseph son of David gives him his name, adopting him (1:20, 25). He is the "Son of Abraham" because it is in him that the entire history of Israel, which began in Abraham, reaches its culmination (1:17).

But the one point Matthew stresses more than any other in this initial part of his Gospel is that Jesus Messiah is the "Son of God." Thus, in chapter 1 Matthew sets forth the divine sonship of Jesus with respect to his origin (1:1, 18): Jesus Messiah is the Son of God because he is conceived by the Holy Spirit (1:18, 20) and born of a virgin (1:23), whose husband scrupulously refrains from having relations with her until she gives birth to her child (1:25).

In chapters 2–4, Matthew continues his discussion of the person of Jesus Messiah, the Son of God, and likewise tells of his mission and filial obedience. In chapter 2, Matthew describes Herod as believing that the new-born "king of the Jews" is simply a political throne-pretender who must be killed (2:2, 13). Through the mouth of the prophet, however, God himself corrects this erroneous judgment: In reality, Jesus Messiah is the eschatological shepherd of "my people Israel" (2:5f.); in fact, this shepherd is none other than "my Son," the ideal Israelite who recapitulates in his infancy travels a segment of the history of the chosen people, who was also "my Son" (2:15; cf. Exod. 4:22f.).

In chapter 3 Matthew depicts John the Baptist as the forerunner of Jesus Messiah but at the same time underlines the superiority of Jesus. John baptizes with water for repentance (3:11), but Jesus is the "Mightier One" whom God at his baptism empowers with the Spirit for ministry (3:16) and calls "my beloved Son" (3:17). In this connection the thing to notice is that with the voice from heaven Matthew brings the entire first part of his Gospel to a climax and also reveals why the title "Son of God" is not found beside "Son of David" and "Son of Abraham" in 1:1: So profound is the truth expressed by this title that it is appropriate for God alone to be the first to utter it openly.[28] Finally, declared by God to be his Son, Jesus Messiah resists the calculated temptations of Satan to effect the loss of his divine sonship, rendering perfect obedience to his Father (4:1–11).

With this overview of the first main part of the Gospel, we are now in a position to appreciate the programmatic role that 1:23 plays. The so-called "Emmanuel passage" furnishes us with a "thumbnail" definition of what it means for Matthew to confess that Jesus is the Son of God: conceived by the Holy Spirit and born of a virgin, Jesus is the one in whom God chooses to dwell among his people. Still, the import of this passage is greater yet; for in Matthew's vocabulary, "God-talk" is not different in kind from "Kingdom-talk." Accordingly, the upshot of our argument is that in 1:23 we also have a preliminary definition of the expression the "gospel of the kingdom": It is the good news that in the person of Jesus Messiah, who is above all the Son of God, God fulfills his promises to Israel and comes to dwell among his own, thus inaugurating the eschatological age of salvation.

In a real sense, the latter two parts of the First Gospel (4:17—16:20;

---

28. Cf. Rudolph Pesch, "Der Gottessohn im matthäischen Evangelienprolog (Mt 1–2)," *Bib* 48 (1967): 416.

16:21—28:20) may be regarded as Matthew's elaboration on 1:23, interpreted as it is by its context (1:1—4:16). Of course this is not to imply that the entire Christology of Matthew can be reduced to the single strain of divine sonship; furthermore, it is the object of the following essay to deal specifically with the christological dimensions of the Gospel. At the same time, because Matthew's Son of God Christology is so central to the message of his Gospel, it is incumbent upon us to pursue this theme for a few additional paragraphs, even at the risk of some duplication of effort.

Important for a proper understanding of Matthew's further presentation of Jesus Messiah as the Son of God is the recognition that Jesus stands before the reader principally as the Son of God also in the chapters following 4:17. To establish this, there are a number of random observations we need to make.

The first is terminological in nature and applies to the whole of the Gospel, namely, it is generally recognized that, whatever their separate origins, such designations as "my [his] Son" (2:15; 3:17; 17:5; 21:37), "the Son" (11:27; 21:38; 28:19), and "Son of God" (8:29) are understood by Matthew to be variant expressions of the more comprehensive designation "the Son of God."[29] Indeed, we have already seen that even the word "son" can be synonymous with the fuller title (cf. 1:21, 23, 25).

The second observation is that "the Son of God" and its equivalent terms do not constitute for Matthew what might be called a "public" title. Thus, unbelievers and enemies never address Jesus with "Son of God," unless it be in mockery or blasphemy (cf. 26:63, 65; 27:40, 43), but with "Teacher" or "Rabbi." Similarly, Jesus, in public or in the presence of one such as a scribe, does not refer to himself as the Son of God but, for example, as the "Son of Man" (cf. 8:20; 9:6). Because, therefore, Son of God is not a "public" title, we should not expect to find it in those pericopes of the Gospel in which Matthew depicts Jesus as interacting with the unbelieving crowds and opponents (cf., e.g., chaps. 5–12).

The third thing to note is that Matthew associates the setting of the "mountain" exclusively with Jesus as the Son of God. The following correlations make this clear: Jesus is tempted on a mountain, as the Son of God (cf. 4:3, 6, 8);[30] Jesus retires to the mountain for prayer, yet the report of

---

29. Cf., e.g., Th. De Kruijf, *Der Sohn des lebendigen Gottes*, AnBib 16 (Rome: Pontifical Biblical Institute, 1962), *passim*. E. C. Colwell ("A Definite Rule for the Use of the Article in the Greek New Testament," *JBL* 52 [1933]: 13f., 20f.) has shown that "the Son of God" is the proper translation of the Greek of this title in such passages as Matt. 4:3, 6; 14:33; 27:40, 54 (cf. 16:16; 26:63).

30. As Evald Lövestam (*Son and Saviour*, ConNT 18 [Lund C. W. K. Gleerup,

this falls within a pericope in which the disciples are said to worship him as the Son of God (14:23, 33); on the mountain on which he is transfigured, Jesus is declared to be God's Son (17:1, 5); and after the resurrection, Jesus meets the eleven disciples on the mountain, and here he refers to himself as "the Son" (28:16, 19). In line with these correlations, it stands to reason that when Matthew describes Jesus in 5:1f. as ascending the mountain to teach and in 15:29–31 to heal he does so not as a new Moses[31] but as the Son of God.

In the fourth place, it is also necessary to recognize that Matthew's description of the disciples as "sons of God" (5:9), "sons of your heavenly Father" (5:45), and "the sons of the kingdom" (13:38) presupposes the understanding that Jesus calls his disciples to follow him (4:18–22) precisely as the Son of God (cf. also 3:17). For inherent in these descriptions is the idea that through Jesus Messiah, who is the Son of God, the disciples of Jesus enter into a relationship of sonship with God.

Finally, equally significant is the circumstance that Matthew ascribes divine authority (exousia) to Jesus in his capacity as the Son of God. This is the thrust of the pericope 21:23–27: The reader is to perceive that because Jesus is the Son of God the "authority" by which he "does these things" is, like that of John, not "from men" but "from heaven," that is, from God his Father (cf. also 11:27; 28:18).

With these random observations in mind, we can trace in bold strokes Matthew's development of the central thought that in Jesus Messiah, the Son of God, God dwells with his own (1:23). In Galilee, Jesus, having been presented at his baptism (3:13–17) and temptations (4:1–11) as the Son of God, is portrayed as embarking upon his messianic ministry to Israel (4:17). He, the Son of God, calls his first disciples (4:18–22), who through him become sons of God (5:9, 45). Accompanied by them he engages in a ministry of teaching and preaching on the one hand and of healing on the other (4:23; cf. 9:35; 11:1). As for his teaching activity, Jesus Son of God ascends the mountain and there provides instruction for his disciples and all Israel (chaps. 5–7). As for his healing activity, he goes about Galilee and performs ten mighty acts of deliverance (chaps. 8–9).

1961], p. 100) and others have pointed out, in the third temptation (Matt. 4:8–10) the title "Son of God" is presupposed but not explicitly mentioned, owing to the nature of this temptation.

31. W. D. Davies (Setting of the Sermon on the Mount, pp. 25–108) and J. M. Gibbs ("The Son of God as the Torah Incarnate in Matthew," Studia Evangelica, TU 102 [Berlin: Akademie Verlag, 1963], pp. 38–41) have demonstrated that Matthew does not, as was once supposed, imbue his Gospel with a new-Moses typology.

In point of fact, in the teaching and healing ministry of Jesus Son of God, the authority of God himself graciously manifests itself (7:28f.; 8:9).[32] In addition Jesus Son of God also authorizes his disciples to go throughout Israel, entrusting them with a ministry of proclamation and healing patterned after his own (10:1, 5–8). And what, at the deepest level, is taking place in the ministry of Jesus Messiah, Son of God? The Son, to whom the Father has given all things, is revealing the Father to those whom he will (11:27).

But Israel does not recognize that in Jesus Messiah, the Son of God, God reveals himself and comes to dwell with his people (chaps. 11—12). Only the disciples of Jesus recognize this (11:25; 12:49f.; 13:11, 16f.). Enlightened by God, they, as will also the Gentiles (cf. the Roman soldiers, 27:54), acknowledge that Jesus is in truth the Son of God (14:33; 16:16f.) and thus articulate what for Matthew's church (16:18) becomes its most exalted confession of faith. Of course this confession is, ultimately, predicated upon the completed work of Jesus Son of God: first, his death on the cross (cf. 27:40, 43, 46, 54) by which he saves his people once for all from their sins (1:21; 26:27f.) and brings to an end the Jewish cult (27:51); and second, his resurrection and exaltation to all power in heaven and on earth,[33] by virtue of which he resides in the company of his disciples to the close of the age, enabling them to carry out their commission to make disciples of all nations (28:16–20).

In broad lines this is the gospel, or message, Matthew proclaims, which is likewise a presentation of Jesus Messiah as the Son of God. In a concluding paragraph we shall attempt to make this presentation fruitful for the objective of this essay.

SUMMARY

We have seen that Matthew describes his writing as the "gospel of the kingdom." In examining its structure we discovered that he develops his concept of the history of salvation within the framework of a topical outline of the "life of Jesus Messiah." The first main part of this outline

---

32. For an explanation as to why Matthew attributes divine authority to Jesus as the Son of Man in 9:6, cf. J. D. Kingsbury, "The Title 'Son of Man' in Matthew's Gospel," CBQ 37 (1975): 193–202.

33. That Matt. 28:16–20 is informed by a Son-of-God and not a Kyrios or Son-of-Man Christology we have attempted to show in "The Title Kyrios in Matthew's Gospel," JBL 94 (1975): 246–55.

(1:1—4:16), which concentrates on the person of Jesus Messiah, portrays him above all as the Son of God. Matthew's concise definition of Jesus as the Son of God is that in his person God inaugurates the eschatological age of salvation in fulfillment of his promises to Israel by coming to dwell with his people (1:23). In seeing how Matthew elaborates on this definition throughout the second and third main parts of his Gospel (4:17—16:20; 16:21—28:20), we learned of the significance it has for him and his church. Briefly, it means all of the following: that Jesus Messiah, the Son of God, reveals God to humankind, authoritatively declaring his holy will and delivering people from the dominion of Satan; that he leads his disciples to perceive his identity and hence to offer their confession of faith; that he saves, through the cross, all who are his from sin, bringing to an end the Jewish cult; and that he, raised by God and exalted to all authority, abides with his own to the end of time as they carry out their great commission. All this, then, is at the heart of the message Matthew intends to promulgate with his document. To round this message out mention must at least be made of the parousia of Jesus Son of Man; nevertheless, on the whole, the message of Matthew proves itself to be indeed the gospel of the Son of God.

7.

The Messiah of
Israel as Teacher of
the Gentiles:

The Setting of Matthew's Christology

LLOYD GASTON

Simple decency, to say nothing of Matthew's law of love, demands that we allow our neighbors to define themselves rather
than impose a caricature on them; and to speak today of the
utter reprobation of the people of Israel is monstrous and
obscene.

The Problem

I

The problem was that Jesus' mission had ended in a complete failure.
Jesus came proclaiming the gospel that "the time is fulfilled and the kingdom of God has come near," that the eschatological hour had dawned
which would see the consummation of all the hopes of Israel, which would
see God's kingship realized universally because his will would be done universally, which would mean not only the redemption of Israel but also
salvation for the nations. In short, Jesus proclaimed that now, in his time,
at the end of history, the prophecy of Deutero-Isaiah (52:7–10) was about
to be finally fulfilled.

But it did not happen. Jesus died without ushering in the kingdom of
God. On the third day history did not culminate in the resurrection of the
dead, for only one man was raised. But this man *was* raised, which seemed
to give divine confirmation to the truth of his message. With great enthusiasm the congregation of the last days continued Jesus' proclamation of the
kingdom to the lost sheep of the house of Israel. Jesus was seen to be not
only the proclaimer but also the bringer of the kingdom, the Savior of
Israel (Acts 13:23; Matt. 1:21), the Messiah of the last days. "Blessed be

78

the Lord, the God of Israel, for he has visited and given redemption to his people, . . . salvation from our enemies and from the hand of all who hate us; . . . to guide our feet into the way of peace" (Luke 1:68–79). And yet toward the end of that first generation of the Palestinian church these words began to sound more and more hollow. Whatever Jesus was to the early church, he was hardly the messianic savior of Israel. The pessimism of the mission speech in Matthew 10 surely represents the experience of the church preaching to Israel, and the messengers seem almost to expect to have their message rejected. Paul reflects something of the anguish of the church over the relative failure of its mission to Israel. This failure of the mission of the church was all the more agonizing because of their expectation that the end was very near, at the end of one generation at the latest (Mark 9:1; 13:30; Matt. 10:23). The problem of the so-called delay of the parousia is really only a subsidiary aspect of the major problem of the unresponse of Israel.[1] And then came the disastrous war with Rome, which ended with the capture of Zion, the destruction of the Temple, the sign of Israel's election, and unbelievable suffering and loss of life. It was an event as momentous for its time as Auschwitz has been for many in our time.

What are we to say to all of this? Has then the word of God failed (Rom. 9:6)? Has God rejected his people (Rom. 11:1)? Are the gifts and the call of God irrevocable (Rom. 11:29)? Is it not blasphemous after the fall of Jerusalem to speak of Jesus as the messianic Savior of Israel? Jesus was after all, not only during his lifetime but also in the activity of his apostles, so different from the messianic expectations in the Old Testament and early Judaism that *either* God misled Israel in the Scriptures and his word is not to be trusted, *or* Jesus was not after all the Messiah and God's revelation in him was not to be trusted. The contrast between the hopes of the Jewish-Christian church and the outcome of their activities and the events of history raised the question of God's trustworthiness in its sharpest possible form.

The situation of the Gentile-Christian church was equally precarious. Salvation for Gentiles depended on the priority of Israel in God's *Heilsgeschichte*. First, "for the sake of God's truthfulness, Christ had to become a servant to the circumcised to confirm the promises given to the patriarchs, in order that," second, "the Gentiles might glorify God for his mercy"

---

1. Johannes Munck has in several publications tried to show the importance of the lack of response in Israel as "the greatest problem faced by primitive Christianity" (*Christ and Israel: An Interpretation of Romans 9–11*, trans. Ingeborg Nixon [Philadelphia: Fortress Press, 1967], p. 20).

(Rom. 15:8f.). First, "God had to send his son, born of woman, born under the law, in order that," second, "we might receive adoption as sons" (Gal. 4:4f., RSV). First, God had to "rebuild the fallen booth of David," in order that, second, "the rest of men may seek the Lord, all the Gentiles who are called by my name" (Acts 15:16f.). God can be trusted to be gracious to Gentiles only insofar as he keeps his promises to Israel. The status of Gentile Christians depended on the prior success of the mission to Israel. Insofar as this mission was unsuccessful, it was essential to assert that this was not the fault of God and his Messiah but of a disobedient Israel, whose guilt had to be magnified. Indeed the unresponse of Israel had even to be shown to be a providential act of God, who deliberately hardened the hearts of his people, as in Romans 9–11 or the use of Isaiah 6:9 in the synoptic Gospels, Acts, and John.[2] God's faithfulness had to be maintained at all costs, even the cost of presenting him as unfaithful to his own people. On the other hand, the decision for the Gentile mission before the arrival of the eschatological time foreseen in the prophets presupposed the prior failure of the mission to Israel. Only when the gospel had been offered to and rejected by all Israel was the church free to take it to the Gentiles (Acts 13:46). This then was the dilemma of the early Gentile-Christian church: The mission to Israel had to be both successful and unsuccessful; God had both to be faithful to his promises and cause Israel to reject the fulfillment of these promises; Jesus had to be the Messiah of Israel even if instead of the messianic kingdom there was disaster, instead of *Heilsgeschichte* there was *Unheilsgeschichte*.

In the face of such a dilemma, one can understand why the church would turn away from Israel completely. When the gospel of Jesus Christ was preached to Gentiles, they heard not the good news of the nearness of God's kingdom, not the good news of the advent of Israel's Messiah, but they "turned to God from idols, to serve a living and true God" (I Thess. 1:9, RSV). Functionally, Jesus meant for the Gentiles what he could never mean for the Jews, the sole revelation of the one God, even God himself. With Pentecost a new factor entered the situation. Liberation, salvation, spiritual gifts were simply part of the experience of Gentile Christians. In their enthusiasm, what need did they have of a history of the promises to Israel, of a Jewish Messiah, Jesus, of commandments of any kind (cf. I Cor.)? The movement was already underway which would end in the

---

2. Cf. Joachim Gnilka, *Die Verstockung Israels: Isaias 6, 9–10 in der Theologie der Synoptiker*, SANT 3 (Munich: Kösel-Verlag, 1961). Paul's concept in Rom. 9–11 of a present remnant and eschatological salvation for "all Israel" cannot be assumed for Matthew.

second-century antitheses: church versus Israel, spirit versus word, Jesus the emissary of the true God versus the God of Israel with his order of creation and tyrannous commandments.

It is against this background that we wish to approach the Gospel of Matthew. This Gospel had for centuries been read as the words of Jesus directed to the Israel of his day and to the church of all times. Then form criticism taught us to hear in the synoptic tradition the kerygma of the earliest church. Now redaction criticism[3] seeks to understand the theology of the final evangelist, as distinguished from that of the tradition. It is precisely this version of a "criterion of dissimilarity" which is used to establish the redactional theology which is the source of major hermeneutical problems. The standard works on New Testament Christology trace the history of the individual titles through the various stages of the history of the early church. Matthew can be and is used as the major source for such investigations. The present task, however, is restricted to outlining aspects of the Christology of the final redaction. The usual assumptions will be made: that the Gospel was written in the period A.D. 80–100, probably in Antioch;[4] that the organization of the material is an important clue to the theology of the redaction;[5] and that this redaction can be distinguished from earlier Marcan, Q, and special Matthean material.[6] In the light of the

---

3. The works that have been considered most important for this study are Wolfgang Trilling, *Das wahre Israel: Studien zur Theologie des Matthäus-Evangeliums* (Munich: Kösel-Verlag, 1964[3]); Günther Bornkamm, Gerhard Barth, and H. J. Held, *Tradition and Interpretation in Matthew* (Philadelphia: Westminster Press, 1963); Georg Strecker, *Der Weg der Gerechtigkeit* (Göttingen: Vandenhoeck & Ruprecht, 1962[1], 1971[3]); Reinhart Hummel, *Die Auseinandersetzung zwischen Kirche und Judentum im Matthäusevangelium*, BEvT 33 (Munich, 1963); W. D. Davies, *The Setting of the Sermon on the Mount* (Cambridge: University Press, 1966); Rolf Walker, *Die Heilsgeschichte im ersten Evangelium*, FRLANT 91 (Göttingen: Vandenhoeck & Ruprecht, 1967); Douglas R. A. Hare, *The Theme of Jewish Persecution of Christians in the Gospel according to St. Matthew*, SNTSMS 6 (Cambridge: University Press, 1967); Jack Dean Kingsbury, *The Parables of Jesus in Matthew 13* (Atlanta: John Knox Press, 1969); Sjef van Tilborg, *The Jewish Leaders in Matthew* (Leiden: E. J. Brill, 1972).

4. Recent scholarship has seen no reason to abandon the arguments of Johannes Weiss, *Earliest Christianity: A History of the Period A.D. 30–150*, trans. Frederick C. Grant (New York: Harper & Bros., 1959), pp. 751–56; and B. H. Streeter, *The Four Gospels* (New York: Macmillan Company, 1925), pp. 500–523; cf. the introductions.

5. The Gospel is not organized in five books to represent the new Torah of the new Moses (cf. Davies, *Setting of the Sermon on the Mount*, pp. 14–108). The outline we follow is that of Jack Dean Kingsbury, "The Structure of Matthew's Gospel and His Concept of Salvation-History," *CBQ* 35 (1973): 451–74; cf. also Ernst Lohmeyer in W. Schmauch, ed., *Das Evangelium des Matthäus* (Göttingen: Vandenhoeck & Ruprecht, 1958[2]).

6. "M" is then basically traditional and not redactional; cf. J. P. Brown, "The Form of 'Q' Known to Matthew," *NTS* 8 (1961–62): 27–42. E. L. Abel, "Who Wrote Matthew?" *NTS* 17 (1970–71): 138–52.

problems just sketched, we shall look at the background of Matthew's
Christology from two distinct perspectives. A brief conclusion will suggest
some of the problems the redaction-critical method poses for theology and
proclamation.

II

On one level Matthew's Gospel is a theological tragedy, the story of the
advent and rejection of the Messiah of Israel. It makes a great difference
from which end one begins, but let us now begin at the beginning and
read through the Gospel from this perspective. "The book of the origin of
Jesus Messiah, the Son of David, the Son of Abraham" (1:1). Coming at
the end of a genealogy beginning with Abraham, Jesus is to be the climax
of the history of Israel, the Messiah of Israel, Son of David, who "will save
his people from their sins" (1:21, RSV). There follows the first of a series
of formula quotations,[7] the point of all of which is christological, to show
that Jesus is the Messiah of Israel, the fulfillment of the prophets. Jesus
has been born as "king of the Jews" (2:2), the "ruler who will shepherd
my people Israel" (2:6). But he was persecuted by Herod the king and
recognized by the Gentile magi, a shadow of things to come.

Also John the Baptist was a fulfillment (3:3f.), who prepared Israel for
its Messiah. "All the prophets and the law prophesied until John [since
then prophecy is being fulfilled]; and if you are willing to accept it, he is
Elijah who is to come" (11:13f., RSV). He preached the same gospel as
Jesus (4:17) and the disciples (10:7): "Repent, for the kingdom of heaven
is at hand" (3:2, RSV), and the same warning against the leaders of
Israel (3:7–10; cf. 7:16–20; 12:33f.). There is only one unified group of
leaders, whether called "Pharisees and Sadducees" or "scribes and Pharisees" or "Pharisees" or "Sadducees" or "scribes."[8] Matthew is dealing not
with history but with types. Jesus was baptized by John in order "to fulfill
all righteousness" (3:15), as he fulfilled the Prophets and the Law (5:17).
At his baptism Jesus was declared to be Son of God, and this term is
immediately defined in the temptation story to mean the representative of
Israel, God's son (cf. Exod. 4:22f.). The title Son of God is for Matthew
equivalent to the title Messiah, as is shown in two key passages, 16:16 and

_wB_

---

7. Cf. Krister Stendahl, *The School of St. Matthew* (Philadelphia: Fortress Press,
1967).
8. Cf. Walker, *Heilsgeschichte*, pp. 11–29; Tilborg, *Jewish Leaders*, pp. 1–7.

26:63. Son of God in Matthew means not power but obedience, not a divine figure but the meek and lowly king.[9] Thus Matthew in his prologue, 1:1—4:16, introduces the person of the Davidic Messiah, the Son of God.

"And he went about all Galilee [all the cities and villages], teaching in their synagogues and preaching the gospel of the kingdom and healing every disease and every infirmity" (4:23 = 9:35, RSV). These two summary statements frame and characterize the intervening material. Jesus' mission was to "their"[10] synagogues, as the Messiah of word (5–7) and miracle (8–9). The Sermon on the Mount is not really an attempt to win Israel to a faith in its Messiah. It begins with an announcement that Jesus' disciples will be persecuted by "them" (5:11) and the demand that the righteousness of the disciples must exceed that of the scribes and Pharisees (5:20). There follows a series of six contrasts, between what was "said to the men of old" and the authoritative word of Jesus, which are usually called by the Marcionite name "antitheses." The antithesis in 6:1–18 is to the behavior of the "hypocrites" who "do all their deeds that they may be seen [praised] by men" (23:5; 6:2, 5, 16).[11] The sermon ends with a final antithesis between Jesus, who "taught them as one having authority," and the scribes (7:29). The most extensive rearrangement of Marcan material is found in Matthew 8–9, in order to present ten miracles illustrating the healing activity of the Messiah, Son of David;[12] but in a saying added to the story of the centurion's servant is sounded for the first time the note of final rejection: "the sons of the kingdom will be thrown into the outer darkness" (8:12, RSV).[13] The miracle collection ends with the contrast of the crowds who say, "Never was anything like this seen in Israel," and

---

9. Cf. Walker, *Heilsgeschichte*, p. 129. It is true that there are other nuances to this title in Matthew (cf., e.g., 8:29; 11:27), and we have barely touched on his use of the title Son of Man, but we are seeking to underline what is characteristic of the Matthean redaction.

10. As in 10:17; 12:9; 13:54; 23:34; cf. "their cities" (11:1), "their scribes" (7:29).

11. Not only is the charge unjustified and inappropriate when applied to the historical Pharisees (cf., among others, G. F. Moore, *Judaism in the First Centuries of the Christian Era* [Cambridge: Harvard University Press, 1927], II, 193), but the concept itself of play acting to win glory from men, contrasting appearance and reality, is typically Greek and not Jewish at all (cf. Tilborg, *Jewish Leaders*, pp. 8–26).

12. On the significance of "Son of David," cf. J. M. Gibbs, "Purpose and Pattern in Matthew's Use of the Title 'Son of David,'" *NTS* 10 (1963–64): 446–64; Bornkamm, *Tradition and Interpretation*, p. 37; Strecker, *Gerechtigkeit*, pp. 118–20; Hummel, *Auseinandersetzung*, pp. 116–22; Walker, *Heilsgeschichte*, pp. 128–32.

13. Differing from Luke 13:28f., it is no longer a call to repentance. The contrast between the Gentiles who come from east and west and the sons of the kingdom as Israel is dictated by the context of the story contrasting the faith of a Gentile with the lack of faith in Israel.

the Pharisees who say, "He casts out demons by the prince of demons" (9:33f., RSV).

The ministry of the Messiah to Israel, the compassion of the shepherd for his sheep (9:36), was continued in the mission of his disciples (9:35—11:1). Like the Messiah (15:24), the disciples were sent only "to the lost sheep of the house of Israel" (10:6, RSV). Like John the Baptist (3:2) and Jesus (4:17), the disciples preach that "the kingdom of heaven is at hand" (10:7, RSV), and like Jesus they perform miracles (10:8). The response to this message is persecution (10:17–23a from Mark 13:9–13), and the period will be brought to a close, before they go through all the towns of Israel, by the coming of the Son of Man (10:23b). As Jesus was called Beelzebul (9:34; 12:24), so also his disciples (10:25). This parallelism of the generation of the Jewish-Christian church with the life of Jesus and to an extent with the activity of John the Baptist is characteristic for Matthew and an important clue to his theology.

Matthew 11:2 speaks of the "deeds of the Messiah," 11:19 of "the deeds of wisdom" which were rejected by "this generation." Because Israel listened to neither John nor Jesus, because they did not repent in response to their deeds, therefore woe and judgment must be pronounced (11:20–24). The crowds were amazed at Jesus' pronouncements in the conflict stories and his miracles and exclaimed, "Can this be the Son of David?" (12:23), but the Pharisees said, "It is only by Beelzebul, the prince of demons, that this man casts out demons" (12:24, RSV; cf. 9:34; 10:25). This is the sin against the Holy Spirit which "will not be forgiven" (12:32). That generation, the brood of vipers, are evil simply by their very nature (12:34). It is "an evil and adulterous generation" that "seeks for a sign," but they will be condemned at the judgment (12:38–42, RSV). It is the case with that evil generation that they will be demon-possessed sevenfold (12:43–45). Even Jesus' family are rejected in favor of those "who do the will of my father" (12:46–50). Finally, Jesus spoke to the crowd in parables *because* they were blind, deaf, and without understanding (13:13, 34). They did not repent because it had not been given to them to know the secrets of the kingdom (13:11; cf. 11:25). The whole section 11:2—13:35 could be comprehended under the heading "Israel rejects her Messiah and is in turn rejected."

The second half of the parable chapter is addressed to the disciples, and 13:53—16:20 largely follows the Marcan outline. We can note in particular three invasions into a Marcan context. Into the controversy story on the traditions of the elders is inserted the remark that the Pharisees were scandalized by Jesus' teaching, and he replies, "Let them alone; they are blind guides of the blind."[14] Into the story of the Canaanite woman has been inserted the programmatic statement of Jesus' mission: "I was sent only to the lost sheep of the house of Israel" (15:24, RSV). Into the discourse on leaven has been inserted the interpretation "He told them to beware not of bread but of the teaching of the Pharisees and Sadducees" (16:12). With 16:21 begins a section of teaching for the disciples organized around the three predictions of the passion; it is clear that the rejected Messiah of Israel must die.

The story of the suffering and death of the rejected Messiah of Israel is played out in Jerusalem. Before entering the city, the Messiah, Son of David, had compassion on two blind men (20:29–34) and then entered the city in lowly royalty as the meek shepherd king of Zechariah (21:1–11). The crowds greeted him as Son of David, and "all the city was stirred, saying, 'Who is this?'" (RSV).[15] The Messiah immediately entered his temple to take possession of it and to heal the blind and the lame, but the chief priests and the scribes[16] were indignant (21:15). Israel, the fig tree, was cursed (21:19). The question concerning the authority of Jesus and John the Baptist is followed by the three great anti-Israel parables, that is, three parables which have been given an anti-Israel interpretation by Matthew.[17] (1) After the parable of the two sons, Jesus says that because Israel did not repent and believe John the Baptist, who came in the way of righteousness, therefore they shall not enter the kingdom of God (21:32). (2) After the parable of the wicked tenants, interpreted even more allegorically than in Mark of the sending of the prophets and the killing of Jesus, comes the final judgment: "He will destroy those wicked people utterly" (21:41), and even more "Therefore, I tell you, God will take from you the kingdom of God and give it to a nation which produces the fruits of it" (21:43). (3) The parable of the marriage feast has been completely allegorized in terms of the sending of early Christian missionaries to Israel, and an awkward insertion into the parable refers to the fall of Jerusalem: "The king was angry and having sent his troops destroyed

---

14. Given the history of Jewish-Christian relations, many Jews may well have wished that this teaching had been followed; they would have been willing to accept the verbal calumny of the second half for the sake of the physical peace of the first.

15. It is not clear whether the confession of the crowd that Jesus was a prophet is meant positively or as an inadequate response.

16. On the chief priests and scribes and elders of the people as the Jerusalem division of the unified opposition of Israel to Jesus, cf. Walker, *Heilsgeschichte*, pp. 29–33.

17. O. H. Steck, *Israel und das gewaltsame Geschick der Propheten*, WMANT 23 (Neukirchen-Vluyn: Neukirchener Verlag, 1967), pp. 289–316, points out the parallelism of 21:28—22:7 and 23:29—24:2 and their connection with the Deuteronomic motif of the murder of the prophets.

those murderers and burned their city" (22:7). Because Israel rejected John the Baptist and Jesus and the early church, therefore God has rejected Israel and destroyed Jerusalem.

The significance of the woes against the scribes and Pharisees (hypocrites, Matt. 23) is to be seen not as actual polemic, with which the tradition undoubtedly begins, but as providing grounds for the unconditional judgment with which it ends. That generation, as successors of those who murdered the prophets (23:29–31), has also as a climax persecuted and killed the early Christian missionaries (23:34). Therefore upon this generation will come all the righteous blood ever shed on earth, from the beginnings of history (Abel) through the Messiah (27:25) down to the end of the history of Jerusalem in A.D. 70 (Zechariah; cf. Josephus *Jewish War* 4.334ff.). Verses 31f. take up again the judgment preaching of John the Baptist (3:7–10) with the very significant omission of "bear fruit that befits repentance"; repentance is no longer a possibility. In an application of a wisdom motif, Jesus says that he would have gathered the children of Jerusalem under the wings of the Shekinah, "but you would not;" therefore, "behold, your house is forsaken" (23:37f.). "For I say unto you, *from now on [ap' arti]*[18] you will not see me until you say, 'Blessed is he who comes in the name of the Lord'" (23:39). These are Jesus' last public words. He who comes will be the Son of Man in judgment. There follows immediately the prediction of the destruction of Jerusalem (24:1f.).

The eschatological discourse (Matt. 24:3ff.) begins with the question "What will be the sign of your parousia and of the end of the age?" Does the question refer to two events or one? The situation of Matthew's church preaching the gospel of the kingdom as a testimony "to all the Gentiles" while being persecuted "by all the Gentiles" is envisaged in 24:9–14. I have suggested elsewhere the possibility that the chapter also describes a kind of parousia of the Son of Man at the destruction of Jerusalem, an event which for Matthew lies in the past.[19] "This generation will not pass away until all these things take place" (24:34, cf. 10:23; 23:36). The strangely unhistorical character of the Gospel makes a decision difficult. In any case, Matthew 25:31–46 portrays the judgment of "all the Gentiles" before the

---

18. On the significance of this "from now on" for the Christology of Matthew, cf. Hummel, *Auseinandersetzung*, pp. 141f.; Walker, *Heilsgeschichte*, p. 70; Trilling, *Das wahre Israel*, pp. 67f.

19. Lloyd Gaston, *No Stone on Another: Studies in the Significance of the Fall of Jerusalem in the Synoptic Gospels* (Leiden: E. J. Brill, 1970), pp. 432f., 483–87.

throne of the Son of Man, which seems to exclude Israel. The criterion for judgment is the love or lack of love shown to "one of the least of these my brethren." The scene is completely universalistic.

Matthew's passion story, in comparison with that of Mark, seeks even more to emphasize the guilt of Israel. Throughout the course of the Gospel the crowds had been undecided whether to follow their leaders or Jesus. At the end it is "all the people" who say, "His blood be on us and on our children" (27:25; cf. 27:22; 21:43). To the question of the high priest, "Tell us if you are the Messiah, the Son of God," Jesus replied, "You have said it; but I say to you, *from now on* [*ap' arti*] you will see the Son of Man sitting at the right hand of Power and coming on the clouds of heaven" (26:64). Jesus died as the Messiah of Israel, the King of the Jews. At the moment of his death the Gentile centurion declared, "Truly this was the Son of God" (27:54). The Gentiles' gain was Israel's loss.

More than any other Gospel, Matthew emphasizes Jesus' messiahship. More than any other Gospel, Matthew emphasizes the utter rejection of Israel. These two emphases are not unrelated. Israel rejected her Messiah; therefore God has rejected Israel. All of this has come upon "this generation," the brood of vipers, the evil and adulterous generation of murderers. This dogma helps Matthew rationalize the failure of the mission of the church to Israel. More important, it helps him to come to terms with the human suffering involved in the disastrous war with Rome; blood simply *was* on the children's heads and cried out for an explanation. Perhaps it also provided Matthew with a solution to the problem of the delay of the parousia, in that he could say that the parousia did occur for that generation in Israel, but it meant judgment. Most of all, though, the concept helped Matthew to understand and justify the shift of the mission of the early church to the Gentiles.[20]

The rejection of Israel freed the way for the Gentile mission, but the connection is not direct. There are many reflections of the church in Matthew's Gospel, but not in opposition to Israel. The church is not the new Israel, not the true Israel, not the heirs of Abraham's faith or the

---

20. Matthew would agree with Heinrich Schlier, "Die Entscheidung für die Heidenmission in der Urchristenheit," in *Die Zeit der Kirche* (Freiburg: Herder, 1942, 1972), pp. 90–107, who names as one of the three basic "presuppositions without which the Gentile mission could not take place: that Israel has rejected the Messiah Jesus and thereby been itself rejected as the elect people." There is a connection with his third thesis: "that the end of the world, which was inaugurated with Christ and makes the time urgent, is not immediately immanent."

grafted branches, not the inheritor of the promises.[21] Insofar as there is continuity, it lies in the concept of the gospel of the kingdom, preached by the Messiah to Israel, the sons of the kingdom, and then taken away from them and made available to non-Israel. But the connection is completely and only christological. Two recent studies of Matthew, that by Strecker and especially that by Walker, attempt to show that Matthew is operating with a rather complex concept of *Heilsgeschichte*. This attempt to impose a Conzelmannian understanding of Luke onto the theology of Matthew cannot be said to have succeeded. In fact, Matthew seems to have no concept of history. His contrast is not between two different periods of history, that of Israel and that of the church, but between two different Christologies, that of the Messiah of Israel and that of the Lord of the Gentiles. The Gospel contains both simultaneously.

For Matthew, Jesus was the Messiah, the Son of David, the King of the Jews. It is not the church but Jesus who was the fulfillment of the Old Testament (cf. the formula quotations). It was Jesus who came to fulfill all righteousness (3:15), who came to fulfill the Law and the Prophets (5:17). As the one who perfectly fulfilled the will of God (26:42), Jesus showed himself to be the obedient Son of God. As the fulfillment in all respects of the Old Testament, and because God in his providence did not allow him to be recognized as that fulfillment, Jesus brought both to its goal and to its end the history begun with Abraham, to free it for new beginnings. Jesus was, but is no more, the Son of David, Son of God, Messiah of Israel.

III

Why should Matthew's Gospel have become the favorite of the emergent Gentile-Christian church? It has commonly been assumed that Matthew is the most Jewish-Christian of the Gospels, largely on the basis of the concern we have just delineated to present Jesus as the messianic fulfillment. But it must be clear that the church is no longer engaged in a mission to Israel.[22] How could they be when they were convinced that Israel had been definitely rejected and that repentance was no longer possible? No one has yet satisfactorily answered K. W. Clark's contention[23] that "this Gentile bias is the primary thesis in Matthew, and such a message

---

21. Cf. Walker, *Heilsgeschichte*, pp. 81–83; and Hare, *Theme of Jewish Persecution*, pp. 156–62.
22. Cf. esp. Trilling, Strecker, Walker, and Hare.
23. "The Gentile Bias in Matthew," *JBL* 66 (1947): 165–72.

would be natural only from the bias of a Gentile author," and more and more scholars have come to agree with him.[24] One also cannot convincingly speak of a polemic against contemporary Judaism because of Matthew's serious misrepresentations. With respect to the antitheses of the Sermon on the Mount, for example, all of which are Matthew's creations,[25] "what purports here to be the Jewish Law or the Jewish way is unrecognizable to Jews, as it would have been for Jesus himself."[26] Of the six, it simply was *not* "said to the men of old" that (6) one should hate one's enemies, or (5) the lex talionis should be applied literally, or (1) only murder is liable to judgment; in the fourth *epiorkeō* is not found in the Septuagint, and it is uncertain whether the reference is to oaths or vows or false witness; and the third on divorce is misquoted. While many parts of Matthew's Gospel are a good source for first-century Judaism, other parts, mainly redactional, show an astonishing ignorance.[27] It is conceivable that for Matthew the Pharisees "are the representatives of the synagogue 'across the street' in Matthew's community,"[28] but if so there was no conversation occurring across that street. It is more likely that the Matthean Pharisees are a theological construct for "that generation" and that if there is any present application it is to a phenomenon within his own congregation. Matthew was written at least for, if not by, Gentile Christians, and the relationship to the Jewish-Christian traditions contained therein is problematic. We examined the Gospel before beginning from the beginning; let us now look at it from the perspective of the end, in terms of (1) its successors in church history, (2) the end of the Sermon on the Mount, and (3) the end of the Gospel, Matthew 28.

Ignatius became Bishop of Antioch in A.D. 83. Matthew is usually dated A.D. 85–100 and localized in Antioch. This means that in all probability Ignatius was bishop of the church in which the final redaction of the

---

24. Trilling, Strecker, Walker, Tilborg, Brown, Abel; and Poul Nepper-Christensen, *Das Matthäusevangelium, ein judenschristliches Evangelium?* (Aarhus: Universitetsforlaget, 1958) (not available to me).

25. Cf. M. Jack Suggs, *Wisdom, Christology, and Law in Matthew's Gospel* (Cambridge: Harvard University Press, 1970), pp. 109–15.

26. Samuel Sandmel, *A Jewish Understanding of the New Testament* (Cincinnati: Hebrew Union College Press, 1956), p. 149. Significant is his spontaneous reaction: "composed . . . by a Gentile" (p. 167).

27. For example, of Sabbath law (12:11), geography (19:1), means of execution (23:24), first-century population (15:22), rabbinic titles (23:9f.), tephillin (23:5, *phylaktērion* = amulet), and especially the Shema (22:37; cf. the evidence but not the conclusion of Joachim Jeremias, *Abba* [Göttingen: Vandenhoeck & Ruprecht, 1966], pp. 255–60).

28. Stendahl, *School of St. Matthew*, p. xi.

Gospel took place. This should be of capital importance for interpreting the Gospel. The church in Antioch as reflected in the letters of Ignatius (ca. A.D. 110) was completely oriented to the Gentiles. Judaism was for him simply obsolete, "for Christianity did not believe in Judaism but Judaism in Christianity" (*Magn.* 10:3), and "if we are living until now according to Judaism (a 'strange doctrine' and 'old fable') we confess that we have not received grace" (*Magn.* 8:1). The prophets after all were disciples of Jesus (*Magn.* 8:2; 9:2); their function was to foretell Jesus' life (*Phld.* 9:2) and preach the gospel (*Phld.* 5:2), and Jesus raised them from the dead (*Magn.* 9:2; cf. Matt. 27:52f.?). Ignatius was troubled by certain heretics who were certainly docetic and probably legalists. "It is monstrous to talk of Jesus Christ and to Judaize" (*Magn.* 10:3). "If anyone interprets Judaism to you, do not listen to him; for it is better to hear Christianity from a circumcised man than Judaism from an uncircumcised" (*Phld.* 6:1). As Weiss said, "the 'Judaizers' were apparently not born Jews but Gentiles."[29] If there was one group of Gentile docetic Judaizers, this might have significance for interpreting Matthew. "But mark those who have strange opinions concerning the grace of Jesus Christ which has come to us, and see how contrary they are to the mind of God. For love they have no care, none for the widow, none for the orphan, none for the distressed, none for the afflicted, none for the prisoner or for him released from prison, none for the hungry or thirsty" (*Smyrn.* 6:2; cf. Matt. 25:31–46). Their lack of love is much more crucial than their opinions. The Christology of Ignatius is related to the situation in the churches. On the one hand it was necessary to emphasize the full humanity of Jesus, that he truly lived and died, for which the appropriate title was Son of David (*Eph.* 18:2; 20:2; *Rom.* 7:3; *Smyrn.* 1:1; *Trall.* 9:1). On the other hand the real significance of the risen Lord for the church is shown in the fact that Ignatius can occasionally call him "our God" (*Eph. Ins.*; 18:2; *Rom. Ins.*; 3:3; *Pol.* 8:3; cf. *Rom.* 6:3; *Smyrn.* 1:1). Uniquely among the early fathers Ignatius regularly calls Christians "disciples"[30] in a manner very reminiscent of Matthew. It is in the correlation between disciple and Lord that we see concretely what is meant by the Lordship of the Son of David. We are to "be firm in the ordinances of the Lord" (*Magn.* 13:1), to act

---

29. *Earliest Christianity*, p. 765.
30. *Mathētēs*, *Eph.* 1:2; *Magn.* 9:2; 10:1; *Pol.* 2:1; 7:1; *Rom.* 4:2; 5:3; *Trall.* 5:2; cf. *mathēteuein*, to make a disciple, become a disciple, *Eph.* 3:1; 10:1; *Rom.* 3:1; 5:1. The significance of the correspondence of usage between Matthew and Ignatius is emphasized by Ulrich Luz, "Die Jünger im Matthäusevangelium," ZNW 62 (1971): 141–71.

only "according to the teaching of Christ" (*Phld.* 8:2), to follow "the commandments of Jesus Christ" (*Eph.* 9:2; *Rom. Ins.; Phld.* 1:2), for we "have the word of Jesus" (*Eph.* 15:2) and "the law of Jesus Christ" (*Magn.* 2:1). What it means to call Jesus Lord and oneself his disciple is perhaps best seen in the title Teacher: "There is one teacher who spoke and it came to pass" (*Eph.* 15:1); ". . . that we may be found disciples of Jesus Christ our only teacher" (*Magn.* 9:1).

Matthew's Gospel ends with the risen Jesus commissioning his apostles (28:19f.). The title of the Didache is "The teaching of the Lord through the twelve apostles to the Gentiles." The work, written probably in Syria sometime in the second century, begins with the ethical catechism of the "two ways," which uses traditional Jewish material and which reminds us of the two gates in Matthew 7:13f. But the author prefaces his traditional ethical material with a heading which summarizes the way of life: the double commandment to love God and the neighbor, and a form of the Golden Rule (1:2). The community has evidently been having difficulties with traveling charismatics, who are to be tested not doctrinally (cf. I John 4:1ff.) but ethically: "From his behavior then the false prophet and the true prophet shall be known" (11:8b). The standard for measuring this behavior is as follows: for teachers, "if his teaching be for the increase of righteousness and knowledge of the Lord" (11:2); or for charismatics, "not everyone who speaks in the Spirit is a prophet, except he have the behavior of the Lord" (11:8a); in general, the community is "to do everything as you have it in the gospel of our Lord" (15:4), "according to the ordinance of the gospel" (11:3), "as the Lord commanded in his gospel" (6:2). Jesus is spoken of as the Lord who commands. One contrast with Judaism is unconsciously comical: "Let not your fasts be with the hypocrites, who fast on Mondays and Thursdays; rather, you should fast on Wednesdays and Fridays" (8:1). Here is perhaps the real parallel with the antitheses of the Sermon on the Mount; one could almost paraphrase: "You have heard that it was said to the men of old, 'You shall fast on Mondays and Thursdays,' but I say unto you. . . ." Similarly the Lord's Prayer is introduced with the words "Do not pray as the hypocrites do, but as the Lord commanded in his gospel" (8:2). It could be said that the major concern of the Didache is to impart to the Gentiles what the Lord commanded them to observe. It is readily understandable as a sequel to Matthew's Gospel; it remains to be seen whether or not it can illuminate that Gospel.

Let us look at the Sermon on the Mount from the perspective not of the beginning, which speaks of righteousness exceeding that of the scribes and Pharisees, but of the end (7:21–23), which warns against charismatic enthusiasm.[31] In a manner not dissimilar to that of Ignatius and the Didache, Matthew has to confront those who claim possession of the Spirit with the injunction to do the will of God. The false prophets (7:15) are Christians, for they come in sheep's clothing, and they are accused of lawlessness (*anomia*). Matthew's understanding of the term is shown by 24:12, "because lawlessness increases, the love of many will grow cold" (cf. also 13:41). These enthusiasts are not antinomians in the sense of lacking law but of lacking love. To them can be applied the warning of John the Baptist that every tree that does not bear good fruit is cut down and thrown into the fire (7:19), a warning that the Baptist directed against the Pharisees and Sadducees (3:10; cf. 12:33–35). The "Pharisees" are accused of being "full of hypocrisy and lawlessness" (23:28). That enthusiasm and legalism (and hypocrisy) are not necessarily opposed but can go hand in hand in the early church has been shown by Käsemann.[32] Matthew's polemic is directed against only one front: lawless, legalistic Christian enthusiasts. The Pharisees do not represent for him contemporary Jews, but in addition to portraying the historical opposition of that evil generation to Jesus, they seem also to represent a factor in Matthew's Gentile-Christian congregation, so that he needs to warn, Do not be like that (6:1; 16:12; 23:3).

It has been persuasively argued[33] that "until all is accomplished" (Matt. 5:17f.) refers to Jesus' life and death, in which Scripture has been fulfilled. There is, however, another sense in which the Law can be fulfilled, that is, done.[34] The content of the demand of "the law and the prophets" is stated unambiguously by Matthew at the end of the sermon: the Golden Rule. He means by that nothing different from the double commandment to love God and the neighbor, for "on these two commandments depend all the law and the prophets" (22:40, RSV). One could also refer to the twice-cited "I desire mercy, and not sacrifice" (9:13; 12:7, RSV) or the

---

31. Cf. Ernst Käsemann, "The Beginnings of Christian Theology," in *New Testament Questions of Today*, The New Testament Library (London: SCM Press, 1969), pp. 82–107; and especially Eduard Schweizer, "Observance of the Law and Charismatic Activity in Matthew," NTS 16 (1969–70): 213–30.

32. "Sentences of Holy Law in the New Testament," in *New Testament Questions of Today*, pp. 66–81. "The antipharisaism of Matthew is in the service of his own ethics" (Tilborg, *Jewish Leaders*, p. 26).

33. Cf. esp. Henrik Ljungmann, *Das Gesetz erfüllen* (Lund: C. W. K. Gleerup, 1954); and W. D. Davies, "Matthew 5:17, 18," in *Christian Origins and Judaism* (Philadelphia: Westminster Press, 1962), pp. 31–66.

34. Cf., among others, Trilling, Barth, Strecker; and Eduard Schweizer, "Matth. 5, 17–20," in *Neotestamentica* (1963), pp. 399–406. "Love is the fulfilling of the law" (Rom. 13:10, RSV; cf. 8:4; Gal. 5:14).

demand for "justice and mercy and faith" (23:23, RSV). The criterion for judgment of the Gentiles is whether or not they have shown love to the hungry, the thirsty, the stranger, the naked, the sick, the prisoner (25:31–46). For Matthew it is very important that Jesus fulfilled the law of Moses; the church, however, should fulfill the law of love.

Finally, let us reflect on the Gospel from the perspective of its end, 28:16–20.[35] (1) "All authority in heaven and on earth has been given to me; go therefore and make disciples of all Gentiles." Although the background of this passage is the exaltation of the Son of Man, in Matthew it has an impressively unhistorical quality. It is not just that the event cannot be located in time, it is essentially timeless. Nothing really has changed in Matthew's Jesus by his exaltation. The authority he now has, he always had; "everything has been given to me by my Father" (11:27). The authority with which he teaches now is the same authority with which he spoke the Sermon on the Mount (7:29; cf. 9:6; 21:23–27). Jesus as the one having authority is Lord, a relational term which is correlate with disciple, and the title with which the disciples constantly address him throughout the Gospel. Jesus for Matthew is the Lord who has authority over the Gentiles, an authority which he did not acquire at a certain point in time, but an authority which he has only because he was the rejected Messiah of Israel (cf. 15:21–28). (2) "Lo, I am with you always, to the close of the age." Not "from now on," but "always," just as the incarnate Jesus could say before: "Where two or three are gathered in my name, there I am in the midst of them" (18:20, RSV). It is customary to refer to Aboth 3:2, "When two sit and there are between them words of Torah, the Shekinah rests between them." In that people gather in Jesus' name, he takes the place of the Torah, but also in that he is in their midst, he takes the place of the Divine Presence. Now the name Emmanuel, God-with-us (1:23), takes on a new meaning. Jesus is given no title in this final scene, but it is appropriate that he be worshiped. It is no accident that a trinitarian formula should appear here more clearly than anywhere in the New Testament. (3) "Teaching them [the Gentiles] to observe all that I have commanded you" (RSV). Here is the clearest reference to the body of the Gospel, now seen under a new perspective. But already then Jesus could speak the words of Matthew 11:28–30 which W. D. Davies very

---

35. On Matt. 28 as the key to the Gospel, cf., among others, Trilling, E. P. Blair, *Jesus in the Gospel of Matthew* (Nashville: Abingdon Press, 1960), and the illuminating essay by Günther Bornkamm, "The Risen Lord and the Earthly Jesus," in J. M. Robinson, ed., *The Future of Our Religious Past*, trans. Charles E. Carlston and Robert P. Scharlemann (London: SCM Press, 1971), pp. 203–29.

appropriately calls "the quintessence of the Matthaean interpretation of Christianity as Gospel and Law." The yoke of the Torah, the yoke of Wisdom, has become the yoke of Jesus. Jesus is in no sense a new Moses giving a new Torah; he is the Torah, the Wisdom of God. The sayings and life of the earthly Jesus have all the authority of Torah, yes, of the will of God which lies behind Torah. Jesus can simply declare what is the will of God: "It is not the will of my Father who is in heaven that one of these little ones should perish" (18:14, RSV). The most appropriate title for the Lord of Matthew's church is only occasionally made explicit: "You are not to be called rabbi, for one is your teacher [didaskalos] and you are all brothers. And you are not to call anyone father on earth, for one is your Father who is in heaven. And you are not to be called teachers, for your teacher [kathēgētēs] is one, the Messiah" (23:8–10). Teacher and Lord are parallel in 10:24, as are their correlates, disciple and servant. The disciples are those who do the will of the Father (7:21; 12:50; 21:31). But the parallel is close between 7:21, "He who does the will of my Father who is in heaven," and 7:24, "Everyone who hears these words of mine and does them" (RSV). Jesus is Lord of the Gentiles, who are called to become his disciples. He is Lord insofar as he is the teacher of the will of God. He is the teacher of that will insofar as he is the direct expression of it. Matthew's Lord, Jesus the Messiah of Israel, functions for Matthew's community in much the same way that Yahweh, the Lord the God of Israel, functions for the Sinai community; but he does not do so directly. Matthew's church was troubled by prophets who were all too able to say "what the Spirit says to the churches" (Rev. 3:22). Matthew's Lord speaks through the words of the earthly Jesus, the Messiah. Therefore it is essential for him to take up the tradition of Jesus' life and teaching, to write a Gospel, to maintain that Jesus was the Messiah of Israel. For reasons we have tried to indicate, Matthew was persuaded that he could affirm Jesus' messiahship only by saying that he was the rejected Messiah. On the one hand Matthew's Christology is well on the way to the doctrine of the Trinity. On the other hand he insists on the authority of the words of the earthly Jesus. For Matthew, then, Jesus was the Messiah, the Son of David, for Israel—and only insofar as he was that is he the Lord, the Teacher of the Gentiles.

IV

A redactional critical study of Matthew presents us with a major hermeneutical problem but also with an important hermeneutical solution.

The problem is that in presenting to the Gentiles the commandment of the risen Lord to love their neighbors, Matthew has forgotten that there were contemporaries who were descendants of the Pharisees and who called themselves Israel. To be sure, "Israel" seems to be for him a theological concept referring to "that generation" and not necessarily to Jews of the present,[36] but the distinction is much too subtle to be helpful. Beginning perhaps with Matthew and continuing down to our day, the Pharisees have become a Jewish stick with which to beat Christian dogs, for legalism and enthusiasm and hypocrisy are essentially Gentile-Christian problems. But when the Matthean picture of that "evil and adulterous generation" is projected onto actual Jews of any age, the consequences are absolutely disastrous. Simple decency, to say nothing of Matthew's law of love, demands that we allow our neighbors to define themselves rather than to impose a caricature on them; and to speak today of the utter reprobation of the people of Israel is monstrous and obscene. There is a great deal in Christian theology which needs to be rethought after Auschwitz, and one good place to begin is with Matthew.

For many, Matthew's theology of *Unheilsgeschichte* for Israel is simply unacceptable.[37] We can be grateful to redaction criticism for underlining more clearly this theological stance so that we can learn to avoid it. Preachers expounding a Matthean pericope should ignore the content and play down the Matthean specifics in favor of the earlier synoptic tradition.[38] Here is the hermeneutical problem: Perhaps we shall have to learn to distinguish between what is apostolic in the New Testament—the genuine Pauline Epistles, the synoptic tradition, perhaps Mark, and, in its own way, John—from what is subapostolic and to give to the latter only a deuterocanonical status. If the redaction critics are right, then the redactor

---

36. This is emphasized by Walker, *Heilsgeschichte*, in various asides.

37. It is remarkable that the redaction critics who elucidate that theology seem not to be troubled by their findings. I have found only one passage which even raises the issue. Trilling in his first edition was criticized by K. Thieme for demonstrating that Matthew preaches the absolute rejection of Israel with no possibility of repentance. He answers in a footnote that "Thieme's criticism is based on a misunderstanding, as if one were taking a position in principle on the guilt and rejection of the elect people rather than speaking only in a very specific sense of the Matthean redaction and its underlying theology. But one must be able to state what he thinks to have found in his exegesis and presents with valid arguments, subject of course to the limitation which governs all such form-critical and redaction-critical work, that the voice which is thereby elucidated is only one voice in the New Testament, which can only be properly understood when heard in connection with the others" (p. 90). But this is not good enough. This aspect of Matthew cannot be harmonized but must be rejected.

38. If our presentation above has been correct, they should also put no stress on the traditional christological titles when proclaiming Matthew's understanding of the real significance of Jesus for the church.

Matthew, as distinguished from the tradition he transmits, can no longer be part of the personal canon of many. As Luther once put it, "Urgemus Christum contra scripturam" (We urge Christ against Scripture).[39]

In what sense is it legitimate to use words of Jesus' originally addressed to a situation in Israel to apply to a congregation made up of Gentile Christians? Here Matthew can be our hermeneutical model. Just as the pastoral Epistles encourage us to apply the teaching of Paul to a later and different situation, so Matthew can encourage us to apply the synoptic tradition to a later and different situation. The redaction of the Gospel is not itself kerygma, but it shows us how the kerygma can be transmitted and applied. Differing from Mark, Matthew wrote a Gospel which consciously presents a Jesus of the past who speaks to his church in the present, not a Christian but a Jewish Jesus. Paradoxically, the same Matthew who taught the church to hate Israel gave to the church a Jewish Jesus, encouraged in it an ethical seriousness, and helped it retain the Hebrew Bible. Even from his perspective of presenting a Jewish Messiah as the authoritative Lord of the Gentiles, his attitude toward Israel ought to have been one of gratitude rather than vilification. Perhaps we do not do Matthew an injustice if we make this correction, for he has much to teach us. We have today our own spirit-filled enthusiasts and miracle-workers and prophets, and perhaps what we need is to learn to listen to the word of God and to do it. In the dialectic between freedom and authority, enthusiasm and commandments, the spirit and the word, perhaps we need today to hear the word, and precisely the word transmitted by Matthew. For our teacher is one, the Messiah; let us take his yoke upon us and learn from him.

---

39. As cited by W. G. Kümmel in W. Eckert et al., eds., *Antijudaismus im Neuen Testament?* (Munich: Chr. Kaiser Verlag, 1967), p. 147.

8.

The Church in Matthew

JAMES P. MARTIN

On the whole, the church of Matthew is characterized more by
the portrait of the disciple community provided in the Sermon
on the Mount than by charismatic activity itself. Nevertheless,
the center for Matthew is neither charismatic action nor ethical
concern, but Jesus Christ.

The fact that a picture of the church appears clearly in Matthew's Gospel
is generally accepted, but its nature is much disputed. For the fact, Bornkamm's judgment is representative: "No other gospel is so shaped by the
thought of the Church as Matthew's, so constructed for use by the Church;
for this reason it has exercised, as no other, a normative influence in the
later Church."[1]

It follows that when scholars attempt to define the "main problem" in
interpreting Matthew, their definitions involve the nature of the church.
Thus, for Trilling, the whole Gospel is to be interpreted in light of the
missionary command of Matthew 28:18–20, and this command, in his
opinion, deals with the institution of the church by the risen Lord.[2]
Trilling's book attempts to show that Matthew wishes to prove that the
church of Christ is true Israel, the people of God. Georg Strecker is concerned to show how the life of Jesus is the presupposition of the church
in Matthew and how therefore Christology and ecclesiology are dialec-

---

1. Günther Bornkamm, "End-Expectation and Church in Matthew," in Günther
Bornkamm, Gerhard Barth, and Heinz-Joachim Held, *Tradition and Interpretation in
Matthew* (Philadelphia: Westminster Press, 1963), p. 38. Wolfgang Trilling, *Das
wahre Israel: Studien zur Theologie des Matthäus-Evangeliums* (Munich: Kösel-Verlag,
1964³), p. 212, says that the picture of the problem of the nature of the church is
difficult in both books. Edward Massaux, *Influence de l'Evangile de saint Matthieu sur
la litterature chretienne avant saint Irenee* (Löwen: Univ. Cath. Lovan, Diss. Theol.
II, 42, 1950), observes that Matthew's Gospel was the most often quoted and the most
influential, especially the Sermon on the Mount. It created the climate of ordinary
Christianity.

2. Trilling, *Das wahre Israel*, pp. 21f., following Otto Michel, "Der Abschluss de
Matthäus-evangeliums," *EvT* 10 (1950–51): 16–26.

tically related.[3] For Eduard Schweizer, the main question for Matthew is in what way the law of Moses is to be obeyed. This question, of course, is crucial for understanding the church in Matthew.[4]

Although we agree that the church appears clearly in Matthew, we may commence our investigation by observing that this Gospel is not a manual on church life, like The Teaching of the Twelve Apostles (Didache), nor is it a legal constitution of the church. It is a gospel, a *vita Jesu* in the sense commonly understood by New Testament students; and this fact poses, therefore, the question of how Matthew's proclamation and report of Jesus' activity and death serve the milieu of the church in which the book was written. Matthew follows Mark as his literary prototype, not James, or the Didache. This demands that interpretation of this church must be faithful to Matthew's form and relate the church to his "life of Jesus." The problem may be posed in terms which emphasize church at the expense of the story of Jesus or which forget the church because of the story of Jesus. Whereas Luke effected a distinction by writing two books, Matthew has given us only one. For both evangelists, however, the time of Jesus and the time of the church belong together eschatologically, because both Gospels are witness to the resurrection of Jesus; and it is the reality of the living Lord of the church which enables them to write the kind of history they present in their Gospels.[5]

Generalizations are to be avoided. The only method by which we may determine how Matthew adapts his tradition to the church situation in which he writes is by careful study of his use of the tradition available to him, especially how he handles his Marcan and Q sources. Careful exegesis is essential for the preacher who wishes to discover the character and shape of Matthew's church and to proclaim it for today's church.[6] Matthew's arrangement of the teaching of Jesus in the form of discourses is not only

---

3. Georg Strecker, *Der Weg der Gerechtigkeit: Untersuchung zur Theologie des Matthäus*, FRLANT 82 (Göttingen: Vandenhoeck & Ruprecht, 1962).
4. Eduard Schweizer, "Observance of the Law and Charismatic Activity in Matthew," *NTS* 16 (1970): 213–30.
5. Rolf Walker, *Die Heilsgeschichte im ersten Evangelium*, FRLANT 91 (Göttingen: Vandenhoeck & Ruprecht, 1967), p. 114, argues that Matthew contains the "life of Jesus" and an acts of the apostles in one book.
6. Joachim Rohde, *Rediscovering the Teaching of the Evangelists*, trans. Dorothea M. Barton (Philadelphia: Westminster Press, 1968), provides a useful discussion of most of the recent interpretations of Matthew. The book is helpful for those who do not read German, but the reader will discover repetitiousness in the works discussed by Rohde, and, while they assist in analysis of some important Matthean problems, the actual character of the church in Matthew remains elusive. We have decided not to repeat these discussions but to try to build upon them.

an important literary feature of his Gospel,[7] but also materially directed to the subject of the church. We have access to the church of Matthew largely through the discourses.[8] By way of introduction then, the Sermon on the Mount (chaps. 5–7) presents the origin of the church in the promise and call of Jesus and the use of the Law for the life of the church. The Mission Discourse (chap. 10), seen in relation to the missionary command of Matthew 28, raises the question of a particularist or universalist church. The Parable Collection (chap. 13) reveals a church in conflict and struggle. Chapter 18 can be called the Church Discourse, so obviously does it deal with the community of Jesus, and, finally, the Eschatological Discourses (23–25) reveal the church under various aspects which present peculiar difficulties for detailed interpretation.[9]

THE PROBLEM OF THE CHURCH

By "problem of the church," we refer to the difficulty of deciding whether the church of Matthew is Jewish or Gentile or some mixture of both. The problem runs through all the materials, both the discourses and the narratives; and the intense discussion it has engendered and the variety of answers given indicates its complexity and intractable nature. We wish to indicate the evidence for the problem and to assume a solution of it for our purposes without going into the detailed argumentation found in nearly all modern studies of Matthew.

The question whether the church of Matthew is Jewish or Gentile is raised by two contradictions in the Gospel. The first is the contrast between the particularist mission of Jesus and the Twelve to Israel (chap. 10), and the universal mission to all nations commanded by the risen Lord (28:18–20). The second contradiction pertains to the Law. Jesus warns against the tradition of the elders and the precepts of men (15:2, 3, 8f.). In 23:2 Matthew describes the scribes and Pharisees as those who sit on Moses' seat, and the disciples are instructed to practice and observe what they say but not do what they do. The Sermon on the Mount focuses on

---

7. Note the formal conclusion to each discourse at 7:28; 11:1; 13:53; 19:1; 26:1. There is much merit, despite disclaimers by many, to Bacon's thesis that the arrangement of five discourses was deliberate.

8. According to Bornkamm, "End-Expectation," p. 15, they show throughout a union of end-expectation and conception of the church peculiar to Matthew. A casual survey suffices to establish this fact as vital to the exploration of the church of Matthew.

9. Not every scholar considers chaps. 23–25 as one discourse; many separate chap. 23 by itself. The concluding formula at 26:1 suggests a unified discourse, but the nature of the unity is open to debate.

the importance of the Law and its validity. What then does Matthew really intend with respect to the Law, and is his intention valid for Jewish Christians only or for Gentile Christians only? To express the problem brusquely, "would the church of Matthew eat lobster?

Mission

The restriction of the mission of the Twelve (10:5, 23) appears to follow the pattern of Jesus' own particularistic mission as he declared it to the Canaanite woman (15:24). The so-called great commission (28:18–20) breaks through this viewpoint and calls for a mission to all nations. How does Matthew intend his readers to understand the relation of these two missions? One solution is to historicize the earlier mission of Jesus and the Twelve, either by conceiving of a Matthean *Heilsgeschichte* which presents a succession of epochs, or by interpreting the particular mission to Israel as part of Matthew's general portrayal of a rejected and guilty Israel.[10] The other solution to the problem of the relation of missions is to understand them to be going on at the same time, to Jews and to Gentiles. Strecker, for example, interprets the "cities of Israel" (10:23) to refer to the cities of the world where Jews live, not only cities within Palestine.[11] This interpretation removes the intolerable tension between the mission and the parousia of the Son of Man and eases the near-expectation of the end; this easing agrees too with the eschatological perspectives of the great commission text which also speaks of the end. Gerhard Barth supports this line of interpretation by showing that in chapter 10 Matthew "bursts open the situation of an historical 'then' during the earthly activity of Jesus" by inserting 10:17–22 from the apocalyptic discourse of Mark 13:1–13. This means that Matthew 10:23 refers to the time between the resurrection of Jesus and the parousia. "In that way," he argues, "the situation of the historical 'then' is left behind, and the missionary discourse now speaks simply of the sending forth of the disciples."[12]

---

10. With respect to method, it is impossible to completely historicize Matthew 10 into a past-historical report; the chapter is clearly directed to the church situation. The question is, For what purpose? Two major solutions are: (1) Matthew presents evidence for a contemporary mission to the Jews by the Twelve, following the pattern of Jesus' own mission. Chapter 10, then, does not only report Jesus' past mission, but also uses it to encourage a present mission to Jews which is encountering fierce difficulties; (2) Matthew reports only the past mission of Jesus in order to demonstrate the hardness of Israel and her rejection of Jesus as the ground of the existence of the (Matthean) Gentile church.

11. Strecker, *Der Weg*, pp. 41f.

12. Gerhard Barth, "Matthew's Understanding of the Law," in Bornkamm, Barth, and Held, *Tradition and Interpretation*, p. 100.

We conclude that Matthew's church was not purely Jewish-Christian, ~Conclu~ but a universal church out of all nations. The passion and resurrection accounts serve the aetiological purpose of explaining the origin and continuing basis of the church's existence as the people of God of the new covenant, as a missionary, baptizing, and teaching community.[13] The historical situation with respect to Israel at the time of Matthew's writing was probably very complex, with deep division within Israel herself, reflected in Matthew's description of the mission of the Twelve in 10:17ff. Simplistic solutions which set all Jews against all Gentiles in deciding on the nature of the Matthean church are out.[14]

Law

Matthew asserts the abiding validity of the Law for his church (5:17–48, esp. vv. 17–20). This assertion is made against those in the church who wish to deny the validity of the Law. Whether the problem with the Law is one of interpretation, or rejection altogether, is not easily decided, because there is evidence for both views. The saying about Moses' seat, a redactional text which introduces the whole of chapter 23, suggests that the evangelist was contesting casuistic interpretation of the Law, not the basic question of the Law's validity. This view is supported by the warning against the tradition of the elders and the precepts of men (15:2, 3, 8, 9). Against casuistry and mere tradition of men, Matthew sets forth the reinterpretation of the Law by Jesus (5:21–48) as the norm for the life of the church. The warnings against scribes and Pharisees (chap. 23) are directed against such spirits in the church of Matthew, not against Jewish religious leaders alone. Whether or not Matthew thought of an actual office of

---

13. It is because Jesus is innocent (according to Matthew's version of the trial) that a mission to Israel must continue, despite the transfer of the kingdom to a people producing the fruits of it (21:43) and despite the guilt of the Jews in the death of Jesus (27:24f.).

14. Walker, *Heilsgeschichte*, amasses an impressive amount of evidence for what he terms Matthew's representation of Israel as a totality of evil and concludes that Matthew, unlike Paul, held no hope at all for any future salvation for Israel (p. 122). He approaches Dispensationalism in his evaluation of the decisive importance for *Heilsgeschichte* of Israel's rejection of Jesus (pp. 212, 138), but differs in his conclusion. For Dispensationalism, the Gospel of Matthew is largely for Jews of a future millennial kingdom; for Walker, Israel is reprobated according to Matthew. Certainly the church of Matthew stands over against some Jewish entity, defined by Matthew's use of Pharisees and Sadducees as a unity (3:7; 16:1, 6, 11f.), and his references to "their synagogues" (4:23; 9:35), but the problem is whether this entity is all Israel or reflects a split within Israel herself. It seems to me that Matthew, like Paul, is troubled, even horrified, at the unbelief of Israel, and regarding the fall of Jerusalem as a divine judgment upon this unbelief, describes Israel's guilt unsparingly so as to warn the church against falling into the same fate.

Christian scribe, some people were entrusted with the responsibility of "interpreting Moses" for the Christian church and apparently were not entirely successful.[15] The lack of success did not pertain to actual interpretation of the law only, however, but probably to the spirit with which the task was performed. Matthew 23:2–8 reflects a polemic against officialdom in the church, a polemic which we shall encounter elsewhere. The practice and doing of these scribes and Pharisees were contrary to those of Jesus, who for Matthew is the only true interpreter of Moses for the church; therefore, Matthew recalls the church to the "one teacher, one master, the Christ" (23:8–12).

Conclusions with respect to the Jewish and/or Gentile character of the church of Matthew drawn from the contradiction concerning missions inevitably interact with similar conclusions about the controversy over the Law. For most Gentile readers of Matthew, it appears natural that the problem over the Law in the Matthean church demonstrates a Jewish-Christian church. This judgment is particularly easy for Gentile Christians brought up on Luther's interpretation of Paul's position on the Law. But in historical fact it is Gentile Christians who have always had difficulty and controversy with the place of Moses in the church of Christ. Gentile Christians seem to oscillate forever between legalism on the one hand and antinomianism on the other, and so rarely arrive at the Jewish enjoyment of the Law. The fact that Gentile Christians so easily accuse Jews of legalism, and so quickly project this evil into every Jewish reference in the New Testament, indicates that the Law is a problem for Gentiles and, correspondingly, that the church of Matthew had many Gentiles in it.[16]

We conclude that the primary difficulty with the Law in the church of Matthew is casuistic interpretation. Antinomianism is probably a secondary difficulty arising out of disregard for ethics on the part of some of the charismatics in the church.[17]

---

15. Reinhart Hummel, *Die Auseinandersetzung zwischen Kirche und Judentum im Matthäusevangelium*, BEvT 33 (Munich, 1963), p. 13, thinks that Matthew does know of Christian scribes; Walker, *Heilsgeschichte*, p. 25, rejects this, citing 23:8 as contrary proof. An alternative view is to take scribes and Pharisees as the post-A.D. 70 Jewish leaders, or even to the post-Jamnia rabbis, against whom, on this view, Matthew was actively fighting. According to this historical interpretation, the kerygmatic address of Matt. 23 would be quite indirect. On this, see Walter Grundmann, *Das Evangelium nach Matthäus*, THKNT (Berlin: Evangelische Verlagsanstalt, 1968), pp. 482f.

16. If Matthew's church were entirely Jewish-Christian, then the Gospel of Matthew would be of historical interest only and have little to offer the contemporary church.

17. Barth, "Matthew's Understanding of the Law," p. 75; "The false prophets are thus clearly designated antinomians" argues that Matthew fights against both legalism and antinomianism. Rohde, *Rediscovering Evangelists*, p. 106, questions the two-front view.

THE CHARACTER OF THE CHURCH

It is surprising that despite the problems attending the decision about a Jewish and/or Gentile constituency of the church in Matthew, its general character appears clearly, as does the character of those whom Matthew regards as false Christians. We wish now to explore this character, keeping in mind that conclusions will always be subject to revision in light of further clarity on the Jewish-Gentile nature of the church.

First, following the pattern of the mission of Jesus as depicted by Matthew, we shall discuss charismatic activity in the church. Second, proceeding from the question of the Law, we shall try to show how this question illumines the character of the church as a community of ethical obedience (righteousness). Before proceeding into the charismatic and ethical aspects, however, it is important to commence with some observations about the kingdom of God in Matthew, because the church can only be properly understood in relation to the coming of the kingdom and its righteousness.

The centrality of the message of the kingdom of heaven throughout all stages of *Heilsgeschichte* is determinative for the self-understanding of the church of Matthew. The kingdom forms the core of the church's confessional stance in the world. The church is exhorted to seek *first* the kingdom of the Father and his righteousness (6:33). It follows that Matthew never equates the church with the kingdom; for him the kingdom of heaven is both present and future reality, the object of faith's possession and of hope, the principle and the goal of ethical living, a total and a normative concept of the reality of salvation. God's reign is presently realized in the reign of Jesus Christ, the Son of Man. The kingdom of the Son of Man is also both present and future. Matthew is more concerned about the identity of content of the kingdoms of God and of the Son of Man than he is about any scheme of successiveness. As Trilling concludes, the kingdom of heaven and the kingdom of the Son of Man are the presuppositions for the theological position of the church of Matthew.[18]

Since the kingdom of heaven is the reality for which the church exists (or better, since God himself is this reality), and since this kingdom is present in Jesus and his history, the gospel form of the *vita Jesu* (from birth to future parousia!) has necessary precedence for Matthew and ex-

---

18. Trilling, *Das wahre Israel*, p. 154, following a discussion of the two kingdoms. While we have summarized the evidence, the exegete should pay careful attention to the peculiarities of Matthew's terminology and description of the kingdom as compared to Mark. Matthew enlarges upon this theme, e.g., he has increased the number of kingdom parables to *ten*; Mark and Luke have *two* each.

plains the form in which he has given us his understanding of the church. Because Jesus is the risen and exalted *Kyrios* to whom all authority in heaven and on earth is given, the word and work of the earthly Jesus is authoritative for the church on earth for all time until the end. This is the thrust of the whole Matthean Gospel.[19] The measure of the true or false church according to Matthew is whether or not the church is faithful to the word and work of Jesus. Matthew would not agree with any "kerygma theology" in which the gospel would be totally identified with the preaching after Easter without being safeguarded by a strict faithfulness to Jesus' own teaching.[20]

Faithfulness to the word and work of Jesus has led the church of Matthew into charismatic mission and ethical obedience, but difficulties have arisen in both areas, and Matthew contests false representations of both mission and interpretation of the Law.

Charismatic Ministry

True discipleship manifests itself according to Matthew in charismatic activity, particularly prophecy and healing.[21] This activity is emphasized because it is a continuation of the work of Jesus himself. Matthew's summarizing of the ministry of Jesus (4:23f.) speaks of healing in an extraordinary way and forms the introductory setting to the Sermon on the Mount. At the outset of Jesus' ministry the evangelist juxtaposes the healing and the teaching work of Jesus and poses the question about the meaning of this combination for the life of discipleship. The summary of Jesus' ministry in 9:35 speaks of his healing and introduces the discourse on the Mission of the Twelve (chap. 10) within the context of the mission of Jesus to Israel. Like Jesus, the Twelve are sent to "heal the sick, raise the dead, cleanse lepers, cast out demons" (10:8, RSV). The miracle stories in chapters 8 and 9 which precede this charge to charismatic ministry and the charge itself lead to the question of John the Baptist about Jesus and Jesus' reply. Jesus' answer speaks of his charismatic ministry as evidence of his messianic activity (11:2–6). This episode is interpreted in terms of the coming of the kingdom of heaven (11:11).[22]

---

19. Cf. Walker, *Heilsgeschichte*, p. 114. "To make disciples" connects the post-Easter and the pre-Easter epochs. See Schweizer, "Observance of the Law," p. 217.

20. Schweizer, "Observance of the Law," p. 217.

21. See Strecker, *Der Weg*, p. 137 n. 4, and Schweizer, "Observance of the Law," pp. 217ff., whose exposition is followed closely in this matter. The term "charismatic" needs to be used with caution and some precision.

22. H. J. Held, "Matthew as Interpreter of the Miracle Stories," in Bornkamm, Barth, and Held, *Tradition and Interpretation*, pp. 214, 239ff.

Matthew's redaction of his tradition reveals that he wishes to affirm charismatic discipleship in a positive way.[23] A charismatic healer must follow Jesus, and to follow Jesus is to be called to a ministry of healing.[24] Jesus' declaration to his disciples that nothing will be impossible for them (17:20) shows, in this context, that the authority of genuine faith is proved in charismatic healing.[25]

The importance of charismatic ministry for Matthew's understanding of discipleship and church is reinforced when we relate the term "disciple" to other terms used to describe them, especially "little ones," "prophets," and "righteous men." Eduard Schweizer concludes that "prophet" refers to the charismatic activity of a disciple, whereas "righteous man" describes the disciple's obedience toward God's law as interpreted by Jesus, and "little ones" is a general description of the Matthean church as "ascetic," "charismatic," and "anti-official."[26]

For Matthew, the life of the church is above all else discipleship. Thus its post-Easter mission is to disciple the nations. This must mean, on the basis of the evidence, that the true church (as Matthew understands it) is characterized by charismatic ministries of healing, exorcism, and prophecy. The ministries are not restricted to the time of Jesus' earthly ministry alone, but through the authority and power of the risen Lord are valid and constitutive for the church until the end of the age (28:19f.).[27]

It is all the more surprising, therefore, to encounter Matthew's forceful denunciation of false charismatics. An astonishing rejection of charismatics is announced near the (literary) end of the Sermon on the Mount: "On that day many will say to me, 'Lord, Lord, did we not prophesy *in your*

---

23. With Matt. 9:8 cf. Mark 2:12; with Matt. 12:7 cf. Mark 2:23–28. Schweizer, "Observance of the Law," pp. 221f., thinks that Matthew's use of Old Testament quotations in Matt. 2 may be intended to portray discipleship according to the ideal of a charismatic itinerant prophet following Jesus in perfect obedience.

24. Schweizer, *ibid.*, p. 223, notes that Matthew omits the Marcan pericope (Mark 9:38–41) of the foreign exorcist.

25. See Matt. 17:16, 18.

26. Schweizer, "Observance of the Law," p. 222. See also his note on *NTS* 20 (1974): 215, where he refers to the *Apocalypse of Peter* from Nag Hammadi, which speaks of a group of "little ones" who are seen (by God) and fight against those who let themselves be called bishop and also deacons as if they had received authority from God, and who recline at table after the Law of the place of honor. Schweizer sees this group continued in the church of Syria, finally merging in the monastic movement of the Catholic church.

27. Interpretation which insists on restricting charismatic ministries to an apostolic age ignores the eschatological realities of the church's existence.

name, and cast out demons *in your name,* and do many mighty works *in your name?'* And then I will declare to them, 'I never knew you; depart from me, you evildoers' " (7:22f., RSV).[28] This rejection is prefaced by the serious warning, "Not every one who says to me, 'Lord, Lord,' shall enter the kingdom of heaven, but he who does the will of my Father who is in heaven" (7:21, RSV).[29] The force of the unexpected rejection is heightened through the threefold repetition "in your name" following the "Lord, Lord."

It is clear that not all charismatic activity is valid in Matthew's view; he knows of false prophets. Charismatic activity by itself is not the complete form of discipleship. Although Matthew expects the final separation of good and evil at the end of this age (13:30, 49), he is not indifferent to the need for distinction and differentiation in the present. The difference between true and false prophet, a sound tree and a bad tree, a house built on sand and a house built on rock, the narrow gate to life and the wide gate to destruction (7:13–20), is *doing* the will of Jesus' Father who is in heaven and *doing* the words of Jesus or *not doing* them (7:24, 26). The doing of the false charismatics, which they themselves describe very well, is incomplete and imperfect because it does not include the doing of righteousness, that is, doing the Law and Prophets as interpreted by Jesus.

Ethical Obedience (Righteousness)

The crucial matter for the church of Matthew is not whether or not there should be a charismatic ministry but whether or not there shall be a complete and perfect discipleship which combines charismatic activities and ethical obedience to Jesus' interpretation of the Law in his word and deed.

The characteristics of the false charismatics, clearly stated in the concluding section of the Sermon on the Mount, show that these persons lack this obedience. The false charismatics are false prophets whose sheep's clothing masks ravenous, greedy hearts (7:15f.);[30] they relax the commandments and teach others to relax them (5:19); they show great signs and wonders but lead the elect astray from the whole way of Jesus (24:11, 24).

---

28. Italics mine. Schweizer commences his study of the church in Matthew from this text.

29. Note the similarity of this language to that describing the judgment by the Son of Man in 25:31–46.

30. They are Christians; they act in Jesus' name and say "Lord, Lord."

Their principal activity is to preach *anomia* (lawlessness).[31] *Anomia* denotes not just a superficial recklessness with the niceties of the Law, but a deep-seated constitutive attitude of the heart which determines the behavior of its practitioners. Neither is *anomia* a genuine form of Christian freedom, but an anarchy of language which leads astray from the true way of Jesus.[32]

The criterion of the ethical difference between the true and false prophet is not trivial.[33] The Sermon on the Mount shows clearly that the criterion is love to the neighbor, including the enemy, as exemplified and taught by Jesus.[34] To be charismatic without love is to be in danger of destruction, as 7:21–23 and the great parable of the judgment of the Son of Man (25:31–46) show. To act in love, even without charismatic gifts and power, is to act truly in the authority and name of Jesus (25:37–40). The true disciple is a true prophet only if he is a righteous person.

The church, then, is a church of (charismatic) prophets who are also righteous. Their righteousness is derived from Jesus' gift of God's rule and righteousness.[35] The church lives by the Sermon on the Mount, not in the abstract or in a legalistic way, but as the community which knows its origins in the promise of Jesus formulated as the Beatitudes, and which understands the Law as a living tradition concerning God's will interpreted by Jesus. Jesus is the true prophet and righteous one, who healed, who wandered from place to place, and who went his way to his cross faithful in his service of God's righteousness.[36]

Discipleship

Jesus called men to discipleship. By his depiction of discipleship, Matthew describes the inner character of the church as truly charismatic and

---

31. *Anomia* (7:23; 13:41; 23:28; 24:12) is variously translated by the RSV. It is not used by the other evangelists and is probably a technical term for Matthew. *Anomia* may mean "without any law at all" or "against a known law." The second meaning would appear more fitting for Matthew's situation, but not to the total exclusion of the other meaning.

32. The "careless words" against which Matthew warns (12:36), directed in context against those who speak lightly or falsely of the source of Jesus' authority, probably indicates the false prophets whose preaching manifests a defective Christology. In 7:17–20, however, it is primarily the behavior of the false prophets which is under attack.

33. E.g., their length of stay, as in the Didache.

34. Schweizer, "Observance of the Law," pp. 224, 227.

35. Righteousness is a key term in Matthew.

36. The church follows Jesus in several respects: in form of ministry-wandering, charismatic and prophetic; in suffering, in true prophecy, and in interpretation of God's law anew in new situations.

truly righteous and truly prophetic.[37] The term "disciple," although not
lacking in the other Gospels and in Acts, is special in Matthew. Unlike its
original meaning, it does not describe persons who freely decide on their
own to become disciples by attaching themselves to Jesus as their Teacher
(*didaskalos*, the correlative term to *mathētēs*); rather, Jesus calls men to
become his disciples.[38]

A normal disciple seeks to become himself a *didaskalos* and thus surpass
the time and the role of discipleship. But in Matthew the relation is per-
manent and not preliminary; discipleship describes a lasting relationship to
Jesus. In Matthew, disciples are not merely students; they are also, and
above all, witnesses to Jesus. Pharisees, strangers, even Judas, call Jesus
"Teacher"; disciples address him as "*Kyrios*."[39] By the title *Kyrios*, the disciples acknowledge Jesus as a wonder-working (charismatic) Savior, but
also as the coming Judge of the world. Eschatological perspective is vital
to Matthew; the church lives under expectation of the coming of the Son
of Man and of judgment. "Disciples" designates the followers of Jesus on
this side of the Last Judgment. In the future kingdom they shall be no
longer disciples but the righteous (13:43; 25:31, 37) or the elect (24:31),
the sons of the kingdom. In the present time the learning of the disciples
is about Jesus and following him in suffering. Their allegiance is to him
and to his teaching.

The dignity of discipleship is the dignity of the learner; they are forever
learning of him who is meek and lowly in heart (11:29); they are servants
(10:25). The life of discipleship is characterized by *faith*. To fail in discipleship is to become of "little faith" (a special Matthean term). To be
of little faith means not trusting Jesus in the difficult situations of the
church's life (8:18–27). Faith, on the other hand, is trusting Jesus, following him anywhere, expecting his power and aid, and therefore being commissioned to make disciples of all nations.

Faith in Jesus characterizes discipleship, but so also does *righteousness.*
The disciples' righteousness exceeds that of the scribes and Pharisees because they have received the gift of God's kingdom from Jesus and have
through him thereby entered upon a new relationship with God (5:20).

---

37. On "disciple," see the article "*Mathētēs*," by Karl Rengstorf in *TWNT* 4:417–
65, and Bornkamm, "End-Expectation," pp. 40ff.
38. Matthew usually uses "disciples" in the plural and describes them often as "his
disciples." The singular form is rare.
39. Thus the terminology is not school language. Jesus does not discuss with his disciples. Only Judas among the Twelve addresses him as "Teacher."

The Sermon on the Mount describes the ethic of true discipleship and therefore of the church of Matthew. The imperative of love for God, neighbor, and enemy arises out of the indicative of Jesus' call and his offer of the kingdom (the Beatitudes). The Beatitudes, which preserve Jesus' offer of the kingdom, are apocalyptic in form, not the wisdom form.[40] They do not offer reward at the end of an effort, but offer God's grace and mercy as the beginning of a new life of righteousness, and as the end of life. Within the entire Gospel of Matthew, Jesus exemplifies poverty of spirit (11:29) and calls his disciples to it.

As a community of disciples the church of Matthew lives in the freedom to which the Beatitudes invite them, and in the power of a new community ruled by Jesus and interpreting its life and all its relations—man and woman, neighbor and enemy, truth and falsehood, hatred and love— according to Jesus' reinterpretation of the Law (5:21–48). The church is therefore concerned with the ethical but delivered from legalism. It is called to be single-minded, of single eye and heart, fixed upon God the Father who in Jesus offers his kingdom (5:48; 6:22–24). Thus fixed upon God and his kingdom, the church is freed from anxiety about eating and drinking and clothing, that is, from considering these of ultimate concern for life's meaning and glory (6:25–33).

On the whole, the church of Matthew is characterized more by the portrait of the disciple community provided in the Sermon on the Mount than by charismatic activity itself.[41] Nevertheless, the center for Matthew is neither charismatic action nor ethical concern, but Jesus Christ.

THE SHAPE OF THE MATTHEAN CHURCH

Community

The Church Discourse in chapter 18 provides a clear view of the shape of the church as Matthew esteems it. Nothing about individual office-bearers of the community is visible, but the church is addressed as a whole through the disciples. In fact, it appears that egotism or aggrandizement of some sort on the part of church officials has led the evangelist to emphatically stress the lowliness, humility, and brotherhood of the whole community. The chapter therefore reveals the problems besetting the

---

40. Klaus Koch, *The Growth of the Biblical Tradition,* trans. from the 2d Ger. ed. by S. M. Cupitt (New York: Scribner's, 1969), pp. 6f.
41. Yet Matthew's literary setting of the Sermon in 4:23–25 stresses Jesus' healing ministry.

church. The discourse provides practical instruction in the realism of the commandment of love worked out in the daily life of the church.[42]

The introductory question "Who is greatest in the kingdom of heaven?" controls the discourse and is answered by all the materials concluding with the decisive word concerning the Father in heaven (vv. 14, 35), who himself cares for the little ones and for forgiveness. This care of the Father in heaven undergirds the whole of church existence and is the true ground of discipleship and therefore of greatness. As Trilling expresses it, God is the formative motive for all required behavior in the community.[43]

Matthew intends the church to understand itself *theologically*. Furthermore, the bond of unity in the church and the basis of its assurance concerning the Father in heaven is Jesus its Lord: The gathering of the church is in his name (18:20); on his authority the church decides to include or exclude (18:17). Jesus is this bond and basis because he is the prototype of the community of the little ones who forgive; he is *the* lowly in heart (11:29) and therefore the greatest, the one to whom God has delivered all knowledge (11:27) and all authority (28:18). Humbling oneself as a child in the community, therefore, is to follow the way of Jesus. Jesus is also the model for pastoral care in the church of Matthew, since he seeks the lost with untiring love (15:24; 18:12–14; 23:37).[44]

Because Jesus is this kind of Lord, and the Father in heaven is this kind of God, the church is above all else a brotherhood of little ones. Jesus himself is brother (25:40). Brotherhood is realized only when no one exalts himself as the greatest, when the lowly are esteemed and not despised, and, above all, where forgiveness of sins rules the common life. Forgiveness of sins reveals the church to be the church of Jesus Christ brought into existence as the community of those whose sins are forgiven by the Father in heaven. Forgiveness occupies a surprising prominence in the instruction on church order. This prominence reveals a situation in the church which

---

42. The exegetical discussion of chap. 18 is complex. See Walter Grundmann, *Evangelium nach Mattäus*, pp. 411ff. Grundmann considers the section 17:24—20:28 under the heading "Life and Order in the New Community." Trilling describes Matt. 18 as a "Hausordnung Gottes" in his book of the title *Hausordnung Gottes: Eine Auslegung von Matthäus 18* (Düsseldorf: Patmos-Verlag, 1960). Wilhelm Pesch, "Die sogenannte Gemeindeordnung Mt 18," *BZ* 7 (July 1963): 220–35, follows Trilling and divides chap. 18 into two major divisions: a section on the little ones (vv. 1–14) and a section on true brotherhood in the community (vv. 15–35). He observes that *paidion* and *mikroi* are only in vv. 1–14, while *adelphos* controls vv. 15–35, and that both sections conclude with a declaration concerning the Father in heaven. See also Trilling, *Das wahre Israel*, pp. 106–23.

43. Trilling, *Das wahre Israel*, p. 155.

44. *Ibid.*

called for this word of the Lord.[45] Trilling concludes that sonship, discipleship, and brotherhood are the three realities which form the church according to Matthew 18.[46]

To summarize, the church of Matthew is the flock of the followers of
Jesus (4:18–22; 19:27) who belong to him (12:46–50), are totally bound
to him (8:21–27; 14:22–33), and confess him (14:33; 16:16). Much of
this is in open contrast to Israel, which rejected Jesus' messiahship.[47] The
church of Jesus is the community of disciples of the kingdom of heaven
(13:52), servants and brothers under the one Lord (18:15–20; 20:20–28;
23:8–12) who participate already in Jesus' time in his mission to Israel and
even after A.D. 70 in a mission to Jews, and who share Jesus' fate (10:5–25;
23:34!). Matthew wants the church to keep always in view the story of
the passion of Jesus, for the origin and continuing basis of the church's
existence as the people of God of the new covenant does not rest upon
any religious disposition, but upon the self-offering of Jesus. The passion
narrative also preserves the record of betrayal and denial among the disciples and thus warns against resting upon the shifting sand of religious
experience.

Order

Is Matthew at all interested in what we would call church order or in
constitutional considerations? The discourse of chapter 18 suggests some
clues about external form. The church gathers together for prayer and may
act to exclude a member from the fellowship (18:17–19). These indicators
do not lay down any law of assembly, yet assembly and order are surely
indicated in the use of the word "church" in 18:17.

The saying to Peter, used by Matthew for the occasion of Peter's confession of Jesus at Caesarea Philippi, occurs in a context which warns the
disciples against the teaching of Pharisees and Sadducees (16:12) and
which grants authority to Peter to "bind and to loose" (16:19). This authority is also granted to the whole church (18:17).[48] The connecting fac-

---

45. Matthew includes the Lord's Prayer with the instruction in righteousness in chap.
6. Matt. 6:14 reinforces the stress of chap. 18 on forgiveness. The church of Matthew
must have been riddled with unforgiving spirits.

46. Trilling, Das wahre Israel, p. 156.

47. Walker, Heilsgeschichte, p. 83, who has much to say about the disciples' vocation re the call to the kingdom of God.

48. Ekklesia denotes a local congregation in 18:17, a common use in the New Testament. The meaning in 16:18 is more debatable. The context and the terminology are
to be carefully considered. Matthew is using tradition here as the special terms indicate:
rock, build, church, gates, Hades, overcome, keep, bind, and loose.

tor in the special language of the Petrine saying is the person and function of Peter, so that much depends on how the statement "You are Peter" is interpreted in relation to this language.[49] This saying must be considered, in turn, in conjunction with Matthew's representation of Peter in general, both in his special material and in his handling of tradition.

What is true about all disciples in Matthew is especially emphasized with respect to Peter—faith and failure; courage and cowardice; total dependence on the saving power of Jesus (14:31; 26:75 with 28:16–20), recipient not originator of God's revelation (16:17). In rejecting the suffering of Jesus (16:22, 23), Peter becomes a stumbling-block and an instrument of Satan. In all of this he is a true representative of the disciples who comprise the church of Matthew.[50]

The fact that Jesus' word about Peter as rock is bracketed by the story of his little faith on the water and by his satanic misunderstanding of Jesus' way of suffering indicates that he is of particular importance to the church of Matthew as an example of the true leader of the community.[51] Peter is a leader because he is par excellence a "little one," with no privileges in or of himself except those given in faith. He represents the true confession of Jesus and exemplifies the qualities of greatness required of officials in the church. His special position thus agrees with Matthew's polemic against false greatness which rests upon charismatic display or which arrogates hierarchical power. It is Peter's weakness which qualifies him for primacy among the disciples and disqualifies him from the model of greatness provided by Gentile lords (20:28). Peter does not have the authority of sole teacher of the church, for this would contradict Matthew's express denial of such a role (23:8).[52]

Jesus remains the builder of his church; the church remains always the church of Jesus. What Jesus does give to Peter is the power of the keys of the kingdom of heaven, the authority to bind and to loose. It is clear that

---

49. Trilling, *Das wahre Israel*, p. 158, says that v. 18 is model language whereas v. 19 is juridical.

50. It is difficult to make a clear decision whether or not Matthew wishes to stress Peter's failures or to heighten his leadership role. A comparison with Mark will yield results on both sides, e.g., Matt. 15:15 and Mark 7:17; Matt. 21:20 with Mark 11:21; Matt. 28:7 and Mark 16:7. Peter's failures are underlined in Matt. 16:22f. and 26:69–75. Peter alone walks on the sea and alone succumbs to the failure of "little faith" (14:28–31), but all the disciples succumb in 8:26.

51. If Matthew took over the word about Peter as rock from tradition, as seems evident, then he has given it his own meaning by placing it in his own context.

52. The saying about greatness occurs frequently in Matt. 18:3, 4; cf. 16:25; 20:26f.; 23:8–12.

this function is related to Jesus' building his church. The binding and loosing probably means the forgiveness of sins mediated through the proclamation of the gospel of the kingdom. Since the forgiveness of sins is important to Matthew, it is noteworthy that this responsibility is shared by the whole church (18:18). The power of the keys, therefore, denotes the proclamation of the gospel of the kingdom. The mission of Peter's preaching, representative of all the disciples (28:18-20), will provide access to the kingdom of heaven. The mission of the church, contrasted with the mission of Pharisees, who succeed in making proselytes who are twice as much children of Gehenna as they are themselves (23:15), encounters fierce opposition. The gates of Hades are open and the powers of death attack the church, but Jesus' promise that these powers shall not overcome his church is sure because he is with it always until the end of the age (28:20).

Although we may discern in the church of Matthew order, office, authority (i.e., responsibility), and mission, we do not find a constitution for them. We discover instead a description of their inner significance, provided with remarkable depth and sobriety. Matthew knows the dark side of the church: tares, false prophets, false Christs, self-seeking charismatics, despisers of the "life" of Jesus, enemies of his cross, lovelessness, hate, officialdom, pagan greatness. The church is in danger of sinking into mere Christianity. Matthew exhorts the church to be different (5:14, 48); he does not give up to despair; his ecclesiology is grounded upon Christ, not itself.

Ministry

Although Matthew does not give a constitution with hierarchy or offices listed, he does know ministry. His understanding of it, a general ministry of the whole church and a specialized ministry, must be derived from his description of the disciples. By calling the Twelve to himself (4:18-22) rather than by merely appointing them to offices, Jesus indicates the representative character of ministry as ministry for the whole church.[53]

Matthew knows a ministry of the Eucharist: established by the Last Supper (26:17-29); anticipated by the feedings in 14:16-21 and 15:32-38; given by Jesus whose disciples (ministers) distribute what they have received from him (15:36); expressed through the activity of the risen Lord

---

53. In this section, I am indebted to Otto Piper's unpublished mimeographed lecture notes on the church in the New Testament, n.d.

(15:32); and eschatological in that it points to the consummation of the age (26:29).

The church of Matthew knows and practices a ministry of baptism which, as the frequency of his references indicates (3:11; 3:13–16; 20:22–23; 28:19!), is important to Matthew. Christian baptism rests upon the baptism of Jesus and continues the eschatological baptism inaugurated by John the Baptist.

Matthew's church is decidedly a ministry of the Word; his concern for the teaching of Jesus indicates as much, as well as his interpretation of the Old Testament. The parable of the sower is in fact a parable of this ministry. The word of Jesus is the foundation of the church and of true ministry (7:24; 13:19). The ministry of the Word functions in the mission of the church to proclaim the gospel of the kingdom to all nations as sign of the inaugurated reign of the Son of Man (24:14).[54]

To summarize, ministry is a divine office by virtue of the delegation of Jesus to his disciples (10:40). The efficacy of ministry, therefore, does not rest upon any human disposition to serve God, but upon God's election of persons to become disciples and agents of his Son. The disciples of Jesus have the privilege of leading people to pursue the real goal of God's kingdom and righteousness and to escape aimlessness; to establish community on the basis of a new collectivity of the people of Jesus; to liberate persons from the powers which enslave, destroy, and prevent them from becoming human after the image of the Son of Man who comes to all in the guise of the hungry, the thirsty, the naked, the prisoner, as stranger, and as neighbor (25:31–46).

---

54. Matthew's stress upon the words of Jesus and his manner of arranging them has suggested to some a worshiping church concerned with liturgy or lectionaries, and to others a scribal church concerned with Old Testament interpretation or with catechetics. There is a measure of truth in all these views, but not the whole truth in any one of them.

9.

Mark as Interpreter of the Jesus Traditions

PAUL J. ACHTEMEIER

> The hermeneutical key to reading and interpreting the Gospel of
> Mark is the role which the evangelist has given to the passion
> of Jesus as the primary perspective for understanding all the other
> traditions about Jesus incorporated in the Gospel.

There is a growing consensus among students of the New Testament that
the author of the shortest Gospel, unknown despite some early guesses in
the tradition, was a person of considerable creativity and theological insight. As we read what may appear to be an uncomplicated, even simplistic,
narrative we can easily lose sight of the seriousness and complexity of the
problems faced by our author and of the creativity he (or she—women
played a prominent role in the early church) brought to their solution.
Among the crises facing the evangelist—the fall of Jerusalem, imminent
or very recent, growing pressure on Christians from an increasingly hostile
environment—perhaps the most subtle was the potential loss of the traditions about Jesus of Nazareth to interpretations that would conform him
to the mold of the more popular Hellenistic religious heroes, miracle-
workers, and/or philosophers. There is evidence that such a radical accul-
turation of the figure of Jesus was already under way in the primitive
church. We get some clue to the dimensions of that problem from our
earliest Christian source, the letters of Paul.

We know that Paul had some knowledge of the traditions about Jesus:
information about his birth (Rom. 1:3–4), his teachings (I Cor. 7:10f.;
9:14; cf. Gal. 5:14 with Matt. 22:27–40), his lowly life (Phil. 2:7b–8),
events connected with his passion (I Cor. 11:23–25), his death on a cross
(I Cor. 2:2), and his resurrection (I Cor. 15:3–8). Yet the form Paul used
in recounting this information makes it clear that he did not yet have any
of our Gospels. The problems associated with having traditions about Jesus

in small units is evident in the difficulty that arose in Corinth over the Lord's Supper. It is clear that when Paul preached to the people in Corinth, he quoted sayings of Jesus and told stories about him. Paul also practiced baptism (I Cor. 1:14–16) and introduced the Eucharist in his efforts to establish a Christian community. Knowing that the Eucharist celebrated events leading up to Jesus' resurrection, the Corinthians got so carried away in their celebrations of this joyful event that the Eucharist became a wild party, with people drinking so much they became inebriated (I Cor. 11:21f.). Obviously, this had nothing to do with the Eucharist Paul had intended to inaugurate among them, as he very quickly and forcefully let them know. Yet the way the Eucharist could be misinterpreted shows the problem of stories told about Jesus apart from any controlling context. They were open to the wildest kind of misunderstanding. Obviously, if the traditions about Jesus were to be preserved in any recognizable form, they had to be placed in a context that would provide a check against such obvious misinterpretation. If Jesus were to be protected against being understood, because of his miracles, as another Hellenistic magician (cf. Acts 8:9–19), or as another philosopher because of his reputation as a teacher (cf. Acts 17:18–21), such a context was necessary. I should like to urge that it was just such a context that Mark set out to create when he wrote his Gospel.

The significance of the kind of solution Mark achieved can be better appreciated when we realize that he had no models to follow. The research into the kind of literature Mark was writing, and what sort of genre he might have been following, has consistently yielded negative results. There were no formal models in either the Jewish or Greek cultural circles in the early to mid-first century that Mark seems to have followed. The idea of collecting the traditions about Jesus into a story whose order and arrangement itself would provide, with a minimum of editorial comment, the context for understanding and interpreting those traditions is apparently the invention of Mark himself.

That insight is a key to understanding the way in which our author composed the Gospel. Rather than choosing a form in which incident was interlaced with comment on the way the incident was to be understood, Mark chose to let the traditions speak for themselves. It was the interpretative context that was to be the key, not the author's own theological expositions. In that way, the traditions would remain free to make their original points, but the way they were arranged and juxtaposed would provide the clue as to the overall context within which those points were to be understood.

The hermeneutical key Mark chose was the passion of Jesus, his death and resurrection. We can see that operate in a little collection of independent stories which we find in Mark 2:1—3:6. It is clear that Mark has done little to integrate these stories with one another. A simple comparison of, say, Mark 2:13–17 with the way Luke used those same traditions in 5:27–32 (Luke probably got them from Mark) will show how much more Luke was interested in integrating the traditions into a more coherent narrative. Among other things, the confusion in Mark (2:15) about in whose house the meal was held is nicely clarified in Luke (5:29). What Mark was interested in, however, was the result of the kind of conflicts reported in those stories, and that result is indicated in the last verse of the last of the five stories, Mark 3:6. It was clear enough that the kind of conflict portrayed in any one of those five independent units of the Jesus traditions would lead to Jesus' condemnation by religious and civil authorities. Mark emphasized that point by assembling five of them and placing at the conclusion the reference to counsel shared by both Pharisees and Herodians. That is the clue that the meaning Mark found in these events lay in the fact that they led to Jesus' passion and death. That point is made less by editorial comment than by the cumulative effect of the arrangement of the traditions (an effect Mark repeats, with similar stories, in 12:13–27). That is the way Mark has chosen, it seems, to make his point here.

Mark makes that same point in a number of other ways in his Gospel, the point, namely, that the hermeneutical framework within which Jesus is to be understood is cross and resurrection. The bulk of this article will explore three ways in which Mark sought to accomplish that. We will look, in turn, at the way Mark treated a character (John the Baptist), the way he arranged his traditions (3:20—4:20), and the way he constructed a theme (the disciples' relationship to Jesus) in his efforts to bring the Jesus traditions under the hermeneutical control of the cross of Jesus.

I

The first verses of Mark make it clear how important John the Baptist was to our author's understanding of Jesus. One could paraphrase that opening by saying, "The beginning of the gospel of Jesus Christ was John the Baptist who appeared, fulfilling prophecy, in the wilderness. . . ." By beginning in this way, Mark made clear that one could not comprehend Jesus apart from an understanding of John. Part of John's significance for Mark can be seen in the description of John, which recalls the figure of Elijah. Mark 1:6 uses language that very closely parallels a description of

Elijah found in the Greek translation of II Kings 1:8 (LXX, IV Kings 1:8). The hairy mantle was the sign of the true prophet (Zech. 13:4; for a false prophet to wear one was an attempt to deceive). John, for Mark, is the long-awaited Elijah, whose appearance signals the onset of God's final rule; and in that role as Jesus' forerunner, John announces Jesus to be the fulfillment of that expectation. That John the Baptist is to be understood as Elijah returned is later made clearer by a saying of Jesus himself (Mark 9:13). By placing a tradition about John first in his Gospel, Mark shows that Jesus belonged to Jewish expectations of God's rule, and indeed that he was the fulfiller of them.

Mark saw another significance for John as Jesus' precursor, however. Not only does John tie Jesus to God's past dealings with his chosen people, but he also foretells Jesus' final fate. That becomes apparent in Mark 6:14–29. In a discussion about the way the public perceived Jesus, several possibilities of identification are mentioned: he is Elijah, he is another of the prophets. But the major identification is with John the Baptist. In fact, it is as John the Baptist that Jesus is finally identified by Herod (6:16), a tradition immediately followed in Mark by the story of the execution of John. It is hardly accidental, and the significance of that juxtaposition is clear: just as John was Jesus' forerunner in his life, so was he in his death. As the significance of Jesus' career was announced at its inception by John the Baptist, so the final outcome of Jesus' career is subsequently announced by John: Jesus will die at the hands of ambivalent civil authorities (note especially 6:20). Yet, in Mark, it is not for political crimes that John died. Such a tradition was current in first-century Palestine, and we can read it in Josephus (*Ant.* 18.5.2): John was executed because Herod feared him as a potential political revolutionary, but in Mark, John died because of the religious content of his message (6:17f.). Running afoul of the authorities because of his attacks on their application of the law, or lack of it, John, like Jesus who was to follow, met his death. That John is necessary for an understanding of Jesus is confirmed, finally, in Mark 11:27–33, where Mark has placed a tradition making just that point in the setting of Jesus' last days in Jerusalem.

John was important to Mark as Jesus' forerunner, and part of John's activity, indeed the climax to it, was his violent death. By that use and arrangement of the traditions concerning John the Baptist, Jesus' forerunner, Mark has shown that Jesus' death was a necessary, indeed inevitable, climax to his career. John the Baptist thus played a continuing role (chaps. 1, 6, and 11) in the story of Jesus; and it was a role whose significance is to be found, in the final analysis, in the fate John shared with Jesus.

II

Our discussion of John the Baptist has already called attention to one of the major hermeneutical techniques employed by Mark in his effort to gain control over the independent traditions circulating about what Jesus did and said, namely, the way he arranges the traditions. That is a technique Mark used frequently, and often with subtlety and sophistication. The interpreter of Mark underestimates the theological sophistication and literary skill of Mark only at his or her own peril. The absence of extensive editorial reworking of the traditions (as in the case of, say, the Gospel of John) is not to be construed as lack of theological wit or sophistication on the part of Mark. An examination of Mark 3:20—4:20 will show how Mark employed that technique and the theological acuity he brought to his task of writing this Gospel.

The first group of verses, 3:20–35, shows the common Marcan technique of "bracketing" one tradition with another in order to interpret them. In this case, an account of the disbelief of the scribes in Jesus' miracles (vv. 22–30) has been bracketed by an account of the judgment on Jesus by his own family as a result of hearing some of the things he was doing (vv. 21, 31–35; v. 30 is Mark's introduction, emphasizing the crowds around Jesus). In this case, it appears that the tradition which is doing the bracketing is to be interpreted by the material it brackets. There is no question that a negative evaluation is put on the reaction of the scribes. To say that Jesus acts with the power of Satan, however illogical that may be (the burden of Jesus' comments in 3:23–26), is to perform the one sin that is unforgivable (thus Mark in v. 30 interprets the saying of Jesus in vv. 28f.). To attribute to Satan the power of God which is able to overcome Satan (the point of v. 27: Satan has been overcome by Jesus, who by God's power is stronger) is to cut oneself off from the one who alone is able to rescue one from Satan through the forgiveness of sin. It is to put Satan in the place of God.

That is obviously a serious matter, and it is around that point that Mark has arranged the tradition of the questioning relatives. In such a context, we know that we are not to interpret the attempt of Jesus' relatives to lay hold of him in any innocuous way. The juxtaposition of the traditions shows that the family shares, in some manner or another, the viewpoint of the scribes: a negative judgment on Jesus. One may not, therefore, in Mark's context, interpret the coming of the immediate family to Jesus in verse 31 as motivated by incipient belief or sympathy toward what Jesus was doing and teaching. Both the context (the scribes' mistaken judgment) and the content (Jesus' physical family contrasted with his true family) make clear that Jesus' family shares in the negative view of him held by the scribes. Opposition to Jesus is growing (cf. 3:6), and it now includes a powerful religious group (scribes) and even his own family. What fate can Jesus expect if that is the kind of reaction he is provoking? Even here, the cross, however dimly, looms in Jesus' future.

There is a further significance in verses 31–35, and that is the contrast between those who are "outside" and those who are "around Jesus" (v. 32: his family is "outside"; v. 34: those who sit "around Jesus"). We have just learned, in Mark's account, the names of some of those who are "around Jesus" (the Twelve, 3:13–19), and now we have learned who some of those are who are on the "outside" (scribes, immediate family). We are introduced here to two groups of people, characterized by their reaction to Jesus: those who reject him and those who associate themselves with him. The groups themselves are also noteworthy. Those who know Jesus best, or should (his immediate family), and those who know religious matters best, or should (scribes), are just the ones who reject him. Those who ought to be closest to him are the ones from whom he has the most to fear. Jesus is without honor "in his own country, and among his own kin, and in his own house" (6:4, RSV). That bears ominous import for Jesus' further career. Will the same thing occur among those who now know him best, namely, his disciples? Will they, like family and religious authorities, turn against him at some future point? Who will support him then? What fate would await one abandoned by all? Clouds are already forming on the horizon of the Marcan narrative.

The next segment of the narrative we must examine, 4:1–20, begins again with the characteristic Marcan remark that Jesus was surrounded by a crowd (v. 1). It is also evident that Mark thought the parable of the sower was of critical importance for understanding Jesus. He bracketed the parable with admonitions to listen closely (Mark added the imperative "listen" to the "pay attention" with which the parable itself began, and at the conclusion he added a saying he apparently thought important, since he used it again at v. 23) and identified this parable as the key to all the parables Jesus taught (v. 13). The parable tells about the ordinary actions an ordinary Galilean farmer would undertake in order to scratch out his normal crop of some seven- to tenfold. What is striking are not the actions of the farmer but the prodigious result of those actions. What had on first observation seemed so ordinary really was the prelude to something quite extraordinary. The contrast is between that ordinary activity and that extraordinary result, not between the amount of seed wasted (vv. 4,

5, 7) and that which yielded grain; in the Greek the word for "seed" is in the singular in verses 4, 5, and 7, and it is in the plural only in verse 8.

For Galilean listeners, the surprise would apparently have come only at the conclusion. Up to that point things ran their ordinary course for a sower. It would have been easy to mistake that sower for any other sower who went through the same motions but got only the ordinary harvest. Something extraordinary began when this sower set out on his work, but that was not clear at the beginning, only at the culmination. Had one applied the normal criteria one had developed over years of observing sowers, one would have missed the significance of this one and would have been shocked at the end result. The parable contains within itself a warning, therefore, not always to trust normal perceptions or normal judgments on what appear to be ordinary actions. In the context, that means, clearly, a warning against reacting to Jesus as did family and scribes. They judged him by normal criteria. Any ordinary person doing what Jesus was doing would have to be, in his family's judgment, "beside himself" (i.e., not in full control of his own words and actions). Any ordinary person performing the exorcisms Jesus was doing would have to be, in the scribes' judgment, in league with Satan. They, and others who judge Jesus similarly, have missed the point of his connection with God's coming rule; and when that kingdom comes in power, they will be shocked beyond measure. Only those who recognize that in Jesus something special is occurring will hold fast to him until the startling conclusion of his activity: the inbreaking of God's rule.

The explanation of the parable, 4:14–20, is identified at its beginning (v. 13) as the key not only to this but to all of Jesus' parables. That "explanation" emphasizes to the exclusion of all else the need to listen carefully and to hold fast to what Jesus says, regardless of the difficulties that may later ensue. Mark wants us to understand that the point of the parables is how one listens, and responds, to Jesus. That is also the point of 4:10–12. Again, one must note carefully that the question asked of Jesus in Mark is not "Why do you use this form of teaching [i.e., parable]?" Rather, the question asked "concerns" the parables, that is, what does this parable, the key to them all, mean? The answer is simply another statement that those who know what is going on in Jesus (the secret of v. 11: Jesus' connection to God's coming rule) do not err in their judgment of what he says and does, while those who make the mistake of judging him by ordinary criteria fail totally to understand anything about him (v. 11). They see what he does, but do not really perceive it; they hear what he says, but cannot really understand it.

These verses (11–12), introduced in a way Mark uses to incorporate independent sayings of Jesus into his narrative ("And he said to them," v. 11; cf. vv. 13, 21, 24), are in obvious relation to 3:20–35. It was precisely there that we had examples of those who could not perceive what there was to see about Jesus (the scribes and his miracles) and of those who could not understand what they heard from and about Jesus (his family). Because they thought they could judge Jesus in the same terms as they judged others who might have done what he did (the ordinary sower!), they are fated to be uncomprehending observers of these events of incredible import (4:12). Familiarity with Jesus or with religious matters will not guarantee that one understands him. Those who refuse to see his connection with the kingdom (the secret, 4:11), remain outside (the same word in vv. 3:31, 33; 4:11). Those who see in Jesus something worth following will possess, one day, that secret (the kingdom); they are the ones who are "around him" (the same word in 3:34; 4:10).

Mark has taken a group of individual traditions[1] and by arranging and connecting[2] them has created a unit of his Gospel which portrays positive and negative reactions to Jesus, but which by the close juxtaposition of Jesus' choice of followers to be "with him" (3:14) and the traditions of rejection of Jesus by scribes and also of family, foreshadows Jesus' final abandonment by all.

All of this simply means that if we are to understand Mark we must be aware that he is a creative author who has chosen to make his points by the way he uses and arranges traditions rather than by actual composition of his own prose. His task is to preserve the individual traditions by putting them in a larger interpretative framework; and he has chosen, in doing that, to preserve the original traditions as faithfully as he can. In fact, it is only because of that decision that it is possible to recognize and to some extent recover those traditions in their pre-Marcan form. Yet Mark is also creative enough to give the reader hints about how he thinks the material is to be understood. By bracketing one tradition within another, he tells us he thinks they share some point, clearer, usually, in one of them than the other. By repetition of vocabulary (those "outside" and "around him" in our passage, even the use of the word "parables" in 3:23; 4:2, 10, 11, 13) he calls our attention to what he thinks belongs together. By general

---

1. There is some agreement among scholars that independent traditions may be found in 3:21, 31–35; another unit in 3:22–27, and perhaps another in 3:28f.; another unit in 4:3–8; another in 4:11f.; yet another in 4:14–20, which shows signs of the missionary language of the primitive church.

2. Editorial work is probably to be found in 3:20, 30; 4:1f., 9f., 13.

arrangement he prepares us for the final fate of Jesus, the cross, which Mark sees as the hermeneutical key for understanding the traditions about Jesus. That same hermeneutical control over his materials is also evident in various themes in Mark's Gospel, and we must now turn to that consideration.

III

The theme of discipleship, exemplified in the Twelve, is of major importance in our Gospel. We will limit ourselves here to a consideration of some of the elements that go to make up Mark's treatment of the Twelve. We will seek to understand how Mark weaves that theme throughout his whole Gospel, making the point he feels must be made about discipleship in general and the Twelve in particular.

A recurring theme throughout the Gospel bears on the inability of the disciples to understand Jesus. Again and again, in obvious and less obvious ways, changes are rung on that theme. A number of scholarly studies and books have been devoted to such a topic, seeing in it in one way or another the key to Mark's Gospel. Yet one point must be clearly borne in mind through it all, and that is that we are not dealing here with personal vacillation or psychological aberration. We are dealing, in this theme, with God's plan as it is being worked out in Jesus.

It is abundantly clear, first of all, that the disciples cannot understand Jesus prior to his cross and resurrection. Let one example suffice. The account of the transfiguration (Mark 9:2–8) is of great significance in Mark's narrative, for it shows the importance of Jesus in God's total plan of salvation: He is to be understood in terms of Elijah and Moses and is named by God as his Son who must be heeded (vv. 4, 7). Indeed, the event is so central that only after the resurrection is it to be told (v. 9), an indication that the true nature and role of Jesus depends on that event for its comprehension. In that framework, verse 6 is enormously revealing. In the midst of all this, Peter remains confused and afraid. Even as direct witness to this event, he is unable to comprehend it.

That tells us more about Mark's understanding of discipleship, however, than it does about Peter. At issue is not the constancy of Peter's character or the level of his religious intelligence. What is at issue is how and when it is possible to understand Jesus, and the answer is, not during his earthly ministry: not until the climax (recall the parable of the sower). That is in its turn not due to human misfeasance or lack of commitment. It is because that is the way God meant it to be. That is apparent in the conclusion of the story of Jesus' walking on the stormy sea (6:45–52). The astonishment of the disciples there is due not to their unwillingness to comprehend but to their sheer inability to do so. They could not understand because "their hearts were hardened." For whatever reason, the very ability to understand what Jesus was about was withheld from them. Mark thought this so important that he picked it up again in a summary he composed after the two accounts of the feeding (8:17). Ominously enough, Mark 4:11 is paraphrased in 8:18, but this time it concerns the disciples. Jesus' fate is closing in around him. Even those closest to him now belong to "those outside." Yet it is something over which they have no control. Jesus' fate is not determined by the mental acuity, or lack of it, of his followers. His fate is in God's hands, and hence his suffering is not accidental.

That point is made again in the predictions of Jesus' passion. In the first of the three predictions (8:31), Jesus says that the Son of Man (Mark's favorite title for Jesus) *must* suffer. The whole of God's plan for him is thus announced. The second and third predictions (9:31; 10:33–34), with their statements about the future, have about them the ring of certainty. Suffering in Jerusalem is not probable ("The Son of man may be delivered over," RSV), it is certain ("The Son of man *will* be delivered over," RSV). But even in the midst of such certainty the incomprehension of the disciples remains unsullied (9:32).

This incomprehension is shown in other ways by Mark. We will limit ourselves to two of them. First, a section which deals with Jesus' teaching on discipleship is bracketed by the two stories in Mark which recount Jesus' healing of people who were blind (8:22–26; 10:46–52). In that way Mark has formed an *inclusio*, a device well known in ancient writings which indicates that a section thus bracketed is to be regarded as a unit. In itself, it is significant that the framework for instructing disciples deals with curing blindness. That is what Jesus was really about, curing the blindness of sinful humanity to the truth of God's grace and love, but it would be untrue to Mark's normal intention to wax allegorical on that point.

The material in this unit begins with the confession of Peter that Jesus is the Anointed One, that is, the Christ. The confession in itself is of course correct. Mark shares with other primitive Christians the conviction that Jesus is in fact the promised Anointed One of God (cf. Mark 1:1). The difficulty lies in Peter's inability to include the dimension of suffering in his use of the title, and that inability is demonic (8:32–33). Clearly, unless one understands the dimension of suffering that belongs essentially to Jesus' mission, one can only misunderstand Jesus.

This pattern of the announcement by Jesus of his impending (and necessary) suffering which is met by the incomprehension of Peter becomes a repeated pattern in the section on instruction to and about disciples and discipleship. The pattern consists of a prediction, evidence of incomprehension of the dimensions of the prediction, and then words of Jesus on the nature of true discipleship (see 8:31–38; 9:31–37; 10:33–45). Between the first and third repetitions of this pattern (i.e., 9:1–30 and 9:38–10:32) Mark has included a variety of stories, all of which deal, in one way or another, with the theme of discipleship. Even the story of the boy possessed by a demon (9:14–29) points to Jesus' disciples and their inability to do what others think disciples should be able to do (cf. vv. 14, 18b, 28f.).

In short, the section in Mark's Gospel which deals specifically with discipleship is structured by a pattern of incomprehension by the disciples of what Jesus says about himself and about his true followers. These traditions are being used in the service of Mark's point about discipleship: One can understand Jesus, and follow him, *only* in the light of his cross and resurrection. Until those events occur, no one understands him; indeed, no one *can* understand him.

The same failure of the disciples is vividly portrayed in the account of Jesus' final hours with them. Perhaps the most striking feature of this portrayal is the stark contrast between what the disciples express as their intention and what they finally do. The first element in that contrast occurs in the setting of the Last Supper, when Jesus solemnly announces that one of them will betray him. The answer of the disciples represents what must be one of the most frequently misinterpreted verses in Mark. The English translation "Is it I?" (RSV) could, and has, given rise to the idea that this question brings each of them to the sudden realization that each could be capable of such a thing; and that sudden insight prompts them to the reflective question "Is it I?" Stung by the realization of the evil in the depth of every human being, each asks the anxiety-laden question about his own future: Would he be the traitor he secretly knows himself capable of becoming? Such an interpretation of the question runs in just the opposite direction, however, of the clear intention of the Greek. One can phrase a question in Hellenistic Greek in such a way that the questioner can indicate unequivocally the kind of answer he or she thinks proper to that particular question. Thus, a "yes" or "no" answer can be built into the question. The question in Mark 14:19 is constructed in such a way that a "no" for an answer is built into it. Each of the disciples clearly expects Jesus to answer "No, of course it will not be you" to his question. Far from showing a reflective self-probing on the part of the disciples, the question indicates that each of them is fully convinced that that future act would be impossible for him.

The events which follow in Mark's narrative cast a painfully brilliant light on the gulf that yawns between what the disciples claim for themselves and what they do in the face of the need to redeem those claims. The gulf begins to show in the scene in Gethsemane when Jesus, in deadly agony, returns from prayer to find his companions sleeping. While God's own son faces the final penalty of their sin, they can do nothing better than sleep. This foreboding of their true reaction to Jesus' fate is brought to full flower in the following scene when Jesus is arrested. There is some small resistance; a bystander draws a sword and wounds one of those who have come to arrest Jesus, but Mark does not name Jesus' defender. Only later tradition, perhaps seeking to ameliorate Mark's unbroken gloom, attributes to Peter that much bravery. Faced with the need to match with deeds their brave and loyal words, Mark tells us, "They all forsook him, and fled" (14:50, RSV).

Even with that, the scene is not yet played out. The spokesman for the disciples, Peter, the "rock," has a chance to redeem himself. Unable to remain in ignorance about the fate of Jesus, Peter followed him anonymously and from a distance, wanting to know without being known. Yet even that final coverlet over his betrayal of his master is denied Peter. Asked by a girl if he were Jesus' follower, Peter denied it, and then again, and a third time when questioned by others. As though to match the three-fold prediction of the passion of Jesus, Peter denies his Lord three times.

In that way Mark makes it clear that human resolve and intended loyalty come to grief in their supreme test. Yet much more is at stake here than a psychological study of human values and actions under stress. Rather, what Mark has done is describe in full detail the sheer inability of those closest to Jesus to follow him before the events of cross and resurrection. That such following became possible after those events is clear enough. The existence of the traditions Mark used in writing his Gospel shows that the disciples did in fact later publicly announce what Peter in the courtyard had denied: They were followers of Jesus, crucified and risen. Their renewed fellowship with him is announced in Mark 16:7 with the angelic promise that they would be reunited with the risen Jesus upon their return to Galilee.

In that way, using the theme of the disciples' inability to understand Jesus during his earthly career, Mark again makes his point about the passion as the interpretative key for an understanding of the Jesus traditions.

Despite all Jesus taught them, despite their intimate association with him, despite all they had seen him do, the disciples *could not* understand Jesus prior to his climactic fate on the cross. Only in the light of that event is it possible to understand and interpret correctly the traditions about Jesus of Nazareth.

We have now investigated three ways in which Mark has used his traditions to carry out his task of providing the hermeneutical framework for the traditions about Jesus: by the development of a character (John the Baptist), by the juxtaposition of traditions, and by the treatment of a theme. Mark of course did not isolate these ways of interpreting the tradition. Peter is also a character in the Gospel, and an analysis of him in that role would be as revealing as the examination of John the Baptist. Similarly, the theme of the disciples' failure to comprehend the significance of Jesus prior to his passion is worked out in several instances by the way various traditions are arranged, and a study of this latter phenomenon would be as useful in understanding Mark as our investigation of the theme of the disciples' incomprehension. Even the examples we chose could easily have been enlarged; much more could be said about the unity Mark created in the portions of chapter 4 which we were unable to examine. Much remains to be learned from the Gospel of Mark. What we have done is simply take some test-borings, as it were, into the landscape of the Marcan narrative.

IV

If much yet remains to be done in the matter of exploring the theological picture of Jesus which Mark paints for us, we can perhaps at this point draw at least three conclusions about the way Mark feels Jesus is to be understood and hence about how we are to understand ourselves in relationship to Jesus.

First, it is clear that for Mark there is no real comprehension of Jesus apart from knowledge of his final fate on the cross and the subsequent resurrection. As we have seen, that theme pervades Mark's narrative from the outset, and in countless ways Mark finds renewed opportunities to drive it home. Thus the climax of Jesus' career becomes also the key to understanding that career; and Mark seeks to deny anyone the possibility of seeing in Jesus primarily a wise teacher, a compassionate friend, or a worker of wonders. He was of course all three, and more, yet primarily for Mark he was the crucified and risen Lord. For Mark, to ignore as central the cross of Jesus is to miss the meaning of the revelatory drama in which Jesus played the central role.

Second, if there is no Jesus without the cross, there is for us no Jesus apart from faith. Seeing Jesus was not enough, as Mark was at pains to show. One could observe his miracles and conclude he was working by demonic rather than divine power. One could hear about his activities and conclude that, rather than inspired, he was mentally unbalanced. One could hear his teachings and fail to comprehend what precisely Jesus intended to say, or even what in the most general way Jesus was trying to teach. If it could happen to those who saw and heard him in person, Mark seems to say, is it any wonder that it remains possible to misunderstand Jesus? No, for Mark, unless faith in Jesus as God's act of redemption is present, one can only miss the significance he bore. For Mark, we continue to walk by faith, not by sight, even on the Easter side of resurrection. Indeed, we can only walk by faith, since both sight and hearing are far too ambiguous to be of significant aid. Mark makes this point, again, in subtle but powerful ways. There are, for example, no resurrection appearances in Mark, only the promise that the disciples will yet see him at some future time. The ambiguity that cloaked the earthly Jesus remains drawn over the risen Jesus until his return in glory. Only then will his significance become inescapable (see 13:24–26). Until that time, only faith can penetrate that ambiguity. Sight will not help. Persecution will continue to cause his followers to fall away, as will the temptation of other ways of interpreting life (see 4:16–19). Only faith can anticipate that final day when the abundant crop will appear (4:8), when the tiny seed becomes the tree (4:30–32), when the harvest is fully ready (4:26–29). Only at the end will we be able finally to see. Until that time, only faith that what Jesus said is true, only confidence that he worked by God's, not Satan's, power, only affirmation that his death on the cross was triumph, not defeat, will enable us to perceive the true reality of Jesus.

If there is no Jesus without the cross, and if there is no Jesus without faith, then it is also true, third, that there is no faith without the cross. If faith means to follow Jesus, it means to follow him, if need be, to the cross itself. It is abundantly clear in Mark that those who follow Jesus must follow him with a total commitment of their lives. That point is made inescapable in 8:34–38. To become a disciple of Jesus means so to put him at the center of life that he, not one's own self-interest, becomes one's dominant theme. To try to construct ourselves into whole human beings, to think that we can achieve through self-fulfillment schemes of whatever kind a life of discipleship, is stridently denied in those words about discipleship. The goal of life is Christ, not self; that is the uncompromising demand Mark enunciates. To follow Jesus, even to the cross, is the only way to God. To be ashamed in any way of that kind of affirmation means to suffer shame in turn in the final judgment Mark is so sure is on the way. To set as the goal of life its gain is surely to lose it; to lose that life in the pursuit of the goal of following the crucified and risen Jesus is surely the only way to find it.

No Jesus without the cross, no Jesus without faith, no faith without a cross—those are hard themes, and they are as hard now to hear, and accept, as they must have been when Mark first enunciated them. Perhaps Mark felt that that was the only way to recover the true picture of Jesus, a picture obscured by the desire to find in Jesus an easier way to God or a surer way to personal fulfillment and happiness. Perhaps Mark felt that only in that way could the full impact of Jesus be felt on the easy and self-indulgent life which seemed to be the goal of the Greco-Roman world he knew. If that be true, then what Mark says will have its impact even yet in our familiar world.

V

There is plainly much more to be said about Mark than has been said in these few pages. The flood of books and articles which have appeared in the recent past, and which continue to appear, bear eloquent testimony to that fact. We have seen some of the results that can be achieved by taking Mark seriously as theologian, while recognizing the unique way he has chosen to make his theological points. Yet despite the efforts devoted to the study of this Gospel in the past decades, many who study Mark have the impression that we are only beginning to see the depths of theological insight which our unknown author has poured into his attempt to provide a means to interpret the ancient traditions about Jesus. The essays on Mark herein will review work already done, give an insight into work currently underway, and point to work yet to be done. To accept the invitation to make this journey into understanding is to sense something of the excitement of others who travel the same route, and perhaps to catch a glimpse of insights that yet remain to be uncovered and exploited. Mark is a rich lode to be mined by students and preachers alike, and that effort will be rewarded with new knowledge and with new insights into self and with new awareness of the ways of God with his people. Mark has yet more light to shed on the Christian life.

10.
Mark's Gospel in Recent Research

HOWARD CLARK KEE

The history of recent research on the Gospel of Mark can be seen as the record of an attempt to discern the aim of the evangelist and so to discover the perspective which gives coherence to all the features of the Second Gospel.

The major issues that concern recent interpreters of Mark were, in fact, posed by scholars a half-century ago. What is new is how those issues are being perceived within the context of the primitive church, and accordingly what solutions are currently being proposed for what have been perennial questions about the intention and meaning of Mark.

The centrality for Mark of Jesus' announcement of the imminent end of the age and of the cosmic conflict that would culminate in the coming of the kingdom of God was discerned against the background of Jewish apocalypticism by Johannes Weiss in 1892.[1] It was a constitutive element in William Wrede's study of the messianic secret in Mark;[2] its potency in the message and activity of Jesus furnished Albert Schweitzer with his clue for understanding the historical Jesus.[3] Of continuing significance for more recent interpreters of Mark has been Wrede's conviction that the theme of eschatological secrecy in Mark was to be traced to the evangelist rather than to Jesus. Thus the ground was already laid by the turn of the century for a view of Mark as interpreter rather than as archivist or neutral reporter.

---

1. Originally published in 1892; available in English translation by D. L. Holland with introduction and notes, *Jesus' Proclamation of the Kingdom of God* (Philadelphia: Fortress Press, 1971).

2. English translation by J. C. G. Greig, *The Messianic Secret* (Cambridge: J. Clarke, 1971). Originally published in German in 1901. Wrede's preface and a new introduction are included with the translation.

3. *The Quest of the Historical Jesus: A Critical Study of Its Progress from Reimarus to Wrede* (New York: Macmillan Company, 1968).

By the end of World War I, the method known as form criticism had emerged, with Martin Dibelius and Rudolf Bultmann insisting that the sayings and narrative material included in Mark were taken over by him from originally oral tradition that had developed in the interests of early Christian preaching, instruction, and worship.[4] The question of the relationship of this material to the historical Jesus was left open, by and large. Mark was regarded by Dibelius as not fully in control of his material,[5] while Bultmann acknowledged that Mark had made some progress toward a theological framework for interpreting Jesus, erected on the basis of Paul's Hellenistic kerygma.[6] Karl Ludwig Schmidt's study of the summarizing passages and narrative links in Mark had shown that these were to be attributed to Mark rather than to historical recollection, so that there was no sure basis for tracing a development or even a sequence in the career of Jesus.[7] That viewpoint was supported theologically by the suggestion of Martin Kähler—offered in a footnote in passing—that the gospel narrative is a passion story with an extended introduction, since it is the Christ of the kerygma not the Jesus of history who is of significance for the church.[8]

The period between the two world wars saw some proposals for refinement of Wrede's theory about the messianic secret,[9] and some efforts to define not only the aims of Mark but the circumstances of writing as well. The form-critical term *Sitz im Leben* ("setting in life" or "life-situation"), however, was handled as though all that mattered was the theological setting of the Marcan tradition. Ernst Lohmeyer sought to trace the origins of Mark to that segment of the primitive Christian community that expected the return of Christ in Galilee. Neither Lohmeyer nor R. H. Lightfoot,[10] who arrived independently at similar conclusions about Mark, provided a perspective in which the Gospel in all its parts could be given a

---

4. Martin Dibelius, *From Tradition to Gospel* (New York: Scribner's, 1935); Rudolf Bultmann, *History of the Synoptic Tradition*, trans. John Marsh (Oxford: Basil Blackwell, 1963).

5. Dibelius describes Mark as essentially conservative of the tradition but touched up the material so as to make of it a "book of secret epiphanies." Only "to the smallest extent" are the evangelists authors (*Tradition*, pp. 225, 230, 21).

6. Bultmann, *History*, pp. 347f.

7. *Der Rahmen der Geschichte Jesu* (Berlin: Trowitzsch & Sohn, 1919).

8. Martin Kähler, *The So-Called Historical Jesus and the Historic, Biblical Christ*, trans. C. E. Braaten (Philadelphia: Fortress Press, 1964), p. 80 n. 11.

9. E.g., H. J. Ebeling, *Das Messiasgeheimnis und die Botschaft des Markus-Evangelisten* (Berlin: A. Töpelmann, 1939).

10. Ernst Lohmeyer, *Galiläa und Jerusalem* (Göttingen: Vandenhoeck & Ruprecht, 1936); R. H. Lightfoot, *Locality and Doctrine in the Gospels* (London: Harper & Bros., 1938).

consistent interpretation, however. Meanwhile commentaries on Mark were produced—some of them detailed (such as the learned tome by Vincent Taylor[11]) and others of a more popular nature, such as those by B. H. Branscomb (1937) and A. M. Hunter (1949). But as W. G. Kümmel ruefully remarked, "A clear explanation of the aim of the evangelist has not yet been elicited from the text."[12]

I

The attempt to elicit that aim has been made, however. In 1956 Willi Marxsen published his study of Mark, in which the focus was on Mark's adaptation of the tradition ("redaction") rather than on the attempt to discover the historical material behind the text. His plea was that Mark be examined as a whole, "within the context of Mark's point of view as gleaned from his scenic framework and programme."[13] The intention was more impressive than the results. The analysis leads to more aphorisms than insights: "Insofar as Jesus is the content of the tradition, he is also the content of the Gospel";[14] "Mark transforms apocalyptic into eschatology";[15] in contrast to the Gospel of Matthew, which is a collection of sermons, "Mark is one sermon."[16] In accord with traditional Lutheran and rationalistic prejudices, Marxsen is eager to deliver Jesus—or at least Mark —from sharing the Jewish sectarian notion of apocalyptic expectation of the imminent end of the age. It is sufficient that the eschatological act of deliverance has already begun; only the finale remains.[17]

The enduring insight of Marxsen was that Mark's Gospel is what he calls "a representation" of Jesus; the Gospel confronts Mark's readers with the reality of Jesus. It is not a report about Jesus but an encounter with the Risen Lord.[18] But what it is the Risen Lord is seeking to say to the community of Mark is largely left unanswered by Marxsen.

In 1957 James M. Robinson, in response to the rise of redaction-history

---

11. *The Gospel according to St. Mark* (London: Macmillan Company, 1953).

12. W. G. Kümmel, *Introduction to the New Testament*, trans. H. C. Kee (Nashville: Abingdon Press, 1975), p. 92.

13. Willi Marxsen, *Mark the Evangelist: Studies on the Redaction History of the Gospel*, trans. J. Boyce et al. (Nashville: Abingdon Press, 1969).

14. *Ibid.*, p. 138.

15. *Ibid.*, p. 189.

16. *Ibid.*, p. 204.

17. *Ibid.*, p. 189; here Marxsen closely approximates the viewpoint of W. G. Kümmel, *Promise and Fulfillment: The Eschatological Message of Jesus*, trans. Dorothea M. Barton (Naperville: A. R. Allenson, 1957).

18. Marxsen, *Mark*, pp. 130f.

and the then surging interest in the historical-Jesus question, offered *The Problem of History in Mark*. In it he sought to show that Mark's view of history is very different from modern positivistic understandings: according to Mark, the story of Jesus is to be seen "in its unity as the eschatological action of God," inaugurated at Jesus' baptism by John and carried forward through his various modes of struggle with evil, culminating in the cross and the decisive victory over evil achieved in the resurrection, whereby "the force of evil is conclusively broken and the power of God's reign is established in history."[19] But apart from his general observation that in Mark "ethical teachings are constantly parallel to christological or eschatological affirmations," Robinson does not show how the diverse components of Mark—narratives, parables, sayings, passion story—are bound together in a unity of purpose.

Taking his cue from the factor of secrecy which pervades the Gospel of Mark, T. A. Burkill noted that Mark's two stories of healing of the blind (8:22–26 and 10:46–52) not only serve as important transitions in the Marcan narrative, but also have a symbolic function in that they stand in sharp contrast to the adjacent accounts of the disciples who are told the truth about Jesus—especially about his suffering and death—but cannot perceive it as God's purpose for Jesus.[20] The confirmation of what Jesus discloses about his own future is provided by the documentation from Scripture and by the detailed nature of the predictions concerning what Mark then goes on to describe as occurring in the trial and death of Jesus. Jesus is portrayed as not knowing one thing: the exact hour of his parousia, but the basic thesis of the Gospel is assumed to be that his suffering and death are the divinely ordained prelude to his ultimate exaltation.[21] What is lacking in Burkill's analysis of Mark is an effective way to integrate the teachings of Jesus, and especially his ethical instructions, with the story of the passion.

Quentin Quesnell, as the title of his study, *The Mind of Mark: Interpretation and Method through Exegesis of Mark 6:52*,[22] suggests, proposes that the key to understanding the aim of Mark is to be found in the enigmatic comment in 6:52: the disciples did not understand concerning the loaves

19. James M. Robinson, *The Problem of History in Mark* (Naperville: A. R. Allenson, 1957), p. 53.

20. *Mysterious Revelation: An Examination of the Philosophy of St. Mark's Gospel* (Ithaca: Cornell University Press, 1963), pp. 142, 186.

21. *Ibid.*, p. 227.

22. Quentin Quesnell, *The Mind of Mark: Interpretation and Method through Exegesis of Mark 6:52* (Rome: Pontifical Biblical Institute, 1969).

following the miraculous feeding and Jesus' having walked on the water; Quesnell sees this incident as a eucharistic scene ("he blessed, he broke, he gave . . ." 6:41), as have other interpreters of Mark. But he considers this to be both an important transition in the literary development of the narrative ("one step along his path of paraenetic development, pointed at delivering the full impact of the gospel in the second half of his composition," p. 276) as well as the seminal center out of which the whole meaning of Christianity is to be unfolded: "The full meaning of the Eucharist is the full meaning of Christianity. It means death and resurrection with Christ. It means the union of all men in one Body. It means His abiding presence. . . . None of this could be seen before the event, and before the central Christian reality of faith which clarified the event as salvific."[23] Presumably Quesnell means that "the event" is the death of Jesus and "the reality" is the Eucharist which furnished the meaning of the death.

Similar concentration on the passion event as the central clue to understanding the aim of Mark is to be found in the collection of essays edited by Werner H. Kelber, *The Passion in Mark*.[24] A new perspective has been introduced, however, as a departure from standard form-critical assumptions: rather than regarding the passion narrative as a unit that Mark has taken over from the tradition, John Donahue (writing in the Kelber volume of essays) describes the passion story as "itself the final product of a varied and complicated development." He asserts further that the account "owes its final form and coherent structure and meaning to Mark," which cannot be determined in isolation from the other sections of the Gospel.[25] The thesis about the Marcan origin of the passion story in its present form has been demonstrated in greater detail by Donahue elsewhere in his *Are You the Christ?*[26] He has shown that Mark worked with traditional materials but has given the material the formal structure of a trial and has then interwoven other elements such as the theme of the predictions of judgment on the temple, the portrayal of Jesus as apocalyptic Son of Man, and the obtuse perfidy of Peter into the narrative. Donahue and others have seen that an important factor in Mark's fashioning of this section of his Gospel has been Christian interpretation of Scripture, whereby accounts of

23. *Ibid.*, pp. 276f.
24. Werner H. Kelber, *The Passion in Mark* (Philadelphia: Fortress Press, 1976).
25. *Ibid.*, p. 20.
26. *Are You the Christ? The Trial Narrative in the Gospel of Mark*, SBLDS 10 (Missoula: Scholars Press, 1973).

events are shaped or even created to conform to what the early church perceived as it read the Jewish Scriptures.[27]

Donahue and Kelber, in their contributions to the volume *The Passion in Mark*, make clear that Mark is at the same time interested (a) in portraying Jesus and (b) in addressing the Christian community of his own time. Thus, as Kelber has seen, the response of the disciples to Jesus' disclosure that his role as Messiah–Son of Man inevitably involves suffering is not only a statement about the theological meaning of the death of Jesus as an event in the past; it is also warning that the coming of the kingdom of God is not to be accomplished by a show of power but by the acceptance of trial, suffering, and death—for the Christian community.[28] Mark's reinterpretation of the Son of David messianic expectation has direct implications for the Marcan community as well, according to Donahue: "For Mark the final assumption of total power and the handing on of royal authority will take place when Jesus returns as Son of Man." In his revision of the Davidic tradition, the new Son of David builds a new temple, as the older one did (Solomon), but this role is fulfilled "in the transformed sense that the Temple is the future community."[29] Similar conclusions were reached by Don Juel in an independent study, *Messiah and Temple: The Trial of Jesus in the Gospel of Mark*.[30] Sharing the view of his mentor, Nils A. Dahl, that "the starting point for the tradition of the trial and crucifixion is the inscription 'the king of the Jews,' " Juel[31] is inclined to think of Mark more as interpreter of tradition than as the creator of it. But he shares with Donahue the conclusions that the royal motif is central in the trial narrative and that the tie with the temple presupposes the Christian conviction that their community is the new temple of God. Accordingly, divine judgment has replaced Israel and its temple as the locus of the link between God and his covenant people.[32]

T. J. Weeden sets forth in summary form the thesis which he developed

27. Cf. H. C. Kee, "The Function of Scriptural Quotations and Allusions in Mark 11–16," in E. E. Ellis and Erich Grässer, eds., *Jesus und Paulus* (Göttingen: Vandenhoeck & Ruprecht, 1975), pp. 165–88. Similarly, Eta Linnemann, *Studien zur Passionsgeschichte* (Göttingen: Vandenhoeck & Ruprecht, 1970), rejects the theory that there was a pre-Marcan passion narrative. Mark has produced a report rather than reproducing an existing connective account.

28. Kelber, *Passion*, p. 60.

29. John Donahue, in *ibid.*, p. 77.

30. Don Juel, *Messiah and Temple: The Trial of Jesus in the Gospel of Mark*, SBLDS 31 (Missoula: Scholars Press, 1977).

31. *Ibid.*, p. 213.

32. *Ibid.*, pp. 212f.

more fully in his earlier study, *Mark: Traditions in Conflict*.[33] Building on
the observation of the form critics that there is a certain tension in Mark
between the passion theme and the desire of the disciples to employ their
miracle-working capacities to move into positions of power (e.g., Mark 10:
35–45), Weeden has proposed that Mark is combatting a triumphalist
movement within the church of his time by showing how Jesus put down
the disciples when they were making such proposals and instead called to
their attention his—and ultimately their—role as suffering servant of God.
Weeden claims that the power-hungry group had adopted a "divine man
christology," which Mark is trying to counter with his suffering Son of Man
Christology. According to this theory, the miracle tradition "seeks well-
being by conquest, leading to dominance or destruction of others,"[34] while
the path of servanthood leads to self-effacement and self-giving love.

The notion of a divine-man Christology builds on the work of others not
directly concerned with Marcan studies. The term itself was employed by
Dieter Georgi in his study of Paul's opponents in Corinth, where it is proposed that miracle-working followers of Jesus were promoting the representation of him as a divinized man (*theios anēr*) whose chief characteristic
was that of power, as evident in the miracles performed by both him and
his followers.[35] Closely related to the voguish divine-man Christology is the
theory that a widespread literary phenomenon of the Greco-Roman world,
the aretalogy, was used to depict divine men, especially the miracles performed by the *theios anēr*.[36] One writer went so far as to describe an
aretalogy as biographical writing in which an impressive teacher possessed
of supernatural powers encounters the hostility of the authorities and is
martyred.[37] If the case could be made for the conceptual model of "divine
man" and for the literary model of "aretalogy," then obviously the links
with Mark would be of great importance for understanding the aim and
background of our oldest Gospel. Careful studies of these alleged models, however, show that the evidence will not support these scholarly
suppositions.

The concept of divine man and the related figure of the charismatic
miracle-worker in the Greco-Roman world have been subjected to thorough

---

33. T. J. Weeden, *Mark: Traditions in Conflict* (Philadelphia: Fortress Press, 1971).

34. "The Cross as Power in Weakness," in Kelber, *Passion*, p. 132.

35. Dieter Georgi, *Die Gegner des Paulus im zweiter Korintherbrief* (Neukirchen-
Vluyn: Neukirchener Verlag, 1964).

36. Moses Hadas and Morton Smith, *Heroes and Gods: Spiritual Biographies in Antiquity* (New York: Harper & Row, 1965). Also Helmut Koester, "One Jesus and Four
Gospels," *HTR* 61 (1968): 230–36.

37. Hadas and Smith, *Heroes*, p. 3.

study. David L. Tiede's investigation *The Charismatic Figure as Miracle Worker* included the phenomenon of divinization in both Greek and Jewish literature of the Greco-Roman period. He has shown that there are two distinct strands in this material: (1) portrayals of divine wise men; (2) accounts of miracle-workers. Thus Plato stresses that it was Socrates' love of wisdom that brought him into communion with the divine, while Xenophon and others emphasize the divine signs in the form of augury, oracles, and extraordinary coincidences as evidence of divinity.[38] The dominant feature of the literary tradition about Socrates, as late as the time of Plutarch, is that he was a courageous moral philosopher, disciplined in thought and act, voluntarily poor, who persevered to the death in his commitment to philosophical truth.[39] Only in the second century A.D. and subsequently are the figures of wise men and miracle-workers blended; as Tiede phrases it, only later do Philostratus and Porphyry in their lives of Apollonius of Tyana and Pythagoras produce "an uneven mixture of miraculous and philosophical traditions rather than a unified blend of homogenous elements."[40] The attempt by Morton Smith and others to utilize Philostratus' *Life of Apollonius of Tyana* as a paradigm for the gospel writers' portrait of Jesus is a gross anachronism, even if one were to allow the appeal to the alleged sources that Apollonius is supposed to have used.[41] In the mythological traditions of the Hellenistic world that report the acceptance of Hercules among the gods, it is his qualities as model of philosophical virtue and as exemplar of wise ruler that lead to his elevation to heaven as a just reward for his labors.[42] Later, in the early centuries of the empire, the figure Hercules is transformed from one whose labors demonstrate athletic prowess to one whose struggles achieve victory over the powers of evil.[43] Thus the Hellenistic apotheosis of Hercules is *parallel to* rather than *precedent for* the figure of Jesus as one who triumphs over evil through the demonstration of supernatural powers.

In Jewish literature of the Greco-Roman period, Moses is portrayed as agent of God, whose divine enablement empowers him to perform extraordinary deeds. But his special relationship to God is to be seen in his wis-

---

38. David L. Tiede, *The Charismatic Figure as Miracle Worker*, SBLDS 1 (Missoula: Scholars Press, 1972), pp. 28–38.
39. *Ibid.*, pp. 40–42.
40. *Ibid.*, p. 61.
41. Howard C. Kee, *Community of the New Age: Studies in Mark's Gospel* (Philadelphia: Westminster Press, 1977).
42. Tiede, *Charismatic Figure*, pp. 72–79, quoting from Marcel Simon, *Hercule et le Christianisme* (Paris: Strassburg, 1955).
43. Simon, *Hercule*, p. 77.

dom more than in his deeds. And there is no effort to picture Moses as a divinized man. Tiede's research and conclusions[44] have been confirmed by the detailed analysis of *theios anēr* in the writings of Philo of Alexandria carried out by Carl Holladay. In his portrayal of Moses as king—just as in Josephus' representation of Moses and other patriarchs of ancient Israel—Philo's intent is to show that they exemplified the wisdom of the truly virtuous man or the wise ruler of the Cynic and Stoic philosophical traditions.[45] Both maintain a clear distinction between the human and the divine. Only in death does Moses become immortal, but Philo goes out of his way to show why the statement in Exodus 7:1 that Moses is *theos* cannot be taken literally.[46] It is unwarranted, therefore, to assume that there was in Hellenistic Judaism a paradigmatic figure of a divinized miracle-worker to which the early Christian image of Jesus was made to conform by Mark's opponents[47] or by anyone else in the New Testament.[48]

Before undertaking an analysis of Mark along the lines implied by Holladay,[49] however, we may consider other approaches that have been suggested to provide insight as to the aims Mark had for writing his Gospel.

II

The first group of these studies of Mark consists of literary analyses of four types: (1) studies of the literary relationships among the Gospels (new approaches to the old synoptic problem); (2) attempts to identify the literary genre or model used by Mark; (3) efforts to employ contemporary literary criticism—especially in relation to narrative—in interpreting Mark; (4) detailed study of component elements of Mark. These can only be sketched here in broad outline and the results assessed briefly.

The most comprehensive study and critique of the hypothesis that Mark's is the oldest Gospel, and the major source for Matthew and Luke, have recently been carried out by Hans-Herbert Stoldt.[50] Combining his-

---

44. *Charismatic Figure.*

45. Carl Holladay, *Theios Anēr in Hellenistic Judaism: A Critique of the Use of This Category in New Testament Christology*, SBLDS 40 (Missoula: Scholars Press, 1977), pp. 78, 195.

46. *Ibid.*, p. 155.

47. Weeden, *Mark.*

48. Georgi, *Gegner.*

49. *Theios Anēr in Hellenistic Judaism*, p. 239.

50. Hans-Herbert Stoldt, *Geschichte und Kritik der Markus-Hypothese* (Göttingen: Vandenhoeck & Ruprecht, 1977).

torical description of the rise and development of the theory of Marcan priority with evaluation of the arguments offered to support the hypothesis, Stoldt shows that a major motivational factor was the attempt to establish a fixed historical basis for the life and teachings of Jesus. As the least explicitly theological gospel—lacking both virgin birth stories and post-resurrection narratives—Mark served well as a minimal historical base, and literary arguments were brought forward to shore up this historical strong-hold. Stoldt's arguments about unworthy and defensive motivations among synoptic scholars defending Marcan priority are in many cases valid, but his attempts to discredit their literary conclusions are considerably less than convincing. Stoldt must account for Mark as "a spiritual New Creation of an independent character"[51] and take refuge in a mystery to account for the sources of Matthew and Luke: "a yet unresolved riddle."[52]

Other analyses of the relationships among the Synoptics have resulted in more cautious conclusions: that Mark and the so-called "Q" source (non-Marcan material common to Matthew and Luke) overlap, and that there are extensive minor agreements of Matthew and Luke against Mark.[53] But a persuasive case has yet to be made that Mark can be accounted for on the hypothesis of dependence on Matthew (or Luke) in a way that is more plausible than the reverse—which remains the over-whelmingly dominant synoptic theory.[54] For technical analysis of the relationships among the Gospels, the most valuable resources are Frans Neirynck's study *The Minor Agreements of Matthew and Luke against Mark*[55] and Robert Morgenthaler's statistical synopsis of the relationships among the first three Gospels.[56] Neither of these scholars is led by the evidence to reject the priority of Mark. What is called for instead is to replace a rigidly literary method of sorting out sources by an approach which takes more fully into account the creativity of the evangelists.[57]

We have already touched on the search for literary models for Mark's Gospel. "Aretalogy" is an unsuitable candidate, unless we ignore the an-

---

51. *Ibid.*, p. 234.

52. *Ibid.*, p. 235.

53. E. P. Sanders, *The Tendencies of the Synoptic Tradition* (Cambridge: University Press, 1969); Thomas R. W. Longstaff, *Evidence of Conflation in Mark? A Study in the Synoptic Problem,* SBLDS 28 (Missoula: Scholars Press, 1977).

54. Kümmel, *Introduction;* full documentation and bibliography, pp. 38–80.

55. Frans Neirynck, *The Minor Agreements of Matthew and Luke against Mark* (Leuven: University Press, 1974). Neirynck shows that evidence adduced by W. R. Farmer in his allegedly objective *Synopticon* (Cambridge: Cambridge University Press, 1969) is in fact prejudiced against Marcan priority, pp. 41f.

56. Robert Morgenthaler, *Statistische Synopse* (Zurich: Gotthelf-Verlag, 1971).

57. Neirynck, *Minor Agreements*, p. 322.

cient use of the term and settle instead on a modern scholarly construct.[58] But do other authentic ancient genre models help in accounting for the style and structure of Mark? The most comprehensive recent assessment of the possibilities is by C. H. Talbert, under the title *What Is a Gospel? The Genre of the Canonical Gospels*.[59] After exploring and rejecting several proposals for models for the Gospels, Talbert comes down on biography, which he defines as prose narration about a person's life, presenting supposedly historical facts which are selected to reveal the character or essence of the individual, often with the purpose of affecting the behavior of the reader.[60] It is not at all clear, however, that Mark's major aim is to portray the "character" of Jesus.

Much less likely is the proposal of Dan O. Via that Mark is patterned after Hellenistic comedy. Indeed, Via must quickly shift his terminology to tragi-comedy, since the passion story is so central for Mark. His insistence on a single theme, a single plot (death followed by resurrection), requires him to leave out of account most of Mark. Adopting the methods of structuralism—especially the literary approach which denies that sociohistorical factors share in the emergence of literature—Via locates the structure of Mark in the evangelist's mind,[61] which unfortunately is not available for analysis.

French literary critics and biblical scholars have sought to employ structuralist methods in interpreting the Bible, and in particular the Gospel of Mark. A prime instance is the analysis of the story of the Gerasene demoniac in Mark 5 by Jean Starobinski. The promise is great: it is claimed that structuralism represents a Copernican revolution in analysis of texts, culture, societies.[62] The results are commonplace observations, however, or explicit allegorization or both: "The fall of the pigs into the lake is a *figure* for the fall of the rebellious spirits into the abyss."[63] Or, the demoniac's life among the tomb is a symbol of alienation.[64] In spite of the admirable announced intention to allow the text to speak for itself,[65] the explanation of the parable of the sower in Mark 4:10ff. is seized upon as

58. Howard C. Kee, "Aretalogy and Gospel," *JBL* 92 (1973): 402–22.

59. C. H. Talbert, *What Is a Gospel? The Genre of the Canonical Gospels* (Philadelphia: Fortress Press, 1977).

60. *Ibid.*, p. 17.

61. *Kerygma and Comedy in the New Testament: A Structuralist Approach to Hermeneutic* (Philadelphia: Fortress Press, 1974), p. 93.

62. Thus François Bovon, quoting F. de Saussure in *Cours de Linguistique Général* (Paris, 1916), in *Analyse Structurale et Exegèse Biblique*, ed. F. Bovon (Neuchâtel Delachaux et Niestlé, 1971), p. 13.

63. Jean Starobinski in Bovon, *Analyse*, "La Démoniaque de Gérasa," p. 72.

64. *Ibid.*, p. 78.

65. Bovon, *Analyse*, p. 20.

justification for allegorical interpretation of the whole of Mark, with the result that the great achievement of employing "scientific method" for exegesis of Scripture[66] comes to nothing more than differentiating the "literal" from the "spiritual" meaning of Mark. The advantage of this process, according to its advocates, is not only to reveal the "moral" meaning of the narrative, but by this method also "one senses that the historicity of the narrative is dissipated."[67] Thus, the story of the demoniac's cure "is no longer an episode in the earthly ministry of Jesus, a moment from his life within time, but it is a timeless victory to which every individual is able to appeal for deliverance from his temporal torment."[68] Like the existentialist hermeneutics of the sixties, one can expect that this new psycho-allegorization will flourish in some quarters, but its anti-historical stance encourages intellectual irresponsibility and its use of the text as a point of departure belies the announced aim of the method's proponents: to direct attention to the text alone.[69]

Far more suggestive and illuminating are those literary approaches to Mark which treat the work as narrative, seeking to account for what stands in the text against the background of the dynamic of narrative as a literary strategy.[70] Tannehill has studied the narrative techniques of novelists and fiction writers—though without labeling Mark as fiction—with noteworthy results. Examining the role of the disciples as depicted in Mark, he shows that the writer has with great skill portrayed them at first in a way that highlights their authority as commissioned by Jesus and implicitly commends them for their devotion to him, and then turns to an increasingly severe criticism of them for their lack of understanding and finally their abandonment of him. The literary adroitness of Mark is seen by Tannehill in the emphasis by means of repetition: three commissioning stories (1:16–20; 3:13–19; 6:7–13, 30); three boat scenes linked with two feeding scenes, which lead to the denunciation of the disciples for their blind lack of understanding (8:14–21). In spite of the special revelation that has been given to them ("the mystery of the kingdom of God," Mark 4:11), they are as blind as the outsiders (4:12). Thus Mark's portrayal of the disciples requires them to engage in self-examination: "The recognition of the disciples' behavior and the search for an alternative way become the search

---

66. *Ibid.*, p. 25.
67. Starobinski, "La Démoniaque de Gérasa," p. 88.
68. *Ibid.*
69. Bovon, *Analyse*, p. 20.
70. See esp. Robert C. Tannehill, "The Disciples in Mark: The Function of a Narrative Role," *JR* 57 (1977): 386–405.

for a new self who can follow Jesus faithfully as a disciple."[71] It is Tanne-hill's exploration of character portrayal in narrative that alerts and sensi-tizes him to discern how Mark is using narrative provocatively to challenge his readers to accept the demands of discipleship. Even when one agrees with Erich Auerbach and Amos Wilder, who, as literary critics, adjudge Mark's Gospel as a whole to be a new literary genre,[72] Tannehill's work shows that there is great value in literary analysis of Marcan detail. Indeed, Auerbach's own study of Mark richly demonstrates the evangelist's narra-tive skill.[73]

III

Extensive research and theorizing have been devoted to the component elements that make up Mark's Gospel. Two comprehensive studies of the process of composition of Mark come to radically different conclusions. Etienne Trocmé, in *The Formation of the Gospel according to Mark*,[74] denies that Mark was able to "set his own imprint to any great extent on the material he received from the 'doctors' of his church and from the Galilean storyteller."[75] Indeed, "the author of Mark was a clumsy writer unworthy of mention in any history of literature."[76] One may wonder in passing why, if this assessment is accurate, the author of this judgment bothered to write a book on Mark, or why a distinguished literary figure such as Auerbach would hold the work in such high esteem for its rhetori-cal power. Trocmé thinks that the Gospel was produced by a missionary movement which broke away from the mother church in Jerusalem and was carrying on evangelism among the common people of Palestine. The original edition of Mark consisted of chapters 1–13. To these "an anony-mous ecclesiastic of the Roman community" attached chapters 14–16, which may have been based on a small document from Jerusalem and which lent to the whole the authority of Peter and the name of Mark.[77]

---

71. *Ibid.*, p. 395.
72. Amos Wilder, *Early Christian Rhetoric: The Language of the Gospel* (Cambridge: Harvard University Press, 1964), p. 36. Also Erich Auerbach, *Mimesis: The Representa-tion of Reality in Western Literature* (Princeton: Princeton University Press, 1953).
73. *Mimesis*, pp. 40–49.
74. Etienne Trocmé, *The Formation of the Gospel according to Mark*, trans. Pamela Gaughan (Philadelphia: Westminster Press, 1975).
75. *Ibid.*, p. 72.
76. *Ibid.*, p. 73.
77. *Ibid.*, pp. 246f.

Piling conjecture on conjecture, Trocmé speculates that the group represented by Mark is linked with the seven who in Acts 6 are chosen for servile roles in the church, and that the real author of the original "Mark" is Philip the evangelist of Acts 6:5 and 8:26ff. The theories are ingenious, but lack both plausibility and evidential support, as well as being of no value in accounting for Mark in the form in which it has come down to us. The missionary outreach of the Marcan community is said by Trocmé to have been launched in obedience to "the command of the Risen Christ,"[78] although in fact the risen Christ never appears in the Marcan narrative.

Werner Kelber's forthcoming work, *The Making of Mark*, promises to be a breakthrough on the question of how forms of oral tradition (as reconstructed and analyzed by Dibelius and Bultmann) were incorporated into the Marcan Gospel. Basing his critical judgments on both general studies of oral transmissions of tradition in various cultures and specific analyses of the gospel tradition in the New Testament and in the second century,[79] Kelber shows that oral tradition develops in a variety of ways: clusters of sayings or miracle stories form by association, while other sayings float independently; some traditions are elaborated, while others are reduced to a stark minimum. A fixed form emerges only at the crucial shift from the oral to the written stage. Incorporating the insights of Gerd Theissen about the important role of itinerant charismatic-prophetic leaders in the early church,[80] Kelber proposes that by reproducing the Jesus tradition in written form Mark has sought to bring to an end the free-wheeling transmission of the Jesus tradition by wandering prophets, who place their claims on at least as lofty a level as that of Jesus; the central opponents whom Mark is attacking are the false prophets and false Christs of Mark 13:3, 21–23 with their wild pronouncements. By reducing the tradition to writing, Mark fixes the figure of Jesus in the past and leaves the time of fulfillment in the open-ended future. The appearance of Mark's Gospel did not bring to an end the free prophetic tradition with its utterances "in my name," but it did give a fixed form to the tradition— although the other evangelists felt free to alter Mark.

The title of Karl-Georg Reploh's study *Mark, Teacher of the Com-*

---

78. *Ibid.*, pp. 215ff.
79. For this point Kelber builds on the research of H. Koester, *Synoptische Überlieferung bei den apostolischen Vätern* (Berlin: Akademie-Verlag, 1957).
80. Gerd Theissen, "Wanderradikalismus: Literatursoziologische Aspekte der Überlieferung von Worten Jesu im Urchristentum," *ZTK* 70 (1973): 245–71. Eng. trans. in *Radical Religion* 2 & 3 (Berkeley, 1975), 84–93.

munity[81] discloses the author's basic thesis that Mark was not written to give an account of the past but to address the Christian community of his own time through the Jesus tradition, collected and adapted for this purpose. Mark's primary aim is not to depict the earthly Jesus but to show the present obligations of the community that calls itself by his name, how they are to be formed and built up in the work which they have undertaken in his behalf.

Viewed as a document for a self-conscious community, there are rough but useful analogies, therefore, between Mark and certain of the Dead Sea writings. In both there are esoteric interpretations of the Jewish Scriptures, which point to the coming of the founder of the community of the new covenant and promise that beyond his suffering and death lies divine vindication. There are regulations for the ongoing life of the community, as in the Dead Sea Scroll of the Rule. There are oblique references to worldly powers as well as to the demonic powers and the struggle with them in which the community will be involved. These conflicts are depicted in the War Scroll and the biblical commentaries at Qumran on the one hand, and in Mark 13 on the other. What we have in Mark, therefore, is a foundation document for an apocalyptic community.[82]

IV

Theological studies of Mark have proved useful in some cases to illuminate details. Ernest Best seeks to show that the Marcan understanding of the death of Jesus is not based on the Hellenistic redeemer model, as Bultmann and his pupils have insisted, but on the obedient son tradition of Judaism, especially Isaac, whose obedience unto death was regarded in first-century Judaism as "the one perfect sacrifice by which the sins of the people of Israel were forgiven."[83] Clearly Mark has shifted the emphasis in Jesus' role as Son of Man from triumph to suffering; precedent for the suffering of the Son of Man is already established in Daniel 7:13, 21, 25, 27, as Best and others have noted.[84] Overlooked by Best, however, is the

---

81. Karl-Georg Reploh, *Markus, Lehrer der Gemeinde*, SBM 9 (Stuttgart: Katholisches Bibelwerk, 1969).

82. This is the basic thesis presented in Kee, *Community*.

83. Ernest Best, *The Temptation and the Passion: The Markan Soteriology*, SNTSMS 2 (Cambridge: University Press, 1965). See also Nils A. Dahl, "The *Akedah* of Isaac," in *The Crucified Messiah* (Minneapolis: Augsburg Publishing House, 1974).

84. Best, *Temptation*, p. 164.

fact that in Daniel and in Mark the suffering that is undergone by the Son of Man is assumed to be an inevitable stage moving toward the vindication of God's agent and his people.[85] Suffering and vindication of the Son of Man are not antithetical but divinely ordained steps in the fulfillment of his redemptive role.

Two other studies of Marcan Christology claim to be based on Jewish messianism rather than on Hellenistic redemptive motifs, but both are covertly or unconsciously grounded in Bultmann's existentialist interpretation of the cross. Philipp Vielhauer saw connections between Mark's portrait of Jesus as the suffering Messiah and the ancient Near Eastern pattern of enthronement of the divine king. Johannes Schreiber adopts Vielhauer's basic position but adds to it the notion that Mark has conformed his picture of the suffering Jesus to that of the redeemed redeemer of Gnosticism, even though that image has long been shown to be a modern scholarly construct rather than an operative concept in the ancient world.

V

In spite of the lack of critical clarity, much less consensus, about the aims of Mark, there has been no dearth of commentaries on this Gospel. The most comprehensive is that of Ernst Haenchen[86] (*The Way of Jesus*), which is filled with brilliant insight on details of Mark but does not provide any overall view of the book or of the author's objectives. Eduard Schweizer's commentary, translated in English as *The Good News according to Mark*,[87] declares that there were three main tendencies in first-century Christianity's understanding of Jesus which Mark was seeking to correct: to regard him as a rabbi, whose teachings were to be recalled and transmitted; to exalt Jesus as a cosmic redeemer, thereby losing sight of his earthly ministry; to depict him as a divinely endowed wonder-worker, whose fanatical followers emulate his charismatic achievements. In seeking to combat these distortions, Mark sets out to preserve the memory of what

---

85. Kee, *Community*, pp. 135f. On the background of the suffering Son of Man, see F. H. Borsch, *Son of Man in Myth and History* (Philadelphia: Westminster Press, 1967). On the various categories of Son of Man sayings in Mark and the Synoptics, see Heinz-Eduward Tödt, *The Son of Man in the Synoptic Tradition*, trans. D. M. Barton (Philadelphia: Westminster Press, 1965).

86. Ernst Haenchen, *Der Weg Jesu: Eine Erklärung des Markus-Evangeliums und der kanonischen Parallelen* (Berlin: A. Töpelmann, 1960²).

87. Eduard Schweizer, *The Good News according to Mark* (Atlanta: John Knox Press, 1970).

Jesus said and did, culminating in his act of self-giving, which discloses "the unprecedented and incomprehensible incarnate love of God."[88]

A lively, readable, popular commentary is that of Dennis E. Nineham in the Pelican Commentary Series.[89] A thorough analysis of Mark from a scholarly, conservative point of view is that of William L. Lane in the New International Critical Commentary. The late Norman Perrin was at work on a commentary on Mark at the time of his death in 1976. Clues as to the direction in which his thinking was moving are evident in his analysis of Mark in his *The New Testament: An Introduction*,[90] where stress is laid on the apocalyptic outlook of Mark: "Mark takes the bold and imaginative step of telling the story of the ministry of Jesus so that concerns of the risen Jesus for his church in the present come to the fore. For him the ministry of Jesus in Galilee and Judea, the ministry of Jesus in the present in the churches for which Mark writes and the ministry of Jesus that will begin with his parousia in 'Galilee' are all the same ministry and can all be treated together in a narrative in which past, present, and future flow together into the one apocalyptic time."[91]

There have been important studies of certain components of Mark's Gospel, such as Paul J. Achtemeier's reconstruction of cycles of miracle stories that underlie the Marcan narrative,[92] and the insightful analyses of the Marcan apocalypse by Hartmann,[93] and by Jan Lamprecht.[94] Studies of the parables bear on our understanding of Mark; notable are those written from a structuralist standpoint by Via[95] and J. D. Crossan.[96] Fresh and perceptive is the investigation of parables from a literary perspective by Madeleine Boucher.[97] Idiosyncratic and highly conjectural is Morton Smith's *The Secret Gospel*, in which it is claimed that the original Mark was written for a secret community that gathered for nocturnal baptisms,

---

88. *Ibid.*, p. 385.

89. Dennis E. Nineham, *The Gospel of St. Mark* (Baltimore: Penguin Books, 1963).

90. Norman Perrin, *The New Testament: An Introduction* (New York: Harcourt Brace Jovanovich, 1974).

91. *Ibid.*, p. 162.

92. "Pre-Markan Catenae," *JBL* 89 (1970): 270ff.

93. Lars Hartman, *Prophecy Interpreted*, trans. Neil Tomkinson (Lund: C. W. K. Gleerup, 1966).

94. Jan Lamprecht, *Die Redaktion der Markus-Apokalypse*, AnBib 28 (1967).

95. Dan O. Via, *The Parables: Their Literary and Existential Dimensions* (Philadelphia: Fortress Press, 1967).

96. John Dominic Crossan, *In Parables: The Challenge of the Historical Jesus* (New York: Harper & Row, 1973).

97. Madeleine Boucher, *The Mysterious Parable: A Literary Study* (Washington, D.C.: Catholic Biblical Association, 1977).

including hints of homosexual practices.[98] Smith's publication of the portion of the text of this document, allegedly preserved by Clement of Alexandria and rediscovered recently at the Monastery of Mar Saba near Jerusalem, is a model presentation of an ancient document.[99] A convenient survey of some major theses about the theological aims of Mark are to be found in Joachim Rohde's, *Rediscovering the Teaching of the Evangelists*.[100] Ralph P. Martin's survey, *Mark, Evangelist and Theologian*, is a useful compendium and bibliographical review, though it is marred by the traditionalist stance of the writer and by his undue concern for the elusive factor of historicity.[101]

VI

Though one cannot yet, if ever, speak of scholarly consensus regarding the Gospel of Mark, certain directions seem to be emerging. Although Mark was influenced as any writer would be by literary styles and genres of his own time, he shaped a new model in writing his Gospel. Its style resembles that of ancient narrative, but its aims and structure seem to have been most influenced by sectarian Jewish apocalypticism, especially that of Qumran, whose sacred writings recounted God's miraculous acts of deliverance as signs of his eschatological vindication and whose members saw in the teachings and the sufferings of their founder models and guidelines for their own communal life and possible martyrdom in the face of the eschatological conflicts that lay ahead. The pervasive elements of secrecy and eschatological vindication are essential features of the self-understanding of a community that believes itself to have been granted by God access to the "secret of the kingdom of God."[102]

---

98. Morton Smith, *The Discovery and Interpretation of the Secret Gospel according to Mark* (New York: Harper & Row, 1973).

99. Morton Smith, *Clement of Alexandria and a Secret Gospel of Mark* (Cambridge: Harvard University Press, 1973).

100. Joachim Rohde, *Rediscovering the Teaching of the Evangelists* (Philadelphia: Westminster Press, 1968).

101. Ralph P. Martin, *Mark, Evangelist and Theologian* (London: Paternoster Press, 1972).

102. Detailed documentation of this interpretation is offered in Kee, *Community*. For a brief statement of the methodological procedure employing sociological models and analyses for historical reconstructions of the early Christian communities, see also Kee, *Jesus in History: An Approach to the Study of the Gospels* (New York: Harcourt Brace Jovanovich, 1977²), pp. 1–8.

11.

Jesus as the Parable of God in the Gospel of Mark

John R. Donahue, S.J.

Mark's Gospel is a narrative parable of the meaning of the life and death of Jesus which draws the reader into the personal engagement that takes place in interpretation and appropriation of the text in a life of discipleship.

A number of years ago Helmut Koester published an article entitled "One Jesus and Four Primitive Gospels," which discussed the unity of the Jesus tradition within its different permutations.[1] Even a cursory look at the proliferation of recent works on the Gospel of Mark would suggest as a title for our presentation "One Gospel, Four (or more) Jesuses."[2] Still, modern scholars are excused for their continuing quests for Mark's Jesus, for he is the first New Testament author to hand on an explicit christo-

---

1. Helmut Koester, "One Jesus and Four Primitive Gospels," *HTR* 61 (1968): 203–47. Also in James M. Robinson and Helmut Koester, *Trajectories through Early Christianity* (Philadelphia: Fortress Press, 1971), pp. 158–204.

2. Some of the more recent presentations are: W. J. Bennett, "The Gospel of Mark and Traditions about Jesus," *Encounter* 38 (1977): 1–11; M. Horstmann, *Studien zur Markinischen Christologie*, NTA 6 (Münster: Aschendorff, 1969): Jan Lamprecht, "The Christology of Mark," *BTB* 3 (1973): 256–73; U. Luz, "Das Jesusbild der vormarkinischen Tradition," in *Jesus Christus in Historie und Theologie*, ed. G. Strecker (Tübingen: J. C. B. Mohr [Paul Siebeck], 1975), pp. 347–74; E. Martinez, "The Identity of Jesus in Mark," *Communio* 1 (1974): 323–42; Norman Perrin, A Modern Pilgrim image in *New Testament Christology* (Philadelphia: Fortress Press, 1974); H. Sahlin, "Zum Verständnis der christologischen Anschauung des Markusevangeliums, *ST* 31 (1977): 1–19; Ernst Trocmé, "Is There a Markan Christology?" in *Christ and the Spirit in the New Testament*, ed. B. Lindars and S. Smalley (Cambridge: University Press, 1973), pp. 3–14. Three excellent, less technical presentations are: Paul J. Achtemeier, *Mark*, Proclamation Commentaries (Philadelphia: Fortress Press, 1975); C. F. Evans, *The Beginning of the Gospel* . . . (London: SPCK, 1968); H. C. Kee, *Jesus in History* (New York: Harcourt Brace Jovanovich, 1977²).

logical question: "Who do men say that I am?" (8:27). With a certain prophetic clarity this question becomes a paradigm for subsequent christological investigation. The question is precipitated by what Jesus has done, and asks who he is. The responses come from contemporary models of those who might be God's anointed. The proper answer is confessional and is understood only by personal engagement in the events of the suffering and death of Jesus.

In approaching Mark's presentation of Jesus, we will offer a brief, mainly bibliographic, overview of some of the ways the Jesus of Mark has been understood in recent study. We will attempt no adequate or exhaustive criticism of these views, but rather direct our attention to a way of reading Mark. Building on Leander Keck's evocative comments about the historical Jesus as the parable of God,[3] we will apply some of the categories and insights of contemporary parable exegesis to Mark's presentation of Jesus. Since parable has now become not simply a description of a select group of sayings of Jesus, but an independent hermeneutical and theological category, we will propose that Mark's Gospel can be presented as a narrative parable of the meaning of the life and death of Jesus.[4]

PRESENTATIONS OF JESUS

Jesus as Hellenistic Savior

Over fifty years ago Bultmann proposed the view that Mark is the conflation "of the Hellenistic kerygma about Christ, whose essential content consists of the Christ myth as we learn of it in Paul with the tradition of the story of Jesus."[5] Variations of this view continue to surface. For J. Schreiber, Mark's Jesus is the "redeemed redeemer" who empties himself in descending to earth, remains hidden during his sojourn, and is killed by demonic powers; but his death is paradoxically his exaltation (return) and epiphany as Son of God.[6] U. Luz, Leander Keck, and Hans-Dieter Betz

---

3. Leander Keck, *A Future for the Historical Jesus* (Nashville: Abingdon Press, 1971), pp. 243–49.

4. The relation of parable and theology is developed in S. McFague, *Speaking in Parables: A Study in Metaphor and Theology* (Philadelphia: Fortress Press, 1978); D. Tracy, *Blessed Rage for Order* (New York: Seabury Press, 1975), pp. 119–45; "Paul Ricoeur on Biblical Hermeneutics," *Semeia* 4 (1975).

5. R. Bultmann, *History of the Synoptic Tradition*, trans. J. Marsh, rev. ed. (New York: Harper & Row, 1968), p. 348.

6. J. Schreiber, "Die Christologie des Markusevangeliums," *ZTK* 58 (1961): 154–83, also developed in his *Die Theologie des Vertrauens* (Hamburg: Furche Verlag, 1969).

propose modifications of this theme,[7] suggesting that in Mark there are two major images of Jesus in constructive dialogue: one a Hellenistic "divine man" or demi-god figure, the other the suffering servant and prophet of the Palestinian tradition. Mark takes over the more naïve Hellenistic Christology but combines it with the title for the eschatological messianic king (*Christos*). Jesus' power is not his because of his "nature" as divine/human but because of his anointing by God and because of his exaltation at the resurrection. The aura of power which characterizes his earthly life is proleptic of the resurrection. His life is, as Dibelius asserted, a "secret Epiphany."[8]

While Luz, Keck, and Betz see "divine man" motifs as contributing positively to Mark's portrayal of Jesus as a figure of power, other authors, most prominently Theodore J. Weeden, see Mark engaged in a heated polemic against these same motifs.[9] The heresy which employs this image of Jesus consists in claims of false messiahship, a reliance on signs and wonders, a misguided realized eschatology, and an over-reliance on the presence of the risen Christ. Mark counters this heresy by representing the disciples in the Gospel as its advocates and then rejecting them by having them move from a stage of unperceptiveness (e.g., 6:52), through misconception of the necessity of suffering (e.g., 8:32–33), to outright betrayal (14:44), flight (14:50), and denial (14:66–72).[10] Positively Mark offers a theology which stresses that the way of discipleship is to be the way of suffering, and that the cross is crucial for human existence. Mark also stresses by omitting a resurrection narrative that it is not Jesus present in power but present only in hope who is the good news.[11]

Jesus as the Fulfillment of the Old Testament

While the above perspectives stress the Hellenistic setting of Mark, another group of interpreters stress the continuity of the Gospel with its Jewish heritage. This becomes most obvious in the careful way in which the life of Jesus is seen as the fulfillment of Scripture and his death is

---

7. Leander Keck, "Mark 3:7–12 and Mark's Christology," *JBL* 84 (1965): 341–58; "The Introduction to Mark's Gospel," *NTS* 12 (1966): 352–70; U. Luz, "Das Geheimnismotiv und die Markinische Christologie," *ZNW* 56 (1965): 45–74; H.-D. Betz, "Jesus as Divine Man," in T. Trotter, ed., *Jesus and the Historian* (Philadelphia: Westminster Press, 1968), pp. 114–33.

8. M. Dibelius, *From Tradition to Gospel*, trans. B. Woolf (New York: Scribner's, n.d.), p. 230.

9. Theodore J. Weeden, *Mark: Traditions in Conflict* (Philadelphia: Fortress Press, 1971). Weeden's position on the disciples has not met with general acceptance.

10. *Ibid.*, pp. 26–51.

11. *Ibid.*, pp. 159–68.

placed under divine necessity.[12] More specifically, Jesus is seen in correspondence to types or figures from the Old Testament. The leading contenders for an Old Testament prototype have been the Suffering Servant of Deutero-Isaiah, especially of Isaiah 52:13—53:12, and the suffering just one of the psalms and wisdom literature.[13] Jesus is seen as the servant in his election by God (Isa. 42:1; Mark 1:11) and most importantly in his atoning death for many (Mark 10:45; 14:24). The suffering just one who is persecuted by unjust oppressors, remains silent, is mocked, and thought foolish, but who is vindicated by God, provides a model for many individual parts of the passion narrative.[14] Finally there is a resurgence of Davidic motifs used to describe the Jesus of Mark.[15] Though Mark does not favor the exact title "Son of David" (12:35–37) (perhaps because of political overtones), many of the actions of Jesus in the Gospel conform to a Davidic model.

Jesus, Messiah: Son of God, Son of Man

By far the most dominant mode of identifying Jesus as God's anointed in Mark has been through the use of the titles. The procedure as represented by Cullmann, Hahn, and Fuller has been to describe the pre-Christian use of the title, its origin as a Christian confession, and its presence in Mark as an index of a stage of Christian usage.[16] Christology was

12. On Mark's use of Scripture, see A. Suhl, *Die Funktion der alttestamentlichen Zitate und Anspielungen im Markusevangelium* (Gütersloh: Gerd Mohn, 1965); and H. C. Kee, "The Function of Scriptural Quotations and Allusions in Mark 11–16," in E. E. Ellis and Erich Grässer, eds., *Jesus und Paulus* (Göttingen: Vandenhoeck & Ruprecht, 1975), pp. 165–88. The necessity (*dei*) of Jesus' death is found at 8:31; 9:12; 14:27; 14:49.

13. On Suffering Servant see C. Maurer, "Knecht Gottes und Sohn Gottes im Passionbericht des Markus," *ZTK* 50 (1953): 1–51; M. Hooker, *Jesus and the Servant* (London: SPCK, 1959), esp. pp. 62–103; J. Jeremias, "*Pais theou*," *TDNT* 5:654–717; *New Testament Theology*, trans. J. Bowden (London: SCM Press, 1971), I, 286–99. On the "suffering just one" see L. Ruppert, *Jesus als der leidende Gerechte*, Stuttgarter Bibelstudien 59 (Stuttgart: Katholisches Bibelwerk, 1972).

14. For example, enemies conspire to kill him (Mark 14:1; Ps. 31:4; 35:4; 38:12; 71:10; Wis. 2:10ff.); friends betray him (Mark 14:18, 43; Ps. 55:14–21); false witnesses arise (Mark 14:56ff.; Ps. 27:12; 35:11; 109:2); the just one remains silent (Mark 14:61; 15:5; Ps. 38:14–16; 39:9); and enemies mock him (Mark 15:20, 29; Ps. 22:7; 31:11; 109:25; Wis. 2:19). See J. Donahue, "From Passion Traditions to Passion Narrative," in W. Kelber, ed., *The Passion in Mark* (Philadelphia: Fortress Press, 1976), pp. 4–6.

15. S. E. Johnson, "The Davidic Royal Motif in the Gospels," *JBL* 87 (1968): 136–50; D. Juel, *Messiah and Temple*, SBLDS 31 (Missoula: Scholars Press, 1977). Donahue, in *Passion*, pp. 72–79.

16. O. Cullmann, *The Christology of the New Testament*, trans. S. Guthrie and C. Hall (Philadelphia: Westminster Press, 1959); R. Fuller, *The Foundations of New Testament Christology* (New York: Scribner's, 1965); F. Hahn, *The Titles of Jesus in Christology*, trans. H. Knight and G. Ogg (London: Lutterworth Press, 1969).

viewed according to a geographical and evolutionary schema: The former consisted in locating a title either in the earliest Palestinian community, in Hellenistic Jewish Christianity, or in Hellenistic (Gentile) Christianity. The evolution involved four stages: An initial stage of the hope for the imminent return of Jesus and the application to him of titles from Jewish apocalyptic for the eschatological deliverer. The second stage was seen as a two-level Christology where Jesus who was Son of David, according to the flesh (Rom. 1:4–6), by virtue of his resurrection became "Lord" and Son of God in power. A third stage consisted of depicting Jesus as already endowed with that power which was to be his by virtue of the resurrection. The final stage (most vivid in John's Gospel) involves a theology of pre-existence and a similarity of nature between Jesus and the Father. The journey to Nicaea and Chalcedon has begun. According to this picture Mark is a Hellenistic document and represents the third stage in the evolutionary schema. While major aspects of this geographical and evolutionary schema are being dismantled, it remains valuable for sorting out the different threads which are woven into the final tapestry which is Mark's Christology.[17]

In the work of Philipp Vielhauer and Norman Perrin, title research receives a new focus. They discuss not simply Mark's handing on of the titles, but his creative use of them. Vielhauer suggests that Mark organizes his Gospel around three uses of "Son of God" which follow the pattern of a Near Eastern enthronement ritual. The baptism of Jesus is seen as a royal adoption (1:11), the transfiguration as a proclamation (9:7), and the crucifixion and centurion's confession as an acclamation (15:39).[18] Perrin has brought title research in Mark to its fullest development by suggesting that Mark uses Son of God and Son of Man in dynamic interrelation.[19] Son of God establishes rapport with the readers; Son of Man gives a proper interpretation to Son of God. It also provides a christological unity to the Gospel by identifying the earthly Jesus who suffered and died with him who is to come in power and glory, a power which he exercised prolep-

---

17. For a critique of this schema see H. R. Bälz, *Methodische Probleme der Neutestamentlichen Christologie*, WMANT 25 (Neukirchen-Vluyn: Neukirchener Verlag, 1967); Philipp Vielhauer, "Ein Weg zur neutestamentlichen Christologie?" in *Aufsätze zum Neuen Testament* (Munich: Chr. Kaiser Verlag, 1965), pp. 141–98 (extended critique of Hahn). M. Hengel's short monograph *The Son of God* (Philadelphia: Fortress Press, 1976) represents a modification of the schema.

18. "Erwägungen zur Christologie des Markusevangeliums," in *Aufsätze*, pp. 199–214.

19. Especially in "The Creative Use of the Son of Man Traditions by Mark," *Modern Pilgrimage*, pp. 84–93, and "The Christology of Mark: A Study in Methodology," in *ibid.*, pp. 104–21.

tically on earth, but which can be understood only by those who follow the way of the cross.

Jesus as Prophetic Teacher and Apocalyptic Seer

One of the paradoxes of Mark's Gospel is that while both absolutely and in proportion to its size it contains far less actual teaching of Jesus than the other Synoptics, it still contains far more reference to Jesus as teacher. *Keryssein* (proclaim) and *didaskein* (to teach) appear more often in Mark than in any other New Testament book, and *euaggelion* is distinctive of Mark.[20] Mark also in places describes Jesus as teaching, but gives no specific teaching.[21] The major blocks of teaching are not clear *didachē*, but are in the parabolic teaching of chapter 4 and the enigmatic discourse of chapter 13.

Undoubtedly Mark as author was familiar with the tradition of Jesus as teacher. What he does is give it a particular and important slant. This slant appears in the first miracle of the Gospel, the exorcism of 1:21–27. Though the miracle concludes with the normal amazement of bystanders, the narrative emphasizes the action of Jesus as "new teaching with authority," even though there has been no explicit teaching.[22] In 2:1–12 a controversy story is joined with a miracle so that the *exousia* of the Son of Man is not simply his power to heal, but his teaching on forgiveness. In the story of the rejection at Nazareth, the relation of teaching and mighty works is stressed when the townspeople ask, "What is the wisdom given to him? What mighty works are wrought by his hand?" (6:2). The reaction of surprise and wonder is in response to the teaching *and* the miracles of Jesus. Teaching is brought under the same aura of power which characterizes the person of Jesus in the miracle stories.

By doing this a number of things are accomplished. Jesus is now seen not simply as a Hellenistic thaumaturge but as a divinely authorized spokesman for God, a prophet. As such an authorized spokesman, Jesus is able to announce and effect a forgiveness of sin which exists apart from the Torah. He breaks the barrier between clean and unclean (7:1–23) and declares the temple now a place of prayer for all peoples (11:17).[23] He teaches a new

---

20. Evans, *The Beginning*, pp. 46–49; Achtemeier, *Mark*, pp. 60–70.
21. Mark 1:21; 2:13; 6:2, 34; 10:1; 12:35; 14:49.
22. On paradigmatic importance of these verses, see R. Pesch, *Das Markusevangelium*, HTKNT 2 (Freiburg: Herder, 1976), I, 127.
23. Werner H. Kelber, *The Kingdom in Mark: A New Place and a New Time* (Philadelphia: Fortress Press, 1974), pp. 59, 98–102.

ethic of entry in the kingdom (10:23–30) and like the prophets of old
defends a poor widow (12:41–44). By joining word and power Mark is able
to invest the tradition of the sayings of the historical Jesus with authority
to speak to the needs of the community of his time.[24]

Not only does Jesus in his ministry act and teach with authority, but as
apocalyptic seer he hands on visions of the end time. In chapter 13 Jesus
describes the toils of the end time (13:1–8), but both cautions against
identifying any historical event with the end (13:7) and warns against false
prophets (13:5, 22). Here Jesus teaches not only about the events surrounding the end time, but also about the conduct of his followers.[25] They
are to be faithful in suffering, which will be a means of spreading the
gospel (13:10–13); they are to reject false speculation (13:21), but are to
be watchful guardians of a trust (13:32–37). Just as in the first half of the
Gospel, Mark has brought the miracles under the authority of the word
of Jesus, so here he subsumes apocalyptic speculation to Jesus' authoritative
word. It is not the apocalyptic events about which the reader is to be concerned, but the return of the Son of Man. Just as this Son of Man suffered
betrayal, trials, and juridical murder, so too will his disciples. By portraying Jesus as an apocalyptic seer who gives a testimony to his faithful ones
and warns them about the future, Mark brings this future under the power
of the word of Jesus. In his earthly ministry, in his suffering, and in the
future of the community Jesus is powerful in word and work. No other
mighty work, no signs and wonders, and no apocalyptic speculations are
to preempt his place.

Despite the different images of Jesus in the Gospel and the differing
perspectives of commentators, there are striking convergences. The tradition which has always seen Mark's Jesus as a figure of power, whether it is
expressed in Bultmann's description of the Gospel as a sequence of revelations or of Dibelius' "secret epiphanies," continues to surface in emphasis
on the divine-man Christology and on Jesus as mighty teacher. Mark
clearly presents the earthly Jesus as already in his lifetime what he was in
virtue of the church's proclamation. At the same time Mark stresses the
emptying of Jesus. Suffering, both in its horror and in its divine necessity,

---

24. That Mark orients the teaching of Jesus to his own community is emphasized by
K.-G. Reploh, *Markus—Lehrer der Gemeinde*, SBM 9 (Stuttgart: Katholisches Bibelwerk, 1969), esp. pp. 227f.

25. The literature on Mark 13 in the last decade has been extensive. While disagreeing on details, most commentators now recognize that the chapter is an indispensable
entrée to problems confronting Mark's community and is also a key section for understanding the eschatological posture of the evangelist.

is not mitigated. Though he is faithful Son, Jesus dies abandoned and forsaken.

All the authors discussed agree that the church in its developing Christology as represented by Mark turned to a wide variety of materials with which to express the mystery of Jesus. In trying to re-present Mark's view of Jesus, it is a mistake to seek a perfectly unified or dominant picture of Jesus. D. Moody Smith's view that John's Gospel offers a multidimensional picture of Jesus is equally true of Mark.[26] What we now undertake is not an extensive evaluation of the above presentations of Jesus, nor do we offer an alternative picture. We will suggest, rather, a way of reading the Gospel which is parabolic. Such a reading means that the Gospel's presentation of Jesus is always "open-ended" and always calls for revisioning and restatement.

PARABLE AND MARK'S GOSPEL

Concomitant with the explosion in Marcan studies has been a flowering of theological and literary reflection on parable and metaphor.[27] In a break with Jülicher, who viewed metaphor as aligned with allegory, contemporary scholars now study parable in the context of literary studies on metaphor. In a now classic essay, Robert Funk describes the parable as metaphor which "because of the juxtaposition of two discrete and not entirely comparable entities produces an impact upon the imagination and induces a vision of that which cannot be conveyed by discursive or prosaic speech."[28] J. Dominic Crossan describes parable as a metaphor or figurative language which proposes a referent so new that this referent can be grasped only within the metaphor itself.[29] In describing Jesus as the parable of God, Keck describes the parable as "a metaphoric life situation with disclosure potential."[30] Paul Ricoeur proposes a full-scale hermeneutics of metaphor applied to biblical narrative.[31]

---

26. D. Moody Smith, "The Presentation of Jesus in the Fourth Gospel," *Int* 31 (1977): 376.

27. *Supra*, n. 4; Norman Perrin's *Jesus and the Language of the Kingdom* (Philadelphia: Fortress Press, 1976) contains an excellent survey of the shifting currents of parable research. Also, W. J. Harrington, "The Parables in Recent Study," *BTB* 2 (1972): 219–41; J. Kingsbury, "Major Trends in Parable Interpretation," *CTM* 42 (1971): 579–96.

28. Robert Funk, *Language, Hermeneutic and the Word of God* (New York: Harper & Row, 1966), p. 136.

29. John Dominic Crossan, *In Parables: The Challenge of the Historical Jesus* (New York: Harper & Row, 1973), pp. 13–15.

30. Keck, *Future*, p. 246.

31. *Supra*, n. 4.

In adopting metaphor and parable to the Gospel of Mark, we are not claiming that the work is a product of a sophisticated and subtle imagination which weaves metaphor throughout the text. What we are claiming is that the Gospel, like any literary or religious text, is the product of an author's imagination in the sense stated by Dame Helen Gardner:

> By the time we have read through the Gospel of St. Mark nothing has been proved, and we have not acquired a stock of verifiable information of which we can make practical use. In that sense reading the Gospel is like reading a poem. It is an imaginative experience. It presents us with a sequence of events and sayings which combine to create in our minds a single complex and powerful symbol, a pattern of meaning.[32]

While accepting Gardner's view of Mark as poetry, we will adopt C. H. Dodd's definition of parable since it is the most accurate and comprehensive description:[33] "At its simplest the parable is a metaphor or simile drawn from nature or common life, arresting the hearer by its vividness or strangeness, and leaving the mind in sufficient doubt about its precise application to tease it into active thought."

". . . is a metaphor or simile"

As we noted the language of metaphor is referential; it points beyond its obvious meaning to another level of meaning. At the same time it is not dispensable, for only by engagement in the concreteness of the metaphor does the new referent present itself. Two of the major metaphors by which Jesus is presented in the Gospel of Mark are the picture of Jesus as proclaimer of the kingdom and as Son of Man.

In taking over the proclamation of the kingdom of God, Mark is doubtless close to the historical Jesus. However he does not simply record this tradition but makes kingdom into a major theological motif which spans the whole Gospel.[34] Jesus' initial proclamation is in terms of the kingdom (1:14–15); the final question posed to him by an adversary is "Are you the King of the Jews?" (15:2, RSV), and he dies placarded as king (15:26). With the exception of 15:43, kingdom sayings, like Son of Man sayings, are always on the lips of Jesus. The chapters on the way of discipleship (8:27—10:52) convey a heavy concentration of requisites for entering the

---

32. Dame Helen Gardner, "The Poetry of St. Mark," in *The Business of Criticism* (Oxford: Clarendon Press, 1959), p. 102.

33. C. H. Dodd, *The Parables of the Kingdom* (New York: Scribner's, 1961), p. 16.

34. In addition to Kelber, *Kingdom,* the other major work on the kingdom of God in Mark is A. Ambrozic, *The Hidden Kingdom,* CBQMS 2 (Washington, D.C.: Catholic Biblical Association, 1972).

kingdom.[35] The kingdom is imminent, calling for belief and conversion, and it is still future (1:15; 9:1). Jesus' private instruction of his disciples is described as the mystery of the kingdom (4:11).

Therefore kingdom evokes a whole series of cross referents within the Gospel itself. This is clear from a closer look at Mark 1:14–15: "Now after John was arrested, Jesus came into Galilee, preaching the gospel of God and saying, 'The time is fulfilled, and the kingdom of God is at hand; repent, and believe in the gospel'" (RSV). While reproducing the substance of the teaching of Jesus, these verses have been certainly reworked by Mark.[36] They have reverberations throughout the Gospel. Structurally they conclude the prologue (1:1–15), but introduce the following chapters, which deal with the proclamation in Galilee. The use of the term "gospel" takes the reader back to verse 1 and effects that identification of Jesus and his kingdom preaching with the message of the Gospel, which will be taken up again (10:29; 14:9).

The verses effect a parallelism and a distinction between John and Jesus.[37] Both are heralds preaching a message of repentance (1:4, 14); both are handed over to death as the innocent just one; both are laid in a tomb by faithful disciples (cf. 6:14–29; chap. 15). At the same time they are distinguished. John's function is to prepare the way; Jesus' function is to follow the way. John points to the future; Jesus announces that the *kairos* is now fulfilled and then unfolds a new future. John calls for repentance, but Jesus calls for repentance and faith in the gospel. These verses effect also a parallelism between Jesus and his followers. Just as the time of John and Jesus was to be characterized by preaching and being delivered up, so too the followers of Jesus are to proclaim the gospel "to all nations" and are to be delivered up (13:9–13).

By making the kingdom proclamation and sayings such a dominant motif and integrative factor in the Gospel, Mark gives a radically new referent to kingdom. The kingdom of God is not simply as Perrin notes a "tensive symbol" for God's sovereignty, but is now a metaphor of that power manifest in the life and teaching of Jesus. Jesus is the proclaimer of the kingdom, but in Mark's presentation the kingdom also proclaims Jesus.

The second major symbol Mark uses to convey the parabolic nature of Jesus' life and teaching is Son of Man. As noted, this "title," though adopted from the tradition, is given a distinctive shape and usage by

---

35. Explicit entry sayings are found at 9:47, 10:15, and 10:23–25. Entry into kingdom involves a reversal of normal expectations.
36. Kelber, *Kingdom*, pp. 3–15.
37. Perrin, *Introduction*, p. 144.

Mark.[38] It serves to unite the three stages of Jesus' life—his coming in power and glory, the hiddenness of this power during his suffering and death, and the proleptic exercise of it during his ministry. Son of Man also gives the proper interpretation to Son of God and provides a structural unity to the Gospel. The Gospel begins when Jesus is acclaimed by the heavenly voice as Son of God. Throughout the Gospel until the trial narrative this description is expressed by a voice from the heavens or by those with some kind of preternatural knowledge. Son of God characterizes Jesus as he performs mighty works, but Mark subsumes these mighty works under that power which Jesus exercises as Son of Man. In the important middle section of the Gospel (8:27—10:52), the three Son of Man sayings show in what sense Jesus is the beloved and chosen Son, that is, as one who follows God's preordained will to the way of the cross.

While throughout the Gospel these titles given Jesus have been related, they have not been found together until the trial narrative (14:53–65). Here, in response to the question of the high priest "Are you the Christ, the Son of the Blessed?" (RSV), Jesus answers with the theophanic revelational formula "I am" and identifies himself with the exalted and returning Son of Man. The Gospel reader now knows in what sense Jesus is Son of God; and when at the cross the centurion utters the proper Christian confession "Truly this man was the Son of God" (15:39, RSV), the confession affirms the presence of God not simply in the manifestation of works of power, nor even in the eschatological finale, but in the brokenness and abandonment of God's chosen one on the cross.

Like kingdom, then, Son of Man has several references. It brings from the tradition a connotation of one who is both an individual and a corporate figure who will be exalted after a period of struggle.[39] The story of Jesus is also to be the story of his followers. Mark uses the title to give a particular theological understanding to Jesus as Son of God too. From the Jewish tradition and from other Christian writings, we know that Christians as well were called sons and daughters of God (Rom. 8:14; Gal. 4:6–7). Mark, by showing in what sense Jesus is to be Son, shows in what sense also his followers are to be "son." Ultimately then the christological titles in Mark are not simply descriptions of Jesus but are metaphors of

---

38. Perrin, *Modern Pilgrimage*, pp. 84–93, 104–21; J. Donahue, *Are You the Christ?* SBLDS 10 (Missoula: Scholars Press, 1973), pp. 150–77.

39. On Son of Man as a corporate figure see C. Colpe, "*Ho huios tou anthrōpou*," *TDNT* 8:423; and Howard C. Kee, *Community of the New Age: Studies in Mark's Gospel* (Philadelphia: Westminster Press, 1977), pp. 134f.

what God has done in Jesus. Mark's Jesus points to the mystery of the divine-human encounter; he is a paradigm of that encounter.

". . . drawn from nature or common life"

As imaginative literature the parables speak out of the concreteness of their images. Erich Auerbach demonstrates that the individuality and concreteness of the Gospel stories explain their enduring quality, and literary critics have noted that the imaginative appeal of poetry lies in its ability to depict the concrete universal.[40] Amos Wilder has underscored the religious dimension of this kind of language by noting that the realism of the parables calls attention to the everyday as the arena of God's intrusion into human life.[41]

The realism of Mark emerges in his presentation of Jesus with a series of strong emotions: pity (1:41), violent displeasure (1:43), anger (3:5), indignation (10:14), groanings and deep sighs (1:41; 8:12), surprise at unbelief (6:6), and love (10:21), all of which Matthew and Luke omit in retelling the same stories. There are places where Jesus shows ignorance, for example, about who touched him (5:31–32) or of what the disciples were discussing (9:33), features which are also altered by Matthew and Luke. Most dramatically the famous "ignorance of the day" voiced by Jesus (Mark 13:32) is omitted by Luke and most likely by the original text of Matthew.[42]

Further, in contrast to Matthew and Luke, there is a sober realism which permeates the passion narrative, especially the latter portion. In the first part of the passion narrative, until the arrest in 14:43, Jesus is the constant initiator of action and the subject of the verbs. After 14:42 he is passive and the object of the verbs. In the first part of the narrative Jesus speaks thirteen times, while after 14:42 he speaks only four times, and then in short cryptic statements (14:28, 62; 15:2, 34). The character of the narrative as passion or something done to Jesus is dramatically communicated by its language. Unlike the Lucan Jesus who remains teacher (22:24–30), healer (22:51), and salvation-bringer (23:43), and unlike the Matthean

---

40. E. Auerbach, *Mimesis: The Representation of Reality in Western Literature,* trans. W. R. Trask (Princeton: Princeton University Press, 1953), pp. 40–49; "Concrete Universal" is the expression of W. K. Wimsatt, *Verbal Icon* (New York: Noonday Press, 1953), pp. 69–83.

41. A. Wilder, *The Language of the Gospel* (New York: Harper & Row, 1964), p. 82.

42. V. Taylor, *The Gospel according to St. Mark* (London: Macmillan Company, 1966), p. 522.

Jesus, who can summon more than twelve legions of angels (26:53) and whose innocence is revealed in a dream (27:19), in Mark, the passion of Jesus is the radical emptiness of one who died in the form of a slave.[43]

As Vincent Taylor aptly remarks: "The sheer humanity of the Markan portraiture catches the eye of the most careless reader."[44] In Mark, Jesus is truly the parable of God, but the way to God is not through any docetic circumvention of the human Jesus. In the case of Jesus himself, no less than in the parables he utters, the scandal of the human is the starting point for the unfolding of the mystery of God.

". . . arresting the hearer by its vividness or strangeness"

The parables take the everyday as a vehicle for mediating the transcendent. In so doing, however, the everyday is put somewhat askew.[45] There is a surprise element or strange twist in every parable which is most often the point at which the revelatory or disclosive power of the parable comes into play. It is ordinary, for example, that a person be mugged on the way to Jericho (Luke 10:33–37), and it may be ordinary that someone stop to help. What is extraordinary is that the helper is a Samaritan. It is ordinary that a younger son would go off and live an independent life (Luke 15: 11–32), fall on hard times, and return home downcast and repentant. It is extraordinary that the father would not only show him unmerited acceptance, but would restore him to a dignity higher than his original state. It is through things like surprise and paradox that the hearer is shaken out of ordinary existence and so is open to revelation. In the Gospel of Mark there are two major devices by which this shaking occurs: (a) the explicit reference to shock and surprise and (b) the use of situational irony and paradox.

Along with other motifs which span and unify the diverse elements Mark includes in the Gospel, such as anticipations of the suffering of Jesus and the disclosure of Jesus' messiahship, is the motif of surprise, wonder, awe,

---

43. On distinctive viewpoints of different passion narratives see H. Conzelmann, "History and Theology in the Passion Narratives of the Synoptic Gospels," *Int* 24 (1970): 178–97; J. Donahue, "Passion Narrative," *IDBSup* 643–45.

44. *St. Mark*, p. 121.

45. Funk, *Language*, pp. 158f.; Tracy, *Blessed Rage*, pp. 129–31; Ricoeur, "The Specificity of Religious Language," *Semeia* 4:114–22, speaks of the extraordinary within the ordinary and says that it is the paradoxical quality of religious language which "dislocates our project of making a whole of our lives," a project which Ricoeur identifies with the Pauline boasting (pp. 125f.).

and fear. There are over thirty-four places in the Gospel where Mark records such a reaction.[46] These reactions embrace all the major aspects of Jesus' ministry: (1) as a conclusion to the miracles of Jesus, 1:27; 2:12; 4:41; 5:15, 20, 33, 42; 6:50, 51; 7:37; (2) as a reaction to the teaching of Jesus, 1:22; 6:2; 10:24, 26; 11:18; 12:17; (3) in narratives of divine epiphanies, 4:41; 6:50–51; 9:6; 16:5; (4) fright of the disciples over Jesus' predictions of suffering, 9:32; 10:32; cf. 14:33; and (5) reactions of opponents, even during the passion of Jesus, 11:18; 12:12; 15:5, 44. Even though a reaction of surprise and wonder may be a formal element of the miracle stories and may be pre-Marcan in some cases, this cannot explain the prevalence Mark gives to it. Mark's own theology of fear and wonder comes out especially in the resurrection account (16:5, 8) and in the jarring ending to the Gospel, "for they were afraid." This motif, which throughout the Gospel establishes rapport with the reader and which dictates how the reader should respond to Jesus, now becomes a symbolic reaction to the whole Gospel. Mark's reader is left not with the assurance of resurrection vision but simply with numinous fear in the presence of divine promise. These reactions of wonder and surprise accompany the revelation of God in Jesus, and they signify the power of this revelation to unsettle and change human existence. At the same time the wonder is a fascinating and attracting wonder.[47] People are surprised and glorify God, they are led to question who Jesus is (4:41); it characterizes the following of Jesus (10:32). These motifs in the text call for a parabolic reading of Mark; for an approach to Mark's Jesus with a sense of wonder, awe, and holy fear; for an openness to the extraordinary in the midst of the ordinary; for a suspension of belief that true faith may occur.

The second major way Mark communicates vividness and strangeness is by the use of irony and paradox. Kelber writes, "If there is one single feature which characterizes the Markan Jesus, it is contradiction or paradox," and in another context I have stated, "Irony is the rhetorical medium through which Mark conveys his message of faith."[48] While the intensity and nuances of paradox and especially irony are pointed out by literary critics, we are working with the generally accepted understanding of irony as language or situations which "express a meaning directly opposite that intended" and paradox as "a seemingly self-contradictory statement, which

46. Pesch, *Markusevangelium*, II, 150–52.
47. *Loc. cit.*
48. Werner H. Kelber, *The Passion in Mark* (Philadelphia: Fortress Press, 1976), p. 179; Donahue in *ibid.*, p. 79.

yet is shown to be (sometimes in a surprising way) true."[49] Common to both devices is a reversal of surface expectations created by the text.

While a full-scale study of irony and paradox in Mark is to be desired, we can simply indicate some aspects of his paradoxical picture of Jesus. The expectations about who the Messiah should be and what he should do are shattered. The day of the Lord's rest becomes the day of the Lord's labor (2:27—3:5). Clean is declared unclean (7:1–23); children who do not ever bear the yoke of the kingdom (the law) are to enter God's kingdom (10:13–16). The one who rules is to be the lackey, the last will be first (10:42–45), the appointed followers are blind, and the blind see.[50] Jesus' way to death is really his way to being raised up. In condemning him, Jewish officials are condemning themselves to judgment (14:62–63); in seeking to preserve their priesthood, they destroy its function—the veil is now split, their role as mediators is ended (15:38). Jesus is mocked as a false prophet at the very moment his prophecy about Peter is being fulfilled (14:65, 72).[51] Pilate and the bystanders ironically call him king (15:2, 32), while the centurion expresses the true meaning of his kingship (15:39). A woman anoints him, but it is really for his burial (14:3–9). The women and Joseph take great pains to bury him whom no tomb will hold.[52] He is risen, but he is not here.

We have offered an admittedly incipient and scattered picture of irony and paradox in Mark. Nonetheless, the examples are adequate to suggest that to enter the world of the Gospel the reader must be willing to have preconceptions shattered and to be open to having Jesus himself presented as "the mystery of the kingdom of God" (4:11).[53] Mark's parabolic and

---

49. R. Lanham, *A Handlist of Rhetorical Terms* (Berkeley: University of California Press, 1968), pp. 61, 71. For a fuller discussion of irony, see J. Jónsson, *Humor and Irony in the New Testament* (Reykjavík: Bókaútgáfa Menningarsjóds, 1965), esp. pp. 16–34, 90–165; and D. C. Muecke, *The Compass of Irony* (London: Methuen, 1969). William F. Lynch, *Images of Faith* (Notre Dame, Ind.: University of Notre Dame Press, 1973), pp. 77–108, discusses irony and theology.

50. The section, which deals with the inability of the disciples to comprehend Jesus' teaching on suffering, is framed by two "giving of sight" narratives, 8:22–26 and 10:46–52. In the second of these, in contrast to the disciples who hesitate to follow Jesus on the way to the cross, Bartimaeus "followed him on the way." See V. Robbins, "The Healing of Blind Bartimaeus (10:46–52) in the Marcan Theology," *JBL* 92 (1973): 224–43; and E. Johnson, "Mark 10:46–52: Blind Bartimaeus," *CBQ* 40 (1978): 191–204.

51. Don Juel, *Messiah and Temple: The Trial of Jesus in the Gospel of Mark*, SBLDS 31 (Missoula: Scholars Press, 1977), p. 72.

52. Gardner, "Poetry of St. Mark," pp. 109f.

53. That Jesus himself may be the "secret [*mysterion*] of the kingdom" is suggested, among others, by Achtemeier, *Mark*, pp. 69–70: "The content of Jesus' teaching, therefore, is Jesus himself. . . . The mystery of the kingdom given to Jesus' followers is also clearly Jesus himself"; and Peter von der Osten-Sacken, "Streitgespräch und Parabel

ironic imagination is a counter, as Paul Ricoeur notes, to any attempt to make a project of our lives or to reduce Jesus to concepts about him or to take his life as a program initiated by him. Mark's Jesus is presented as gift ("to you is given") but also as challenge.

"leaving the mind in sufficient doubt about its precise application to tease it into active thought."

One of the elements contained in Dodd's seminal description of parables which has received intensive discussion is their "open-ended" quality.

Despite attempts within the synoptic Gospels themselves to close off the meaning of individual parables through allegorization, moralizing application, or incorporation into the theological perspective of the whole work, the parables originally were without application and gain meaning only through the closure the hearer gives to them. The parable functions as event of revelation only when the hearer enters the new world of the parable and as actor in the parable looks from within it backward to a previous understanding and forward to new possibilities. Mark's presentation of Jesus is no less open-ended.[54]

What New Testament critics say about the text as word event and the need for the meaning of the text to be completed by the reader is very close to Wolfgang Iser's observations on the phenomenology of reading.[55] Iser notes that what gives a literary text its enduring and aesthetic quality is its ability to engage the active participation of the reader. He further notes that it is "the 'unwritten' part of a text which stimulates the reader's participation."[56] He then describes various devices which effect this participation. The text may contain various perspectives among which the reader is forced to choose. Apparently trivial and schematic scenes often have a hidden significance which must be discovered. The reader must make connections between disparate parts of the texts. There are often hiatuses or "gaps" in the text which must be filled in. Iser calls these gaps the basic element of aesthetic response and says, "It is only through inevitable omissions that a story gains its dynamism."[57] Another important fac-

---

als Formen markinisher Christologie," in *Jesus Christus in Historie und Theologie (supra,* n. 2), pp. 375–94, esp. 386–91.

54. *Supra*, n. 45.

55. W. Iser, *The Implied Reader* (Baltimore: Johns Hopkins Press, 1974), esp. chap. 11, "The Reading Process"; and "Indeterminacy and the Reader's Response in Prose Fiction," in J. H. Miller, ed., *Aspects of Narrative* (New York: Columbia University Press, 1971), pp. 1–45; *The Act of Reading* (Baltimore: Johns Hopkins Press, 1978).

56. *Implied Reader*, p. 275.

57. *Ibid.*, p. 280; "Indeterminacy," pp. 11–14. Though he does not allude to biblical interpretation, Iser's observations are close to certain approaches of the New Hermeneu-

tor is a process of retrospection and anticipation, created by individual parts of the text. Finally, Iser discusses the formation of illusions by readers as they move through texts, along with the subsequent breaking of these illusions, which creates a dynamic rapport between the reader and the said and the unsaid part of the text.

Again, as in the case of irony and paradox above, we can offer nothing more than suggestions about devices in Mark by which the text and the reader are engaged. ("Paradoxically" many of these devices are those very things which cause literary critics to characterize Mark's Gospel as primitive or unliterary.)[58] One of the major devices both in the theology and structure of the Gospel and by which the reader is engaged are the *Sammelberichte*, or summary statements.[59] These come at strategic places and often serve to join disparate elements of tradition. Their very schematic and allusive quality, such as the statement in 1:28 that "his fame spread throughout all Galilee" or that crowds from all Palestine came to him (3:7, RSV) or that he went about among the villages teaching, call on the reader to fill in the gaps, to make a judgment about who Jesus is. By location and content these summary statements recapitulate the preceding section and anticipate what is to come.[60]

Another way in which Mark engages readers in working out things for themselves is by sowing early in the narrative seeds which will blossom throughout the text.[61] The first appearance of Jesus is accompanied "immediately" by the rending of the heavens and a voice declaring him beloved son (1:11); "otherworldly" salutations of Jesus reappear through-

tic and existentialist exegesis; see P. Achtemeier, *An Introduction to the New Hermeneutic* (Philadelphia: Westminster Press, 1969), pp. 54–148. His analysis is also similar to that of H.-G. Gadamer, *Truth and Method*, trans. G. Barden and J. Cumming (New York: Seabury Press, 1975), pp. 301–4. .

58. Taylor, *St. Mark*, pp. 112f. For recent views on Mark primarily as a collector, see J. M. Robinson, "The Literary Composition of Mark," in M. Sabbe, ed., *L'Evangile selon Marc: Tradition et rédaction*, BETL 34 (Gembloux: Duculot, 1974), pp. 11–19; and E. Best, "Mark's Preservation of the Tradition," in *L'Evangile selon Marc*, pp. 21–34. For a counterposition, see Perrin, "The Evangelist as Author: Reflections on Method in the Study and Interpretation of the Synoptic Gospels and Acts," *BR* 17 (1972): 5–18; and "The Interpretation of the Gospel of Mark," *Int* 30 (1976): 115–24.

59. See Taylor, *St. Mark*, p. 85, for complete list. The major summaries are: 1:14f.; 3:7–12; 6:6b, 30–33. A recent study of the importance of these to Mark's redaction and theology is W. Egger, *Frohbotschaft und Lehre: Die Sammelberichte des Wirkens Jesu im Markusevangelium*, Frankfurter Theologischen Studien 19 (Frankfurt am M.: J. Knecht, 1976), esp. pp. 158f.

60. This technique of Mark has most recently been noted by R. Tannehill, "The Disciples in Mark," *JR* 57 (1977): 390.

61. The way in which Mark's narrative technique involves the reader is developed by Tannehill, *ibid.*, and in his "The Gospel of Mark as Narrative Christology," *Semeia* 16

out the narrative (1:24; 3:11; 5:7; 9:7), but the true meaning of "son" is held in suspension to the very end of the narrative (15:39). Jesus' first public act is to call disciples (1:16ff.). Even though scenes of explicit dealing between Jesus and his disciples come at structurally important places in the narrative,[62] for major portions of the book the disciples function as scenery or backdrop and reappear as recipients of an unfulfilled promise at the end of the Gospel (16:7–8). The ultimate fate of Jesus is hinted at in the parable of the bridegroom (2:20) and in the conspiracy of the Pharisees and Herodians (3:6) but is held in suspension until the passion narrative. Two important predictions, the promise that Jesus will baptize in the spirit (1:8) and the meeting in Galilee (14:28), are not fulfilled though others (8:31; 9:31; 10:32; 14:18, 30) are. Mark has a penchant for duality and for recounting spatially separate scenes in a similar manner (e.g., 11:1–6; 14:12–16).[63] All these devices, the holding of suspension of theological motifs, the use of the fulfillment and non-fulfillment of prophecy, and the juxtaposition and parallelism of accounts engage the reader in personally working out the connections and enable one to become part of the world of the text.

In its own way Mark's presentation of Jesus offers a progression in the creation and shattering of illusions. In the first part of the Gospel the reader identifies with a figure of power and renown. Jesus joins successful combat with demonic forces. He exercises power over death, sickness, and natural forces. He offers bread to the hungry and solace to the bereaved. In the middle section the reader sees that this illusion is to be shattered. The figure of power is to be handed over to people who will kill him. Yet even this new illusion is to be shattered, for the brokenness of the cross is itself broken by the message "He is risen." And yet the final illusion is shattered. "Risen" does not mean a return in power and presence to the community. The community must continue to struggle with illusions (with false christs, false messiahs) until they finally "see" him (13:26; 16:7).

The Jesus of Mark truly does leave the mind in sufficient doubt about his precise meaning to tease it into active engagement. What in the text itself is portrayed as discipleship, complete with its successes and failures, is, in subsequent history, the personal engagement which takes place in interpretation, in representing the text to one's self, and in appropriating

---

(1979): 57–95; and by N. Petersen, *Literary Criticism for New Testament Critics* (Philadelphia: Fortress Press, 1978), pp. 49–80.

62. Mark 1:16–20; 3:13–19; 6:7–13; 8:27ff.; 11:1ff.; 13:1ff.; 14:12ff.; and E. Schweizer, *The Good News according to Mark*, trans. D. Madvig (Atlanta: John Knox Press, 1970), pp. 384f.

63. F. Neirynck, *Duality in Mark: Contributions to the Study of the Markan Redaction*, BETL 31 (Leuven: University Press, 1972). P. Achtemeier calls attention to the

it in a life of discipleship. The Gospels of Matthew and Luke exemplify the first testimony we have to this engagement.[64] The lived experience of individuals and communities represents its continuance. As an open-ended parable the Gospel of Mark will constantly receive new statements and new closures. Exegesis which deals with the "said" portion of the text can describe certain parameters within which such closure may occur; it can never exhaust the positive ways in which the Jesus of Mark may be present and may be presented.

RE-PRESENTING MARK'S PARABLE

In Mark, Jesus is the parable of God who is present in privileged time (*kairos*) and who summons those who hear him to radical faith and radical conversion (1:14). This Jesus is a figure of power in conflict with the powers of the cosmos and the powers of hardness of heart (3:5; 6:52; 8:17).[65] Yet broken, and abandoned by the source of all power, he dies as the radically powerless one. During his life his power is manifest yet hidden.[66] His disciples and followers are also to be empowered with his spirit (1:10; 13:11). They will confront evil powers and spread the gospel (13:10), but will also die, broken by betrayal and suffering (13:11–13). Their power, too, is hidden.

Jesus *as* good news and the good news which he proclaims are an intrusion into everyday life. His mission in the world is not one of an isolated prophet, but involves the engagement of others called out of the ordinary way to follow his way. He does not exist except in community with others. The summons he gives to those he calls is "to be with him" and to do the things he has done (3:13–19).[67] To share in his power is not to possess power of prestige and playing lord over others, but is to practice the self-emptying service which becomes the source of liberation to the many (10:41–45).

---

dual cycle of miracle stories which are incorporated into chaps. 4–8, "Toward the Isolation of Pre-Markan Miracle Catenae," *JBL* 89 (1970): 265–91.

64. As we noted in the case of the realism of Mark's presentation of Jesus, Matthew and Luke remove ambiguity. They also create different kinds of documents by appending birth narratives and resurrection appearances.

65. Stressed by J. M. Robinson, *The Problem of History in Mark*, SBT 21 (London: SCM Press, 1957).

66. We have not contained an explicit treatment of the Messianic Secret. See W. C. Robinson, "The Quest for Wrede's Secret Messiah," *Int* 27 (1973): 10–30; Pesch, *Markusevangelium*, II, 36–47, feels it is no longer a helpful descriptive term.

67. K. Stock, *Die Boten aus dem Mit-Ihm-Sein: Das Verhältnis zwischen Jesus und den Zwölf nach Markus*, AnBib 70 (Rome: Pontifical Biblical Institute, 1975), esp. pp. 177–91.

Response to this parable puts the ordinary askew. It involves a challenge to the total fiber of life. Riches and the security they offer as well as the love and trust which come from family life (brother will betray brother) are problematic. Rejection and suspicion by religious and civic leaders and a brutal juridical murder await the caller and the called. Mark offers his readers a human, realistic Jesus who is also a figure of power and mystery, who has broken down the barrier between God and sinful humans, and who is now present to the community as word of promise. He does not present the lordly teacher of Matthew (5:1) or Luke's compassionate healer. Mark's Jesus is for those who stand between promise and presence, who like the trembling women are afraid and often do not know what to do with the message they have received.

Neither responding to the call nor entering the world of the parable nor sharing its power assumes fidelity to the call. Those first called, first failed. The way of discipleship in Mark is not the way of the perfect; it is the way of a pilgrim, failing people. It is the Pauline paradox of strength in weakness (II Cor. 12:10), of life amidst death (II Cor. 4:7–12). Responding to the parable of Jesus in Mark is engagement in the ultimate paradox of the Christian faith.

12.

The Portrayal of the Life of Faith in the Gospel of Mark

Eduard Schweizer

Mark speaks of the life of faith by using the notion of "following Jesus" as a metaphor to bring to light all the profound dimensions of the relation which the gospel inaugurates between believer and living Lord.

When we try to describe what the title of this essay expresses, we might pick up this or that favorite word of Jesus handed down in Mark, or we might prefer to keep to the stories about Jesus, or we might rather start from some comments of the evangelist himself. Whatever we would do, it would be a more-or-less casual choice of our own. Should we not, first of all, look at the totality of his Gospel in order to detect what he has to convey to us? As John—not being directly dependent on the first three Gospels—shows, there was probably a pre-Marcan tradition which was moving toward the new literary form which appears in Mark's Gospel. Nonetheless, he is the first one to have written in this new genre. Therefore, looking at the structure of his book will reveal to us something of the reasons why he wrote it in this way, how he understood his task, and, hence, what his message, and especially his portrayal of the life of faith, is.

Now I certainly do not dream that everybody will agree with my way of looking at this Gospel. Therefore, I shall not only excuse any reader who skips the following detailed pattern with its Roman numbers and capital or small ABC's to get at the relevant three points at the end, but I shall even expect most readers to do so. This is why I shall summarize the gist of it in three short paragraphs. Those, however, who are interested in the basis of my arguments, and have also the time to look at it, may examine, critically of course, the details of the structure of Mark's Gospel as I see them:[1]

I. 1:15 Introduction
    A. 1:1–8   Fulfillment of the Scriptures, time of salvation
    B. 1:9–13   The Son of God on earth, between God and Satan
    C. 1:14–15   Transitional summary: The nearness of the kingdom in Jesus' teaching

II. 1:16—3:12 First activity in Galilee: Jesus' authority and the blindness of the Pharisees
    A. 1:16–20   The call of the disciples
                    a. 1:21–45   Jesus' authority over demons and illness
                    b. 2:1—3:5   Jesus' authority over sin and law
    B. 3:6   Rejection by the Pharisees
    C. 3:7–12   Transitional summary: Jesus' healing

III. 3:13—6:6 Around the Lake of Galilee: Parables and signs and the blindness of his fellow citizens
    A. 3:13–19   Selection of the Twelve
                    a. 3:20—4:34   The parables
                    b. 4:35—5:43   The signs
    B. 6:1–6a   Rejection by his fellow citizens
    C.   6b   Transitional summary: Jesus' teaching

IV. 6:7—8:26 Journeys: Influence even on Gentiles and the blindness of his disciples
    A. 6:7–13   Sending of the Twelve
                    a. 6:14–31   Death of John, return of the Twelve
                    b. 6:32–56 & 8:1–13   Jesus' miracles and the demand of signs
                    c. 7:1–37   Promise for Gentiles who do not keep the Law
    B. 8:14–21   Rejection by the disciples
    C. 8:22–26   Transitional pericope: The opening of blind eyes (in Bethsaida)

---

1. I have suggested the main lines of this structure in *Anmerkungen zur Theologie des Markus*, in my *Neotestamentica* (Zurich: Zwingli Verlag, 1963), p. 100 n. 32, and outlined it in a more detailed way in *Die theologische Leistung des Markus* (*EvT* 24 [1964]: 337–55; cf. NTS 10 [1963–64]: 421ff.). Since then, I have learned some more details from Norman Perrin, who followed more or less my pattern, "Towards an Interpretation of the Gospel of Mark," in Hans Dieter Betz, ed., *Christology and a Modern Pilgrimage* [1971], pp. 5f., 11f.). Cf. my essay "Towards a Christology of Mark?" in *God's Christ and His People: Festschrift Nils A. Dahl* (Oslo, 1977), p. 32, and the pattern on p. 214 of the fourth edition of my commentary NTD 1 (1975), which is almost identical with the one presented here. R. Pesch, *Das Markusevangelium*, HTKNT 2 (1976), and F. G. Lang, *Kompositionsanalyse des Markusevangeliums*, ZTK 74 (1977): 1–24, differ in some points.

V.   8:27—10:52 Unveiled revelation and the call to follow Jesus
     A. 8:27–32a   First prediction of suffering, death, and resurrection (in
                     Caesarea Philippi)
     B. 8:32b—9:1   Misunderstanding of the disciples and call to follow Jesus
                     a. 9:2–8   Transfiguration (on a *high mountain*)
                     b. 9:9–13   Elijah and the suffering of the Son of Man
                     c. 9:14–29   The problem of faith
     A' 9:30–32   Second prediction of suffering, death, and resurrection
                     (in *Galilee* [*Capernaum*])
     B' 9:33–50   Second misunderstanding of the disciples and call to fol-
                     low Jesus
                     a. 10:1–12   About marriage (in *Judea and beyond the
                                  Jordan*)
                     b. 10:13–16 About children
                     c. 10:17–31 About wealth
     A" 10:32–34   Third prediction of suffering, death, and resurrection (on
                     the *way to Jerusalem*)
     B" 10:35–45   Third misunderstanding of the disciples and call to follow
                     Jesus
     C" 10:46–52   Transitional pericope: The opening of blind eyes—fol-
                     lowing Jesus (in *Jericho*)

VI. 11:1—16:8 Suffering, death, and resurrection
     A. 11:1—13:37   The Temple in Jerusalem: Open conflict, destruction of
                     the Temple, and the coming kingdom
     B. 14:1—16:8   Passion and resurrection

Even those who would disagree about some of the details would agree on
three main points made by this structure of the whole Gospel:

1. Jesus is, throughout the Gospel, rejected by men. The first half of his
activity is portrayed by three complexes, each of which ends with his rejection, first by the authorities (3:6), then by his fellow citizens (6:1-6),
finally by his own disciples (8:14–21).[2] The second half of Mark's description of the life of Jesus is subdivided by the three prophecies of his rejection in Jerusalem (8:27–32a; 9:30–32; 10:32–34), but even in the period
of open revelation of his destiny his disciples misunderstand him.

2. Man is called to follow Jesus. With the call to follow him the work
of Jesus starts in 1:16–20. In a specified way this call is repeated at the
beginning of the next two subdivisions, in 3:13–19 and in 6:7–13. In the
second half of Jesus' activity the call to follow him forms again, three
times, the answer of Jesus to the misunderstanding by the disciples of his
prophecy of suffering (8:34–9:1; 9:35–50; 10:41–45). Finally, the transi-
tional pericope which connects this part of the Gospel with the passion

---

2. Cf. 8:18 with 4:12.

story tells of the blind man who was healed by Jesus and "followed him on the way," an echo of the statement in 10:32 that Jesus and those who "followed him" were "on the way" to Jerusalem (and to the cross!).

3. Jesus cannot be understood without his cross. In the first half of his work in Galilee and its surroundings he constantly forbids the proclamation of his signs (1:44; 3:12; 5:43; 7:36; 8:26); in the second half and in Jerusalem itself no signs are told except in 9:14–29, which is much more a treatise about unbelief and belief than a miracle story, and in 11:20, which is actually a prophecy of the end of Jerusalem and its Temple. This is coupled with the fact that even his disciples do not understand Jesus during the first period in Galilee (4:13; 6:52; 7:18; 8:14–21) and misunderstand him as soon as he teaches them about the way he will suffer, die, and rise again (8:32f.; 9:33f.; 10:35–40). Even the so-called confession of Peter, who has detected the messiahship of Jesus (8:27–29), is in fact not a confession but rather a misunderstanding. Peter has, according to Mark, not even reached the level of the demons, who have long before recognized that Jesus is the Son of God. Jesus orders him not to tell anybody about that (8:30), and although Peter's detection is quite correct, his reaction to Jesus' prediction of suffering and death shows how little he understood what this correct title of "Christ" really meant. The first confession to Jesus' divine sonship (about which the demons knew from the beginning) is, strangely enough, that of the Roman officer before the cross (15:39). This means that, in the view of Mark, nobody can understand Jesus in a non-demonic way until he has learned that Jesus' divine sonship reveals itself primarily in his rejection, his suffering, and his dying. Looking at his signs or even at his glory as revealed in his transfiguration leads, by necessity, to a mere misunderstanding as long as it is not a glory which follows the shameful death of Jesus on his cross (9:9, 12). To learn this is, for Mark, not so much a matter of theoretical insight as a matter of practical behavior; only the one who follows Jesus personally on his way to the cross will be able to experience also the power of his signs and miracles.[3]

---

3. As early as 1966 I doubted whether a Hellenistic "divine man" (in the sense of miracle-worker) ever existed in the first century A.D. (ZNW 57:201 n. 5). W. v. Martitz has, on my request, confirmed my doubts (TWNT 8:339, 29ff.). One should therefore not speak of a divine-man Christology in Mark or before him (cf. also Pesch, Markusevangelium, I, 277–81). Yet the "man of God" who works miracles (without becoming divine) is known since II Sam. 6:6f.; I Kings 17:16, 22; 18:38; II Kings 2:14, 21, 24; 13:21(!), etc., and men like Philo have Hellenized this picture so that the borderline between God and man of God may not always have been drawn clearly. As for Mark, he certainly estimates miracles highly, but only the disciples who know Jesus' way to the cross, and even follow him there, are able to understand them; cf. my "Christology" (n. 1), pp. 29–31.

FOLLOWING JESUS

(a) 1:16–20 and 2:14

All three stories are told in a very typical way; they have probably been told and retold until they retained like a woodcut only those features which were really important. In all three passages the starting point is Jesus. He "passes along" by the Galilean lake or the customs office or "goes a little farther." Then comes the elective act of Jesus: he "sees" Simon and Andrew, James and John, and Levi, just as God "sees" David in order to call him (I Sam. 16:1), the elders of the Jews in order to protect them (Ezra 5:5), the house of Judah in order to save it (Zech. 12:4). Long before those whom God or Jesus will call, protect, or save have any presentiment, he has started his work with them. The next step is Jesus' entrance into their conscious lives: He "calls" them. Again, this is the miracle of God's unexpected grace; they are in no way prepared for this call. They are not in any holy state; they are doing their everyday work of fishing or mending the nets or calculating taxes. They do not even belong to the ("churchgoing") people that listened to Jesus' preaching (1:14f.). His word hits them unprepared, but it hits them like the call of the creator who "calls and there it is" (Ps. 33:9). It creates their obedience; immediately they leave their nets and their father, they rise and follow him. This is not only true at the beginning; it is also true that Jesus will remain the active power in their whole lives of following and serving him: "I will make you become fishers of men."

(b) 8:34–9:1

The call to Levi shows that it is not only the Twelve that are called to follow Jesus in a literal sense. To be sure, this is not asked of everybody; the man in Gerasa who wanted "to be with him" (exactly as it is said of the Twelve in 3:14) is sent back to his home (5:18f.). In 8:34 Mark states explicitly that Jesus, before exhorting them to follow him, had called "the people together with the Twelve." Thus, following him seems to be a demand for all of his disciples, including those who are not to do so in a literal way.

Now, the exact distinction between the role of the Twelve and that of all the "disciples" in the Second Gospel is one of the most difficult problems. On the one hand, Mark speaks of a special call to the Twelve to be with him and to be sent to preach and to be given the authority to cast out demons (3:14f.). Here he may have thought of their historically unique function as witnesses to the life, death, and resurrection of Jesus, which makes them the foundation of the proclamation of the gospel and of the faith of the church. On the other hand, as we have seen, Levi does not belong to the Twelve (differing from Matt. 9:9; 10:3), nor does the Gerasene, who, nonetheless, is sent to preach, even though not to be with Jesus. Finally, the exorcist who has not "followed" Jesus and his disciples at all is authorized by Jesus himself for his healing work (9:39).[4] Whereas 8:34 mentions the Twelve and the multitude, Jesus addresses (9:35) only the Twelve, although he is doubtless speaking to all believers in the following passage. In a similar way, this is also true for 10:41-45, especially since immediately afterward the blind man who was healed joins the group of the Twelve "to follow him on the road" (10:52, as in 10:32). Thus, according to Mark, there are different tasks for different disciples; not all of them are obliged or allowed to be with him in a bodily way. Some, inside and outside of the group of the Twelve, are sent to preach, some to heal, some to other tasks. Following Jesus, however, is not an obligation or a privilege of only the Twelve.[5]

What, then, does this mean? It is described in 8:34 as "denying himself and taking up his cross." Centuries of Christian tradition and reinterpretation have certainly falsified these terms. Denying oneself is not the same as repressing everything which would make us happy, and taking up one's cross is not the same as bearing patiently all kinds of aches and problems. In 14:71-72 Peter "denies" Jesus by declaring, "I do not know him." Taking up one's cross describes the moment in which the convict knows that all possibilities of appeal or clemency are exhausted and that this is now his end. Following Jesus leads, therefore, according to this verse, to a life in which he becomes so important that our ego comes to its end, as far as it is not directed toward him, and receives from him a value and an importance that surpasses all previous value and importance. The following sentence describes this in an even clearer way: clutching to one's life leads to the loss of it; becoming free to give oneself to others leads to real

---

4. Matt. 12:30 shows the difference between not following Jesus himself, which is impossible for a disciple, and (as Mark 9:39 states it) not following his group (i.e., the church of Mark's time), which is possible.

5. K. G. Reploh, *Markus—Lehrer der Gemeinde*, SBM 9 (1969), pp. 56-58, stresses the "typological" character of the Twelve, who represent all believers: G. Schmahl, *Die Zwölf im Markusevangelium—Eine redaktionsgeschichtliche Untersuchung*, Trier Theologische Studien 30 (1974), contrariwise, stresses their unique historical importance; similarly K. Stock, *Boten aus dem Mit-Ihm-Sein*, AB 70 (1975), with emphasis, however, on the fact that only disciples who have gone through a real experience of Jesus are able to mediate his whole work to the church.

life (v. 35).[6] Now, this is an experience which everybody could have. Life becomes senseless and empty as soon as it is no longer being lived for the sake of somebody or something. Hence, even the greatest egoist persuades himself that he actually lives for his business or for the progress of science or for his family, perhaps even for the common weal. Indeed, gaining the whole world does not help him if his life becomes meaningless (vv. 36f.). And yet, this does not mean that the world should be of no interest to the disciples of Jesus, that they should rather abandon it. On the contrary, the world has new interest for them, although they no longer try to gain it for themselves, but rather for their master and his gospel (13:10). Mark has added, in verse 38 and in 9:1, a warning from Jesus against not drawing the consequences: the only criterion of our way of life will be the Son of Man himself. There will be but one question in the definite, last judgment of our lives: Have we lived after the model of Jesus?

The comparison of (a) and (b) states the main problem clearly: Is following Jesus a mere gift from heaven without any cooperation of man, as the first pericope suggests, or is it a performance of man in which his own will is of first importance, as the second one suggests? Before attempting to answer this problem, we may briefly look at the three remaining passages.

(c) *9:34–35 and 10:42–45, 46–52*

In 9:34 Mark refers to a discussion of the Twelve about who is the greatest among them. This is very human; man has to find his identity; somewhere he has to be great. And this is not wrong; Jesus accepts that and even gives his guidance to reach that goal: Whosoever wants to become great has to become servant to all (9:35). This is contrary to all general rules and all normal experiences. Generally, only great men exercise authority (10:42), and yet, in contrast to the accepted opinion, Jesus repeats his statement (10:43f.). At this place Mark inserts the decisive word about the Son of Man's coming to serve and to give up his life as a ransom for many (10:45). Then follows the story of the blind man who has been healed by Jesus so that he might be able "to follow him on the road," the road to Jerusalem and to the cross (10:46–52).

This, I think, is Mark's answer to our problem and his most meaningful symbol of what the life of a disciple will be. It is Jesus' own answer

---

6. Luke 17:33 and John 12:25 do not include the clause "for my sake and the gospel's"; thus, Jesus probably spoke the word without this clause. His statement is true also in this very general way, but it becomes only practicable in his wake.

and his own symbol.[7] For many years I have used the imagery which the Swiss mountain town in which I was allowed to serve as a minister for nearly ten years provided me (in the highlands of Papua–New Guinea, I had to shift the locale to a father cutting a path through the jungle with a machete): When a heavy snowfall sets in, the boy who had gone to his friend's after school instead of going home cannot get home until his father comes, with his strong shoulders, and breaks the way through three feet of snow. The boy "follows him" in his footsteps and yet walks in a totally different way. Father is not merely his teacher or example—otherwise the boy would have to break his own way, only copying the action of the father —nor is it a vicarious act of the father—otherwise the boy would just remain in the warm room of his friend and think that his father would go home instead of himself.

The imagery is unimportant, but not so the point it should, like Mark, bring home to us. No doubt, a life that is lived according to "Jesus" and becomes a "following him" is totally God's gift and never our performance. It is he who breaks through and clears the way. So much is it so that he even, in doing this, gives us also our important part in this act, our "being in it." He does not come over us like an avalanche which simply sweeps us down in its course—and probably as corpses. He comes into our lives in the same way love comes into the life of man, namely, in such a way that he really gives us our lives, changes us, shapes us. Not as corpses but as loved creatures are we with him. Therefore, our response becomes relevant, but not as a condition that we have to fulfill before or after his coming. It is, rather, like music which becomes music only if and when we let it move us, if and when we learn to hear it; otherwise, it remains a sequence of insignificant noises. It is only and exclusively the musicians who play, and yet, the same music is music for one and mere noise for another. So seriously does Jesus take our following that he does not even

---

7. Cf. Martin Hengel, *Nachfolge und Charisma*, BZNW 34 (1968). In *Erniedrigung und Erhöhung bei Jesus und seinen Nachfolgern*, ATANT 28 (1955, 1962²) (cf. *Lordship and Discipleship* [London: SCM Press, 1960], chap. 1b), I have pointed to the following facts: the verb "to follow" is to be found in Mark, Q, and John, always connected with the earthly Jesus (except, perhaps, Rev. 14:4); its usage is quite different from the Greek one: in the Old Testament it is used for "following the idols [or Jahweh]." In *Jesus Christus*, Siebenstern-Taschenbuch 126 (1968, 1976⁴), p. 43 (cf. *Jesus* [London: SCM Press, 1971], p. 40), I have stressed the difference from the usage by the rabbis, who did not call disciples. Only in I (III) Kings 19:20 the Greek verb is used once for Elisha "following" Elijah and is, as Hengel, *Nachfolge*, pp. 18–20, shows, taken up in Jesus' time by Josephus, who also refers to the idea of "following" Yahweh in the holy war (*ibid.*, pp. 20–23); Josephus is clearly influenced by the existence of charismatic leaders of his time.

rebuke Peter who exclaims, "Lo, we have left everything and followed you" (RSV), although such boasting is not quite appropriate just after Jesus' statement that God alone makes possible that which is impossible for men (10:27f.).

We have to go one step further. Besides the traditional liturgy of the Lord's Supper in 14:24, 10:45 is the only place where Mark refers to Jesus' death "for many." Although the structure of the whole Gospel is determined by his repeated references to the rejection, the suffering, and the death of Jesus, Mark is very reticent when it comes to a definition of the cross as reconciliation. He seems to be afraid of a misunderstanding, as if reconciliation were a matter of simply accepting a doctrine or performing a rite. What Mark wants to convey to us is rather something similar to what happens to a man—to use our imagery again—who has cut the path through the jungle for days in order to lead a group of prisoners back to freedom and life and then dies of exhaustion when arriving there. He would have died "for many," although this would not mean that the many simply had to acknowledge this theoretically or in a symbolic rite. They were with him on this march, and yet he was the only one who was strong enough to open the way and he died in doing so. To be sure, Mark would not reject the idea of "ransom," but he would not want the idea taken out of the context of his whole Gospel and cast into the plaster of paris of a doctrinal statement; then it would lose its flexibility and perhaps its life. How does Mark describe a man who follows Jesus and is with him in such a way that Jesus goes ahead of him and opens the road for his journey?

A LIFE IN FAITH

We have seen that in all cases in which a man really followed Jesus it was always the call of Jesus himself that started him, and not simply the decision of the disciple. Something similar is true even for those who were healed by Jesus. Certainly there are some who received healing because they trusted in him, even asked him on their knees (1:40; 5:22f., cf. 27, 34). However, even they were attracted by him and by his reputation, and Mark does not say whether this is more than any physician or miracle-worker could have done. In many cases, it is the friends and relatives who bring the sick one to Jesus (2:1; 7:32; 8:22). In other cases, the sick man fends off any help from Jesus (1:24; 5:7). When Mark explains this by putting such a cry of resistance into the mouth of the demons, he simply expresses the strange fact that man, even in his hopeless illness, puts up fierce resistance against God's help. Mark knows something about the "demonic" character of man and thinks that man is not naturally open to God. Different is the Gentile woman in 7:25, who succeeds just because she knows her position as a woman and as a Gentile gives her not the slightest right to beg Jesus for help and that she has no achievement of her own to boast about (v. 28). Toward the end of the Gospel, we find some striking evidence for this character of real faith. It is, according to Mark, not a disciple who buries Jesus (and by so doing renders him the last service) but one of those "anonymous" Christians[8] who never came to a definite decision in his faith. Finally, it is a Roman officer who first confessed Jesus as the Son of God, though all he saw was Jesus die with a loud cry which sounded like desperation; it was a Gentile, a military man who could not keep his hands pure but was just leading an execution-squad in a highly unjust case. All this shows how strongly Mark is convinced of the quality of the gift which inheres in faith. Faith is indeed the deep conviction of God's unmerited act toward a man who, without him, would not even be able to accept the gift. If it is considered a human merit, it ceases to be faith.

And yet, to use the image again, music is to be heard, faith is to be lived. Because faith is understood as the gift of God, it takes such an important place in the Gospel. Mark's miracle stories differ from the Hellenistic ones in their structure:[9] Faith is placed at the beginning of the story, not at the end when the listeners are admonished to believe in the miracle-worker whose miracles were told. Sometimes the Marcan stories emphasize that faith has to persevere against different obstacles. The leper has to approach Jesus against all the rules which prohibit his drawing near (1:40). The bearers of the paralytic have to get to Jesus in spite of the crowd (2:4). The man with the withered hand has to come and stretch out his hand in the presence of a critical audience, knowing that healing is not allowed on a Sabbath (3:1–5). The disciples in the storm have to carry a sleeping Jesus with them who does not seem to care at all (4:38), or leave him behind on the safe shore (6:47f.). The demons in the Gerasene man even attack Jesus and repulse his interference (5:7; cf. 1:23). The woman healed of her hemorrhage has to come forward with fear and trembling before she can realize that what she has done is an act of faith (5:33f.). Jairus receives the message of his daughter's death and is told not to trouble Jesus any longer (5:35). The disciples must be aware of seemingly

8. For instance, K. Rahner, *Grundkurs des Glaubens: Einführung in den Begriff des Christentums* (Freiburg: Herder, 1976), pp. 32–34 and often.
9. Cf. G. Theissen, *Urchristliche Wundergeschichten*, SNT (1974), pp. 139–43, 163–74.

insurmountable difficulties and must discuss helplessly the ways to solve the problem before they see Jesus feeding the multitude (6:35-38; 8:2-5). The Syrophoenician woman has to accept first a refusal by Jesus (7:27). None of them has awakened faith in himself by any special method of his own; faith came over them, but they had to let this happen and had to try, without giving up and returning to trust in their own power, to start living by this gift.

The most explicit treatment of this question of faith is perhaps the story of the epileptic boy (9:14-27). Mark alone has understood the very center of this story, because only he refers to the cry of the boy's father: "I believe; help my unbelief!" (RSV). He has seen that the faith of the boy's father manifested itself precisely in his perception of his unbelief; because he knew that he could not believe by his own effort, he started really to believe. The same truth becomes visible in the disciples who are unable to heal the boy (v. 18) and have to learn that prayer alone will do it: faith which expects everything from God and nothing from its own piety or power. This is, for Mark, the core of all these stories: Life in faith is nothing more than following Jesus, letting him go ahead, sticking to his lead, expecting everything from him so that all our abilities or inabilities, all solutions or obstacles, become secondary to him.

This explains the second anomaly in the Marcan stories. As a rule, a miracle story ends with the praise of the miracle-worker who is proclaimed Lord or Son of God. There is no acclamation of that kind in Mark before 15:39, the acclamation of the Roman officer. This is extremely important for Mark: It is the crucified one, not the miracle-worker, who elicits the first confession from one who really understands God's mighty deeds in Jesus. Not even an extraordinary experience of God's healing or saving power leads to genuine faith, but rather the spiritual poverty of a Gentile who realizes that Jesus had to go to this length to open for him a way of life. It is the same spiritual poverty that was found in a Gentile woman who spoke of the crumbs of bread which are given to the dogs under the table (7:28), or in the man who believed by pointing to his unbelief (9:24). Contrariwise, those who might think they possess a right to approach Jesus fail: his family that comes to seize him (3:21), his fellow citizens who know him from his youth on (6:3), even his disciples who have seen his deeds (8:17-21) but are unable to heal (9:18) and are not present at the cross. He, and he alone, will be their help after Easter (16:7).

It is therefore of prime importance for Mark that Jesus refuses a sign to those who seek one from him (8:11-13). Faith certainly may beg for a sign, hope for it, and praise God when it gets one, but it cannot require it. It is the same as a husband seeking proofs that his wife loves him; even if he hired a private eye and got all the proofs he wanted, it would not be the beginning but the end of his love. Therefore, the reasoning of the onlookers under the cross is impossible: "Let the Christ come down from the cross that we may see and believe" (15:32). This would, in contrast to the acclamation of the officer in verse 39, be an attempt to dodge the challenge to faith, since believing on the ground of indubitable proofs makes it impossible to give oneself totally to trusting God. Following Jesus is never a matter of clever calculation; it is, for Mark, a divine gift which leads to going after him whether seeing his power or not. Only with empty hands is man able to approach God expecting him to fill them. It may therefore often be necessary even to experience such poverty in a concrete way: The disciples have to begin their mission without bread, bag, or money (6:8); and when they are charged and brought to trial, they have to wait for the Spirit, without having a well-prepared defense or an adequate rhetoric at their disposal (cf. n. 3).

This explains also the stress which, in Mark's Gospel, is laid on Jesus' attack against all legalism. Wherever man thinks that he may gain God's grace by his merits, by his observance of all the laws, he fails. Mark pictures this in the model of the Pharisees,[10] who cannot believe in an unmerited forgiveness (2:6, 16) or in a Sabbath observance which is not primarily a law but a gift for man (2:27; 3:4). In this respect it is impossible to combine an old garment with a piece of new cloth or old wine skins with new wine, as it is impossible to fast in the presence of the bridegroom (2:18–22). Perhaps the most shocking saying of Jesus, reported by Mark, is 7:15: "There is nothing outside a man which by going into him can defile him" (RSV). Not even the disciples understood it (v. 18), because if this is true, all the laws of purification are no longer valid and the frontiers between Israel and the Gentile world would break down. Then, there is nothing left to distinguish the pious from the godless.

In the light of what we have said, one of the most peculiar features of

---

10. When Mark (or one of the other evangelists) speaks of Pharisees, he sees the adversaries of the church around or after A.D. 70, when, forced by historical developments, they had to emphasize the Mosaic law in its totality lest Israel lose its identity among the nations. At the same time, the church had to distinguish itself from the Jewish nation and synagogue. This situation has doubtless sharpened the picture of the controversy of Jesus with the Pharisees. One should not forget, though, that originally and to some extent still in the time of Jesus, Pharisaism was a popular movement emphasizing individual piety over against a mere liturgical correctness (cf. M. Hengel, *Judentum und Hellenismus*, WUNT 10 (1969), pp. 321–30, 557f.)

Mark's Gospel becomes, perhaps, understandable. The time after Easter is, for Mark, a time without Jesus. Nowhere does the Second Gospel speak of the presence of the exalted Lord in his church, although it does speak, and at some length, of that time in chapter 13. According to 13:34 the Lord has gone abroad and left his servants in charge, and the picture of the future in verses 5–23 is a picture without a present Christ until he comes again in his parousia (vv. 24–27).[11] Now, even during his earthly ministry, Jesus was never simply available. He was sleeping during the storm or had stayed behind on the shore; or, conversely, the disciples were sleeping while he prayed in Gethsemane. On that same evening, he was even taken away from them by the soldiers; if they had not fled they could have seen him, but seen in total powerlessness, tried, spat at, flogged, crucified, with no kingdom, power, or glory being visible. Even this, they have missed.

Does not something of this "unavailability" of Jesus run throughout his teaching also? The parable of the sower certainly speaks of the final great harvest, but more than two-thirds of the story tells of failure; for a long time only the crows which devour the seed, the rocks which refuse it, the thorns which choke it are visible, not the living seed which succeeded in getting into the ground (4:3–8). The parable of the self-growing seed speaks of the time between sowing and harvesting in which the farmer simply has to wait patiently (4:27), and the parable of the mustard seed emphasizes that this is the smallest of all seeds on earth (4:31).[12] These parables show that in some way the powerlessness of Jesus continues after Easter. True, the disciples were to see him in Galilee (16:7),[13] but this did not change the fact that the post-Easter period was a period of wars (13:7), persecution (13:9), betrayal and hate (13:12f.), tribulation (13:19), and deception (13:21f.). The final parable in this chapter (13:24–27) reveals something of Mark's theology. There is a touch of desolation and of fervent expectation of the final salvation in the parousia: The lord has gone and the doorkeeper stays awake for his return. But this, perhaps the

---

11. I have learned this point from T. Weeden, *Mark: Traditions in Conflict* (Philadelphia: Fortress Press, 1971), pp. 81–90, although disagreeing with him strongly in many points (cf. pp. 32–36 in my "Christology" [n. 1]).

12. This, of course, is not correct biologically, but shows, just because of this fact, the emphasis which Jesus lays on the smallness of the seed which is now sown.

13. Mark may have reported some epiphany stories after 16:8, which have been lost either accidentally or because they were rejected later on (E. Schweizer, *The Good News according to Mark*, trans. D. Madvig [Atlanta: John Knox Press, 1970], pp. 366f.; for a contrary view cf. Pesch, *Markusevangelium*, II, 536–43; H. Anderson, ed., *The Gospel of Mark*, New Century Bible [Greenwood, S.C.: Attic Press, 1976], pp. 351–54]. To E. Linnemann's essay, cf. W. R. Farmer, "The Last Twelve Verses of Mark," SNTSMS 25 (1974), pp. ix–x.

oldest, layer is not the dominant one. Over it lies a second layer: all the servants have been charged, each one with his work. That they do it in the meantime is what the lord expects from them. Thus, the time between Easter and parousia is a period of probation, full of tribulation, and yet not of total desolation.

Just the fact that the lord charged his servants with work shows that he is, in some different way, still present in his word. Therefore, God's own voice has urged the disciples to listen to him (9:7), and all that do listen to him are as his mother and brothers (3:34).[14] Had not Jesus himself told them that only praying out of a heart which seeks all help from God would lead them to deeds like the ones he performed (11:17, 22–25)? Even more, Jesus will still be present with them after Easter in his name. Not only for them but for all who trust him, although, perhaps, they may not have the correct church membership and confession (9:38f.). Finally, he promises them that the Spirit will teach those who do not know what to say (13:11). In short, Mark underlines both sides of the truth: The time after Easter is, even more than the time of the earthly ministry of Jesus, a period in which he and his help are not simply available and visible, but it is also a period in which he and his help are to be found in his word and in his name and in the teaching of the Spirit.

SUMMARY

Following Jesus means "to be with him" (3:14) in such a way that he remains the lord who goes ahead and breaks the way for his followers. It means to follow him to the lonely places where he prays (1:35f.; 14:32f.; cf. 6:31f.). It means to follow him to the tribunal (14:53f.; 13:9), even on the road to the cross (8:34; 10:52). It means to go with him into the midst of the storm, and it means experiencing there his mighty help (4:37–39; 6:47–51). It means to become trained in faith by such experiences (4:40f.; 6:51f.). This includes following Jesus in a life of service to others. Simon's mother-in-law "served them" after being healed (1:31). The Gerasene went to proclaim Jesus in his homeland (5:20). The "little ones" are entrusted to Jesus' disciples in the most emphatic way (9:41f.). The poor widow's copper coins are an example for them (12:41–44). To God should be given what belongs to him, as well as to Caesar what belongs to him (12:13–17). Thus, the twofold commandment to love God

---

14. This is probably the original saying of Jesus (omitted by Luke!), and v. 35 a later, more cautious interpretation.

and one's neighbor is the summary of the whole law and whosoever lives according to that commandment is near the kingdom of God, as, for instance, is the Jewish scribe who agreed with Jesus in this point (12:28–34). In Mark this saying marks the end of the conflict stories, but not the end of the conflict itself. It is this conflict which brings Jesus to the cross and it is, therefore, never to be forgotten that, in the view of Mark, such love becomes possible only for those who follow Jesus, who, in his perfect love to God his father and to the many for whom he has opened this new way to real life, has "shed his blood of the covenant for many" (14:24).[15]

---

15. I suppose that Mark knew of post-Pauline (docetic?) tendencies (Schweizer, *The Good News according to Mark*, pp. 380–83; also R. P. Martin, *Mark, Evangelist and Theologian* [Exeter: Paternoster Press, 1972], pp. 153–62). If his *Sitz im Leben* was simply the tradition which continued Jesus' proclamation of the kingdom of God (G. Dautzenberg, *Zur Stellung des Markusevangeliums in der Geschichte der urchristlichen Theologie*, Kairos 18 [1976], p. 291; also *Die Zeit des Evangeliums*, BZ 21 [1977]: 233f.), it would be even more important that his gospel "differing from Paul in a substantial way, nonetheless preaches a *theologia crucis* of its own" (my "Christology" [n. 1], p. 39).

13.

Interpreting the Gospel
of Luke

ARLAND J. HULTGREN

> Study and exposition of Luke's Gospel can raise our conscious-
> ness to see that God's saving activity has been disclosed in cer-
> tain foundational events which are the basis and clue to his mis-
> sion in history and to his ultimate salvation at history's end.

The writings of Luke (Luke-Acts) have gained a renewed interest in
recent years, and the scholarly work on them has proliferated at an enormous pace. Our purpose in the present essay is not to provide a survey of
such activities, but to examine the Gospel of Luke itself in terms of its
structure, features, and general significance. Naturally, the way one looks
at Luke in terms of these concerns is determined to one degree or another
by what he has read and reacted to.[1] Nevertheless, what follows is less a
survey of research and more by intention an invitation to the interpretation
of Luke's Gospel within the context of the church.

THE STRUCTURE OF LUKE'S GOSPEL

In discerning the structure of Luke, the question has to be asked whether
the author himself gives any hint of how he conceives the general con-

---

1. Although space does not allow full documentation in footnotes, the specialist will
see that in addition to the works cited below the author is informed by and reacts to
many important works in Lucan studies, including Hans Conzelmann, *The Theology of
St. Luke*, trans. Geoffrey Buswell (New York: Harper & Bros., 1960); several essays
collected in Leander E. Keck and J. Louis Martyn, eds., *Studies in Luke-Acts* (1966;
reprint ed., Philadelphia: Fortress Press, 1980); Jacob Jervell, *Luke and the People of
God: A New Look at Luke-Acts* (Minneapolis: Augsburg Publishing House, 1972), and
others. The following are cited as resources for study and exegesis.
Commentaries in English (and in print), written from various perspectives, include
G. B. Caird, *The Gospel of St. Luke* (Baltimore: Penguin Books, 1963); Frederick W.
Danker, *Jesus and the New Age: According to Luke* (St. Louis: Clayton Publishing

tours of Jesus' career and its significance. It is fruitful in this quest to look at Acts—which contains several speeches (2:14–36; 3:12–26; 4:8–12; 5:29–32; 10:34–43; 13:16–41; 14:15–17; 17:22–31) setting forth apostolic preaching—and compare the structure and content of these speeches with the Gospel account as a whole. It is beside the point whether these speeches are based on reminiscences of what was said, or whether they are simply Lucan compositions. In either case—whether they inform Luke, or whether Luke has composed them (or both, i.e., that they are based on traditions, but have been given their present form and wording by Luke)— these speeches are Luke's estimate of the apostolic preaching and the form it took.

To claim direct parallels in structure consistently between the speeches and the Gospel cannot be done. Nevertheless, striking similarities do occur in terms of both structure and theological point of view. Aside from the incidental fact that frequently the speeches open with a direct address to their various audiences (2:14; 3:12; 4:8; 13:16; not so in the speeches of 5:29–32; 10:34–43), as does the Gospel (1:1–4), there are four contact points of similarity in terms of structure and affirmations concerning the career of Jesus. First, each of the speeches contains quotations from, or allusions to, Scripture, or at least an account of redemptive history based on the Scriptures, and these are gathered at the beginning and/or end of the christological kerygma (2:16–21, 34f.; 3:13a, 22–25; 4:11; 5:30; 10:43; 13:17–22, 33–37, 41). Likewise in the Gospel the scriptural quotations and allusions are concentrated largely at the beginning (the nativity stories and Jesus' inaugural sermon at Nazareth) and at the end (the passion and post-

---

House, 1972); E. Earle Ellis, *The Gospel of Luke*, rev. ed., New Century Bible (Greenwood, S.C.: Attic Press, 1974); Norval Geldenhuys, *Commentary on the Gospel of Luke*, NICNT (Grand Rapids: Wm. B. Eerdmans, 1951); A. R. C. Leaney, *The Gospel according to St. Luke*, Harper's Commentaries (New York: Harper & Bros., 1958); Leon Morris, *The Gospel according to St. Luke*, Tyndale Commentaries (Grand Rapids: Wm. B. Eerdmans, 1974); and I. Howard Marshall, *The Gospel of Luke*, New International Greek Testament Commentary (Grand Rapids: Wm. B. Eerdmans, 1978).

Among these the commentary by Ellis deserves special comment. It has the usual features of a standard critical commentary, but also reports and reacts to contemporary Lucan studies and seeks to describe the "teaching" of Lucan pericopes. Unfortunately the commentary by John M. Creed, *The Gospel according to St. Luke* (London: Macmillan Company, 1930), is no longer in print.

Studies especially useful to get an orientation to Lucan studies include C. K. Barrett, *Luke the Historian in Recent Study*, Facet Books, Biblical Series 24 (Philadelphia: Fortress Press, 1970); Frederick W. Danker, *Luke*, Proclamation Commentaries (Philadelphia: Fortress Press, 1976); I. Howard Marshall, *Luke: Historian and Theologian*, Contemporary Evangelical Perspectives (Grand Rapids: Zondervan Publishing House, 1970); and Bo Reicke, *The Gospel of Luke*, trans. Ross MacKenzie (Atlanta: John Knox Press, 1964).

resurrection appearance narratives). Second, the thesis is set forth in the speeches that it was Israel's authorities who, being ignorant of the Scriptures and opposed to the divinely endowed ministry of Jesus, brought about Jesus' death (2:23; 3:14, 17, 25f.; 4:10; 5:30; 10:38f., 43; 13:27f., 41), but whose actions were the very means by which the divine plan could be fulfilled (2:23; 3:18; 4:11; 13:27, 29). Similarly, in the Gospel it is the Jerusalem authorities who are portrayed as behind the proceedings against Jesus (22:66—23:5, 10, 13, 18–25); yet it is through the death of Jesus that the divine plan is fulfilled (24:25–27, 46f.). Third, the career of Jesus is said to be inspired by the Spirit in Acts (10:38) or endowed with divine power (2:22; 10:38), which is also the case in the Gospel (Spirit: 4:1, 14, 18; 10:21; power: 4:14, 36; 5:17; 6:19; 8:46; 9:1). And, finally, all that has happened is to be proclaimed to bring about repentance and forgiveness of sins (Acts 3:19, 26; 5:31; 10:43; 13:38), which is the closing note of the Gospel too (24:47).

Although it must be emphasized that there are variations in the speeches and that the picture given here is at places composite (i.e., not every speech has all elements), the similarities indicated help to delineate the structure of the Gospel more clearly. Going in this direction, one can conclude that the Gospel has a structure which, while partly determined by the sequence of Mark, is cast into three parts. Following upon the Address (1:1–4), the following structure can be seen:

I. The Days of Preparation among the Faithful in Israel in Fulfillment of the Scriptures, 1:5—4:13
II. The Days of the Messiah in Israel, Endowed by the Spirit and Divine Power, 4:14—21:38
   A. The Days of Manifestation in Galilee, 4:14—9:50
   B. The Days of Consolidation and Division in Israel, 9:51—19:44
   C. The Days of Manifestation of the Messiah in the Temple, 19:45—21:38.
III. The Days of Fulfillment of the Scriptures in Israel for the Salvation of the World, 22:1—24:53.

The structure of the Gospel, seen in this way, conforms generally to that of the speeches in Acts. The emphasis upon the fulfillment of the Scriptures is at the beginning (I) and end (III). The ministry of Jesus itself (II) is portrayed as the time in which he is endowed with the Spirit and divine power (cf. Acts 10:37–39a) to carry on his activities in Galilee (II-A), on the way to Jerusalem (II-B), and in the Temple (II-C). Luke expected his readers to see that the circumstances of Jesus' coming into the world and his departure from it took place in accordance with the divine plan as presented in the Scriptures and that his intervening ministry was conducted in accordance with the divine plan through Jesus' endowment by the Spirit (4:14, 18; 10:21) and divine power (4:36; 5:17; 6:19; 8:46; 11:20) and as he sought the Father's will in prayer (5:16; 6:12; 9:18, 28f.; 11:1). In terms of Christology this implies a functional subordinationism of Jesus to the Father; he is the eschatological and Spirit-endowed prophet like that Moses promised in Deuteronomy 18:15 (Luke 4:18, 24; 7:16; 13:33; 24:19; Acts 3:22–26; 7:37) and the Lord's servant (Luke 22:37; Acts 3:13, 26; 4:27, 30).

Two explanatory comments in regard to the structural analysis are necessary. First, the word "days" appears in the designations for parts of the structure. The reason is that the term "days" is expressive of Luke's style. Luke writes his Gospel to account for "things which have been accomplished among us" (1:1, RSV) in days past. He looks back upon the "days" of Jesus and the early church from the standpoint of the third generation. Frequently in Luke-Acts there are references to times past, and these are spoken of in various phrases employing the term "day(s)": "in these days" (Luke 1:39; 6:12; 23:7; 24:18; Acts 1:15; 6:1; 11:27) or "after these days" (Luke 1:24); "in those days" (Luke 2:1; 4:2; 9:36; Acts 9:37); "in the days of" Herod, Luke 1:5; Elijah, 4:25; Noah, 17:26; Lot, 17:28; the census, Acts 5:37; David, 7:45; "until the day" of John's manifestation, Luke 1:80; "on one of the [or "those"] days" (Luke 5:17; 8:22; 20:1); and "when the days . . . drew near" (Luke 9:51; cf. Acts 1:22). All of these are found in special Lucan materials or editorial connections, except Luke 17:26 (Q). But even there, whereas Matthew reads, "as were the days of Noah" (24:37, RSV), Luke has "as it was in the days of Noah" (RSV), thereby setting "the days of Noah" more firmly into a time prior to "the days of Jesus." To write of the past in terms of given "days" in which events took place can, in sum, be considered characteristic of Luke.

Second, the term "Israel" appears in the headings for various sections of the structural outline (I, II, II-B, and III). The reason again is due to Lucan vocabulary and style. From Luke's standpoint it is among the faithful who are conscious of their place in the ongoing life of Israel that the Messiah is expected (1:16, 54, 68; 2:25, 32, 34; 24:21); it is, in retrospect, to Israel that the Messiah came (Acts 10:36; 13:23); and it is the repentant of Israel who form the nucleus of the people of God (Jervell). Luke places a positive emphasis on Israel. He does not relegate Israel to a past era which has come to a close with the ministry of Jesus, nor does he think of the church as a "new Israel" which has replaced the "old." The ministry of Jesus took place in Israel, and it is the faithful of Israel, to whom the promises are considered fulfilled, who constitute the church— along with Gentiles incorporated into their fellowship. For Luke the church is not a new Israel, but Israel having come to realize the fulfillment of its own heritage.

DISTINCTIVE FEATURES IN A SURVEY OF LUKE'S GOSPEL

Part One: 1:5—4:13

Contrary to Mark, Luke does not begin immediately with John the Baptist, the baptism, and the outset of Jesus' ministry in a compact way. He shows that all which is to be related concerning the career of Jesus had a foundation in time (1:5; 2:1f.; 3:1–3, 23) and space (2:4; 3:2f.) among certain faithful persons of Israel. Such persons were righteous and devout (1:6; 2:25), given to prayer (1:13; 2:37), receptive to God's word and will (1:38, 60, 63; 2:25, 36f.; 3:2), prompt (and on occasion filled with the Holy Spirit) to articulate joy and praise (1:41, 67; 2:20, 27–32, 38), looking for the time when God will bring about repentance and salvation to Israel (1:16f., 47–55, 68–79; 2:30, 38), obedient to the law of the Lord (1:6, 9; 2:21, 22–24, 39), and of notable family heritage (1:5, 27; 3:23–38).

In chapter 3 Luke begins making contact with the sequence of Mark and only there also (cf. Luke 3:7–9 with Matt. 3:7–10) begins making use of the Q document. From here to the end of the section (1:5—4:13), attention is first upon John the Baptist (3:1–22), followed by the genealogy (3:23–38) and temptation (4:1–13). In each of these passages certain Lucan features emerge. First, the role of John the Baptist is drawn sharply by Luke. As in Mark (1:4), Matthew (3:2), and Q (Matt. 3:7–10//Luke 3:7–9), John is a preacher of repentance. But in Luke alone John's ministry explicitly anticipates the universal significance of the Messiah.[2] Furthermore, as in Mark (1:1, 3, 7f.; and in Matt. 3:1–12), John the Baptist is the forerunner of the Messiah and belongs to the "beginning of the good news of Jesus Christ" (Mark 1:1). But against Mark (and Matthew), Luke records the imprisonment of John relatively early (3:19f.), even before recording the actual baptism of Jesus (3:21f.). Apparently Luke did so to remove John from the stage before the ministry of Jesus begins and to cast

---

2. Luke adds to Mark's quotation (1:3) of Isa. 40:3 the words of Isa. 40:4–5 which include "and all flesh shall see the salvation of God."

John into a subordinate role. John belongs to the "beginning of the good news," but only to its initial stage—the time of preparation. The recording of John's imprisonment before Jesus' baptism can cause one to wonder whether Luke intended that Jesus' baptism was performed apart from the activities of John. But the text does not support that, for the baptism of Jesus is linked with that of "all the people" (3:21). What we have here is undoubtedly an instance of Luke's literary style. Elsewhere Luke closes a section, but then he adds subsequent material which is to be understood as falling within the section just closed.[3] The same is the case here. Having finished the account of John's ministry, Luke closes it (the imprisonment reference, 3:19f.), and then the spotlight falls upon Jesus.

Luke's genealogy (3:23–38) differs from that of Matthew (1:1–16) in three major respects: (1) it runs from Jesus back, while Matthew's runs from the past to Jesus; (2) his list of ancestors differs; and (3) while Matthew traces the ancestry of Jesus to Abraham, Luke traces it beyond Abraham to Adam and even on to God (3:38). While the latter may well express Luke's "universalism" (i.e., Jesus' link to all mankind through Adam), the fact that the genealogy falls after the voice from heaven attesting Jesus' unique sonship (3:22) and links the human race by sonship to God (3:38) establishes the potentiality for fallen mankind to be restored to God through the Son at the parousia (cf. Acts 3:21).

Luke's temptation account (4:1–13) is based upon Q (cf. Matt. 4:1–11). It differs from Matthew's mainly in that the second and third temptations are in reverse order from that of Matthew. Which evangelist departed from the order of Q is debatable, but it is plausible that Luke did in order to have the last take place at the Temple.[4]

Part Two: 4:14—21:38

This section portrays the Days of the Messiah in Israel, Endowed by the Spirit and Divine Power (II). Jesus is portrayed, as Acts 10:37–39a sum-

---

3. At 8:37 Jesus leaves the country of the Gerasenes, but the sequel (8:38f.) belongs in that setting. At 11:53 Jesus leaves a certain place, but then it is said that the scribes and Pharisees provoke him, and he teaches the multitudes—all apparently in the same setting as 11:53. At 23:54 the Sabbath is said to be beginning; yet the women take time to check the tomb and the body, return to the city, and then prepare spices and ointments (23:55f.)—all before the Sabbath actually begins. Similarly, at 9:51 it is written that "the days were near for him to be received up" and that "he set his face to go to Jerusalem," but it takes ten chapters to get there. Luke has what might be called "narrative addenda" which have not been given sufficient attention.

4. Luke ends blocks of material with Jesus or other persons in the drama on location at the Temple. Besides the present verse (4:9), there are the following: 2:46 (the end of the birth and infancy narratives); 21:37f. (the end of Jesus' ministry of public teaching); 24:53 (the end of the Gospel); Acts 2:46 (the sequel to Pentecost); 5:20–42 (the end of the account of the earliest congregation's activities in Jerusalem).

marizes, as preaching the word, going about doing good, and healing all oppressed by the devil in "the country of the Jews and in Jerusalem" (RSV), anointed with the Holy Spirit and power.

The first subdivision (4:14—9:50) portrays the Days of the Messiah's Manifestation in Galilee (II-A). It opens with Jesus' returning to his homeland in Galilee "in the power of the Spirit" (4:14, RSV). What follows has aptly been called Jesus' "inaugural sermon" (4:16–21), in which he declares that the Scripture passage read in the synagogue (Isa. 61:1f.; 58:6) has been fulfilled. Reference to the Spirit (4:18) alludes to Jesus' baptism (3:22), and the works which the Spirit empowers him to do (4:18–19) are to be accomplished in the ministry to come. Time and again—by redactional summaries, compositions, and through use of his special traditions—Luke portrays the ministry of Jesus in Galilee as fulfilling the words of Isaiah: he goes on from place to place to "preach the good news" (4:43; 8:1); he heals with the "power of the Lord" (5:17); he sends out the Twelve to "preach the kingdom of God and to heal" (9:2), which they do (9:6); and he speaks of the kingdom to the crowds and heals (9:11; contrast Mark 6:33f.). He has "power" to heal (4:36; 5:17; 6:19; 8:46; cf. 11:20) and manifests the "majesty" of God (9:43). He is declared to be a prophet (7:16; cf. 4:24; 7:39). All of these are specifically Lucan touches, as are the occasions on which Jesus is portrayed in prayer (5:16; 6:12; 9:18, 28f.).

Finally, it is in this section that Luke includes the Sermon on the Level Place (6:17–49). The sermon follows upon Jesus' praying upon a "mountain" (6:12; not among the "hills" as in the RSV and NEB)—a place of special revelation corresponding to Sinai, where Moses received revelation (Exod. 19:3, 20; 24:13–18). But, contrary to Matthew 5–7, the sermon is not given on the mountain (since that is reserved for special communication with God). As Moses descended to meet with the people (Exod. 32: 15; 34:29), so Jesus and the Twelve descend (6:17) to a level place to meet with the people—a great multitude who come from "all Judea" and even from Tyre and Sidon (6:17). Luke thereby underscores the breadth and inclusiveness of Jesus' ministry.

The second subdivision (9:51—19:44) portrays the Days of Consolidation and Division in Israel (II-B).[5] It opens with reference to the "days"

---

5. The section clearly opens at 9:51, but where does it end? The following have been suggested by various scholars: 18:14; 19:10, 27, 28, 44, 46, and 48. The first suggestion (18:14) has nothing in its favor except that at 18:15 Luke resumes using Mark. Other places (19:10, 27, 28) short of 19:44 must be rejected, since each is followed by a resumption of travel (19:11, 28, 41). The last two (19:46, 48) fall within the ministry of Jesus in the temple. The section closes at 19:44.

drawing near for Jesus to be "received up" (9:51).[6] Within the entire section there are few temporal notations. Those which do occur are quite general. All but one are found within Lucan redactional links and consist of such phrases as "after this" (10:1), "in that same hour" (10:21), "in the meantime" (12:1, RSV), "at that very time" (13:1), "on the [or "a"] Sabbath" (13:10; 14:1), and "in that hour" (13:31). The remaining time reference is in a logion from Luke's special material concerning "today, tomorrow, and the day following" (13:32f.). The impression given is that the whole account is cast within a few days' time. The Sabbath references (13:10; 14:1) alone give a chronological appearance to the section, but even they appear only for the sake of the pericopes they introduce (Sabbath healings). Apart from them the journey to Jerusalem is portrayed more as a decisive moment—the days just prior to the final events (from crucifixion to ascension)—than a duration of time having true chronological sequence. Likewise, although there are geographical references in the section (9:52; 10:38; 13:22; 17:11f.; 18:35; 19:1, 28f., 41), there is no real progress toward Jerusalem; at 17:11, for example, Jesus is no closer to Jerusalem than at the outset. Attention is focused on Jerusalem as the goal, (9:51, 53; 13:22, 33f.; 17:11; 18:31; 19:11) so that the cross, resurrection, and ascension are anticipated. Neither chronological nor geographical references serve to provide an actual "itinerary" of Jesus between his Galilean ministry and the events to follow in Jerusalem. The whole section sets forth thematic motifs which fall basically into two categories:[7] instruction for Jesus' disciples as forerunners of the new community within Israel (hence, consolidation) and disputation with opponents (hence, division). The section is almost entirely didactic and polemical. It contains some twenty parables, together with many other sayings having to do with discipleship (e.g., 9:60, 62; 11:2–4, 28; 12:8–13, 14f., 22–34; 14:25–27; 16:10–13, 18; 17:1–6, 20f.; 18:15–17, 24–34); and—for polemical purposes—it contains conflict stories (11:14–23; 13:10–17; 14:1–6) and harsh words against Jesus' opponents (e.g., 10:13–15; 11:29–32, 37–52; 12:1–3; 16:14f.). The fact that the section portrays Jesus as on his way to his suffering and death indicates also that Jesus is equipping his disciples for carrying on his work after his death and resurrection.

---

6. What does "received up" mean? While some commentators say it refers to the ascension alone, others (rightly) say that it refers to the whole course of events (crucifixion, death, resurrection, and ascension) by which Jesus passed from earthly to heavenly existence (cf. the reference to Jesus' "exodus" in 9:31).

7. Bo Reicke, "Instruction and Discussion in the Travel Narrative," in *Studia Evangelica*, TU 73 (Berlin: Akademie-Verlag, 1959), I, 206–16; and *Luke*, pp. 38f. Cf. also Ellis, *Luke*, pp. 146–50, and Marshall, *Luke*, pp. 152f.

The third subdivision (19:45—21:38) sets forth the Days of Manifestation of the Messiah in the Temple (II-C). It begins and ends with Jesus in the Temple (19:45, 47; 21:37f.) and begins and ends by saying that Jesus taught there daily (19:47; 21:37). Contrary to Mark, in which Jesus conducts part of his ministry (after initially entering the Temple) outside the Temple (11:11–14, 19–26; 13:1–37), Luke has the entire section of the Judean ministry after the triumphal entry (19:28–44) take place in the Temple. A saying from Mark in the passion narrative refers back to this section. There Jesus addresses the Temple authorities, reminding them that he had been "daily in the temple," and yet they did not seize him (Mark 14:49//Matt. 26:55//Luke 22:53). Luke has apparently edited his materials in 19:45—21:38 by a literal reading of the saying. Jesus teaches "the people" (19:48; 20:1, 9, 45; 21:38) or his disciples (20:45) there. Conflict stories appear—taken from Mark (11:27–33; 12:13–17, 18–27, 35–37)—in which Jesus is interrogated by Temple authorities (20:1–8, 20–26) and Sadducees (20:27–40, 41–44), but Luke emphasizes more than Mark that, while the Temple authorities are determined to have Jesus done away with, they cannot because of his consistently positive acceptance by the people (19:47f.; 20:6, 19, 26). The subdivision as a whole (19:45—21:38) falls within the larger unit (4:14—21:38) of the Days of the Messiah in Israel (II). It sets forth a final manifestation in the Temple. The cleansing and the teaching are the means by which the Temple is claimed as the place to which the faithful of Israel—witnesses of the resurrection—return (24:53; Acts 2:46; 3:1–3; 5:20, 25, 42) for prayer and teaching—"daily" (Acts 2:46; 5:42).

Part Three: 22:1—24:53

This section portrays the Days of Fulfillment of the Scriptures for the Salvation of the World (III). It contains the narratives of the passion and post-resurrection appearances, as well as the commission to preach to all the nations, followed by Jesus' departure. The sequence—passion, death, and resurrection—is conceived as an unfolding of the divine plan in fulfillment of the Scriptures (24:26f., 44–46; Acts 2:23, 25–36; 3:18, 22–26; 4:11; 13:27–29), concerning which the witnesses are to bear testimony (24:47–49; Acts 1:8; 2:36; 3:15; 4:10; 5:32; 10:39; 13:26, 32, 38).

Luke's distinctive features in connection with the passion, death, and resurrection narratives cannot be traced in detail here. It is important to notice, however, that Luke sets into paradoxical relationship the ideas that (1) the death of Jesus was predetermined by God, but that, nevertheless, (2) it occurred as a result of evil. More than Mark, Luke emphasizes that in Jesus' passion, death, and resurrection the words of the Scriptures were being fulfilled (18:31; 20:17; 22:37; 24:26f., 44, 46). But at the same time Luke emphasizes the onslaught of Satan's power (22:3) and the power of evil against Jesus (22:53). Jesus is accused before Pilate of political insurgency (23:2, 5, 14), but Pilate is not convinced (declaring Jesus innocent three times, 23:4, 14f., 22); nor are a fellow victim of crucifixion (23:41), the centurion (23:47), and Joseph of Arimathea (23:51).

It has been observed that Luke does not teach a "theology of the cross" to the degree of Mark and Paul. He omits, for example, Mark 10:45, which speaks of Jesus' death as a "ransom for many." With his emphasis on Jerusalem, the divine necessity of Jesus' death, and the narration of the passion, however, Luke does focus attention on the cross, albeit in his own way. The death of Jesus is portrayed more in the manner of a martyrdom. In his dying moments Jesus, as the perfect martyr, forgives his enemies (23:34; cf. Stephen in Acts 7:60) and commits his spirit to the Father (23:46; cf. Stephen in Acts 7:59). Pathos is there, but an explicit affirmation that Jesus died for our sins is not. The death of Jesus is portrayed as a background for the resurrection, the divine reversal. Jesus' exaltation is made possible only through his death. As in the Gospel of John, therefore, death and glorification are inseparably connected. The difference between Luke and John is that while in the latter the death is itself a part of the glorification, for Luke the cross is a necessary step (i.e., a prelude or background) for glorification through the resurrection of Jesus from the dead (24:26).

The narrative of the post-resurrection appearances and Jesus' departure in chapter 24 is based on special Lucan traditions, although there are points of contact between Luke's story of the empty tomb (24:1–11) and that of Mark (16:1–8). Luke goes beyond Mark to give accounts of Jesus' appearance on the road to Emmaus (24:13–35), his appearance to the eleven in Jerusalem (24:36–49), and his departure (24:50–53). What is established in this chapter is that God has reversed the consequences of evil, which brought about Jesus' death, in accord with his will and plan given in the Scriptures (24:25f., 32, 44–47). But Easter provides not only the denouement of past redemptive history (24:46); it is also the foundational event for the future of redemptive history: "repentance and forgiveness of sins should be preached in his name to all nations" (24:47, RSV). The proclamation of Jesus crucified and risen shall become the pledge of divine grace for all who repent from here on out. The risen Christ departs (24:50–53), but he promises the gift of the Spirit (24:49) and bestows a blessing (24:50f.). The result is that the proclamation of the church is to set forth the story of the divine vindication of Jesus, who is now enthroned, and to declare forgiveness of sins in his name to those who repent and believe (cf. Acts 2:38; 3:19, 25f.; 5:31; 10:43; 11:18; 20:21).

THE SIGNIFICANCE OF LUKE FOR
THE CHURCH TODAY

Insofar as the church of today stands in continuity with its past, it is indebted to Luke in many ways. In particular, there are the well-known Lucan themes which have had a formative impact on Christian thought, devotion, mission, and preaching.[8]

Such themes can be augmented by two others which could have importance for some interpreters today. The first is what can be called Luke's "urbanism." The word "city" (*polis*) appears thirty-eight times in Luke's Gospel, and "village" (*kōmē*) twelve times.[9] In the course of his ministry Jesus passes through cities and villages (8:1; 9:6; 13:22). Early in his ministry, after prayer, he resolves to preach the good news of the kingdom to cities (4:43). Crowds from the cities come to hear him (8:4). The mission of the seventy is essentially to cities (10:1, 8, 10–12). Over against Mark (1:40), Luke places the healing of a leper in a city (5:12) and again (con-

---

8. These include (1) Luke's universalism, i.e., that God's salvation is available to all persons and nations (2:31f.; 3:6; 4:24–30; 13:29f.; 14:15–24; 24:47), which is given concrete expression in concern for "sinners," "Samaritans," and other outcasts of society (5:1–11; 7:36–50; 10:29–37; 15:1–32; 17:11–19; 18:9–14; 19:1–10; 23:39–43); (2) interest in women within the divine plan of salvation (Elizabeth, Mary, and Anna in chaps. 1 and 2; see also 23:49, 55; 24:6–11) and as persons capable of spirituality, faith, and responsibility before God (7:11–17, 36–50; 8:2f.; 10:38–42; 11:27f.; 13:10–17; 23:27f., 49, 55; 24:6–11; cf. also the parables at 15:8–10; 18:1–8); (3) interest in the poor (1:48, 52; 3:11; 4:18; 6:20f.; 7:22; 12:33f.; 14:13, 21; 16:19–31; 18:22; 19:8); (4) the dangers of wealth and its proper use (3:11–14; 6:24f., 30; 12:15–34; 14:12–14; 16:1–13, 19–31; 18:22–25; 19:8); (5) joy (1:14, 44; 2:10; 15:7, 10; 24:41, 52); (6) the Holy Spirit (prior to Jesus' birth, 1:35, 41, 67; 2:25–27; in Jesus' career, 4:1, 14, 18; 10:21; promised to witnesses, 24:49; cf. 11:13); and (7) prayer (5:16; 6:12; 9:18, 29f.; 11:1–13; 22:32, 39–46). Luke's themes (twenty of them) have been explored comprehensively by John Narvone, *Themes of St. Luke* (Rome: Gregorian University Press, 1970).

9. Of the 38 instances of *polis*, 3 are from Mark and 6 from Q, leaving 29 in the special Lucan materials. Of the 12 instances of *kōmē*, 2 are from Mark, none from Q, leaving 10 in the Lucan special materials. Mark uses *polis* 8 times, *kōmē* 6 times. Matthew uses *polis* 27 times (3 from Mark; 6 from Q), *kōmē* 6 times (3 from Mark).

trast Mark 6:30–32) places the feeding of the five thousand at Bethsaida
(9:10–17). Certain Lucan parables make reference to city-dwellers (14:21;
18:2, 3) or rulership over cities as a reward (19:17, 19). The conception
of Jesus as essentially an agrarian and pastoral figure—so common even in
our own times—can be derived from Luke only by failing to notice his
pronounced urbanism. Luke sensed the importance of Jerusalem, cities, and
villages as places of strategic importance (which is also the case in Acts),
and he also considered them populated by persons capable of response and
witness. For Luke, "city folk" are not less likely than "country folk" to
respond positively to Jesus and his emissaries, nor are they less "humble"
or less "simple" in their faith and love. True, it is at Jerusalem that Jesus
meets opposition, but this is from the leadership (19:47; 20:19; 22:2; 23:
1f., 5, 14), not from the "daughters of Jerusalem" (23:27f.) and "the
people" (19:48; 20:1, 6, 9, 19, 26, 45; 21:38; 22:2). Luke alone of the
Gospel writers tells of Jesus' weeping over the city of Jerusalem (19:41),
not because its general population is unresponsive but because its spiritual
leaders cannot see the significance of the divine visitation taking place
(19:39, 42, 44). Nothing in Luke suggests a negative view of cities and
their populations per se.

Another point of interest in terms of themes is that in Luke's Gospel
there is a profound, paradoxical relationship between the "charismatic"
and the "institutional" or regulated. On the one hand, Luke, more than
the other evangelists, portrays the coming of the Spirit upon persons to
empower them to speak and perform deeds. But, on the other hand, it is
Luke who has been singled out among the evangelists as a representative
of "early Catholicism." The term suggests—not incorrectly—that for Luke
the Spirit's activity is restricted first to the ministry of Jesus (the Gospel,
after 1:1—3:21) and then to the leaders of the apostolic church (Acts).
But it must be emphasized that in the Gospel (and Acts) the Spirit is
nevertheless a free gift from above. What we have, in sum, is the free
manifestation of the Spirit among persons divinely elected for specific
roles in redemptive history, who worship God in the temple (Luke 1–2;
24; Acts 1–7), and among those whom Christ has appointed to carry on
the apostolic ministry (Acts). The institutional does not by itself guarantee the presence of the Spirit. The facts are, as Luke sees them, that the
Spirit mobilizes those who are receptive to its power, and the institutional
is the earthly matrix in which those endowed by the Spirit act.

Aside from these thematic contours of Luke, it is necessary to ask about
Luke's significance in broader terms for the contemporary theological cli-

mate and for preaching today.[10] Naturally that is a question too broad and sweeping to handle here, since it is difficult to describe a common "theological climate," and one person's preaching situation is not another's. Nevertheless, some comment is in order concerning the way the question has been posed in recent discussion.

It has become widely accepted today that Luke has adjusted the traditional eschatology in the gospel tradition so that the parousia, already delayed, is thought to belong to an indeterminate and distant future. Along with this consensus has come an evaluation of Luke as a theologian of the first century, and sometimes that evaluation has been negative. As others have reported,[11] these evaluations have come about chiefly among those who have contrasted Luke with Paul. They tend to see Paul as one who proclaims a "pure kerygma" of existential address, and for whom history has come to its end, while Luke is seen to be a theologian of redemptive history for whom eschatology is an inane doctrine of last things. Luke has "corrupted" the Pauline gospel of existential address.

But the contrast between Luke and Paul has been overdrawn. One cannot say that Luke has "de-eschatologized" the gospel tradition without qualification,[12] nor can it be said that Paul is devoid of a redemptive-historical perspective. On the one hand, while it is the case for Paul that those in Christ belong to the new age and its righteousness (Rom. 3:21f.; 7:5f.; 8:1; II Cor. 5:17; Gal. 4:7), share in the life of the eschatological

---

10. Several volumes based on the "new lectionary" (or "new lectionaries," since there are some differences among denominations), and which attempt to connect exegesis and proclamation, have appeared recently, but these are of uneven quality. Three helps, which take exegesis seriously, are particularly worthy of mention: Reginald H. Fuller, *Preaching the New Lectionary: The Word of God for the Church Today* (Collegeville, Minn.: Liturgical Press, 1974), has done exegesis of texts for all three years (A, B, and C) and has given suggestions for preaching. Gerard Sloyan, *Commentary on the New Lectionary* (New York: Paulist Press, 1975), has provided commentary for all three years; he does not suggest homiletical themes explicitly, but he does make connection between exegesis and broader theological and historical questions. These works by Fuller and Sloyan are based on the Roman Catholic *Ordo Lectionum Missae*, with which the lectionaries of other denominations have a high degree of commonality. Finally, *Proclamation: Aids for Interpreting the Lessons of the Church Year*, Series C, 8 vols. (Philadelphia: Fortress Press, 1973/74) and *Proclamation 2: Aids for Interpreting the Lessons of the Church Year*, Series C, 8 vols. (Philadelphia: Fortress Press, 1979/80) provide the most in commentary and suggestions for homiletical development.

11. Ulrich Wilckens, "Interpreting Luke-Acts in a Period of Existentialist Theology," in *Studies in Luke-Acts*, pp. 60–83; Werner G. Kümmel, "Current Theological Accusations against Luke," *ANQ* 16 (1975): 131–45.

12. While there are passages in Luke in which the delay of the parousia is assumed or affirmed (contrast Luke 9:27 with Mark 9:1, and Luke 21:8 with Mark 13:6; see also 12:49f.; 17:20f.; 19:11; 21:9, 12, 19, 20–24; 22:69), there are others in which it is set forth as imminent (10:9, 11; 12:38–40, 41–48; 12:54—13:9; 18:8; 21:32).

gifts of the Spirit (Rom. 7:8; 8:23; II Cor. 3:18; 5:5; Gal. 5:5, 16–26), and
live "as though not" in the world and its entanglements (I Cor. 7:29–31),
it is also the case that the passing of time brings one closer to the day of
salvation (Rom. 13:11); the time between Easter and the parousia is a
time of mission (Rom. 15:19); and salvation is explicitly or implicitly referred to on some occasions as future (Rom. 8:18–25; I Cor. 7:29; 11:26;
15:51–58; II Cor. 5:5; I Thess. 4:13—5:11). The difference between Luke
and Paul is not that of redemptive history vis-à-vis kerygmatic existential
address, but lies in the fact that Luke has given more conscious reflection
upon redemptive history, which is implicit and to some extent explicit
already in Paul.

Giving attention to Luke means that one will give his schema of redemptive history its due. Some would argue that therein lies a danger: The
hearer is not called upon to make a decision about his own situation
coram deo; he is not called upon to decide about his life and commitments,
nor is he invited to participate in salvation offered "here and now." But,
on the other hand, the recital of the acts of God in history has had an
enduring place in the worship of Israel and the church, and for good
reason. By re-presentation of the remembered-in-faith-past of what God
has done, rehearsed in liturgy and proclamation within the community
which rejoices in it, the individual participant and hearer can realize that
salvation is a gift from beyond (and rejoice in it) no less than the individual to whom is proclaimed the message that God's salvation in Christ
is offered to him in his present moments of decision, perpetually renewed.
To use a current expression, the recitation of redemptive history can offer
an experience of "consciousness raising" (as opposed to existential self-
understanding). The hearer is not asked to consider new possibilities for
his own self-understanding but is called upon to look "up, back, and
ahead" to see that God's salvation has been revealed in certain "foundational events" of the past which are the basis and clue to his mission in the
course of history and to his ultimate salvation at history's end. While an
existential interpretation of the gospel is still with us—also for good reasons
—a careful reading of Luke-Acts can expand the horizons of the Christian
community to behold in faith what God has accomplished and is doing
in history, and will accomplish at history's end. If there is danger here of
ecclesiastical false security, there is also opportunity here for the church
to come to terms with its own mission to mankind in the passing of time—
with Jesus and the apostolic church as paradigms.

14.
Shifting Sands:
The Recent Study of the
Gospel of Luke

CHARLES H. TALBERT

> The approach to the Gospel of Luke which seemed certain to prevail twenty years ago has been challenged in all its significant features. The crucial questions concerning the critical interpretation of the Third Gospel are awaiting new answers.

Prior to 1950 Luke was generally viewed as a historian, and research on the Third Gospel focused on source criticism. By 1966, W. C. van Unnik could speak of the "new look" in Lucan studies that had come from Germany. Since 1950, he said, Luke-Acts has become "one of the great storm centers of New Testament scholarship."[1] As a result Luke no longer appears "as a somewhat shadowy figure who assembled stray pieces of more or less reliable information, but as a theologian of no mean stature who very consciously and deliberately planned and executed his work."[2]

The roots of this shift from Luke the historian to Luke the theologian lay in Bultmann's *Theology of the New Testament.*[3] There Bultmann treated Luke-Acts in the section "The Development toward the Ancient Church," which focused on the ecclesiastical, doctrinal, and ethical deviations from the early Christian kerygma. Luke, he said, has lost the original eschatological understanding of Jesus. He has surrendered the original kerygmatic sense of the Jesus tradition and has historicized it. The third

---

1. "Luke-Acts, a Storm Center in Contemporary Scholarship," in L. E. Keck and J. L. Martyn, eds., *Studies in Luke-Acts* (1966; reprint ed., Philadelphia: Fortress Press, 1980), p. 16.
2. *Ibid.,* p. 23.
3. Rudolf Bultmann, *Theology of the New Testament,* 2 vols. (New York: Scribner's, 1951, 1955).

197

evangelist endeavors as a historian to describe the life of Jesus.[4] Further, the ecclesiastical office has become a guarantor of the apostolic tradition (e.g., Acts 20:18ff.).[5] In *Theology of the New Testament*, therefore, one finds already a view of Luke's stance which includes eschatology and early Catholicism as the central points of interest. It remained for the Bultmann school to work out the details of the position.

Ernst Käsemann developed Bultmann's view that Luke-Acts belonged to those early Christian writings which reflected a loss of the original kerygmatic sense of the Jesus tradition. He said, "I can acknowledge as earliest Christianity only that which still has its focus in an eschatology determined by the original imminent expectation in its changing forms. When this focus shifts, a new phase is to be established. That is undoubtedly the case with Luke. . . ."[6] Luke has replaced primitive Christian eschatology with salvation history. The Third Gospel is the first life of Jesus.[7] When Acts is added, the apostles become guarantors of the gospel tradition.[8] Käsemann says he first became aware that Luke-Acts was not to be read primarily as history but as theology in 1941–42, but the war and immediate post-war period prevented his pursuing the literary study of the problem himself.[9]

It was Hans Conzelmann who undertook the literary study necessary for the elaboration of Bultmann's view of Luke.[10] His task was facilitated by form criticism, which had shown that the Gospel framework was not a part of the original Jesus tradition but was secondary. As long as the scholar's concern was primarily historical (e.g., the quest for the historical Jesus), the study of the framework would be neglected. It remained for Conzelmann to raise the question about the interpretation of the framework as an entity in its own right. What is the structure of Luke's complete work, and what is the essential meaning of that structure? "Can we see in the outline of the Gospel the real purpose of Luke's work as an author?"[11] The distinctive Lucan perspective, he asserted, can be seen from a comparison

---

4. *Ibid.*, II, 116f.

5. *Ibid.*, II, 140.

6. Ernst Käsemann, "Paul and Early Catholicism," in *New Testament Questions of Today* (Philadelphia: Fortress Press, 1969), p. 237 n. 1.

7. Ernst Käsemann, "The Problem of the Historical Jesus," in *Essays on New Testament Themes* (London: SCM Press, 1964), p. 29.

8. Ernst Käsemann, "Ministry and Community in the New Testament," in *ibid.*, p. 89.

9. "Paul and Early Catholicism," p. 236 n. 1.

10. Hans Conzelmann, *The Theology of St. Luke* (New York: Harper & Row, 1960).

11. *Ibid.*, p. 16.

of Luke with his primary source, Mark.[12] The door was now open to read Luke-Acts as theology rather than as merely history. Conzelmann believed, moreover, that Luke's position had to be located in the context of the development of the church. That is, the Lucan *tendency* had to be related to the *occasion* of the writing.[13]

It is Conzelmann's contention that an examination of the way in which the third evangelist handled his sources indicates that the Christian tradition has been recast so as to eliminate the primitive Christian expectation of an imminent end of the age. In the place of this expectation, the evangelist substituted a three-stage history of salvation (Israel—Jesus—church) at the distant end of which lies the hoped for parousia. The Lucan *tendency* is the recasting of primitive Christian eschatology into a history of salvation, removing the parousia to a distant future. For Conzelmann, that factor in the Lucan milieu which *occasioned* such a tendency was the consternation of the church caused by the delay of the parousia. In order to deal with the shock experienced by the church of his time over the delay, the author of Luke-Acts wrote, reshaping as he wrote, the primitive tradition so as to eliminate the expectation of an imminent parousia.

In pursuing his teacher's thesis that the Lucan writings reflected the loss of the original Christian eschatological perspective, Conzelmann had evolved a method, redaction criticism. He presupposed the priority of Mark and so had a point of comparison by which to discern the Lucan editorial tendency. He presupposed a Gentile-Christian setting for the work.[14] In the course of his argument for a three-stage salvation history in Luke-Acts, Conzelmann had virtually rejected Luke 1–2 as an original part of the Third Gospel.[15]

Taken together, the work of Käsemann and Conzelmann gives us the "new look" in Lucan studies which emerged from Germany after 1950.[16] Luke is a theologian whose distinctive perspective can be discerned by careful attention to his modification of his Marcan source. The Lucan theological achievement was set in Gentile Christianity's struggle to deal with the problem of the delay of the parousia by substituting the presence of the Holy Spirit in the third stage of a three-stage salvation history. Unfor-

---

12. *Ibid.*, p. 15.
13. *Ibid.*, p. 13.
14. *Ibid.*, p. 147, e.g.
15. *Ibid.*, pp. 18 n. 1, 75 n. 4, 118, 172.
16. Of course, on Acts groundbreaking work was done by others also, e.g., Philipp Vielhauer, "On the 'Paulinism' of Acts," in *Studies in Luke-Acts*, pp. 33–50; Ernst Haenchen, *The Acts of the Apostles* (Philadelphia: Westminster Press, 1971).

tunately, the loss of the original eschatological orientation reduced the kerygmatic Jesus tradition to a historian's life of Jesus and changed the apostles into guarantors for the truth of the tradition. Such changes placed Luke-Acts in the early Catholic camp and marked it as a deviation from the true gospel.

So compelling did this "new look" appear that C. H. Dodd, in a private letter to J. E. Yates, supposedly said, "I suspect we shall have to give (the Lucan writings) over, so to speak, to Conzelmann."[17] Only ten years later, however, Ward Gasque could conclude his exhaustive survey with the assertion "There is no general agreement among scholars on even the most basic issues of Lukan research."[18] What happened to the Bultmannian view of Luke that seemed destined to carry the day in the mid-sixties? The remainder of this essay will attempt in five sections to describe the shifting sands.

THE TEXT TO BE INTERPRETED

In this section we must consider two questions: (1) textual-critical matters and (2) the problem of Luke 1–2. We begin with the issue of the correct text of Luke.

Conzelmann, in his book on Luke, worked from a Greek New Testament edited before the publication of P75.[19] In 1961, V. Martin and R. Kasser published *Papyrus Bodmer XIV*, which contained Luke 8, 10–17, 22–24 almost in their entirety and parts of 3–7, 9, 18.[20] This codex, dated between A.D. 175 and A.D. 225, is our oldest known copy of the Third Gospel. Although it does not support any one type of text entirely, it agrees more frequently with B than with any other single manuscript.[21] P75 is rarely in agreement with D when this manuscript stands alone.[22] For example,

17. Cited by R. R. Williams, "Church History in Acts: Is It Reliable?" in *Historicity and Chronology in the New Testament* (London: SPCK, 1965), p. 150.

18. *A History of the Criticism of the Acts of the Apostles* (Tübingen: J. C. B. Mohr [Paul Siebeck], 1975), p. 305.

19. *Theology of St. Luke*, pp. 50, 173 n. 3, e.g.

20. Geneva: Bibliotheque Bodmer, 1961.

21. Bruce M. Metzger, "The Bodmer Papyrus of Luke and John," *ExpTim* 73 (1961/62): 202.

22. J. A. Fitzmyer, "Papyrus Bodmer XIV: Some Features of Our Oldest Text of Luke," *CBQ* 24 (1962): 174.

P75 omits Luke 22:43–44, the fuller version of the prayer in 11:2–4, and the fuller version of 9:55, all of which are *found* in D but not in B. P75 also has Luke 22:19b–20,[23] 24:3 "of the Lord Jesus"; 24:6 "He is not here but is risen"; 24:12[24] and 24:36 "And he said to them, 'Peace to you' "; 24:40 and 24:51 "And he was carried up into heaven"; 24:52 "worshiping him," all of which are *omitted* by D but found in B.

These eight particular instances where P75's reading is longer than D are the most important. Since D has the tendency to give the longer reading when compared with *Sinaiticus* or B, Westcott and Hort thought when D contained the shorter text it was significant. Hence they preferred the reading of D in these eight instances where it gives the shorter text. Largely as a result of P75, Westcott-Hort's so-called "Western noninterpolations" are widely rejected as the authoritative readings today.[25] For example, in the twenty-sixth edition of Nestle/Aland the decision goes consistently against D and for P75.

A word of caution is in order here. E. C. Colwell taught us years ago that neither preferring the reading in the largest number of manuscripts nor choosing the text of the oldest manuscript was a proper criterion for modern textual criticism.[26] Generally, an eclecticism based on the internal criticism of readings is acknowledged as proper procedure.[27] It is difficult to escape the impression that phrases like "the overwhelming weight of evidence" mask a return to criteria not otherwise acceptable.[28] When decisions are made solely on the basis of intrinsic probability, the results do not always support P75. For example, G. D. Kilpatrick, in a forthcoming book on the Eucharist in the New Testament, forcefully argues for the

---

23. E. E. Ellis argues that the longer text is original (*The Gospel of Luke* [London: Nelson, 1966], pp. 253–55; so also P. Benoit, H. Schürmann, P. Parker, J. Jeremias, etc.).

24. K. P. G. Curtis argues against v. 12 as original ("Luke 24:12 and John 20:3–10," *JTS* n.s., 22 [1971]: 512–15). John Muddiman ("A Note on Reading Luke 24:12," *ETL* 48 [1972]: 542–48) and Frans Neirynck ("The Uncorrected Historic Present in Luke 24:12," *ETL* 48 [1972]: 548–53) support v. 12 as part of the original text of Luke.

25. Klyne Snodgrass, "Western Non-Interpolations," *JBL* 91 (1972): 379, appealing to Aland and Jeremias esp.

26. *The Study of the Bible* (Chicago: University of Chicago Press, 1937), pp. 57–64.

27. Cf. M. M. Parvis, "Text, NT," *IDB* 4:612; G. D. Kilpatrick, "The Greek New Testament Text of Today and the Textus Receptus," in H. Anderson and W. Barclay, eds., *The New Testament in Historical and Contemporary Perspective* (Oxford: Basil Blackwell, 1965), pp. 189–208.

28. E.g., Metzger, *A Textual Commentary on the Greek New Testament* (London: United Bible Societies, 1971), p. 176. Cf. the criticism of this by J. M. Ross, "The United Bible Societies' Greek N.T.," *JBL* 95 (1976): 121.

shorter text of the Last Supper in Luke on the basis of intrinsic probability:
(1) the shorter text is the more difficult; (2) the language favors the shorter
text (Kilpatrick's strongest evidence); and (3) elsewhere Luke is verbally
independent of the Pauline Epistles. At the same time, Kilpatrick just as
ably defends the longer text of passages like Luke 24:51. Although at the
moment there is strong impetus to accept the readings of P75 *in toto* at
the points where Westcott-Hort chose D, due caution will resist and re-
affirm a method based on intrinsic probability. In any case, there have been
shifts in the text of Luke since Conzelmann wrote.

Conzelmann's work on Luke ignored the first two chapters and did not
treat them as integral to the Gospel.[29] The response to this position has
been unanimously negative. On the one side, some scholars have accepted
Conzelmann's general scheme of salvation history and have tried to fit the
birth narratives into that scheme.[30] Still others have used the birth narratives to challenge Conzelmann's picture of Lucan salvation history.[31] Critics
on both sides agree, however, that Conzelmann's claim that Luke separates
John the Baptist from Elijah is erroneous, given Luke 1:17, 76.[32] Today
the infancy narratives are taken as integral to Luke-Acts. Assuming their
integrity, discussion centers on questions of sources,[33] structure,[34] and nature of the material.[35]

---

29. *Theology of St. Luke*, pp. 118, 172, 75 n. 4, 18 n. 1.

30. E.g., H. H. Oliver, "The Lucan Birth Stories and the Purpose of Luke-Acts,"
NTS 10 (1964): 202–26; W. B. Tatum, "The Epoch of Israel: Luke 1–2 and the
Theological Plan of Luke-Acts," *NTS* 13 (1967): 184–95.

31. E.g., Paul S. Minear, "Luke's Use of the Birth Stories," in *Studies in Luke-Acts*,
pp. 111–30.

32. E.g., W. C. Robinson, Jr., *The Way of the Lord* (a doctoral dissertation submitted to the theological faculty of the University of Basel, privately published, 1962),
pp. 3–19; S. G. Wilson, "Lukan Eschatology," *NTS* 15 (1970): 330–47.

33. There are at least four basic positions regarding the sources of Luke 1–2: (1)
One source: e.g., Paul Gaechter, "Der Verkundigungsbericht Lk 1:26–38," *Zeitschrift
für Kirchliche Theologie*, 91 (1969): 322–63, 567–86. (2) Two sources: e.g., A. R. C.
Leaney, *The Gospel according to St. Luke* (New York: Harper & Bros., 1958), pp. 26f.
(3) Multiple sources: e.g., Rudolf Bultmann, *The History of the Synoptic Tradition* (Oxford: Basil Blackwell, 1963), pp. 294–301. (4) Free composition by the evangelist: e.g.,
M. D. Goulder and M. L. Sanderson, "St. Luke's Genesis," *JTS*, n.s., 8 (1957): 12–30.

34. René Laurentin, *Structure et theologie de Luc 1–2* (Paris: Gabalda, 1957); C.
H. Talbert, *Literary Patterns, Theological Themes and the Genre of Luke-Acts* (Missoula: Scholars Press, 1974).

35. E.g., Jean Daniélou, *The Infancy Narratives*, trans. Rosemary Sheed (London:
Burns & Oates, 1968), agrees with Laurentin and Goulder-Sanderson on the midrashic
nature of the material but also wants to affirm its historical basis. Much more careful
is R. E. Brown's "Luke's Method in the Annunciation Narratives of Chapter One," in
J. W. Flanagan and A. W. Robinson, eds., *No Famine in the Land* (Missoula: Scholars
Press, 1975).

THE THEOLOGY OF LUKE

Any description of Lucan theology will inevitably include Acts along with the Third Gospel. Our sketch will develop in five brief units.

1. Salvation History and Eschatology

Conzelmann found a three-stage salvation history in Luke-Acts (Israel—Jesus—church). He connected it with the supposed elimination of references to an imminent end by the evangelist. Luke, he said, has substituted salvation history for the expectation of an imminent end because of the delay of the parousia. Research since Conzelmann has generally supported his recognition of Lucan salvation history, though not his claim that it is unique to Luke-Acts.[36] Our understanding of salvation history in Luke-Acts has been further refined, moreover, by seeing that the age of the church was divided by Luke into two eras, the apostolic age and the post-apostolic age.[37] Research since Conzelmann has not been so kind with reference to his claim that the third evangelist eliminated reference to the imminent end to deal with the delay of the parousia. There has been a widespread agreement that an expectation of the imminent end is found in Luke-Acts.[38] Furthermore, a diversity of occasions has been inferred for the Lucan eschatological concern. For example, H. W. Bartsch thinks Luke faced two problems, an over-realized eschatology on the one hand and a loss of eschatological hope on the other.[39] Talbert sees Luke involved in a battle with only one front, over-realized eschatology.[40] F. W. Danker and E. E. Ellis also posit one-front war but think it is apocalypticism.[41] S. G. Wilson

---

36. Oscar Cullmann (*Salvation in History* [London: SCM Press, 1967]) and I. Howard Marshall (*Luke: Historian and Theologian* [London: Paternoster Press, 1970]) are adamant that Luke stands in continuity with other New Testament writers.

37. Talbert, *Literary Patterns*, chap. 6.

38. E.g., F. O. Francis, "Eschatology and History in Luke-Acts," *JAAR* 37 (1969): 49–63; C. H. Talbert, "The Redaction Critical Quest for Luke the Theologian," in *Jesus and Man's Hope* (Pittsburgh: Pittsburgh Theological Seminary, 1970), I, 171–222; A. J. Mattill, Jr., "*Naherwartung, Fernerwartung*, and the Purpose of Luke-Acts," *CBQ* 34 (1972): 276–93; R. H. Hiers, "The Problem of the Delay of the Parousia in Luke-Acts," *NTS* 20 (1974): 145–54; Eric Franklin, *Christ the Lord: A Study in the Purpose and Theology of Luke-Acts* (London: SPCK, 1975). Gerhard Schneider, however, sides with Conzelmann (*Parusiegleichnisse im Lukas-Evangelium* [Stuttgart: Katholisches Bibelwerk, 1975]).

39. *Wachet aber zu jeder Zeit* (Hamburg: Herbert Reich, 1963).

40. "Redaction Critical Quest," pp. 171–222.

41. F. W. Danker, *Jesus and the New Age according to St. Luke* (St. Louis: Clayton Publishing House, 1972); Ellis, *Gospel of Luke*, p. 59.

assumes two fronts in Luke's battle, apocalypticism and loss of eschatological hope altogether.[42] General agreement is limited to this: the evangelist writes in terms of a salvation history which includes within it the hope for an imminent end.

2. Christology

Conzelmann's views on Christology include both a stance on proper method and a certain content. Regarding method he says, "The special elements in Luke's Christology cannot be set out by a statistical analysis of the titles applied to Jesus."[43] Rather, Lucan Christology is seen in the context of the total view of salvation history. The content of Luke's picture of Jesus he sets out in terms of past, present, and future.[44] The historical Jesus has been relegated to the past as bearer of the Spirit, preacher of the kingdom, and gatherer of the witnesses. The exalted Christ of the present is bestower of the Spirit. He is not only present to his church as a figure from the past by means of the picture of him presented by tradition but also is active through such means as the power of his name, which, for example, heals, and through his appearances to his apostles. In the future, moreover, Jesus will be the eschatological judge.

Research since Conzelmann is divided over exactly how one goes about discerning Lucan Christology. Does one concentrate on the titles used for Jesus,[45] or does one look for the overall structure of the Lucan picture of Jesus?[46] The difference such an approach can make is remarkable. If, for example, one focuses on the title "Lord" and notes that in the use of this title Luke makes no distinction between the historical and the exalted Christ, one may be led to conclude that for Luke there is no distinction between the earthly and the exalted Lord.[47] If, however, one looks at the overall pattern of Jesus' career in Luke-Acts and notes that it conforms almost exactly to the myth of immortals in Greco-Roman antiquity, one may be led to conclude that for Luke the ascension marks a radical change in the status of Jesus.[48]

---

42. *The Gentiles and the Gentile Mission in Luke-Acts* (Cambridge: University Press, 1973), chap. 3, esp. pp. 83f.

43. *Theology of St. Luke*, p. 170.

44. *Ibid.*, pp. 177, 179, 186, 194, 204 n. 1.

45. E.g., D. L. Jones, "The Title *Christos* in Luke-Acts," CBQ 32 (1970): 69–76; idem, "The Title *Kyrios* in Luke-Acts," SBL Seminar Papers 1974, ed. George MacRae (Missoula: Scholars Press, 1974), pp. 85–101.

46. C. H. Talbert, "An Anti-Gnostic Tendency in Lucan Christology," NTS 14 (1968/69): 259–71.

47. Jones, "*Kyrios* in Luke-Acts," p. 96.

48. C. H. Talbert, "The Concept of Immortals in Mediterranean Antiquity," JBL 94 (1975): 419–36.

A more precise formulation of the shape of Lucan Christology has resulted from two contributions from the Greco-Roman background of the two-volume work. On the one hand, the Lucan Jesus has been related to the mythology of immortals.[49] In Mediterranean antiquity near the beginning of our era a distinction was drawn between two types of divine beings, eternals (like Zeus) and immortals (like Dionysus or Hercules). The immortals had originally been mortal, but at the end of their careers there occurred a transformation or ascension so that they obtained the same honors as the eternals. Some evidence of the ascent was usually given. Either an immortal's ascent to heaven was witnessed or there was no trace of his physical remains. That the absence of the hero's physical remains pointed properly to an ascent to heaven was known from (a) predictions/ oracles during the hero's lifetime that he would be taken up; (b) a heavenly announcement at the end of his career stating or implying that he had been taken up; and (c) appearances of the hero to friends or disciples confirming his new status. In addition, another feature frequently present in the description of the immortals was a reference to the man's being begotten by a god of a human mother or his being the child of a goddess and a human father. When one spoke of an immortal in the Greco-Roman world, therefore, he meant a mortal who had become a god, and this was expressed in terms of an extraordinary birth and an ascension into heaven. The other side of his deification, the immortal, could and did intervene on behalf of his favorites.[50] Given the Lucan portrayal of Jesus, there is no way a Mediterranean person could have missed this as a portrayal of Jesus in the mythology of the immortals.

On the other hand, the Lucan Jesus has been related to the Greco-Roman image of the wandering philosopher.[51] Though fluid, this image frequently contained the following elements: (a) the philosopher was pictured as a wandering preacher whose journeys were sometimes the result of a divine command; (b) the philosophy he expounded was a way of living rather than an explanation of life; (c) his philosophy was learned by imitation of his life-style as much or more than by remembering his precepts, a learning procedure he consciously cultivated; and (d) in the controversy over the true and the false philosopher, succession lists and narratives often functioned to designate where the "living voice" could be

---

49. *Ibid.*

50. E.g., Dionysus of Halicarnassus, *Roman Antiquities* 6.13.1–4, tells the legend of how Castor and Pollux, twin immortals, appeared during a battle, aiding the Roman cause and announcing Roman victory.

51. Talbert, *Literary Patterns*, chap. 6.

found, that is, where the way of life was lived as well as expounded. Again, a Mediterranean person looking at Luke-Acts as a whole would have difficulty avoiding the impression that Jesus was a philosopher figure who founded the community which succeeded him. It is significant, moreover, that in antiquity lives of philosophers were sometimes told in terms of the myth of immortals.[52] Taken together, these two concepts furnish the best means for understanding the Lucan Jesus.

3. The Death of Jesus

Conzelmann said that Luke did not develop a positive doctrine of the redemptive significance of the passion or the cross. There was no connection with the forgiveness of sins.[53] Recent research has either sustained this judgment[54] or modified it only slightly.[55] In Luke-Acts, Jesus' death is viewed primarily as part of the divine plan and as a martyrdom of a righteous man, which serves as the dominical basis for Christian suffering.[56] For Luke, it is the glorification-exaltation of Jesus that enables him to be a cause of salvation for men.[57]

4. Salvation

Conzelmann said that just as the eschaton, for Luke, no longer signified present but future circumstances, so also eternal life is removed into the distant future.[58] Research since Conzelmann has shown that whereas in Paul Sōzein usually refers to final salvation (e.g., Rom. 5:9f.), in Luke-Acts it applies almost exclusively to the present. Salvation includes healing as well as forgiveness. It is associated with faith. It comes about through hearing the word, which includes the miraculous.[59]

5. The Church

Conzelmann's description of the Lucan understanding of the church did not go as far as that of Käsemann and others. The church, he said, is not

---

52. E.g., "Empedocles," in Diogenes Laertius, Lives of Eminent Philosophers; Philostratus, Life of Apollonius of Tyana.

53. Theology of St. Luke, pp. 196, 197 n. 3, 201.

54. Richard Zehnle, "The Salvific Character of Jesus' Death in Lucan Soteriology," TS 30 (1969): 420–44.

55. Marshall, Luke: Historian and Theologian, pp. 171–75.

56. C. H. Talbert, Luke and the Gnostics (Nashville: Abingdon Press, 1966), chap. 5.

57. Zehnle, "Salvific Character," p. 431; Marshall, Luke: Historian and Theologian, p. 169.

58. Theology of St. Luke, p. 230.

59. B. H. Throckmorton, "Sōzein, sōteria in Luke-Acts," SE 6:515–26 (Berlin: Akademie Verlag, 1973); P. J. Achtemeier: "The Lucan Perspective on the Miracles of Jesus: A Preliminary Sketch," JBL 94 (1975): 547–62.

yet considered as a factor in salvation in the sense of its being an object of faith. It appears only as the necessary medium of the message to us. Further, the present office-bearers are authorized by the Spirit, not yet by any particular succession.[60] Research since Conzelmann has been divided on these points. On the one side, some have agreed with Conzelmann, denying any thought of succession to Luke.[61] On the other side, others have agreed with Käsemann that a succession motif is found in Luke-Acts.[62] At present, the issue is moot.

Though incomplete, an outline of the Lucan theological perspective seems to be emerging among scholars. Nevertheless, redaction criticism has been unable to delineate either the Lucan purpose or the Lucan *Sitz im Leben*. The usual procedure has been to trace a theological theme through Luke-Acts and then, on the basis of one's results, to infer an occasion for it. Problems arise (a) when one has to arbitrate among the many competing themes in the two-volume work and assign positions of relative importance to them;[63] (b) when one has to do an analogous thing among the proposed occasions; and (c) when one has to decide an elementary question such as whether the readers are Gentile or Jewish Christians.[64] In sum, redaction criticism has enabled us to see the author as a creative theologian with a perspective of his own and to discern parts of that point of view. It has not enabled us to grasp Luke's purpose in the context of his *Sitz im Leben*. The issue before us today is, How can one discern the unity of the author's thought and thereby infer what are the central problems of his time and place?

THE ESTIMATE OF LUKE'S THEOLOGY

Conzelmann, although he has since affirmed the contrary,[65] at first seemed to regard Luke's theology as a departure from primitive Christian-

---

60. *Theology of St. Luke*, pp. 218, 225.

61. C. K. Barrett, *Luke the Historian in Recent Study* (London: Epworth, 1961), pp. 73, 76.

62. Schuyler Brown, *Apostasy and Perseverance in the Theology of Luke* (Rome: Pontifical Biblical Institute, 1969), p. 129, *passim*.

63. E.g., salvation history (Conzelmann), salvation (Marshall), ecclesiology (Jervell), orthodoxy (Talbert).

64. Ellis (*Gospel of Luke*, pp. 52f.) and Jacob Jervell (*Luke and the People of God* [Minneapolis: Augsburg Publishing House, 1972]) see Jewish-Christian links for the Lucan writings. Any such claims must deal with passages like Luke 5:17–26, 6:46–49. and 8:16, where the signs point to Gentile readers. Cf. G. B. Caird, *Saint Luke* (Baltimore: Penguin Books, 1963), pp. 95, 107, 119.

65. *An Outline of the Theology of the New Testament* (New York: Harper & Row, 1969), pp. 149–52.

ity. Certainly in the "new look" to Luke-Acts that emerged from Germany after 1950 Lucan theology was generally regarded as suspect. It represented early Catholicism (so Käsemann, Vielhauer, Haenchen, Grasser, e.g.). After 1945 the predicate "early Catholic" was used by the Bultmann school in order to differentiate writings, layers, and elements in the New Testament from its kerygmatic center, the actual gospel. The roots again go back into Bultmann's *Theology of the New Testament*. This two-volume work must be read against the background of the old Protestant view of church history. According to this view, there was originally an ideal New Testament church which was followed by a fall away into Catholicism. So in Bultmann's *Theology of the New Testament* one meets a normative Christian stance in Paul and John, after which there is a fall away. In contrast to the old Protestant view, however, in Bultmann's work this fall away already begins in the New Testament itself. In polity, doctrine, and ethics, the developments after Paul and alongside John reflect this falling away. This means that the New Testament contains at least two strata— a kerygmatic center (the true gospel) and a layer which has deserted the kerygmatic understanding of existence. In the Bultmann school this second layer has been called "early Catholicism." Into this early Catholic layer various scholars have included II Peter, Jude, Ephesians, the Pastorals, parts of Matthew, and Luke-Acts.[66]

W. G. Kümmel has recently attempted a summary of the debate in Germany.[67] To the five basic criticisms made of Lucan theology (he knows nothing of the near expectation of the kingdom, does not understand Jesus' death as a saving event, holds to the notion of "succession," and therefore, thinks there are guarantees for the Christian tradition; thus, faith's assurance is handed over to human accomplishment, and he misunderstands the kerygma evidenced by the existence of Acts after the Gospel), Kümmel has summarized also the responses made to them: Luke does know the expectation of the near end;[68] does not entirely remove the redemptive significance of Jesus' death (cf. Luke 22:19b–20; Acts 20:28) though his chief emphasis is on Jesus' death as corresponding to God's will;[69] does not reflect on apostolic succession;[70] and he recounts the history of Jesus not as a mere historian but as do Matthew and Mark, with the aim of proclama-

---

66. Talbert, "An Introduction to Acts," *RevExp* 71 (1974): 443.
67. "Current Theological Accusations against Luke," *ANQ* 16 (1975): 131–45.
68. See n. 38.
69. That Luke does not develop a doctrine of atonement does not mean that he works with a *theologia gloriae*. Cf. Marshall, *Luke: Historian and Theologian*, p. 209. If, however, one assumes the contrary, there is then a theological need to retain the long text of the Supper in Luke.
70. See nn. 61, 62.

tion.[71] Finally, since the kerygma Paul received (I Cor. 15:3ff.) presupposes that the resurrection experience of witnesses must also be reported in designating the basis of Christian faith, the presence of Acts is no betrayal of a primitive Christian stance.[72]

Kümmel concludes that it is wrong to say that Luke's theology is illegitimate/early Catholic. Luke remains, in the main lines of his theology, in agreement with the central proclamation of the New Testament (i.e., Jesus, Paul, John). Without a doubt, Luke belongs to the most important, and for us normative, witnesses to the New Testament proclamation.

From a vantage point outside the Bultmann school, it appears that the basic problem is the ambiguity of the term "early Catholic."[73] Sometimes it is used so loosely that it can mean Luke-Acts reflects a canon concept, a concept of a summary or summaries of faith, and a concept of episcopacy committed to preserving the true faith. In this case, Luke is probably early Catholic. At other times, however, the term is used to denote such things as (a) moralization of the faith and a conception of the gospel as a new law (legalism); (b) a trend toward sacramentalism; and (c) a conception of the ministry as the authoritative teaching office which legitimates the Word. In this case, Luke is not early Catholic.

What is needed are two sets of categories: one to describe the new forms of Christianity which emerged after the first generation and the other to designate the varieties of Christianity possessing essential discontinuity with early Christianity's understanding of Christian life and faith. Early Catholic is an appropriate term for the emerging form of Christianity that was characterized by canon, creed, and episcopacy. It is necessary, however, to follow the lead of the old Catholic church in its process of canonization and to distinguish between two types of early Catholicism, normative and non-normative. When this is done, Luke-Acts can be accurately designated as normative early Catholic. Its view of Christian life and faith does not represent a fall away from Christian truth. In this we may agree with Kümmel.

THE QUESTION OF METHOD

How does one arrive at the theology of Luke? Conzelmann said: "We must start from a methodical comparison with his [Luke's] sources, in so

---

71. This is strongly argued by Talbert, "The Redaction Critical Quest for Luke the Theologian," pp. 211f.

72. Jervell, "The Problem of Traditions in Acts," in *Luke and the People of God*, pp. 19–39, makes the best case on this point.

73. Barrett, *New Testament Essays* (London: SPCK, 1972), pp. 99f.

far as these are directly available or can be reconstructed."[74] Assuming the two-source theory, Conzelmann believed Luke's theology could be discerned especially from Luke's alterations of Mark. This methodology has been widely accepted. The scholar notes a particular change made by Luke. If he is aware that the effect of this change is consistent with the effect of changes Luke has made elsewhere, then he makes the inference that the change reflects a tendency of the evangelist.[75] At the same time, at least three challenges to this method have been raised.

In the first place, it has been argued that since Luke uses traditions other than Mark and Q, some differences in pericopes where Luke parallels Mark are not due to Lucan redaction but, in part at least, to variant traditions. Tim Schram's Der Markus-Stoff bei Lukas argues that one must distinguish two groups of material in Luke where Luke runs parallel to Mark. Group one contains material which comes from Mark so that all differences from Mark are due to the third evangelist.[76] Group two consists of material that is under the influence of variant traditions.[77] In this second group the task is to distinguish between Mark, the pre-Lucan tradition that is non-Marcan, and the redaction of the evangelist. Here divergences from Mark cannot, without further evidence, be taken as due to the evangelist. In this case, literary criticism attempts to serve as a corrective to redaction-critical work on Luke. Schram's point that not every difference from Mark that one finds in Luke where they run parallel is a reflection of the evangelist's editorial activity is one that has been made for years by advocates of the Proto-Luke hypothesis generally and by contenders for an independent Lucan passion narrative in particular.[78] Given these contentions, deriving Luke's theology from an observation of changes he makes in his Marcan source becomes extremely difficult.

In the second place, it has been asked whether Lucan theology should be sought only in the places where the evangelist differs from tradition instead of also in the areas where he reproduces tradition with little or no

---

74. Theology of St. Luke, p. 12.

75. E.g., G. W. H. Lampe, "The Lucan Portrait of Christ," NTS 2 (1956): 160–75, esp. 160.

76. Tim Schram, Der Markus-Stoff bei Lukas (Cambridge: University Press, 1971). Group One: Luke 4:31–44; 5:27–32; 6:(1–5), 6–11; 8:11–15, 19–21, 26–39, 40–56; 9:7–9, 46–50; 18:15–17, 18–30, 35b–43; 19:45–48; 20:1b–8, 20–26, 41–47; 21:1–4, 37f.; 22:1–13.

77. Group Two: Luke 5:12–16, 17–26, 33–39; 6:12–19; 8:4–8 (9f.), 16–18, 22–25; 9:1–6, 10–17, 18–22 (23–27), 28–36, 37–43a, 43b–45; 18:31–34 (35a); 19:28–38; 20:(1a), 9–19, 27–40 (46); 21:5–36; (22:3).

78. E.g., Vincent Taylor, The Passion Narrative of St. Luke (Cambridge: University Press, 1972); Schneider, Verleugnung, Verspotting und Verhör Jesu nach Lukas 22: 54–71: Studien zur lukanischen Darstellung der Passion (Munich: Kosel-Verlag, 1969).

change. Howard Marshall and Frieder Schütz argue that the fact that Luke took over tradition shows he regarded it as important. Hence the traditions he took over should not be regarded as awkward intrusions into his work but rather its basis. If we confine our attention to what can clearly be identified as redactional, we stand in danger of producing an eccentric picture of Lucan theology.[79]

In the third place, since 1963 there has been a significant assault on the "two-source theory."[80] Although the alternatives proposed have not proved convincing, enough difficulties with Marcan priority have emerged to render its position as an "assured result" of criticism suspect and to make it a questionable control on redaction-critical work. Employing Mark as a control today is about as compelling as using Colossians and II Thessalonians to describe Paul's theology. It may very well be legitimate to do so, but so many have problems with the procedure that such an assumption narrows considerably the circles with whom one can converse.

To do redaction-critical work as Conzelmann did, using all variations of Luke from Mark in pericopes where they run parallel as indications of the Lucan mind, is problematic on three counts. The issue before us today is, How can one study the distinctive perspective of the third evangelist without assuming any source theories? In this regard, the problem is the same as that faced with Mark and John all along.

ISSUES FOR FUTURE RESOLUTION

In the preceding survey two issues for future resolution emerged: (a) How can one discern the unity of the evangelist's thought, given the many different themes isolated by redaction criticism? and (b) How can one delineate the distinctive perspective of the author without assuming any source theories? Joachim Rohde has observed: "The history of the study of the synoptic gospels is . . . the history of the changing methods used in the endeavour to obtain fresh knowledge."[81] Since redaction criticism associated with the "new look" in Lucan studies[82] has been unable to resolve the first issue and has not attempted to deal with the second, the question

---

79. Marshall, *Luke: Historian and Theologian*, pp. 19f., 218; Schütz, *Der leidende Christus: Die angefochtene Gemeinde und das Christuskerygma der lukanischen Schriften* (Stuttgart: Kohlhammer Verlag, 1969), p. 19.

80. Cf. Reginald H. Fuller, "The Synoptic Problem after Ten Years," *PSTJ* 28 (1975): 63–68, for an estimate of the situation today.

81. *Rediscovering the Teaching of the Evangelists* (Philadelphia: Westminster Press, 1968), p. 1.

arises whether or not we are at a point where a new methodology would contribute significantly to our understanding of Luke-Acts.

In the last decade literary critics have seen that a particular text standing alone is a problem because it lacks meaning. The interpretative rule "What is said must be understood in its context" works well for a word in a sentence, for a sentence in a paragraph, for a paragraph in a section, and for a section in the document as a whole. But what is the context for the whole? This question has led criticism to the attempt to view the individual text (i.e., the document as a whole) in terms of a universal type or configuration which is constructed on the basis of an *inductive* grouping of texts with common features. It is the particular text's participation in the universal type that gives it a first level of meaning. The particular text's transformation of the universal type-structure-genre is then seen as a further way of saying something about the meaning of the document taken as a whole.

If a critic searches for those unconscious structures that are rooted in the human mind as such, as structuralists seem to do, then boundaries of time, geography, and culture mean nothing. The universal type-structure-genre is constructed from texts of virtually any time and place and civilization.[83] If the critic looks for those structures that have a definite function in a specific social and cultural context, as genre critics seem to do, then the boundaries of time, geography, and culture are crucial. The universal type-structure-genre is constructed from texts that come from a specific locale during a specific era. In either case, the critic's task is seen as viewing the individual writing in terms of a universal type of configuration constructed on the basis of an inductive grouping of texts with common features.

Although no structuralist interpretation of Luke-Acts has yet been made, there has been one attempt at genre criticism.[84] With what writings in the Mediterranean world from 300 B.C. to A.D. 300 can Luke-Acts be grouped? The closest thing in antiquity to the two-volume Lucan work is a type of

---

82. W. G. Thompson attempts to do redaction criticism without presupposing any source theories (*Matthew's Advice to a Divided Community*, Mt. 17:22—18:35 [Rome: Pontifical Biblical Institute, 1970]).

83. Dan O. Via, Jr. (*Kerygma and Comedy in the New Testament* [Philadelphia: Fortress Press, 1975]) claims this method works on the text as a whole (pp. 72f.) and without presupposing any view of sources (p. 6). It would appear tailor-made for our needs. The preoccupation with esoteric terminology is so great as to be frustrating and the pay-off so meager that hope is dashed. Once one has shown that there is a structural-generic relationship between Mark, the Pauline kerygma, and classical comedy in that all are informed by a death-resurrection motif (comedy), what has one contributed of real significance to our understanding of Mark?

84. Talbert, *Literary Patterns*, chap. 8.

biography of the founder of a philosophical school which has within it, after the founder's life, a list or narrative of his successors and selected other disciples, whose function was to delineate where the true and living tradition of the school was to be found in the present. If Luke-Acts is seen as belonging to this universal type-structure-genre, then its very participation indicates the first level of the document's meaning. The social function of such a text in antiquity was to speak a word, in the context of controversy, about where the true tradition was to be found in the time after the founder. A second level of meaning can be discerned from the changes the evangelist makes in the genre, for example, in his expansion of the narrative of successors and selected other disciples so that it is roughly the same length as that of the founder's life and loosely parallels it in content and sequence. Such an insight, if accurate, provides the clue for the relative ordering of the various themes isolated by redaction criticism and for the primary occasion which prompted the document. It is significant, moreover, that this methodology need presuppose no source theories for Luke-Acts.

Lucan studies in the last twenty years have been like shifting sands. At present, widespread agreement is difficult to find, except on the point that Conzelmann's synthesis is inadequate. Until the scholarly community can agree on a proper procedure for studying Luke-Acts, there is little likelihood that another synthesis will fare any better.

15.

Salvation and Discipleship in Luke's Gospel

RALPH P. MARTIN

The salvation present in and through the person of Jesus is an organic motif of Luke's Gospel. It encompasses the offer of new life and the demand for disciplined living.

What follows is a modest exercise in redaction criticism with reference to key ideas in Luke's Gospel: salvation and discipleship. The first term sums up a major theme of Luke, so we must look first at the evangelist's distinctive use before setting the ideas on a wider canvas. Attention will be confined to the Gospel, with only occasional allusion made to Acts.

SALVATION IN LUKE'S GOSPEL

W. C. van Unnik has provided a survey of the data from which it will be sufficient to deduce the following conclusions: (1) " 'Salvation' lies at the center of Luke's Gospel; it represents the dominant idea of his message."[1] (2) The evidence for this statement clusters in the infancy narratives (1, 2) which, drawn from Luke's special source and cast in Septuagint (LXX) style, contain references to God as "savior" (1:47; cf. Hab. 3:18, LXX) and promise that the forerunner will bring the "knowledge of salvation" in the Messiah's offer of forgiveness (1:69, 71, 77). The birth of Jesus is hailed as the advent of a "savior" (2:11), Messiah the Lord (cf. 2:26 and Ps. Sol. 17:32; 18:5).[2] Simeon gives thanks, in his song, for the appearing of "salvation" in the birth of the child (2:30). Throughout these chapters the term "salvation" is drawn from Jewish eschatological expec-

---

1. "L'usage de SOZEIN 'Sauver' et des derives dans les évangiles synoptiques," reprinted in *Sparsa Collecta: The Collected Essays of W. C. van Unnik*, part one (Leiden: E. J. Brill, 1973), pp. 16–34 (32). See too E. M. B. Green, *The Meaning of Salvation* (London: Hodder and Stoughton, 1965), pp. 125–31.

2. On the textual issue, see Paul Winter, "Lukanische Miszellen," ZNW 49 (1958): 67–75.

tation, and Luke is very likely indebted to a liturgical tradition for the precise formulations. (3) Within the body of the Gospel there are four distinctive verses which echo like a refrain since they contain a set formula: "your faith has saved you" (RSV; 7:50; 8:48; 17:19; 18:42: all statements are identical in wording and have the verb in the perfect tense, sesōken). The verses, moreover, come at the end of three pericopes which have to do with Jesus' healing ministry and form the punch line of the dialogue. The pronouncement logion is linked with forgiveness of sins in the fourth instance. (4) In the formulation "Are the ones being saved [hoi sōzomenoi] a few?" (13:23) we meet a participial construction found in other contexts to describe Christian believers (Acts 2:47; I Cor. 1:18). It is important to note the eschatological background of the recorded question. Jesus' reply avoids all discussion of the precise issue and warns about the difficulties of entering the (eschatological) kingdom. He promises, however, an entry to the non-Jews (13:28-29, Q). (5) In 19:9, 10 the present realization of salvation is again assured as Zacchaeus is welcomed as a "son of Abraham." The emphasis falls on Jesus' seeking this man, an unlikely candidate for salvation; and in so doing Luke is underlining Jesus' mission to the outcasts of Israel as he performs the role of the messianic shepherd (Ezek. 34:16). [Cf. 9:56 (Textus Receptus).] Lastly, (6) Luke's usage is illustrated in his verb forms. The nouns ("salvation," "savior") are most likely liturgical in origin; and in any case they do not describe a state or a doctrinal statement, but are closely related to the person of Jesus (Acts 4:12). They point to his gracious activity both in the offer of new life he makes in healing and pardon and in the ensuing demand he imposes (9:24). "Salvation" can sum up the "Christian message" (as in Acts 13:26; 28:28) in both of these aspects.

THE BRINGER OF SALVATION

The structure within which Lucan Christology is set is that of two stages,[3] corresponding to the earthly life and the heavenly status of Jesus. The framework is succinctly contained in the statement of 24:26. The goal to which Jesus moves in this Gospel is his being "received up" (9:51: analēmpsis) in glory at the ascension. The indispensable preliminary to the exaltation is his death and resurrection, seen as one event by which his glorification is accomplished (12:50; 13:32f.). Thus a theologia crucis is a prelude to a theologia gloriae. There are implications of this necessary

---

3. Helmut Flender, St. Luke, Theologian of Redemptive History, trans. Reginald H. and Ilse Fuller (London: SPCK, 1967), pp. 41–56.

connection which relate to Luke's understanding of the Christian life and the way in which the total salvation that Jesus wrought is applied to the church. We may conveniently use these two aspects of Luke's presentation as categories in which to see his Christology displayed.

The Earthly Figure of Jesus

In 1:32 Jesus is hailed as "Son of the Most High," which is a royal title that is amplified in the following line of the stanza. The evidence that, for this evangelist, "Son of God" is a messianic title is seen in the confession of the demons "You are the Son of God!" to which the editorial comment is appended, "But he rebuked them, and would not allow them to speak, *because they knew that he was the Messiah*" (4:41; cf. Mark 1:34). Luke's report of the Q-sayings in the temptation narrative (in 4:3–9) is set in a context already determined by the baptismal proclamation "You are my beloved Son" (3:22) and by the statement (3:38) that the first Adam was "son of God." "Son of God" is Luke's common title, but "sonship" is not in accord with the contemporary expectation implied in "Messiah." This is borne out at the Sanhedrin interrogation (22:70). To the question "Are you the Son of God?" Jesus returns an evasive reply. There is, however, another feature of the Lucan trial story that is important. He has separated the two questions of messiahship (22:67) and sonship (22:70). He has done this apparently to distinguish between "Messiah" as a political title (which he disowns in keeping with his editorial procedure to emphasize the non-political involvement of the message) and "Son of God" as a religious title which, insofar as it can be separated from Messiah, conveys filial relationship. Two examples of the latter occur in 2:49 and the Q-logion of 10:22. So, Luke's stress on filial awareness breaks the mold of a messianic stereotype and puts Jesus' relationship to God on a new footing, with obvious paraenetic application to the Christian as "son of God" in the divine family.

Luke's use of the term "Messiah" is functional, and there are three sections in his Gospel where a technical sense may be suspected, to illustrate and confirm the claim that in Jesus of Nazareth the true hopes of Israel's messianic salvation came to realization—in spite of the seeming contradiction of those claims implied by his rejection and defeat (cf. 24:21).

1. *Jesus' visit to his patris and his rejection* at the Nazareth synagogue (4:16–30) has been placed by Luke at the frontispiece of his account of the public ministry, directly following the temptation pericope. Certain parts of the section stand out, chiefly in connection with Jesus' citation of Isaiah 61:1–2, 58:6. More debatable is the idea, implied in the reference to "the year of the Lord's favor" (4:19), that we are to see an allusion to the

Jubilee year (Lev. 25:10). It is just conceivable that Jesus had this year of Jubilee in mind, both in his reported claim "Today this scripture has been fulfilled in your hearing" (4:21, RSV) and in 7:22 (cf. Matt. 11:4f.) when in response to the Baptist's question "Are you the coming one, or shall we look for another?" he indicated that he was fulfilling the role of the Messiah who would announce the year of Jubilee and set the people free.[4] There can, however, be no certainty as to Luke's intention in this suggestion of a chronological dating. Much more likely is the idea that he is insisting that Jesus is the "anointed one" who began his public career by laying claim to being the "bearer of the Holy Spirit," whose presence was already at work in the anticipations of his birth (2:25f.).

John's disclaimer when it is proposed that he may be the Messiah (3:15) is clearly intended to shift the focus of attention away from the baptizer to the one baptized. He utters the statement "He will baptize you with the Holy Spirit *and with fire*" (3:16, RSV), a version of Mark 1:8 which has been editorially adapted by Luke to bring out the significance of the future baptism conducted by Jesus at Pentecost (Acts 1:5; 2:3, 19).[5] This expectation of a Messiah who would "baptize" the people was already known in Judaism. But the point is being made that the one who will grant the Spirit has himself received the Spirit as a gift. Thereafter in Luke's presentation the Spirit comes upon Jesus at his baptism (3:22). The reader, therefore, is not surprised to read that, at Nazareth, Jesus claimed to be the recipient of the Spirit, since even the intervening activities set between baptism and announcement are themselves directed by the Spirit (4:1, 14). What is exceptional in the Nazareth pericope is the type of Messiah Jesus is claimed to be; and that involves his function as *bringer of messianic salvation to the Gentiles*. Luke's omission of the line (in Isa. 61:2) "the day of vengeance of our God" from the quotation given at 4:19 is deliberate.[6] This has been made to extend the scope of messianic blessedness to embrace the Gentiles—a theme justifiably seen in many places in Luke-Acts and illustrated here by the actions of Elijah and Elisha (4:24–27).

---

4. August Strobel, "Die Ausrufung des Jobeljahrs in der Nazarethpredigt Jesu," in W. Eltester, ed., *Jesus in Nazareth* (Berlin: Walter de Gruyter, 1972), pp. 38–50.

5. E. Earle Ellis, *The Gospel of Luke*, New Century Bible, rev. ed. (London: Oliphants, 1974), p. 90. But see James D. G. Dunn, "Spirit-and-Fire-Baptism," *NovT* 14 (1972): 81–92.

6. To the brief bibliography in the present writer's *New Testament Foundations* (vol. 1, *The Four Gospels* [Grand Rapids: Wm. B. Eerdmans, 1975], pp. 255ff.) should be added James A. Sanders, "From Isaiah 61 to Luke 4," in which attention is again called to the importance of the evidence of 11Q Melch (*Christianity, Judaism and Other Greco-Roman Cults*, part 1, *Studies for Morton Smith at Sixty* [Leiden: E. J. Brill, 1975], pp. 75–106. Cf. M. de Jonge and A. S. van der Woude, "11Q Melchizedek and the NT," *NTS* 12 [1965–66]: 301–26, esp. 309–12).

In summary, Luke shows Jesus as the consecrated Messiah, both gifted by and bearer of the Spirit, who would inaugurate messianic salvation. There is a double edge to his work. He reaches out to the non-Jews or to "Jews who made themselves as Gentiles," and thereby incurs the opposition of Jewish leaders.

2. *The Mosaic-messianic typology* is seen at work in 9:28–36. As the inauguration at Nazareth is a curtain-raiser to Jesus' public ministry, so the transfiguration is a prelude to the travel section in which he sets his face in the direction of Jerusalem and his *analēmpsis* (9:51).

Comparison with the two synoptic accounts (Mark 9:2–8; Matt. 17:1–8) is invited. In particular, we note how Peter's harsh word (Mark 8:32; Matt. 16:22) and his subsequent rebuke (Mark 8:33; Matt. 16:23) are omitted from Luke. Instead, the limpid and verbless confession "The Christ of God" (9:20) is followed simply by an announcement that "the Son of man must [*dei*] suffer" (RSV), a cryptic sentence recalling that Luke uses the verb implying necessity more often than the other evangelists do to point up the scriptural framework in which the Messiah's sufferings and glory are set (24:26, 27, 46).[7] The notion of a *Heilsplan* involving the destiny of the Messiah is the key factor to understanding Luke's version of the transfiguration. This is obviously so as we inspect the wording of 9:31: Moses and Elijah "appeared with glory and spoke of his departure [*exodus*], which he was to fulfill at Jerusalem." The Mosaic-Exodus typology with its nexus of promise and fulfillment is clear in this sentence, peculiar to L. But the LXX influence is just as visible as we see how Luke has edited and revised Mark to portray the scene in the light of Moses' experience on the mountain (Exod. 24, 34).[8]

It is in data such as these that Luke's intention most clearly surfaces; and it allows the conclusion that his understanding of messianic redemption is dictated by Old Testament/LXX terms and idioms. He sets forth Jesus as the expected deliverer of his people, in his role both as a new Moses and a new prophet charged to bring the redeemed people into the promised land.[9] His title to messianic dignity is seen to involve an ap-

---

7. Luke-Acts have 41 or 44 of the 102 occurrences of *dei* in the New Testament, according to Erich Fascher, "Theologische Beobachtungen zu *dei*," in W. Eltester, ed., *Neutestamentliche Studien für Rudolf Bultmann* (Berlin: A. Töpelmann, 1954), pp. 248–54.

8. This feature is well brought out by Eric Franklin, *Christ the Lord: A Study in the Purpose and Theology of Luke-Acts* (Philadelphia: Westminster Press, 1975), pp. 72f.

9. C. F. Evans, "The Central Section of St. Luke's Gospel," in D. E. Nineham, ed., *Studies in the Gospels: Essays in Memory of R. H. Lightfoot* (Oxford: Blackwell, 1955), pp. 37–53.

pointment with his destiny at Jerusalem, where he must suffer before he enters his glory.

3. *The charge-sheet of the accusations brought against Jesus* as he is conducted before Pilate epitomizes Luke's message about messiahship (23:2): "We found this man corrupting our nation, stopping them from paying taxes to Caesar, and saying that he is himself the Messiah, a king!" At previous points in the narrative, Luke has recorded statements which give the lie to these accusations. They have been shown to be false: (1) the nation is already corrupted (9:41); (2) at 20:22, 25 the spies sent out to impeach him are told by Jesus, "Pay what is Caesar's to Caesar"; (3) Jesus has already refused the role of political Messiah (22:67; cf. 4:5-8) and his title, "king of the Jews," is inoffensive to Pilate, who forthwith is ready to release him and will declare him to be innocent three or four times (23:4, 14, 15, 22) and wishes to set him free (23:20). The Jews are to blame, since it is they who maliciously frame these inaccurate charges (as in Acts 17:6b–7).

What stands out on this background of Jewish involvement and culpability is Jesus' messiahship as expressible in non-political terms; and we may see how Luke teaches that Jesus' reign is heavenly and spiritual.[10] He thus uses the medium of Old Testament prophecies but gives a spiritualizing twist to what at first glance looks terrestrial and concerned with existing social structures (1:32f.). This conclusion leads us to consider Jesus' heavenly office.

The Heavenly Lord

"The Lord" (*kyrios*) is Luke's favorite christological appellation, in both his Gospel and in Acts. We note the comprehensive way in which he employs the term, ranging from the birth story, where he is already "Christ the Lord" (2:11), to his exaltation (Acts 2:36).

The controverted issue is to know whether Luke is careful to maintain something of a distinction in his use of the title *Kyrios* between the earthly Jesus and the state of Christ after the resurrection.[11] The data are as follows. We may freely concede that the references in the birth narratives do not prove a great deal in view of their liturgical origin; that there are instances (e.g., 5:12; 9:61; 18:41) where "Lord" (*kyrie*) as an appellation is non-significant, since it is a courtesy title of respect; and that 19:31 need

10. Gerard S. Sloyan, *Jesus on Trial* (Philadelphia: Fortress Press, 1973), pp. 107f.

11. See C. F. D. Moule, "The Christology of Acts," in Leander E. Keck and J. Louis Martyn, eds., *Studies in Luke-Acts* (1966; reprint ed., Philadelphia: Fortress Press, 1980), pp. 159ff., and the critique brought by Franklin, *Christ the Lord*, pp. 49–55.

mean no more than the animal's owner (though 19:34 repeats the *kyrios* title; cf. Mark 11:6 and Matt. 21:6, which omit the second reference). What is worth investigating are those sections which combine the vocative and the title both in narrative form:

10:1—After this the Lord (*kyrios*) appointed seventy(-two) others (RSV)
10:17—The seventy(-two) returned with joy, saying, "Lord" (*kyrie*) (RSV)

10:40—Martha was distracted . . . she came and said, "Lord" (*kyrie*)
10:41—the Lord (*kyrios*) answered her (RSV)

12:41—Peter said to him, "Lord" (*kyrie*); v. 42, the Lord (*kyrios*) said (RSV)

The point seems to be that Luke places in close proximity both the vocative appellation and narrative title in order to suggest a deep association between them. Then there are those passages where "Lord" as a vocative suggests a personal relationship between Jesus and his chosen followers, such as 5:8, 11:1, 17:37, and 22:33 (Peter's bold statement, "Lord [*kyrie*], with you I am ready to go to prison and to death), which is picked up at 22:61 ("the Lord [*kyrios*] turned and looked at Peter, and Peter remembered what the Lord had said"). The conclusion is defensible that *kyrios* (as both a narrative noun and an appellation) is meant to convey the sense of a personal bond uniting Jesus and those committed to him.

It is not disputed that after the resurrection the title *kyrios* takes on a richer meaning, as in 24:34, "The Lord is risen." The suggestion, however, is possible that Luke also uses the title of the earthly life of Jesus not only in his narration but also in a descriptive sense, in order to say that there were personal links between Jesus and his followers in the pre-resurrection period. Even then the disciples' response to Jesus set up a relationship that was akin to the relationship between the exalted Lord and the church in the apostolic age. We may trace herein a Lucan distinctive aim, which was *to clamp together the earthly and exalted epochs of Jesus' appearance and to stress a continuity that the resurrection only deepened and enriched but did not drastically alter.*

The evangelist's message to the church of his own time can be seen in this linkage as Luke deliberately employs the title of exaltation. His theological conviction and his pastoral interest both seek to show that the church lives under the present rule of the risen and exalted Lord whose earthly life still speaks to the evangelist's generation. For Luke the past is not dead, and the offer of salvation that was made in the person of Jesus

Christ in his earthly ministry still holds good, since the same Lord is as active in the post-resurrection and apostolic period as he was in "the days of his flesh." And the past history is related to make that offer a contemporary reality and to lay a claim of response on the present-day hearers in Luke's situation. We may go even further and claim that Luke as an evangelist told the story of the past not as an end in itself but in order to lay a solid foundation (1:1–4) on which the present ministry of Jesus in the church could be built. "Salvation is found," comments Franklin, "not by linking up with a person of the past but by submitting to the Lord of the present."[12] The call to the present availability of his offer and to the need for the hearer's acceptance reverberates in such places as 4:21; 19:5, 9; and 23:43.

MESSIAH'S TASK IN LUKE

The ministry of Jesus centers on the proclamation of God's kingdom. But where Mark has a relatively "simple" framework in which Jesus' work begins with his announcement that God's rule is imminent (1:14f.//Matt. 4:17), Luke has (1) omitted the Marcan summary and (2) introduced some complications to the framework. For one thing, he has placed the promise of the kingdom within the nativity narratives (1:32f.). Then, at the other extreme, he pictures the eleven, even in the post-resurrection period, still concerned with an Israelite kingdom and still anxious to know when it will be set up (Acts 1:6). From these features some momentous conclusions have been drawn.

One is that since Luke follows the statement that Jesus began his ministry with a record of his teaching in the synagogue (4:14f.) we are meant to understand that a decisive shift in eschatological expectation has occurred.[13] From the Marcan idea of imminent awareness that the kingdom is at hand Luke has removed the presence of the kingdom not only into the distant future but to a non-historical, transcendental, and even "timeless" realm. He has done this to change radically the nature of the kingdom's coming to permit an emphasis on the kingdom as a present reality. What has occasioned this shift in eschatological perspective is Luke's attitude to the delay of the parousia. The upshot of this "de-eschatologizing" championed by Luke is that he is seen to be concerned not with the kingdom as near at hand, but with the nature of the kingdom. As Conzel-

---

12. *Christ the Lord*, p. 71.
13. This, of course, is the thesis propounded by Hans Conzelmann in his seminal work, *The Theology of St. Luke*, trans. G. Buswell (New York: Harper & Row, 1961).

mann expresses the conclusion, in reference to the verse (16:16) on which he has placed so much weight, "The coming of John does not mean that the Kingdom is near, but that the time for the preaching of the Kingdom has come."[14]

Critical evaluation of this theory involving Luke's alleged revision of eschatology is still under way.[15] What seems clear, as the smoke clears, is that Luke does not dismiss the hope of an imminent end and that his picture of God's kingdom includes both aspects of its present reality in the ministry of Jesus and the futuristic hope of its imminent, but not immediate, realization in its fullness.[16] The issues, as we address our question to the matter of how Luke envisages Messiah's work, is to inquire how Luke describes the blessings of messianic salvation.

Jesus' Ministry of Exorcism and Healing

Luke's characterization is summed up in Acts 10:38, a verse which closely links God's anointing Jesus with the Spirit and his beneficent ministry. The exorcisms performed by Jesus bring into prominence what Luke otherwise associates with Jesus' healings, namely, his task to overthrow Satan's empire. The special material in Luke is resonant with the theme of a conflict with Satan, who is depicted as Jesus' foe. At the conclusion of the temptation story, 4:13 postpones the further approach of Satan until an "opportune time," presumably to be dated in the Gethsemane episode and providing a superficial justification for Conzelmann's well-known dictum that the central phase of the ministry is Satan-free.[17] But 22:28, with its use of the perfect tense, "you have continued with me in my trials" (peirasmoi), is an indirect proof that such peirasmoi were a feature of the entire ministry and suggests an involvement with demonic powers in such places as 10:18, 11:16–18, and 13:16. The notion of a "tempted Christ" who is yet victorious has obvious practical, hortatory significance for this evangelist, as we shall later observe.

Luke Has an Interest in Jesus' Offer of Forgiveness

The Lucan Jesus stands out as the friend of "sinners." By this term the reader is meant to understand not only the fallen and the socially disgraced,

---

14. Ibid., p. 112.

15. Otto Merk, "Das Reich Gottes in den lukanischen Schriften," in Jesus und Paulus, ed. E. E. Ellis and Erich Grässer (Göttingen: Vandenhoeck & Ruprecht, 1975), pp. 201–20.

16. Franklin, Christ the Lord, pp. 19–21.

17. Theology of St. Luke, p. 80.

but those whom the official Jewish leaders disowned as "Jews who had made themselves as Gentiles," that is, they were unconcerned about the technical details of rabbinic religion, such as tithing, Sabbath observance, and ceremonial cleanness, and had compromised their "Jewishness" by contact with the Gentiles. The actions and parables of Jesus[18] in Luke are consonant with a concern for the social and religious outcasts of his day, particularly in his offer of table-fellowship to "publicans and prostitutes" (5:29–32; 15:1, 2; 19:5–7) that has to be viewed in the light of the expected "banquet of the blessed" in God's kingdom (14:15). Jesus is announcing that his meals with sinners are an anticipatory token of what God intends to do, that is, to receive sinners at his heavenly table. This dimension to his action in eating with sinners seems clearly to explain the innuendo leveled at him as "a glutton and a drunkard, a friend of tax collectors and sinners" (7:33–35, RSV).[19]

His entire life mediated the forgiveness of God, so it is not surprising that Luke should place on his lips words of pardon as he stood at the cross (23:34). It is exactly in keeping with Luke's motif that, in a post-resurrection scene, the mission charge (cast in the creedal form of *oratio obliqua*) laid on the disciples should be "that repentance and forgiveness of sins should be preached in his name to all nations" (24:47, RSV). The final phrase picks up yet another Lucan theme distinctive of Messiah's work.

Jesus' Ministry in This Gospel Reaches Out to Embrace Non-Jews

It is well known how Luke accentuates Jesus' concern for women and children, thus earning him the encomium of Dante, "the scribe of Christ's gentleness." It is just as evident that Luke departs characteristically from any model that would have restricted Jesus' ministry to the Jews. At 2:32, the *Nunc Dimittis* proclaims him "a light to be a revelation to the Gentiles" as well as "glory" for Israel (borrowing language from the servant motif in Isa. 49:6). The citation of Isaiah 40:3–5 (common in part to all Synoptics) is carried forward to include "And all mankind shall see the deliverance [*sotērion*, borrowed from LXX; MT and 1QIs[a] have "glory"] of God" (3:6)—an addition not represented in Matthew (3:3) or Mark

18. Actions: 7:36–50; 9:51–56; 17:11–19; 19:1–10; 23:32, 39, 43; parables: 10: 30–37; 14:15–24; 18:10–14.
19. G. N. Stanton, *Jesus of Nazareth in New Testament Preaching* (Cambridge: University Press, 1975), pp. 138–46.

(1:3). The genealogy of Jesus is traced back to Adam (3:38) as if to emphasize his participation in the common life of all men.

In the exigencies of the ministry, Jesus goes out of his way to show interest in and concern for the non-Jews. In the programmatic announcement of his Nazareth "sermon," both Elijah and Elisha have sympathetic dealings with non-Israelites (widow of Sarepta, Naaman), who appear in a favorable light. Tax collectors who were regarded as no better than Gentiles are shown to be responsive, in their attitudes both to John the Baptist (3:12) and in their acceptance of Jesus' message (7:29f.). The Gentile centurion in Capernaum is praised by both Jews (as a godfearer, after the manner of Cornelius, Acts 10) and Jesus, whose word of commendation is framed (in 7:9; contrast Matt. 8:10, which condemns Jewish unbelief) to make the Gentile an exemplar of faith unparalleled in Israel.

The pericope of 13:22–30 poses special problems. The judgment on Israel, recorded in Matthew 8:11–12 as a sequel to the healing of the Gentile centurion's slave, is transferred from the earlier story in Luke and placed in chapter 13 (vv. 28f.) in connection with the parable of the shut door. But there are differences. The order given in Matthew implying that the Gentiles are included in the kingdom (8:11) and that the sons of the kingdom are ejected (8:12) is inverted. It is as the Jews (first) refused and so were self-excluded that the "door of faith" was opened to the Gentiles (Acts 14:27), and through it they came streaming into the kingdom from all points. As a second feature in Luke's version we should notice his inclusion of verse 30, which is added to enforce the same point, namely, that the mission of Jesus extends to the Gentiles. Finally, the commission in 24:47 specifies the Gentiles as those who heed the call and offer of repentance and pardon. Luke's interest in the Gentile mission is a positive conclusion in recent study, and attempts to deny it have not met with much success.[20]

The Climax of Messiah's Task is Reached in Jerusalem

The framework of the so-called travel narrative (9:51—18:14/19:44)[21] is given for the ostensible reason of explaining how Jesus left Galilee and came to Jerusalem. Jesus is thus brought on his way by a circuitous route

---

20. See the monograph by S. G. Wilson, *The Gentiles and the Gentile Mission in Luke-Acts* (Cambridge: University Press, 1973).

21. For a full survey of recent opinion on the travel narrative, see James L. Resseguie, "Interpretation of Luke's Central Section (Luke 9:51—19:44) since 1856," *Studia Biblica et Theologica* (Fuller Theological Seminary) 5.2 (1975): 3–36.

until at length he stands before the city gates (19:28). The Old Testament testimonium (in v. 38), which is followed by the lament over Jerusalem (19:41–44), suggests that Luke wished to indicate the connection between Jesus' entry and his forecast of rejection in the parable of 19:11–27. At all events, the solemnity of judgment on Israel (seen, e.g., in 20:18, L) is brought out in anticipation of Israel's fateful rejection of its Messiah.

1. *The passion* narrative, starting with the solemn introduction (22:1), designed to prepare them for Jesus' death as a sacrificial offering,[22] is set within a paschal frame (22:7, 11, 15), with the mention of the various cups and dishes (in the longer text) contributing to this emphasis (22:17–20).

2. *The loneliness and humanity of Jesus* are prominent in Luke. Of these features there are several examples, of which we may select 22:28, where Jesus is grateful for human companionship; 22:35–38, on which T. W. Manson's comment is *apropos*, "This short dialogue throws a brilliant light on the tragedy of the Ministry," with verse 36 expressing "the utterance of a broken heart";[23] the vivid detail of the agony in Gethsemane (22:39–46); the placing of the mockery (22:63–65) *before* the trial and not after it (as in Mark 14:65), which highlights the injustice and callousness of the horseplay, suggestive of a piece of buffoonery in which Jesus is called on to "prophesy," that is, name the man who struck him (contrast Matt. 26:68 and Mark 14:65, where the mockery "fulfills" Isa. 50:5f.); the lament on the *via dolorosa* (23:28–31), addressed to the women of Jerusalem; and the presence of "partners in distress" (23:39–43) and the contrition of the crowd (23:48), which add a certain relief to the somber tragedy. With the substitution of the confident cry "Father, into your hands" (23:46) in place of the Marcan-Matthean utterance of abandonment, the Lucan passion narrative closes on a note of quiet expectation that the end is not here. Rather, the cross is the road to glory; already "today" Jesus will be in paradise (23:43).

3. The passion story is told in such a way that *Jewish involvement carries all the marks of culpable responsibility*. When we come to read the actual trial scenario and regard the strange "neutrality" of Pilate, it becomes evident that Luke is implicating the Jewish leaders. He passes over the first interrogation before the council (22:54) that is explicit in Mark-Matthew. In 22:67–71 he is intent on showing that the Jewish trial is a mockery: there are no charges preferred, no accusing witnesses at hand, no testimony,

---

22. Conzelmann, *Theology of St. Luke*, p. 79.
23. *The Sayings of Jesus* (London: SCM Press, 1949), p. 341.

and no formal verdict.[24] Indeed, the travesty climaxes in the cry "Why do we still need evidence? We have ourselves heard it from his own mouth." The latter reference provides the Lucan key: "from his own mouth" takes us back to a series of L passages (4:22; 11:54; 19:22) that describe scenes of self-incrimination.[25] Thereafter (23:26) "they" (i.e., the Jews) carry into execution the non-Roman verdict (23:25) and lead Jesus to his death. The prayer (in 23:34) "Father, forgive them" is apparently directed to the Romans, who are the unwitting agents, but the real guilt stands to the account of the Jews. "This Jesus . . . *you* crucified and killed by the hands of lawless men" (Acts 2:23, RSV; cf. Acts 3:14f.; 7:52; 13:28) sums it up.

4. A well-attested feature of the kerygma recorded in Acts is *the use made of the Old Testament to show that Messiah's death and vindication were foretold*. The language used includes the servant passage as well as the expectation of the Mosaic prophet (Acts 3:13, 21–23, 26; 4:30). Yet the servant of Yahweh is introduced to explain the glorification and enthronement of Jesus rather than his obedience to death, and there is no clearly worked-out soteriology in Acts (except possibly for 20:28).

The same holds true for the Gospel. Luke is just as committed to a scheme of promise-and-fulfillment as are the other evangelists in that he knows that what occurred in the death and resurrection of the Messiah was foretold "in all the scriptures" (24:25–27, 32, 44–46). But there are differences.

Much has been made of the alleged Lucan transposition of Mark 10:45 by which the ransom saying has become an innocuous "I am among you as one who serves" (22:27, RSV), though it is more likely that each evangelist is following an independent tradition. At the Last Supper the "interpreting words" are different, and the Isaianic overtones in Mark (14:24) are replaced by emphasis on the new covenant (22:20, longer text). It is with the covenant that Luke is particularly concerned, as we can see from 22:29, and the assigning-by-covenant (*diatithemai*) of places at the Messiah's table in his kingdom is connected with judging the twelve tribes of Israel. It seems that his understanding of Jesus' death was less that of concern with the significance of atonement than with the practical, pastoral mediation of forgiveness by the establishing of the new covenant of Jeremiah 31:31–34.[26] It is the covenantal aspects of the Old Testament that

---

24. Paul W. Walaskay, "The Trial and Death of Jesus in the Gospel of Luke," *JBL* 94 (1975): 81–93.

25. David R. Catchpole, *The Trial of Jesus* (Leiden: E. J. Brill, 1971), p. 201.

26. But I. Howard Marshall has a more positive appreciation of the soteriological significance of Luke's account of the passion (*Luke: Evangelist and Theologian* [Grand Rapids: Zondervan Publishing House, 1971], pp. 171–75).

interested him most, and it is arguable that the servant passages are more closely tied to Isaiah 49:6–8 than Isaiah 53, which even when it is quoted in Acts 8:32f. does not teach explicitly the atoning significance of the servant's work. The value of this aspect of the servant's ministry, namely, that he unites men in a covenantal relationship with God by the offer of forgiveness, would have special appeal for Luke, for he can apply the vocation of the *ebed Yahweh* in Isaiah 49:6 to the apostolic mission (Acts 13: 47) as well as to the messianic ministry of Jesus (2:32; 4:18f.). And he can demonstrate from the fact that the *ebed* is glorified (Isa. 52:13; 53:11) as God's "righteous" one (23:47; Acts 3:14; 7:52; 22:14) the inevitable consequence of his then being the dispenser of the Holy Spirit (Acts 2:33) at the ascension. A pastoral and paraenetic interest in Luke predominates throughout.

THE COST OF DISCIPLESHIP

The essentially pastoral concerns of the third evangelist are never more clearly visible than in his insistence on the *demands of discipleship*. What J. C. O'Neill says of the six "Amen" sayings in Luke is true of the drift of the entire Gospel: "We are witnessing the beginnings of Pastoral Theology."[27] At all points Luke *is not composing his work as a detached narrator; he is seeking to elicit a response in the present by his recital of past events. For him Jesus is the Savior whose work, begun in his ministry, is now continued in his risen life and exalted ministry in the church.* The ascension is the hinge on which the work of salvation turns. The earthly ministry led up to it (9:51; 13:32; 24:51); the coming of the Spirit is consequent upon it (Acts 2:33), and as living Lord-in-the-Spirit he continues to confront men with his offer and demand of grace in the gospel. We have surveyed briefly the offer of messianic blessedness in salvation; it is time to evaluate the demands the Jesus of Luke's story made and still makes to the church.

The Eschatological Motif

The Lord's parousia is anticipated through the use of an eschatological motif which Luke offers as an incentive to Christian conduct. He emphasizes the present lordship of Jesus and his exaltation as head of the messianic community. But he has still retained the strain of earnest expectation

---

27. "The Six Amen Sayings in Luke," *JTS*, n.s., 10 (1959): 1–9, esp. 9.

that "the end will come" (Acts 1:11).[28] No doubt he is reflecting on and reacting to a situation in the church where the postponement of the parousia was an occasion of perplexity and loss of confidence. To such a predicament he held out the message of hope that, after Jesus had suffered and been rejected by "this generation" (17:25), the day when the Son of Man is revealed (17:30) will occur.

There are several aspects of Jesus' teaching in Luke that are tinged with this eschatological hope, to be fulfilled "soon if not immediately" (21: 32, 36). Parables of watchfulness in 12:13–21 (the rich fool) and 12:35–40 (the ready servant) gain the forcefulness expressed in their punch lines from the fact that the urgent summons comes at an unknown time (v. 20). The trustworthy and prudent steward does not know the hour of his master's return (v. 43), so that even if the "master is a long time in coming" (v. 45) he is continually alert. Luke seems clearly to be answering the implied objection that the delay of the parousia means that he will not come soon.

The section 17:20–37 is composed of Q and L material, and the introductory question implied in verse 20, What is the nature of the kingdom and when does it come?, is answered by the double insistence that (1) there is no parousia without the cross (v. 25); yet (2) the "day of the Son of Man" will come, but not to those who (idly) watch for it (v. 20) or to those who think it will never arrive. The same two objections to problems of the parousia are encountered in Acts 1:9–11. When the day does come, it will be unexpected and destructive to the unwary.

The Interim

Luke's Gospel is replete with warnings against apostasy and loss of faith[29] between the "going" and the "coming" of the Son of Man because it is a period full of danger to the church. The dangers he foresees both from within the fellowship of the church and from the outside fall under the rubric of "time of temptation" (*peirasmos*) (8:13).

External threats are described in 12:1–12, a passage that conflates Mark, Q, and L material. The Lucan emphasis comes at verse 11, where "before synagogues, rulers and authorities" is added; and this setting is made the occasion for the warning, set in a different place in Mark and Matthew, about the "blasphemy against the Holy Spirit" (v. 10). Severe hardships,

---

28. Wilson, *Gentiles*, pp. 84ff.
29. See Schuyler Brown, *Apostasy and Perseverance in the Theology of Luke* (Rome: Pontifical Biblical Institute, 1969).

involving death (12:4f.), were evidently leading to a loss of nerve. So Luke
has both encouragements to persevere (18:1–8) and warnings lest faithful
Christians become censorious of the *lapsi* (17:1–4). God will vindicate the
true believer, mirrored in the widow who persistently cries out for justice.
He will answer "speedily" (18:8), though verse 8b implies that when he
does so it will be unexpectedly (as 17:22–37). If the "Son of Man" is dis-
appointed at faith's absence, how much more will the negligent Christians
be covered with shame?

Total Demands of Discipleship

Luke underscores, above all, that there is a rigorism accompanying the
Christian life, and he illustrates it in several ways. Clearly the bringing together of the various candidates for discipleship in 9:57–62 serves a single
purpose. It is not an easygoing choice that counts (v. 57), nor are excuses
permitted (v. 60), nor can delay in accepting Jesus' call be rationalized
(v. 61). These episodes are from Q, but Luke has driven home the thrust
of Jesus' demand by relating it to the preaching of the "kingdom of God"
(v. 60), which is the criterion underlying his call (v. 62, L). The need to
consider the requirements of true allegiance is spelled out in 14:25–35,
which brings together L parables (the incomplete building, the king going
to battle) and Q material on conditions of discipleship (hating parents and
the metaphor of salt: par. Matt. 10:37f.; 5:13). But there are some differences. Luke has intensified and deepened the cost by his addition of family relations to Matthew's "father or mother" in 14:26. Most of all, he has
added to Q "even his own life also" as a part of the total demand.

This could be interpreted in a non-literal fashion and taken to be a powerful reminder that the would-be disciple must surrender his claim to
wealth (the warning is directed personally to the rich ruler in 18:24: contrast Matt. 19:23; Mark 10:23). This would be consonant with Luke's admittedly ambivalent purpose of being opposed to riches yet teaching their
true value elsewhere in the Gospel.[30] But "self-denial" means far more in
Luke. A reference to "carrying [*bastazein*] the cross" and "coming *after*
[*opisō*] Jesus" in 14:27 suggests an almost literal acceptance of the death
that Jesus died. Luke borrows terminology from the passion story (cf. John
19:17), as though to stress that discipleship may be synonymous with
martyrdom (Acts 7:54–60). Yet he picks up another idea that makes him
an advocate of moral heroism when to Mark's "let him deny himself and

---

30. The *Umwertung* motif is seen at 1:52f., 6:20–26, and 16:19–31, while a more
positive attitude to the use of wealth underlies 16:1–13.

take up the cross and follow me" (8:34, RSV) he adds "daily" (9:23), as though to reflect his knowledge of Paul's constant dangers in a hostile world (I Cor. 15:31; II Cor. 4:11f.). Discipleship is a costly commitment, and there is no easy road to glory. "Through many tribulations we must enter the kingdom of God" (Acts 14:22, RSV) is a caveat just as applicable to the Christian life in the Gospel as in Luke's second volume. There is the promise that as the suffering Jesus has now been exalted (24:26) so the faithful Christian may expect no less (14:11; 21:19).

16.

The Shape
of Luke's Gospel in
Lectionaries

Frederick W. Danker

The way in which the Gospel of Luke is presented in the lectionaries brings out the dominant concerns and purposes of the evangelist himself.

In 1969 the Sacred Congregation for Divine Worship published a three-
year system of three appointed lessons for each Sunday and festival of the
church year. The Protestant Episcopal Church in the United States adapted
this *Ordo Lectionum Missae* for its own constituency in 1970. Presbyterians
followed a similar procedure for their *Worshipbook*, also published in 1970.
And in 1973 an organization of representatives from four Lutheran bodies
of America, known as the Inter-Lutheran Commission on Worship
(ILCW), published their three-year system.[1]

A special feature of all these systems is the fresh attention paid to inter-
relationship of the various parts of the service and to the importance of
following as much as possible the thread of thought in a complete book,
especially the Gospels and some of the Epistles. This means that the worshiper is expected to derive some appreciation of the meaning of a given
pericope from its liturgical as well as its literary context. The fact that there
is a great deal of correspondence between the lectionaries also means that
the worshiper benefits from a broad range of biblical understanding and
scholarly expertise. This circumstance, combined with the church's concern to proclaim what was first written out of a context of proclamation,
suggests that also the scholar, whether professional exegete or professional
proclaimer, may have something to learn from the wealth of the church's

---

1. *The Church Year: Calendar and Lectionary,* Contemporary Worship 6 (Minneapolis: Augsburg Publishing House; Philadelphia: Board of Publication of the Lutheran
Church in America; St. Louis: Concordia Publishing House, 1973).

wisdom, either by way of stimulation for pursuit of fresh directions in understanding his author's mind, or for control of capricious research. Also, it may be hoped, the church will benefit from the scholar's rejoinders in dialogue.

The present study is confined to the mode of treatment Luke's Gospel undergoes at the hand of the framers of the four lectionaries usually cited in *Proclamation: Aids for Interpreting the Lessons of the Church Year*.[2] Particular attention is paid to the question of grasping Luke's multifaceted thought and to the impression that might be conveyed by the liturgical context of Luke's pericopes. For benefit of easy reference for use by proclaimers, the selected pericopes, most of which are located in Series C, are presented according to their sequence of use in the church year.

ADVENT

Luke 21:25–36

All the lectionaries assign Luke 21:25–36 as the first Gospel text in the season of Advent. In the light of the Old Testament lesson, Jeremiah 33: 14–16, the worshiper learns that Luke here approaches a problem perennial in the church: How are the messianic credentials of Jesus to be maintained in the face of historical developments that appear to contradict his claim to be in continuity with Israel's eschatological hopes? The Old Testament lection promised safety for Judah and security for Jerusalem under a Davidic deliverer. This salvation was expected to take place within history and as a triumph for the nation of Israel. Luke takes seriously the literal historical dimension of such messianic hope and incorporates it in the Benedictus (chap. 1, esp. vv. 68–72), in terminology drawn from Isaiah and the psalms. Jesus is the messianic deliverer, Luke affirms, and he would have spelled the promised security to Israel, as the Gospel text for Passion Sunday specifies (19:45). But his nation failed to recognize both his identity (19:42) and its own obligation to enrich the world through him (2:32).[3]

---

2. Published by Fortress Press, Philadelphia, this publication appeared in three major sets, corresponding to the three lectionary systems, each set consisting of seven booklets. Each of the series is distinguished by its concentration on a single Gospel during the Sundays after Pentecost: Series A, Matthew; Series B, Mark; Series C, Luke. The booklets present, with few exceptions, the following four major lectionaries in columns: Lutheran, Roman Catholic, Episcopalian, Presbyterian, and UCC. These are abbreviated below as follows: LC, RC, EP, PR.

3. See Frederick W. Danker, *Luke*, Proclamation Commentaries (Philadelphia: Fortress Press, 1976), chap. 6.

Rejection of the Messiah required therefore a fresh hermeneutic if Old Testament hope was not to be completely shattered, or if the attachment of that hope to Jesus was not to be viewed as misplaced. Luke's answer included the following: (1) all understanding of the Old Testament begins with the life of Jesus as expression of the divine will displayed in the Old Testament Scriptures (cf. 24:27, 44); (2) Jesus is the definitive Messiah and Lord (2:11; Acts 2:36), and Israel's rejection of him does not invalidate Old Testament hope; (3) in the face of rejection, God in his great mercy restores Jesus to Israel and to the world, with possibility for fresh hope (Luke 24:47). In fact, affirms Luke, the kingdom of God comes in two phases: it is reality now but will disclose itself in extraordinary advent at the end of history; therefore, Jesus' followers need not be anxious about his credentials. Even in the face of disasters, as displayed in Luke 21:25–26, Jesus Christ is in charge.

Since apocalyptic hope includes the prospect of justice and righteousness (cf. 1:75), Jesus, in Luke's text for the day, warns his followers not to retreat from the hard responsibility of facing life at its worst. Such retreat can take place through the devil-may-care route of dulling one's brains, whatever the means, or of so immersing oneself in the routines of existence that one forgets, as did the rich fool (12:16–21), the purpose of life. The latter method bears a more respectable facade than does the other, but without appreciable difference in effect, namely, a deadening of sensitivity for the rumble of the future that is to be heard in the shockwaves of the present.

Luke 3:1–6

Association of fervent hope with moral earnestness finds reiteration in the adoption of Luke 3:1–6 as the third lesson on the Second Sunday in Advent. However, the use of Malachi 3:1–4 as the Old Testament reading in the Lutheran rite distorts the shape of Luke's Gospel, for at 3:4–6 Luke is at pains to weed out of his Marcan source any reference to John the Baptist as Malachi's eschatological messenger. Jesus' credentials are not to be subject to the vagaries of any attempt to find a correspondence or lack of it between expectation based on interpretation of Malachi's message and actual historical circumstances.

Luke 3:7–18

To lend force to their understanding of Luke's use of Isaianic prophecy, all the lectionaries include as Gospel lesson for Advent III Luke's recital of John the Baptist's proclamation (3:10–18, with vv. 7–9 included in the

LC and EP). Thus Luke's inferential *oun* (v. 7) is taken seriously, and the association of ideas in verses 7 and 8 is kept in orbit with Luke's further interpretation in Acts 8:21–22 and 13:10. Inclusion of verses 7–9 in the Lutheran and Episcopalian rites not only reveals the artistic unity in Luke's pericope, but suggests that the decisive action spelled out in verse 17 is intimately connected with quality of religious claim. Luke 16:19–31 displays the apocalyptic kickback in shallow appeal to "Father Abraham." Approved liturgical recitation is no warranty for the future. Religious appearances are no substitute for genuine repentance. By calling attention to this theme, these two lectionaries express even more sharply that the outcome of the promise is intimately connected with moral response. Thereby apocalyptic hope is released from fixation on specific prophetic blueprints, and Christian ethics is not at the mercy of fluctuations in eschatological pronouncements or visions.

The use of Zephaniah 3:14–18 alongside the Gospel undergirds appreciation of the ethical integrity of Lucan eschatology. Zephaniah anticipated renewal (v. 17), interpreted by John the Baptist as "fruits of repentance"; and victory over the enemy (v. 15) is now viewed as elimination of all that is opposed to the Holy Spirit (Luke 3:16f.). Thus the lectionaries, in correct apprehension of Luke's understanding of the decisive and therefore eschatological character of God's donation of the Holy Spirit, affirm that Advent is not to be divorced from consideration of the significance of Pentecost.

Luke 1:39–49

Since Luke does not lend support to traditional liturgical interpretation of the protocol of atonement, the lectionaries find it difficult to bring Luke into line with accepted soteriological terminology. Some attempt is made with the use of Hebrews 10:5–10 on Advent IV, but the worshiper might be inclined to conclude that Luke himself sponsors replacement of the old, with special reference to the sacrificial system as a model for understanding the function of Jesus Christ in the economy of salvation. According to Luke, the death of Jesus is not in itself designed by God as the means of solving the human problem. Rather, it is the result of human ignorance and malice in the face of divine donation (cf. Acts 3:13f., 17). However, God exercises executive privilege. Having raised Jesus from the dead, thereby reaffirming his credentials as Messiah and Lord (Acts 2:36), he uses his apostolic emissaries to proclaim pardon in the name of Jesus (see Acts 5:31f.).

Luke 1:26–38

The fact that the church continues such proclamation is evidence for the earnestness with which it understands the story of the annunciation, used in Series B on Advent IV. By incorporating this text in Advent, the lectionaries reveal sensitivity to Luke's understanding of eschatology. The traditional anticipation of a Davidic deliverer finds expression in verses 26–33, but apparently it is understood that the validity of the promise in II Samuel 7:8–11, 16 (the Old Testament reading) is assured by the Holy Spirit's special intervention in the generation of this Deliverer (Luke 1: 34–36). Thus the credentials of Jesus are preserved from contamination by the vicissitudes of history, and the church can ride out change, disaster, and disappointment of explicit prophetic expectations.

CHRISTMAS

Luke 2:1–14(20)

All or part of Luke 2:1–20 appears in Series A and B of most of the lectionaries as the third reading for the Nativity. The Old Testament reading, Isaiah 9:1–6, with its anticipation of deliverance for the oppressed, offers a bridge to the message of the Magnificat, part of which found usage in the Advent cycle.

Against the background of imperial power structures the humble circumstances of the new King provide a remarkable contrast. The shepherds, who similarly qualify for fresh evaluation of identity in the new age, are also models of the faith that is required for recognition of God's new apocalyptic demonstration, now present in its first phase.

Luke 2:21

With the Lutherans, Roman Catholics and Episcopalians alert their worshipers on January 1 to the importance assigned by Luke to the name "Jesus" (2:21). From the Old Testament readings (Num. 6:22–27, LC, RC; Isa. 9:2–4, 6–7, EP) it is apparent that Luke's labored qualification of the name (v. 21b) is to be grasped as an exposition of divine design fulfilled in the birth of Jesus.

Luke 2:22–52

Traditional association of the First Sunday after Christmas with the theme "Holy Family" leads the Roman Catholic lectionary[4] to interpret

---

4. On the citations here, see *Lectionary for Mass* (New York: Catholic Book Publishing Co., 1970), pp. 37–39.

the principals in Luke 2:22–40 (Series B) and verses 41–52 (Series C) as models of piety: Simeon, an exemplary Israelite; Anna, beyond the call of duty, loyal to her marriage vows; and Jesus, wise beyond his years, obedient to his parents. The question is how these function in the thematic framework of Luke's writing.

From the use of Luke's Gospel during the Advent cycle it is possible to isolate a number of leading themes previewed by Luke: (1) The presence of salvation in the person of Jesus; (2) reversal in fortune of the lowly and the mighty; (3) the need of faith in the face of divine unfolding of history; (4) two-phase apocalyptic; (5) necessity of repentance for realization of the reign of God; (6) futility of reliance on religious form without moral vitality; (7) the Holy Spirit as integral factor in eschatological decision; (8) forgiveness as exercise of divine executive privilege; (9) universality of divine generosity.

In the text under discussion, numbers 1, 2, 6, 7, and 8 from above are overtly present. The observations on piety are therefore subordinate to one or more of these themes. Now a dominant interest of Luke's is his desire to document crucial developments through the presence of two or more witnesses (cf. 8:51; 9:28, 30f.; 10:1; 19:29; 22:8; 23:14f.; 24:4, 13). Quite evidently Simeon and Anna are Luke's prime witnesses to the presence of salvation in the person of the infant Jesus. Their piety is especially emphasized by Luke to show that recognition of God's salvation is connected with religious integrity and to demonstrate that Jesus' credentials were acknowledged in Jerusalem by two of the most devout Israelites. Through such emphasis Luke provided a point of contrast for the pondering of Jesus' later rejection in the same city, a rejection anticipated by Simeon himself (vv. 34f.).

Luke 2:36–52

For the first two Sundays after Christmas the Presbyterian lectionary goes its own way and features wisdom as a basic motif, first in 2:41–52 and then in verses 36–40. The choice of Old Testament (Isa. 45:18–22) and New Testament (Rom. 11:33—12:2) readings for the first of the two Sundays, and Job 28:20–28 and I Corinthians 1:18–25 for the second, displays fine insight into Lucan theological presuppositions, including especially the preeminent claim of the Creator on his creatures. Jesus, who is later declared greater than Solomon (11:31), is a prime model of wisdom, for he identifies completely with his Father's will and purpose (2:49). Because of the uniqueness of his commitment, his Davidic credentials are in Luke's record subordinate to his identity as the Son of God (see again the progression of thoughts in 1:31–35). The crucifixion will reveal the depth of his commitment, and that which appears to be God's weak folly will be proclaimed as his powerful display of wisdom (I Cor. 1:18–25).

In Series B the Presbyterian lectionary combines Luke's recitals of the naming of Jesus (2:21) and his presentation in the Temple (vv. 22–24) for consideration on the Second Sunday after Christmas. In association with the Old Testament (Isa. 60:1–5) and New Testament (Rev. 21:22– 22:2) readings the worshiper will sense that the ceremonies cited in the text have significance far beyond their Jewish sphere. Completely imbedded in the liturgical life and customs of Israel, this child is "holy to the Lord" (v. 23) in the unique way mentioned earlier at Luke 1:35, in connection with Advent IV in Series B. At the same time, it is part of the mystery of his person that while being a Jew born and bred he initiates a movement that will ultimately, as Luke is at pains to document, lead to liberation from dependence on the temple and its cult. As anticipated in Isaiah 60:3, the realm of the sacred will embrace the world. Considered from this point of view, Luke would have found congenial the use of Revelation 21: 22–22:2.

EPIPHANY

Luke 3:1–17, 21–22

Luke's recital of circumstances surrounding the baptism of Jesus challenges the proclaimer to be equal to a large assignment. Especially interesting is the Presbyterian lineup of readings for the First Sunday after Epiphany (Gen. 1:1–5; Eph. 2:11–18; Luke 3:15–17, 21–22). In profound appreciation of Lucan thought, this lectionary shows that the universality of Jesus' reign (as documented in the Advent and Christmas cycles) is intimately connected with the universal jurisdiction God enjoys by right of creation (see, e.g., Acts 17:24ff.). The Spirit operative at creation's dawn is the same Spirit who begets Jesus (1:35) and, at Pentecost, the church (1:8). Universality of claim presupposes for Luke universal outreach under the direction of the one Spirit (24:46–49). Receipt of the Spirit apart from standard cultic routines also puts an end to parochial divisions (Acts 11:16f.).

Luke 4:14–21

Luke's programmatic set of pericopes, 4:14–21 and verses 22–30, is so packed with anticipation of his subsequent expositions that his hearers and readers will be grateful to the lectionaries for alerting them to aspects they might otherwise have missed.

For the Third Sunday after Epiphany, the RC and PR lectionaries prompt the worshiper to consider 4:14–21 in the light of Nehemiah 8:1–10. Just as Nehemiah and his associates interpreted the reading of the Law for the people, so Jesus interprets the prophet Isaiah for his townspeople, but with a difference—he himself is the hermeneutic for the old: the prophecy finds fulfillment "today" (Luke 4:21). The RC lectionary ties into this note of fulfillment by prefacing the reading of Luke 4:14–21 with 1:1–4. Thereby the entire Gospel is viewed as a biblical scenario (see also 24:44). The Lutherans and Episcopalians use as Old Testament reading Isaiah 61:1–6, with intent to focus on Jesus' identity as the Servant of the Lord.

Luke 4:21–30

Judiciously set aside for contemplation on a separate Sunday (Fourth after Epiphany) is the sequel (4:21–30) to Jesus' inaugural disclosure at Nazareth. All the lectionaries appear to feature Luke's universal scope for the proclamation of Jesus, who like the prophet Jeremiah (Jer. 1:4f.) received divine appointment prior to his birth. Through juxtaposition of 1:17–19 next to verses 4–5 in the Old Testament reading (others read vv. 4–10) the RC lectionary suggests how central to Luke's Gospel is his awareness of the hostility Jesus is destined to receive from the civil and religious establishments. The stress in the Gospel reading on the activities of Elijah and Elisha indicates how well the prophetic model is adapted for assessment of Jesus and his mission. Having divorced John the Baptist as much as possible from the Elijah-Elisha role, Luke now casts Jesus in that mold, but with a view to demonstrating later (9:18–36) how he transcends any and every prophetic pattern (cf. Acts 3:24).

Luke 5:1–11

Consideration of the placement of Luke 5:1–11 in the church year (Epiphany V) will contribute to fresh appreciation of the function of this pericope in the Gospel. Himself the Servant of the Lord *par excellence*, Jesus selects the first of twelve who are to form the nucleus of Israel in a mission of servanthood to the world. In the face of divine generosity displayed in the tremendous catch of fish, Peter identifies himself as a *hamartōlos*, that is, one who is not accustomed to moving in the circles of the holy. But Jesus, in his response, sets the pattern for his ministry of association with "publicans and sinners" and at the same time pronounces absolution by making Simon a partner in his chief enterprise.

Luke 9:28–36

For observance of the transfiguration all the lectionaries, with the exception of the Presbyterian, use Luke 9:28–36 as Gospel reading. However, the variation in Old Testament readings and in calendric placement suggests different directions for interpretation of the pericope. In the LC rite the observance of the transfiguration climaxes the Epiphany. cycle and anticipates the period of Lent. Thereby Luke's theme of Jesus' suffering (v. 31) as the pathway to glory (see esp. 24:26) finds clear enunciation. Deuteronomy 34:1–12 observes that Moses had no rival as prophet. In keeping with the basic motif of Epiphany, the lectionary shows that Jesus superseded even Moses. If Israel paid attention to Moses, how much more ought the disciples to heed Jesus' announcements of the route he must take to carry out the Father's purpose (Luke 9:35; cf. v. 22).

The EP lectionary uses Deuteronomy 8:1–8, 5–6 as Old Testament reading in observance of the transfiguration. The stress here on obedient attention to Moses suggests that the Lucan pericope comes to focus at 9:35. However, unless the proclaimer heeds the hermeneutical nudge given by his liturgical calendar he might be prompted to engage in a general moralistic discourse on obedience to Jesus.

Roman Catholics use the Lucan pericope both on August 6, a traditional date for observance of the transfiguration, and together with the Presbyterians on the Second Sunday in Lent. In the first instance, August 6, Daniel 7:9–10, 13–14 and II Peter 1:16–19 set the pattern for understanding the pericope in terms of second-phase apocalyptic. Similarly, the choice of Genesis 15:5–12, 17–18 and Philippians 3:17—4:1 as first and second lesson for the Second Sunday in Lent point to the motif of reversal of fortunes: Abraham, a childless nomad, becomes an illustrious ancestor; lowly bodies of Christians are to be transformed into glorious bodies; and Jesus will return as a glorious Son of Man.

Luke 23:35–43

Instead of the traditional text, 9:28–36, the Presbyterians adopt Luke 23:35–43 for observance of the transfiguration. This arrangement contributes a strikingly fresh dimension for the understanding of Luke's line of thought. At this climactic moment of the crucifixion Jesus makes a royal proclamation welcoming the criminal to association with himself in paradise. Thus both the criminal and Jesus experience transfiguration at the very nadir of their lives. The divine voice at the original transfiguration

had said, "This is my beloved Son, listen to him" (9:35). At the crucifixion Jesus' identity as God's Son is made a butt of mockery, but his sonship is confirmed by the Father in extraordinary demonstration (23:44ff.),
and the criminal had in his own way "listened."

The same lectionary's use of I Corinthians 15:20–28 displays a line of
continuity between the theology of Paul and Luke, both of whom inex-
tricably link, albeit in distinctive ways, the believer's destiny with that of
Jesus. The Old Testament reading, II Samuel 5:1–4, reminds the worshiper
that the One who invited the criminal to his royal quarters that day can
boast of the lineage pronounced by the angel at Luke 1:32–33.

LENT

Luke 5:29–35

Presbyterian usage of Luke 5:29–35 as a reading for Ash Wednesday
sheds light on Luke's moral theology. According to Zechariah 7:4–10, the
Old Testament reading, God is more interested in justice, kindness, and
mercy than in fasting. To lead sinners to repentance, Jesus' avowed goal
(Luke 5:32), would mean a desirable increment of righteousness. How
then can the genius of ritual reside in exclusion of the sinner? It is counterproductive and against God's own interests. Moreover, the rescue of the
sinner ought to take place in the context of celebration: "eating and drinking," as the Pharisees deride it (v. 33). The theme is familiar from Luke
15. As Zechariah 8:19 affirms, morality and joy are correlatives. The LC
lectionary for the Fourth Sunday in Lent is similarly oriented in its association of Isaiah 12:1–6 with Luke 15:1–3, 11–32.

Luke 4:1–11

All the lectionaries use 4:1–11 on the First Sunday in Lent. This choice
welds the progression of the church year to the dramatic logic in Luke's
Gospel. The temptation scene will echo with crescendo in the crucifixion
narrative (23:35ff.) when Satan finds his climactic hour (22:53).

Luke 13:1–9

One of Luke's theological linchpins is the Old Testament view of divine
patience (e.g., Wisd. 11:26—12:10; Joel 2:11–14; Tobit 13:6–13). God
does not immediately pounce on the sinner with retributive judgment. This
means, however, that victims of oppression will themselves require patience,
as affirmed by Luke 13:1–9, the Gospel for the Third Sunday in Lent. But,
as Israel's experience under Pharaoh confirms (Exod. 3:1–8, 10:15; RC
drops vv. 9–12), God will finally move in on the sinner. On the other hand,

failure to recognize the mercy of God in the delay of judgment will invite most certain doom. Jesus' followers are therefore cautioned in Luke 13: 1–9 not to lapse into false security, a reminder that finds support in I Corinthians 10:12–13, part of the second reading for the Third Sunday in Lent. The EP lectionary uses I Samuel 16:1–13 to underscore the thought that one is not to appraise divine judgment on the basis of exterior circumstances. Also, it supports the emphasis on divine mercy with the help of II Corinthians 5:17–21.

Luke 22:14–30

Since Isaiah 43:16–21 (the Old Testament reading for the Fifth Sunday in Lent) envisages a new exodus, the PR lectionary uses Luke 22:14–30 as fulfillment of the expectation and at the same time confirms Luke's indebtedness to the Book of Isaiah. The words in Isaiah 43:19 immediately help recall the recitation of Isaiah 40:3–5 in connection with the beginning of Jesus' public ministry (Luke 3:4–6). Moreover, the Old Testament reading, with its motif of celebration, is appropriate for interpretation of Luke's view of Jesus' last Passover as an introduction to the victory that would take place on Calvary's hill. According to Jesus' announcement in Luke 22:16, the arrival of the kingdom is integrated with his own fate. In line with this expectation and with the promise of verse 30, Luke records at Acts 10:41 that Peter and his associates did indeed eat and drink with Jesus after his resurrection (see also 1:4). Engaged in joint servanthood with their Lord, the apostles went on to declare God's praise.

HOLY WEEK

Luke 19:41–48

Only the PR lectionary records a reading from Luke for Monday in Holy Week: 19:41–48. Just as the Temple was cleared for proper worship of God, so, suggests the lectionary through adoption of Hebrews 9:11–15, Jesus purifies his followers for service. Discounting the probability that a view of atonement foreign to the evangelist might be attributed to him by hearers of the second lesson, the worshiper will not fail to grasp Luke's stern message to all religious leaders and their adherents: Jesus was crucified because those who should have known better did not realize the "things that pertained to their peace" (v. 42; see also Acts 3:13f.). But the Christian community is subject to similar myopia (cf. Acts 1:6ff.), and only through awareness of Luke's constant appeal for Christian integrity will the proclaimer protect and discourage his hearers from anti-Semitic chauvinism.

Luke 22:7–20

For Maundy Thursday the LC lectionary uses Luke 22:7–20 as Gospel reading, but like the PR lectionary for Monday in Holy Week adopts a pericope from Hebrews (10:15–39) as the second lesson. However, the cultic symbolism obscures Luke's view of the kingdom as a collegial enterprise of servanthood with mission to the world under the direction of Jesus Christ, the chief servant.

Whatever the origin of the disputed reading in Luke 22:19–20, the evangelist's own view of what constitutes the "new covenant" comes through at verses 28–30 (cf. Acts 3:25f.).

Luke 23:33–46

On Good Friday the PR lectionary again suggests the sacrificial terminology of Hebrews 10:4–18 as hermeneutical medium for understanding the soteriology in Luke 23:33–46. Luke, however, highlights the reality of Jesus' kingship by recording as the culminating act of his career an executive pardon for the criminal. Use of Lamentations 1:7–12 as the first lesson might well alert the worshiper to a basic point in Luke's work: The destruction of Jerusalem is no sign that Jesus lacked valid messianic credentials. If, on the other hand, the more traditional interpretation of Jesus as the "Man of Sorrows" is suggested, then Luke's text is given a direction alien to the express disclaimer in 23:28–31. The death of Jesus is tragedy only for the unrepentant, for repentance is the proper answer to the crucifixion. The criminal (v. 41) and the crowds, who beat their breasts (v. 48) in a gesture reminiscent of the publican's action in the Temple (18:13), exhibit appropriate response.

EASTER

Luke 24:1–35

In keeping with previous awareness of the importance of the Exodus tradition for Lucan theology, the LC (Luke 24:1–11) and PR (vv. 13–35) lectionaries both fix the resurrection of Jesus in the context of Israel's deliverance from Egypt (Old Testament reading, Exod. 15:1–11). However, the Presbyterians, by concentrating on the encounter on the road to Emmaus, bring into prominent relief a favorite Lucan motif: Jesus at meal with his friends. Alertness to this feature in Luke's soteriology will protect the proclaimer from divorcing Easter and Good Friday. The experience of these two disciples is in fact of the same order as that of the criminal who received assurance of close fellowship with Jesus in the royal celestial garden (traditionally reserved for the righteous) before the sun would set on Good Friday. Easter is not the victory itself, but celebration of the victory that extends from and out of history's darkest hours.

Luke does indeed share the universal Christian hope for the resurrection of God's people (see, e.g., 20:27–40), but this is not a primary stress in 24:1–10, as suggested by the Episcopalians, who read Isaiah 25:6–9 and I Corinthians 15:20–26 on this feast day.

Luke 24:13–49

More integrated with Luke's total approach is the direction given by the Lutherans through use of 24:13–49 on Easter Eve or Easter Monday. The first reading for the day (Dan. 12:1c–3) connects expectation of resurrection with acceptance of responsibility for guidance of others in the way of righteousness. A similar association is made in Luke 24:46–47. Jesus' public ministry was, according to Luke, devoted to search for the lost (see, e.g., chap. 15). As the resurrected Lord he commissions his church to participate in his own mission of service to the world. Thus the followers of Jesus also become candidates for the resurrection. Only in identification with Jesus' servanthood does the church have a future and a hope. Such is Luke's antidote to a self-centered *theologia gloriae*.

Luke 24:44–53

Variation in the textual tradition of 24:51 precludes certainty as to whether Luke intended to refer to the ascension of Jesus in verse 51. However, Acts 1:2 suggests that the text is to be understood in this way, and Luke 9:51 anticipates the ascension as an integral part of Jesus' experience in and near Jerusalem. In any event, the liturgical usage points to a fundamental theological position in Luke: The passion and the resurrection are a reciprocal totality of divine purpose. By presenting the ascension, or its equivalent, on Easter Day, Luke underscores the royal terminology employed in connection with the crucifixion. The kingdom has indeed drawn near, as already affirmed in Luke 10:9, 11 and as Isaiah 51:5 had promised. Like Simeon (2:26), Jesus' disciples realized fulfillment of their master's assurance that they would not die until they had seen the kingdom of God (see 9:27).

PENTECOST

The third readings on the Sundays after Pentecost in Series C are taken from the Gospel of Luke and form in the main a *lectio continua*. In this way the worshiper finds exposure to most of the Gospel within one church year. Only the more striking features of the lectionaries and their understanding of Luke's Gospel during this long period of the church's calendar can, however, be discussed here.

Luke 10:25–37

The third lesson for the Eighth Sunday after Pentecost, Luke 10:25–37, raises the question of Luke's theology of ethics. According to Deuteronomy 30:9–14 (the first lesson for the day), the Word of God is understood as something closely related to the worshiper's inner being. As the New English Bible renders it: "upon your lips and in your heart ready to be kept." In other words, Yahweh's will is not a coercive force but is in tune with what it means to be responsively human. The lawyer thinks the law of Moses is an invitation to in-group selectivity. Jesus reminds him that obedience involves absorption of the *person* in the challenge of encounter, and the lawyer had to admit that "the one who showed mercy" was "neighbor" to the half-dead man. Mercy is not a response to law but is an expression of humanity as well as of the heart of God (cf. Luke 6:36). In the Lucan text a remarkable ethical dimension is made clearer through liturgical exposure: obedience to law and being basically human are correlatives. The total context of Luke's Gospel reveals, of course, that Jesus is the supreme demonstration of God's own merciful character.

Luke 11:1–13

Association of Genesis 18:20–32(33) with Luke 11:1–13 on the Tenth Sunday after Pentecost helps relieve the Lucan text of superficial application. As Abraham pleaded for Sodom, so the church is in servant-mission to the world. To carry out that mission it needs the resources and impulsion of the Spirit. Since there is nothing closer to the Father's heart than this mission, he is more than ready to give the Spirit to those who ask.

Luke 12:32–40

The PR lectionary for the Twelfth Sunday after Pentecost includes II Kings 17:33–40 as first reading. This Old Testament text shows how the settlers of Samaria tried to serve both the Lord of Israel and their own national gods. In contrast to such double-mindedness, Luke 12:32–40 emphasizes the importance of integrity as the church awaits the second phase of the kingdom.

Luke 17:11–19

The third lesson for the Twenty-First Sunday after Pentecost (Luke 17: 11–19) prefaces a crucial pericope on the subject of eschatology (vv. 20–37). At 4:27 Luke observed that only one leper, and a foreigner at that, had been healed in the time of Elisha. Now Jesus heals *ten* at one time. The kingdom of God has indeed begun to make its appearance in its first phase (17:21). Like Ruth, who clings to Naomi and her God (Ruth 1: 1–19a in the LC, and vv. 8–19a in the EP), Naaman will worship only the God of Israel. Similarly, the Samaritan acknowledges God's goodness coming through the person of Israel's Messiah.

Luke 18:9–14

Use of Sirach 35:12–14, 16–18 as Old Testament reading for the Twenty-Third Sunday after Pentecost, in the RC and EP lectionaries, sharpens appreciation of the unity of Luke's triad in 18:1–17. The plaintive plea of the widow (vv. 1–8) finds correspondence in the publican's humble petition for mercy in the third lesson (18:9–14) for this day. Also, the Pharisee's self-avowed liberality is put in the communicable category of a bribe.

Luke 19:1–10

Zacchaeus is Luke's model of a repentant person, and the use of Wisdom 11:23—12:2 in association with Luke 19:1–10 (RC and EP, Twenty-Fourth Sunday after Pentecost) spotlights a basic Lucan theme: repentance and faith mean a change in life-style.

Luke 23:35–43

Appropriately the LC, RC, and EP lectionaries use the climactic pericope in Luke's Gospel on the closing Sunday of the church year. In keeping with Luke's motif of the searching shepherd (15:1–7), the LC and EP lectionaries use Jeremiah 23:2–6 as first lesson. The RC lectionary uses II Samuel 5:1–3, which combines the themes of shepherd and king. Jesus, butt of ridicule for his apparent regal failure, is nevertheless the legitimate King, who moves power in the interests of his subjects.

Luke 6:39–45

With a rather unusual association of lessons (Job 23:1–7; I Cor. 15:54–58; Luke 6:39–45) the PR lectionary sounds for this last Sunday a note of victory in the hope of the resurrection and thus offers an easy transition to the proclamation at the beginning of Advent. Censorious criticism is not the way to life. Admission of one's guilt, however, is not hazardous to one's future, for the Father has displayed his mercy in Jesus Christ. This *is* the gospel according to Saint Luke.

CONCLUSION

Extended examination of the lectionaries cited suggests that their framers found the Third Gospel congenial to their interests. Part of the mystique of the church year is its dramatic character, the interplay of past, present, and future. No writer in the New Testament is more equal than Luke to the acceptance of such challenge. However, a few features stand out with special prominence.

Thematically central is Luke's conviction that the kingdom of God has arrived in connection with Jesus Christ. This means that Luke, like the parcelers of the lessons in the church year, is very conscious of the past but considers the contemporary moment unique. Now imperial decrees are not published without authority; but as the creator with sovereign rights, God can decree as he wishes, and in connection with the one name, Jesus, he declares amnesty for humanity. This means the kingdom is reality. But it appears in two phases, and the church with its acceptance of responsibility for the proclamation of the One Name declares that it lives within the first phase. The second phase comes with the end of history. In effect, then, Jesus' earthly life and the church's experience under his leadership within history form a midpoint between prophetic anticipation and apocalyptic consummation. Much of the lectionaries' use of the Old Testament is in documentation of this fact.

Related to Luke's eschatological thinking is the dynamic function he assigns to the Holy Spirit, both in Christology and ecclesiology. Jesus, as servant of the Lord, born of the Spirit, associates his church through the Spirit with himself in collegial servanthood to the world. In identification with such servanthood the church also finds the hermeneutic for understanding the meaning of the resurrection.

Much of the task of the proclaimer during the church year is to help the worshiper keep a cool head as he encounters a myriad of rebel forces calculated to turn back the kingdom claims of God. The lectionaries, therefore, emphasize with Luke the close relationship between ethical responsibility and eschatological sensitivity. Ultimately it is mercy that is the badge of kings. When obedience is weighed in that balance, the kingdom is indeed at hand.

17.

The Audience of the Fourth Evangelist

PAUL S. MINEAR

> Reading the Fourth Gospel in search of its first audience can
> lead to a fresh awareness of the way in which the contemporary
> disciple is its audience.

Work on this essay has strengthened two convictions of mine. First, this
Gospel is of such a character that study usually leads to progressively
greater bewilderment. Each verse, superficially quite simple, conceals a
highly complex thought-structure that resists efforts to absorb it. As soon
as a reader becomes aware of one riddle, that one riddle leads to a dozen
others, none easily solved. From the earliest times this book has baffled the
ablest interpreters; students, therefore, should be prepared for frustration.
A second conviction is this: My own equipment is quite inadequate for
contributing substantially to the solution of any of the major riddles. Johannine research is a field where specialists are in command, and I do not
venture to rank myself with them. My rapport with Johannine modes of
thought is so insecure that when I make an assertion it should properly be
terminated with a question mark rather than with a period.

In what follows, I will be addressing not so much the guild of technical
scholars as the company of pastors whose study of the Gospel is geared
into their work of preaching and teaching. Perhaps I can help you read
this document from a new vantage point by raising a fresh set of questions
to ponder as you read. Our habits of reading can put a straitjacket on our
minds, and the more familiar the text, the tighter the constraints. Active
thinking is often aborted unless we come to the text with fresh questions.
I have in mind some questions which I hope will inveigle you into a slow-
paced search for clues within the Gospel itself: *What stance did the author*
expect his first readers to take as they read his words? What reactions did
he wish to encourage among them? Did he wish to arouse any specific
resonance between his readers and the events he narrated?

If we can answer such questions as these, we may perhaps discover an unsuspected kinship between the modern pastor and this ancient author.

I have spoken of the author. Any student who has survived seminary education will recall how many problems that word "author" releases. It is customary in recent research to take note of several distinct levels of authorship: those persons who were responsible for various oral and written sources; that person or group responsible for collecting those sources into a single consecutive narrative; the person who edited and published the final version. On any accounting, the present Gospel had a jagged oral and written history, the recovery of which is conjectural at best.[1] On this cluster of problems I agree with my colleague Nils A. Dahl: "I am inclined to think that the Evangelist himself was the 'ecclesiastical editor' of the traditions of the Johannine 'school.'"[2] So when I say "John," I have in mind the completed edition which was available to readers by the late first century and which every pastor now has in his library, at least in translation.

The questions I have raised, though often neglected, are fully in line with a long-standing and widely recognized principle of exegesis. J. Louis Martyn has reminded me that it was strongly supported by Walter Bauer: "Before one inquires into the author's intention, he must ask how the first readers are likely to have understood the text."[3] If we can put ourselves in the place of the original readers and discern the changes in attitudes or actions to which they would be impelled, we may be less inclined to twist the text to suit our own predilections and desires. And we may be able to recover accents in the original dialogue which have become submerged in later tendencies to treat the Gospel as the author's monologue.

It must be admitted that even the best of scholars often neglect the role of the first audience in that dialogue. I grant that commentators usually ask whether that audience was composed of Jews or Gentiles, believers or non-believers, Palestinian or Diaspora Jews, Gnostic or anti-Gnostic Christians, even though no single answer is acceptable to all.[4] Less often, however, do commentators press beyond these formal categories to the immediate situations and urgent needs of the first readers. For example, it is clear that, whatever their formal identity may have been, they were con-

---

1. For a recent survey of scholarly opinion, see Robert Kysar, *The Fourth Evangelist and His Gospel* (Minneapolis: Augsburg Publishing House, 1975), pp. 9–81.

2. *Jesus in the Memory of the Early Church* (Minneapolis: Augsburg Publishing House, 1976), p. 119.

3. J. L. Martyn, "Glimpses into the History of the Johannine Community," *ETL* (1977), p. 163.

4. For a recent survey, see H. B. Kosten, *Studies in John* (Leiden: E. J. Brill, 1970), pp. 98–110.

fronted by a situation in which faith in Christ entailed hostility from the "world," a "tribulation" not unlike that of Christ himself. This "world" had continued to reject the Word so vigorously and so violently that such terms as the light and the darkness represented no vapid sentimental clichés but bitter conflicts between the apparent madness of a minority cult and the manifest wisdom of a dominant majority. We must ask how this author read the plight of that minority and how he sought to respond to their needs. In his day, the skeptical attacks of an early Rudolf Augstein must have been both recurrent and effective.[5] So how did John respond to the emerging questions of a community for which such attacks were a matter of daily diet? I urge you to read and reread the Gospel searching for this audience.

FIRST CLUES

In many literary documents, evidence concerning the original dialogue partners may be detected in the opening section, where an author greets his readers, and in the closing section, where he takes leave of them. Often he uses personal pronouns for this purpose. Such pronouns, though scarce, may be found in John. We look first at the prologue. We may note that this prologue stresses a decisive difference between two reactions to Jesus: rejection or acceptance. In which of these two groups did the author place his readers? The answer depends largely upon the intended force of three pronouns: "the Word . . . dwelt among *us* . . . *we* beheld his glory . . . from his fullness *we* have all received. . . ." To exclude the readers from these pronouns would seem to relegate them to the "world" that "knew him not." The other option is to include them among those who believed in his name, who had received authority to become God's children, who had beheld his glory, and who had received from his fullness "grace upon grace."

This second option, I believe, is preferable.[6] Author and audience together constitute a community indwelt by the Word.[7] Because of membership in this community, the dialogue between author and readers can proceed at the deepest conceivable level. If we read the prologue in this way,

---

5. *Jesus Son of Man* (New York: Urizen Books, 1977).

6. Raymond Brown advances a third option, which I find unconvincing. To him, the *us* of v. 14b refers to mankind, the *we* of v. 14c shifts to the apostolic witnesses, while the *we* of v. 16 shifts back to mankind (*The Gospel according to John*, AB [Garden City, N.Y.: Doubleday, 1966], I, 13–15).

7. See my discussion of incarnation in *Int* 24 (1970): 291–302.

we will see that its major function is neither polemic nor apologetic, but confessional and doxological, in this respect comparable to such passages as Hebrews 1:1–4, I Peter 1:3–9, and Ephesians 1:3–10. The author wants his readers to share his awareness of the profound mysteries that inhere in their family life as God's sons.[8] I advance this conclusion tentatively and urge each of you to form your own judgment and then to look with me for additional clues.

Other strategic uses of personal pronouns appear in the closing sections: "This is the disciple . . . who has written these things; and *we* know that his testimony is true" (21:24, RSV). In this case, the pronoun appears to refer to the writer alone, inasmuch as he places a tangible distance between himself, the beloved disciple, and his readers (notice also the "I" in v. 25). I think that this paragraph justifies a whole series of inferences: (1) The beloved disciple had been previously known by this particular audience, who may even have been converted by his preaching.[9] (2) He had been the last survivor of those who had known Jesus before his glorification.[10] (3) His death, which seemed in some way to contradict Jesus' prediction, had dismayed and discouraged them. (4) His death meant that they no longer had direct contact either with Jesus or with anyone who had known him. (5) This made them dependent upon the testimony, whether oral[11] or written, of secondhand reporters, among whom the evangelist himself belonged. (6) This lacuna in the succession of witnesses had resulted in greater confusion and uncertainty about the grounds for faith.

If this set of inferences is adopted, we get a glimpse of an audience similar to that reflected in the prologue: believers, troubled by changes occasioned by the disappearance of the initial disciples. In 21:24, John tried to alleviate that disturbance.

Do we find corroboration in the personal pronouns of 19:35? "He who saw it has borne witness—his testimony is true, and he knows that he tells the truth—that you also may believe" (RSV). We notice again the same implicit recognition of a distance separating the beloved disciple from author and audience. The text implies that neither author nor audience

---

8. Very frequently in John the word *all* (*pās*) connotes all, and not some, members of this community (3:8, 15, 16; 4:13; 6:35–40; 11:26; 12:32, 46; 15:2; 17:2; 18:37). I suggest that in the prologue *all* carries this same reference (1:7, 12, 16).

9. "The Beloved Disciple appears to have functioned as a founder within the Johannine community" (R. A. Culpepper, *The Johannine School* [Ann Arbor, Mich.: University Microfilms, 1974], p. iv).

10. Similar but earlier situations are reflected in I Thess. 4:15; I Cor. 15:6.

11. Even as late as the mid-second century, many Christians preferred oral to written traditions as being more dependable (e.g., Papias in Eusebius *H. E.* 3. 39. 1–7).

had been present at the crucifixion. Because the beloved disciple had been present, author and readers could rely upon his report. There is, however, a significant difference. In this verse, the readers ("you") are being asked to move from a stance of unbelief to belief. Should we infer that the author had non-believers in mind?

The conclusion to chapter 20 may support that inference: "These are written that *you* may believe that Jesus is the Christ, the Son of God, and that believing *you* may have life in his name" (20:31, RSV). It is obvious that the evangelist wants his readers to shift to a position of belief. He writes as if he, but not they, had already received "life in his name," in sharp contrast to the prologue in which author and readers share that life. What are we to make of this contrast? Is it due to different sources or authors? Or to different audiences at different stages of composition? Or are the inferences from chapters 1 and 21 wrong? Or is the notion of believing sufficiently ambiguous to permit 20:31 to refer to unbelieving believers?

Before trying to resolve this apparent contradiction, let us follow a clue which the passages already examined have uncovered: These texts reflect a contrast between two groups—those who had been present in the events narrated and those who had not. Both author and readers appear to belong to the latter group, but the readers are more troubled by their distance from the events than is the evangelist. Let us scan other passages to see if they reflect this same contrast. For purposes of shorthand, we will use the terms "disciples at first hand" and "disciples at second hand."

THE TWO GENERATIONS

We begin with a text in which Jesus himself makes the distinction and in doing so he reveals a powerful concern for the disciples at second hand. This is the intercessory prayer of chapter 17. It is almost impossible to exaggerate the importance which the evangelist attached to this prayer, an importance indicated by its location. It is the decisive turning point between ministry and passion,[12] between Jesus' training of the disciples at first hand and his act of giving life to "all flesh." It announces the hour of his glorification and views that hour both proleptically and retrospectively. One "model" for the construction of this prayer, as for the eucharistic dis-

---

12. I cannot agree with Rudolf Bultmann and other scholars who relocate the prayer after 13:1–30 (cf. *The Gospel of John: A Commentary*, trans. G. R. Beasley-Murray et al. [Philadelphia: Westminster Press, 1971], pp. 457ff.).

courses as a whole, is provided, I believe, by Moses' farewell address to the twelve tribes and his benediction over them in Deuteronomy 29–34.[13] Here the covenant-maker seals an everlasting covenant with the covenant people.

In arranging the prayer in three paragraphs the Revised Standard Version is correct, and we should note carefully the sequence and content of the three. In the first (17:1–5) Jesus prays for the consummation of his own vocation, in which the glorification of the Son will coincide with the glorification of the Father. This glory is both primal ("before the world was made," RSV) and final ("glorify thou me in thy own presence," RSV); as both primal and final it endows Jesus with authority over all flesh and invests the life he gives with the same eternality. His vocation, completed in this climactic hour, thus receives an all-inclusive cosmic range. We may note the emphasis on the "all." God has given to Jesus authority to give life to *all* whom God gives to him; when we ask who were meant to be included in this *all*, we find an answer in the next two paragraphs. Jesus first intercedes for the disciples among whom he is then standing. They have been given to him by the Father, and he is to be glorified in them. They have already received the Word; here they are being consecrated for their vocation in the world. That mission draws the hatred of the world upon them, but that very hatred will become an occasion for the gift of joy. Their message will carry the same truth as his; their sending, following upon his sending, will be validated and empowered as a result of this intercession. That the basic reference is to the disciples at first hand is indicated by the reference to Judas (v. 12). At no point is there any indication that these disciples are readers of the Gospel; rather they are the authorized bearers of the *logos* (v. 20).[14]

Quite different is the second group for whom Jesus prayed: "those who believe in me *through their word*." The prepositional phrase is quite explicit. Although these believers have not seen the Lord, they have nevertheless received the *logos*. They have been linked to Jesus by the disciples at first hand, for the possessive "their" (*autōn*) is a specific pointer to that first generation. Although in one sense all later generations come to faith through the word of that first generation, the evangelist here, I think, is

---

13. See my "The Beloved Disciple in the Gospel of John: Some Clues and Conjectures," *NovT* 19 (1977): 105–23.

14. This paragraph repeats for greater emphasis the conviction that this first generation is linked through Jesus to God by way of the same word (vv. 6, 14, 17) and the same name (vv. 6, 11, 12) and the same glory (vv. 4, 10). These links constitute their oneness. In v. 10 the *all* refers probably, though not certainly, to the disciples at first hand.

concerned with the second only. By the explicit petition of Jesus, a generation gap is recognized in the very effort to overcome it. I suggest, therefore, that the immediate audience of John did not include the first generation, but consisted of the second.

In making this suggestion we part company with two of the foremost exegetes of our time. Bultmann says quite flatly that this verse (v. 20) "does not, of course, only refer to the preaching of the first generation, but to Christian preaching in general" and that "the petition is made for all believers without reference to space and time."[15] In a similar vein, R. E. Brown writes that the words "are directed to Christians of all times."[16] That is a natural way for modern readers to think of this Gospel, inasmuch as we are so far removed from the initial audience, and Christians of many generations have included themselves within the company of those addressed. This way of reading the Gospel, however, ignores the quite specific dilemmas that Christians confronted as soon as the disciples at first hand had disappeared from the scene. I want to insist that John, like virtually every other New Testament author, was addressing a quite concrete set of circumstances which come into view in such verses as 17:20ff. In some respects, these disciples at second hand imagined themselves at a distinct disadvantage in comparison with their predecessors. They would be reassured by Jesus' foreknowledge of their plight and by his pledge to dwell with them no less than with the first disciples. He made their vocation, their sending, a direct continuation of his. The passing of time, with the succession of generations, marked no diminution in glory or in the knowledge and love of God. The prayer reminded its first readers of the inclusive force of the prologue's we. They have the same origin, as children born of God's love, and the same destiny, as messengers called to dwell with Jesus where he is.[17]

To visualize these readers and to read the prayer as they would read it may enable us to catch many fresh nuances in the text. For instance, consider the repeated petition "That they all may be one." That prayer could envisage a unity within itself of this second generation, or it could envisage their unity with the first generation. I am inclined to favor the second alternative. While recognizing three links in the chain of sendings—the Son, the first disciples, those who believe through their word—the prayer

---

15. Gospel of John, pp. 512, 698.
16. Gospel according to John, II, 582.
17. See my essay " 'We Don't Know Where . . .' John 20:2," Int 30 (1976): 125–39.

stresses the oneness of their vocation. God can be trusted to secure their oneness in glory, in truth, and in love. Unless this oneness is maintained, the central purpose would be endangered: "that the world may believe that you have sent me." Jesus prevents any break in the chain, though he appears to distinguish between two links: "I made known to them . . . [the disciples at first hand?], and I will make it known [to the disciples at second hand?], that the love with which you have loved me . . ." (v. 26).

The implication of this way of reading the text is clear: readers who identified themselves with the second generation needed such a reassurance because their distance in time and space from Jesus created difficulties, although the text does not specify the precise nature of these difficulties. Did they feel less certain of their faith because they had never heard or seen Jesus? Did their veneration for the heroic veterans, many of whom had been martyred, make them feel inferior (21:18, 19)? Had the absence of authoritative witnesses increased the gravity of dissensions within the church? Had the hostility of "the world," and especially the animosities from the synagogue, diminished their poise and confidence in Jesus? Had they become less clear about their unique mission and less strongly committed to it? Had their sense of participation in the "glory" of the Father and the Son been dissipated by the routines of living? Had communal frictions eroded their confidence that God loved them, even as he had loved Christ (v. 23)? Conjectures of this sort are provoked by the prayer, though these must remain conjectures only. They may, however, be strengthened when we examine other texts in which the disciples at second hand enter the picture. For this purpose we will look first at the narratives dealing with the glorified Lord, inasmuch as the intercessory prayer anticipates that situation.[18]

In the first account of the resurrection (20:1–18) I think it is uncommonly significant that Mary's question of *where*, reiterated on three occasions, should be answered in such a way as to include all believers; in this respect it echoes the prayer of 17:24 that the disciples at second hand might

---

18. For this audience, then, there existed a distance in space and time between the events narrated and their own work in the "world." For this author, that distance was bridged by those realities mentioned in the prayer: glory, word, name, knowledge, love. Since for him prayer and passion were correlatives, this bridge was composed also of the events of the passion, when the glory of God and the glory of Jesus intersected. Moreover, because this point of intersection was in the *hour*, the *now*, of vv. 1–5, the bridge linked the disciples at second hand to both primal and final realities. See chap. 5 in my *To Die and to Live* (New York: Seabury Press, 1977).

be where he is.[19] A similar nuance can be discerned in the Johannine refusal to set a terminus to the presence of the glorified Lord. In this Gospel there is nothing comparable to the story in Acts of the ascension. In fact, it is probable that all the conversations with Jesus after Mary's dialogue with him (20:17) are post-ascension meetings. In this Gospel it is argued that, although later disciples do not see him, he continues to abide in them and they in him; the two spaces—where he is and where they are—coincide.[20]

So, too, in the account of the first vision of the ascended Lord (20: 19–23), the gift of the Holy Spirit is designed to qualify them to forgive or to retain the sins of believers who are yet to be converted. Jesus had been sent to the first group only in order that they might be sent to others, for example, the readers of the Gospel. Then, too, in the dramatic account of Thomas' doubts, the climax is reached only when the attention shifts from Thomas to those who would not have his advantages (20:24–28). This implies that when in coming days believers would have greater reasons for skepticism than Thomas their faith would be more commendable than his. In some respects they would be able to claim superiority even over Mary, Peter, and the beloved disciple! Whatever the cause of the prevalent sense of inferiority, chapter 20 clearly seeks to erase it.

We should note the parallelism between the benediction of 20:29 and the author's statement of purpose in 20:30, 31. These parallels are too extensive to be accidental. In both cases a special mention is made of those who believe without seeing, in contrast to those who have seen. In fact, the author presents his book as a substitute for the signs, thus recognizing that his readers will have access to faith through reading rather than through seeing. In verse 31, the audience ("you") is distinguished from the disciples of verse 30, but the life in blessedness received through faith will be the same for both groups. John visualizes his mission in writing as a way of enabling readers to take advantage of Jesus' beatitude; he hopes above all else that they will inherit life as a result of their reading. He has accepted for himself a vocation continuous with that of Jesus and the disciples at first hand, although, as we have noted, he does not claim for himself the privilege of having seen.

The weighty symbolisms of chapter 21 also express strong concern for the disciples at second hand. They enter the scene as the fish whom the

---

19. See n. 17.
20. See Eduard Schweizer, *New Testament Essays: Studies in Memory of T. W. Manson* (Manchester: Manchester University Press, 1959), pp. 230–45; also Dahl, *Jesus in the Memory of the Early Church*, pp. 99–102.

disciples, at first unsuccessfully, are seeking to catch, but who, with the Lord's help, are drawn into the nets. Jesus is concerned with the size of the catch, but even more with its unity; the untorn net symbolizes the oneness for which Jesus prayed in 17:20ff. John's readers would associate themselves more fully with the fish than with the fishermen and would be taught by the allegory to trust. They would realize that Jesus himself intended their conversion and that he would continue to be present to their community.

In Jesus' colloquy with Peter, the symbolism shifts from net to flock, but the thrust remains the same. Here the command "Feed my lambs" embodies both the prime concern of Jesus and the prime test of Peter's love for him. The command clearly anticipates the needs of the flock during the period after Jesus' death but before Peter's. That flock belongs to Jesus to such a degree that feeding it is the mode of following him. It is quite natural for all later shepherds to identify themselves with Peter; the evangelist, however, expected his readers to identify themselves with the sheep and, in so doing, to recognize the character of the love that bound them to Jesus, to Peter, and to one another. They should freely recognize their debt to the chain of martyrs—first Jesus, and then Peter—but this veneration should in no wise diminish their sense of full participation in God's glory (vv. 18, 19). I have already commented on the role of the beloved disciple on this same occasion; the readers come into view as "the brethren" who had been disconcerted by his death (v. 23). Accordingly the Gospel tries to compensate for that disappointment by providing in written form a dependable version of the oral witness of that disciple. Hereafter they must rely on the *logos* and not on more direct contact with those who had seen the glorified Lord. In this, as in other passages I have surveyed, the author simultaneously recognizes a generation gap and seeks to bridge it.

SUPPLEMENTARY MOTIFS

Let me repeat my confession concerning the tentative nature of this approach and invite you to test it by referring to other materials. There is, for example, another discourse in which followers are pictured as sheep (10:1–30). Who is it who constitute the flock for whom the good shepherd gives his life? One must include the sheep then present, but also "the other sheep I have which are not of this fold" (v. 16). Only after they have heeded his voice can Jesus speak of one flock, and that will not happen until he has laid down his life for them. When he used this term "other sheep," whom did Jesus (and/or John) have in mind? Dispersion Jews to be united to Palestinian Jews? Jewish Christians in the Dispersion to be united to the "first church" in Jerusalem? Gentile converts to be added to Jewish believers? Deviant Christian minorities to be reunited to the orthodox majority? Exegetes have opted for variant solutions.[21] I suggest still another alternative: The "other sheep" are the disciples at second hand, whose place in a united flock is here assured to be the will and work of this self-sacrificing shepherd. Such an interpretation would align this allegory to Jesus' intercessory prayer and to his final consecration of Peter as shepherd.

An examination of the allegory of the vine (15:1–17) will also yield interesting data if one perceives the subtle relationship of the vine, its branches, and their fruit. The identity of the vine is certain: Jesus. The identity of the branches, though not so certain, is probable: the disciples at first hand. The identity of the fruit: the disciples at second hand. In producing this fruit, the vinedresser, the vine, and the branches collaborate. In fact, the fruit of the branches *is* the fruit of the whole vine, the unity being traced to a mutual laying down of life (v. 13), a unity in love as well as in joy. The whole production is designed not only to yield fruit, but to assure the continued "abiding" of this fruit (v. 16). The chain of being coincides with the chain of mutual dependence and mutual sacrifice. As in the other texts, the momentum of thought moves in the direction not of the original audience of Jesus but the audience of the evangelist. This momentum accords with the saying which in the Johannine context parallels the beatitude of 20:29: ". . . he who receives any one whom I send receives me; and he who receives me receives him who sent me" (13:20, RSV). When they respond positively to the disciples at first hand, the disciples at second hand will entertain both the Son and his Father. There is no more exalted role in any generation, though in every generation that role entails persecution by the world (v. 21).

In your reading of this Gospel let me also ask you to notice the degree to which all followers, those of the first as well as those of the second generation, depended for faith upon someone who is "not the light." According to the prologue, all who believe come to faith through John the Baptist

---

21. Martyn has cogently argued that in this verse "this fold" refers to the Johannine community and that the "other sheep" are "other Jewish Christians who, like those of the Johannine community, have been scattered from their parent synagogues by experiencing excommunication" ("Glimpses," p. 174). I am not yet so persuaded. Where Martyn finds the closest parallel in 11:52, I locate it in 17:20.

(1:7; also 6:41). To him Andrew, the first disciple, was indebted, and only through Andrew's word was Peter enlisted; then only through Philip was Nathanael called (1:35–39). It is quite typical of this Gospel that each disciple should first be enlisted not by Jesus directly, but by another witness.[22] So, in the chain of witnesses that reaches back to the beginning, no link ranks higher than any other, for all respond to the Word and all become mediators of the Word. The stories reflect this interdependence so naturally that it is easy for the reader to miss it. This motif may well be related to the dismay of followers who no longer have access either to Jesus or to the apostles, but who must rely upon the hearsay of later witnesses. In this respect the first generation had found things no easier than the second.

Nor was the second generation unique in confronting massive obstacles to faith. In this regard the embarrassments attributed to the disciples at first hand may have been intended, at least in part, to reassure their successors. Those early heroes had on various occasions vowed their loyalty to Jesus, only to be corrected by him: "Do you now believe? The hour is coming, indeed it has come, when you will be scattered, every man to his home, and will leave me alone" (16:31, 32; RSV). Not a single disciple before the passion had come through his internship with a clean record. Surely it had been no easier for them to understand or to accept their vocation than for their descendants. Peter had not been alone in denials and treacheries (2:23f.; 4:48; 6:2–15; 6:64ff.; 8:31–47; 13:38). In destroying the halos so readily placed on apostolic heads by the second generation (expressive of secret envy and self-pity?), the evangelist had, I believe, a positive message for members of that generation.

It is almost certain that in John's day the hostility of the synagogues was undermining the courage and poise of John's readers.[23] That being so, his portrayal of the earlier situation made it obvious that similar hostility had been present from the beginning. The earlier situation had been as confused and as dangerous and with as many excuses for doubt and betrayal, for self-concern and panic. No cluster of antagonisms more acute could be

22. Unless I have missed count, no person in the Gospel became a disciple save through the mediation of some other person—with one exception: Philip (1:43). However, Martyn has demonstrated on other grounds that the exception is due to the fact that the shape of this verse has been altered, probably before the final redaction ("We have found Elijah," in R. Hamerton-Kelly and Robin Scroggs, eds., *Jews, Greeks, and Christians* [Leiden: E. J. Brill, 1976], pp. 201–8).

23. J. L. Martyn, *History and Theology in the Fourth Gospel* (New York: Harper & Row, 1968), pp. 3–41; and "Glimpses."

imagined than those that had been faced and overcome by Jesus.[24] Even
Jesus' brothers had been opposed (7:5). Many who had believed had refused, out of fear, to admit it. The signs which had reflected Jesus' authority had either misled or offended many who had seen them. If the measure
of Jesus' prophetic work was rejection by his people, the same measure
applied to all whom he called to continue that work, whether they belonged
to the first or to the second generation. As we read the Gospel we should
constantly ask two questions: What factors in the situation faced by John's
readers would lead him to accent this hostility? What attitudes and actions
did he hope to encourage among those readers by his realistic and ominous
narratives?

It was not until after Jesus' "lifting up" on the cross that the disciples
at first hand could fully grasp the nature of his vocation or the conditions
under which their own vocation would be carried out. Neither the Scripture nor the Lord's prophecies were understood until after that event
(2:22; 8:28; 12:16; 13:7). Only then could belief in him be grounded in
full understanding; until then it was highly vulnerable (13:19; 14:29).
Only after his glorification could the Counselor come with his true witness
(15:26; 16:7) and his gift of joy (16:22). Such statements were, of course,
addressed to the disciples at first hand, but the evangelist stressed them
for the sake of his own readers. He wanted them to realize that the ground
of faith, the faith that is inseparable from eternal life, was the same for
them as for their predecessors, whose direct access to Jesus gave them no
substantial advantage. All disciples, without exception, must rely upon the
Word, upon the presence of the incarnate Lord with his own, and upon the
Spirit of truth to "convince the world concerning sin and righteousness
and justice" (16:8).

BELIEF AND LIFE

We are now ready to return to the matter broached earlier: the apparent
contradiction between an audience of believers and John's intention (advanced in 20:30, 31) to persuade his readers to believe. That simple word
"believe" does not carry equal force in all the passages. There are, to be
sure, some passages in which it is used in an unqualified and absolute
sense, as in the famous 3:16. Such a sense seems to imply that every act of

---

24. See 9:34f.; 15:18–25; 16:1, 2, 33; 17:14. John's assurance to his readers is well
summed up in 15:18: "If the world hates you, know that it has hated me before it
hated you" (RSV).

belief automatically conveys the gift of eternal life, as if there were a one-to-one correspondence between them. But there are many more passages in which belief is *not* accompanied by eternal life (2:23f.; 6:2f.; 6:64f.; 8:31–47; 16:31).[25] In fact, it is doubtful whether we should attribute this life to any disciple until after Jesus' hour had come (17:1f.). Knowledge of the truth, a sharing in Jesus' life-giving work, the birth from above, the gift of the Spirit, the beatitude of eternal life—all these became fully accessible only after the departure and the coming again of Jesus.[26] It is in this life-giving sense that John wanted his readers to believe, but his story made him aware of the difficulties in the path of such belief. It required a successive learning of the same kinds of lessons that the disciples at first hand had learned in their contacts with Jesus before his death. This is why the action of believing carries such complex and multiple meanings in this document.

No recent interpreter of the Gospel has seen so clearly this feature of Johannine belief as Bultmann, an insight undoubtedly linked to his appreciation of the existentialist character of the Christian life: "So far as the Evangelist is concerned it is irrelevant whether the possible readers are already Christians or are not yet such, for to him the faith of Christians is not a conviction that is present once for all, but it must perpetually make sure of itself anew."[27] I want to suggest that the multiple gradations and forms of faith were due not so much to the existentialist character of the Johannine witness as to the vocational grounding of his thought. He realized that to accept the Word is to be called into an arduous and hazardous mission of which the terrifying mode is the "lifting up" of the Son of Man. To continue in that Word is to draw upon oneself the hostility of the world, made immediate by the experience of expulsion from the synagogue. Such a vocation does not permit of a "once for all" definition. Only by fulfilling a calling/sending in which eternal life takes the form of total self-giving does a person or community truly *believe* in the name of Jesus. Any notion of believing that falls short of being sent as Jesus was sent fails to do justice to the *double* implication of the familiar statement of John's

---

25. These passages make it hard to accept the dictum of Barnabas Lindars that John knows no middle course between perishing and having eternal life, or between belief and unbelief (*The Gospel of John* [London: Oliphants, 1972], p. 24).

26. The unqualified use of believing, as in 3:16, may be more easily understood and accepted if this verse is taken as uttered from the vantage point of the post-resurrection church. This may be the implication of the first-person pronouns in 3:11.

27. *Gospel of John*, p. 698. To this statement Bultmann appends a note, the truth of which I have already questioned: "A precise circle of readers is obviously not in view."

intention: "that you may believe . . . *that believing* you may have life in his name."

No writing in the New Testament gives to its conception of believing a stronger missiological and martyrological stamp. This factor gives the message of John its existentialist immediacy, but only because at the same time it conceives all true believing as a continuing participation in the vocation of the Son of Man. The purpose of the evangelist is as fully stated in the closing petition of Jesus (17:24f.) as when he speaks in his own role in 20:30, 31. He wants his readers to be with Jesus where he is, to behold his glory, and to share in the love with which the Father loved the Son "before the foundation of the world." This implicit objective becomes quite explicit in First John:

> I write to you, not because you do not know the truth, but because you
> know it, and know that no lie is of the truth. . . . Let what you heard
> from the beginning abide in you. If what you heard from the beginning
> abides in you, then you will abide in the Son and in the Father. And this
> is what he has promised us, eternal life (I John 2:21–25, RSV).[28]

THE TESTING OF THE HYPOTHESIS

Let the Gospel now be read to see if the extended hypothesis just presented enhances one's empathy with the first readers. Do successive episodes in the story of Jesus illuminate their stories? Do Jesus' encounters with "the Jews" reflect hazards which disciples continued to face? Do the misunderstandings of Jesus' message, whether by his enemies or his friends, anticipate their own misunderstandings? Would reading this Gospel help them to accept their role as friends or branches or fish or flock? Would their imaginations be activated to sense in their fellowship the abiding presence of Jesus, along with the empowering guidance of the Counselor? Would they become more self-reliant as they learned how fallible the apostles had been? Would they be freed from envy and despair when the halos were stripped from the heads of those fathers in faith? As their own calling led them toward their own passion, would they receive courage from Jesus' intercessions for them?

Should the approach be found credible, other features of this Gospel may come to light which are designed to bridge the gap between these two generations, for instance, the stress upon doing everything *in the name of*

---

28. The Gospel and the Epistle may not come from the same hand, but they almost certainly represent the same school of thought and the same epoch. In any case, the similarity of intention is striking.

Jesus, a phrase that is repeated in many texts relating to post-ascension situations (14:13, 14, 26; 15:16; 16:23–26; 17:26; 20:31). *Name* is a reality that links Jesus' authority and presence to the authority and presence of God, and simultaneously to the disciples at first hand (17:6, 11, 12). The same reality bridges the distance between God and the disciples at second hand: "I will make known to them thy name" (17:26). Or, to change the figure, to speak of God's name was to speak of the genes which are transmitted from one generation to the next. And no generation was able to pray in that name until *after* it had understood the "lifting up" of the Crucified (16:23, 26).[29]

As with name, so with Spirit. In the absence of Jesus, his presence would be maintained through the coming of the Spirit-Counselor-Judge-Witness. As John tells the story, the glorification of Jesus enabled him to continue his work through the Spirit in the first generation. Even more than this, the presence of the Spirit enabled the first generation to become witnesses to the second (15:26f.). Through their word, the Spirit continues to make the absent Lord present, just as the Gospel of John itself represents the presence of the absent "beloved disciple" (21:24).

Our approach may also help to suggest the original ambience of the upper-room discourse. Was John a protagonist or antagonist of the development of sacramental theology? It is clear that he did not identify the supper (13:2) with either Passover or Eucharist. On the other hand, his audience could hardly fail to sense the relevance of these conversations to their sacred meals. In listening to these discourses, they would recognize the presence of the absent Lord and, simultaneously, their kinship with the disciples at first hand.[30] I do not believe that the author discouraged this resonance. In fact, I think the farewell discourses conveyed to his audience the same covenantal functions that the farewell address of Moses (Deut. 29–34) had conveyed to successive generations in Israel.[31]

Most clearly of all, this concern with John's audience may help us uncover the rationale that led John to his unique stress upon the *logos,* for it was this *word* that bridged the generation gap. It is not enough to characterize Johannine thought as a *logos* theology and Christology; it is

---

29. Dahl, *Jesus in the Memory of the Early Church,* p. 101.

30. Of the present participle in 17:20 "those who believe in me," Brown writes: "If the viewpoint is that of the Last Supper, the present participle is proleptic, having the force of a future. . . . If the viewpoint is that of the time of the Johannine writer, the believers are a present reality" (*Gospel according to John,* II, 769).

31. See n. 13. Brown also compares Jesus' covenant with the Mosaic, pointing out that the rabbis, like Jesus in 20:29, stressed the blessedness of proselytes who had not seen the Sinai signs but who had nevertheless believed in Moses' word (*ibid.,* II, 1048).

also a *logos* ecclesiology and even a *logos* zoology.[32] The word acts as the communicator of life from one generation to the next; a key to this chain of being is the simple declaration "I have given *them thy* word" (17:14). Here the three pronouns are linked together by an act of giving. The *giver* conveys *God's* word to a *group* of recipients in such a way that they in turn become givers of the same word to a new community of recipients, all of these successive groups becoming *one* in an "ecumenism of time" (G. Florovsky). "I have given them thy word" thus becomes a musical canon, a "round" that can be repeated with endless contrapuntal variations. With little change in meaning, one could replace the noun *word* in this canon with such alternatives as name, truth, glory, life, and love.

When they read chapter 17, John's audience would have been reminded of this endless chain of being, generations of faith linked by the transmission of these genes. The word which they had heard (17:20) would remind them of the word which their predecessors had heard (17:14, including the beloved disciple), and they would recognize this word as Jesus himself, the word of life and the word of God. The chain of being thus linked them to the primal action of God (1:1–5) in such a way as to correct the notion that any earlier generation had held any advantage over them. "Early Christian thought is radically protological."[33] By the same token, the chain of being linked the second generation to the future consummation in such a way as to destroy any notion that some later generation might have an advantage over their own. Jesus' intercession assured them of beholding his glory and of being with him. This glory and this presence were radically eschatological. By this word, God provided a bridge over every distance of time and space. Yet this bridge was no timeless escape from temporal existence; it had been grounded in the vocation by which Jesus had glorified God (17:1–5) and in the vocation to which he had called his disciples.

In these last paragraphs I have seemed to shift from speaking of the particular perspective of the disciples at second hand to speaking of all

---

32. There is something misleading in the fact that the RSV capitalizes its translation of *logos* in the prologue and nowhere else. This is exegesis and not translation. It presupposes a difference in meaning in the prologue which is difficult to prove. Many verses in later chapters use *logos* in as profound a way: as God's word; as bearer of the divine glory, grace, and life; as Christ himself indwelling his people; as the bond in the Spirit between God, Christ, and the generations of believers. It would be better not to capitalize the noun anywhere than to insert this invidious distinction between the prologue and many later passages (e.g., 8:31–35; 12:48–50; 14:21–24; 15:3; 17:6, 14, 17, 20).

33. John Meagher, *The Way of the Word* (New York: Seabury Press, 1975), pp. 184f.

subsequent generations. This apparently justifies the conviction of those who interpret John's audience in a general and inclusive way. Quite the contrary. Only because John addressed his own contemporaries in so responsible a fashion have these perennial and universal values accrued to his work. Only when the word is related to the urgent needs of a particular generation does the wider relevance of that word emerge. This, of course, fully justifies later generations of witnesses in their propensity for seeing themselves in the mirror provided by John's Gospel. For in the end Søren Kierkegaard is right: There is no substantial distinction between the disciples at second hand and all later disciples.[34]

34. *Philosophical Fragments* (Princeton: Princeton University Press, 1942), pp. 74–93.

18.

Community and Gospel: Vectors in Fourth Gospel Criticism

ROBERT KYSAR

> Current study of the Fourth Gospel is marked by a growing con-
> centration on the question about the community in whose midst
> it was written.

The concept of "vector" might well be utilized metaphorically to speak
of the directions and movements within the field of Fourth Gospel criticism, for there are indeed "vectors of research" perceptible to the observer.
The most evident of these seem to be moving in one general direction,
namely, toward the elucidation of the Gospel in relation to the community
which gave birth to the document and to which the document itself was
addressed. I propose, therefore, to organize our glimpse into the labyrinth
of monographs and articles dealing with the Gospel around contributions
toward understanding it in its community setting.[1] It is my goal to examine only samples of the most recent Fourth Gospel criticism. But these
current works I will attempt to locate within the broader context of contemporary research.[2]

First we should note several studies which describe *the origin and nature
of the Johannine community.* The most prominent of these is the discussion of *The Johannine Circle* by Oscar Cullmann.[3] Cullmann argues that

---

1. The fact that so much recent Fourth Gospel criticism may be summarized under
the rubric of the Gospel and its community was pointed out to me by Professor R.
Alan Culpepper.

2. For surveys of scholarship on the Fourth Gospel see the following: Wilbert F.
Howard, *The Fourth Gospel in Recent Criticism and Interpretation,* revised by C. K.
Barrett (London: Epworth, 1955); D. Moody Smith, "Johannine Christianity: Some
Reflections on Its Character and Delineation," *NTS* 21 (1975): 222–48; Rudolf
Schnackenburg, "Zur johanneischen Forschung," *BZ* 18 (1974): 272–78; and my
The Fourth Evangelist and His Gospel (Minneapolis: Augsburg Publishing House, 1975).
(See n. 1.)

3. Oscar Cullmann, *The Johannine Circle,* trans. J. Bowden (Philadelphia: Westminster Press, 1976).

the community responsible for the Fourth Gospel had a distinctive origin and development and at the same time understood itself to be cordially related to other forms of early Christianity. It is Cullmann's thesis that the community to which the fourth evangelist belonged took its origin in the conversion of members of a heterodox, marginal Judaism. The non-Christian environment both by heritage and by its actual setting in later years for the Johannine community was this syncretistic and borderline form of Judaism. Converts to Christianity out of this group are identified as the "Hellenists" in Acts 6 and are represented therein in the person of Stephen (Acts 8). The community shared at least three lines of contact with the Christian Hellenists: much of its theology (e.g., Christology), its concern for a mission to the Samaritans,[4] and its dependence on heterodox Judaism. Qumran Judaism, the Baptist sect, and Samaritanism were all means by which Johannine Christianity was influenced by heterodox Judaism in its later development. But the link with marginal Judaism is to be traced in the history of the Johannine circle to Jesus himself, whose affinity with syncretistic forms of Judaism is evidenced in his attitude toward the temple and in his concept of the Son of Man.[5]

Cullmann's thesis surely has its distinctive features, but in many ways this influential study only contributes further to an increasing tendency to see the Fourth Gospel against the background of a form of Judaism quite differentiated from the emerging rabbinical and "normative" Judaism of the first century. Within the past few years, more and more evidence has been produced to demonstrate the affinities between Johannine Christianity and some as yet amorphous sectarian Judaism. However, Cullmann's argument is unfortunately burdened with an almost dogmatic hypothesis that the fourth evangelist is concerned to report the historical facts of the life and ministry of Jesus. He is content even to call the Fourth Gospel a "life of Jesus." One would wish in this connection that Cullmann would have investigated the gospel genre and its peculiar form in the Johannine account. While there is no need to doubt the historical roots of the Fourth Gospel in the life and ministry of Jesus,[6] It is most problematic that one can appropriately call the Gospel a life of Jesus.

---

4. Most recently this possibility has been examined by James D. Purvis, "The Fourth Gospel and the Samaritans," NovT 17 (1975): 161–98. See also my Fourth Evangelist, pp. 160–63.

5. Cullmann, Johannine Circle, pp. 30–62, 89–94. See also Oscar Cullmann, "Von Jesus zum Stephanuskreis und zum Johannesevangelium," in Jesus und Paulus, ed. E. Earle Ellis and Erich Grässer (Göttingen: Vandenhoeck & Ruprecht, 1975), pp. 44–56.

6. Raymond Brown, The Gospel according to John, AB 29, 29a (New York: Doubleday, 1966, 1970), esp. pp. xli–li.

If Cullmann exemplifies one tendency of Johannine studies regarding the community behind the Fourth Gospel, particularly in terms of its original and definitive religious roots, Alan Culpepper represents one who has tried to define the nature of that community. He proposes that the Johannine community was in fact a "school" and then goes about the task of examining the characteristics of ancient schools in the Greco-Roman world. Many of these characteristics, Culpepper contends, are to be found in the community behind the Fourth Gospel. For instance, as was the case in ancient schools, the Johannine community apparently looked back with respect to its founder—the one known in the Gospel as "the disciple whom Jesus loved." With this shared characteristic, as well as others which he is able to isolate, Culpepper concludes that the Johannine community was indeed a school in this ancient sense.[7] Culpepper's work is of great importance in the broader arena of Fourth Gospel criticism because it takes us a step closer to understanding the nature of the community out of which this puzzling and distinctive Gospel comes. While it may seem insignificant upon first glance whether we term the community a school, a sect, or just what, the definition of the community as a school has important consequences. Not only may this understanding enable us to solve some aspects of the enigmatic Fourth Gospel, such as the role of the beloved disciple, but it may also enable us to comprehend how it is that the Gospel could be the literary preservation of a tradition reaching back to decades before it. The school exists among other reasons precisely to preserve the teachings passed on by its founder.

A second vector in Fourth Gospel studies involves those *traditions of the Johannine community*. Surely one of the clearest movements in Johannine scholarship thus far in the second half of this century is the emerging conviction that behind the Gospel there is a tradition. Some propose it was written source(s), while others would prefer to term it an oral tradition.[8] Within the most recent years still another source theory has been offered, this one by Sydney Temple, who has endeavored to isolate what he calls a narrative-discourse source which formed the "core" of the Fourth Gospel. Temple notes that most frequently in the Gospel a discourse is linked to an event which has just been narrated. He isolates what seems to him to have been a source which contained a number of narratives followed in each case by a discourse. For example, 6:1–35, 41–51, 60, and 66–70 constitutes the discernible portion of the core source in chapter 6; while 6:

---

7. *The Johannine School*, SBLDS 26 (Missoula: Scholars Press, 1975).
8. *Fourth Evangelist*, part one.

36–40 and 61–65 are "enlargements" upon the source offered by the evangelist as sort of midrashim in the process of incorporating his source.
There is between the narrative and discourse portions of the proposed
source no stylistic difference. The differences of style occur most notably
between the discourse material from the source and the discourse "enlargements" which the evangelist has added. In addition to the core source and
the evangelist's enlargements upon it, Temple finds that other sources were
employed in the construction of the Gospel (e.g., "The Two Signs—A Cana
Source," 2:1–11 and 4:46–54). Further evidence of the evangelist's redactional work is detectable in his editorial additions to the core source (e.g.,
the explanations found in chap. 6 at vv. 2, 6, 8b, 10b, and 12–13, as well
as elsewhere).[9]

Temple concludes that the narrative-discourse source was an authentic
report of an eyewitness to the ministry of Jesus by one whom Temple believes was a scribe. The narrative-discourse core of the Gospel has a Semitic
flavor and reflects the actual life situation of Jesus. The core material was
"simple down-to-earth reports which . . . give a feeling of authenticity
which has been lost because they have been overlaid by the comments and
enlargements." Temple concludes that the anonymous scribe kept his records during the life of Jesus and that somewhere between 35 and 65 the
Gospel was written. It is most likely the work of John the son of Zebedee,
who used the scribe's records as the core of his work. Thus the Fourth
Gospel was at least concurrent with, if not earlier than, the Synoptics,
which Temple proposes were composed A.D. 40–80.[10]

Temple's work is most surely welcomed as a constructive addition to the
efforts to isolate and delineate the source materials preserved in the Johannine community and utilized by the evangelist. But it is necessary to note
that Temple's methodology does not convince the discriminating reader.
His method comprises what he understands to be a form-critical approach,
but it is persistently vague and imprecise. He does employ style criteria in
his effort (e.g., the use of connectives in the source and Semitic parallelism
forms), but most often applies a comparative study of the Johannine and
synoptic materials in search for what he terms a "realistic narrative." Further, one must ask whether his conviction that the source is an eyewitness
account of Jesus' life and ministry is a conclusion of his study or whether
it is a pre-judgment which he uses to separate the more primitive traditions

---

9. *The Core of the Fourth Gospel* (London and Oxford: Mowbrays, 1975), pp. 37f.,
50–62.
10. *Ibid.*, pp. 50–62, 285–96, viii; quotation, p. 62.

from later materials.[11] Most assuredly Temple's work will need careful scrutiny and should evoke considerable discussion. It might be argued too that his position along with Cullmann and others (see J. A. T. Robinson's proposals[12]) forces us to take a new look at the date and the historical value of the Fourth Gospel.

At present the source hypothesis which seems to attract the most discussion is that of Robert T. Fortna. His proposal that a "signs Gospel" was used by the fourth evangelist has gathered some additional support in recent research.[13] Fortna himself has attempted to apply his theory by showing how redactional criticism on the basis of a signs gospel illuminates the Gospel.[14] Fortna's redactional-critical studies cannot *substantiate* his source theory, but they certainly do present a persuasive implementation of it. The ability of a source theory to produce a convincing and rational view of the evangelist's redactional work is a powerful argument in favor of the theory.

The concern for the community and its traditions invariably raises anew the old question of the relation of the Fourth Gospel and the Synoptics. The proposal that the fourth evangelist knew one or more of the Synoptics persists, in spite of the fact that such a view attracts only a minority of scholars. Still, such a view is championed by no less illustrious a figure than C. K. Barrett.[15] However, more evident than a literary dependence is the growing effort to see the contact between the Fourth Gospel and Synoptics in terms of a common tradition(s). In recent years this view has been presented in two new provocative forms. Günter Reim has proposed that the fourth evangelist employed a "fourth synoptic gospel" which contained many of the traditions found in the three canonical Synoptics but

---

11. *Ibid.*, pp. 68–251.

12. John A. T. Robinson, *Redating the New Testament* (Philadelphia: Westminster Press, 1976), pp. 290–311.

13. E.g., Edwin D. Freed and Russell B. Hunt, "Fortna's Signs-Source in John," *JBL* 76 (1975): 563–79; and John J. O'Rourke, "The Historic Present in the Gospel of John," *JBL* 93 (1974): 585–90. D. Moody Smith has presented a carefully argued rationale for how a miracle source might have been combined in the Johannine community with a passion narrative as an apologetic effort directed toward the Jews ("The Setting and Shape of a Johannine Narrative Source," *JBL* 95 [1976]: 231–41). Cf. Rudolf Schnackenburg, *Das Johannesevangelium*, pt. 3 (Freiburg: Herder, 1975), esp. pp. 463f.

14. Robert T. Fortna, "Christology in the Fourth Gospel: Redaction-Critical Perspectives," *NTS* 21 (1975): 489–504; and idem, "Theological Use of Locale in the Fourth Gospel," *ATR*, Supp. 3 (1974): 58–94.

15. C. K. Barrett, "John and the Synoptic Gospels," *ExpTim* 85 (1973–74): 228–33. See also Barrett's commentary, *The Gospel according to St. John* (London: SPCK, 1955).

in variant forms. He has followed up his imaginative suggestion with specific studies of 4:44 and the farewell discourses.[16] While Reim's proposal is fascinating in many ways, it has yet to be convincingly demonstrated.

The same may be said for an almost equally imaginative endeavor to trace the relationship between the Johannine and Lucan passion narratives. The similarity between Luke and John in the passion-narrative materials has been the subject of considerable discussion in recent years.[17] Hans Klein has compared these passion materials and advanced a complex theory by which the similarities and differences may be understood. There was, Klein suggests, a common tradition comprised of a passion narrative and resurrection appearances. That common source was constructed from the source which Mark used and a source employed by the third evangelist as well. This common source, influenced by Marcan and Lucan sources, was the primary element in the composition of a Johannine *Vorlage* for the passion, and the latter was used in the writing of the Gospel of John.[18] If one insists that the simpler hypothesis to solve a problem is always preferable to the more complex one, then surely Klein, along with Reim, is not to be followed. The complexities of Klein's source development theory are overdrawn. However, these investigations of the relationship between the Fourth Gospel and the Synoptics demonstrate that the question is far from settled, and work on the relationships among especially Mark, Luke, and John must be vigorously pursued.

It is surely evident that the Johannine community did cradle within itself a rich tradition, part of which came to literary expression in the Fourth Gospel. D. Moody Smith admirably summarizes this vector in Johannine studies: "The distinctive character of the Johannine narrative material within the Gospel strongly suggests a principal source (or sources) and one independent of the Synoptics."[19]

The study of the traditions of the community is hardly separable from our third vector: *the theology of the fourth evangelist and his school.* Ef-

---

16. *Studien zum Altestamentlichen Hintergrund des Johannesevangelium* (Cambridge: University Press, 1974); "John IV:44—Crux or Clue?" *NTS* 22 (1976): 476–80; and "Probleme der Abschiedsreden," *BZ* 20 (1976): 117–22.

17. See especially the important article by F. Lamar Cribbs, "A Study of the Contacts That Exist between St. Luke and St. John," Society of Biblical Literature 1973 Seminar Papers (Cambridge, Mass.: Society of Biblical Literature, 1973), II, esp. p. 60; and Anton Dauer, *Die Passionsgeschichte im Johannesevangelium* (Munich: Kösel-Verlag, 1972).

18. Hans Klein, "Die lukanisch-johanneische Passionstradition," *ZNW* 67 (1976): 155–86.

19. "Johannine Christianity," p. 229.

forts at redactional criticism in the Gospel[20] show promise of helping us understand more clearly the theology of the evangelist and his community. An application of redaction criticism is found in what is termed *Gemeinde-theologie*. The best example of this "community theology" approach to the Gospel is the work of Ulrich B. Müller, whose book on the history of the Christology of the Johannine community should receive attention. Müller takes 1:14 and 16 as statements of the christological tradition in the Johannine community. They were portions of a hymn utilized by John's community. "The hymn, John 1:14, 16, is stamped with a one-sided christology of glory which ignores the possible offense of the death of Jesus." The community theology represented in these verses is a special soteriological view: The revelation of the glory of the Logos mediates grace to the believers. From the divinity of the revealer divine life can be appropriated. But the death of Jesus is ignored in order to protect this divinity. The evangelist, however, was concerned with the fact of Jesus' death and the temptation of his community to ignore this fact; hence he attempts in the Gospel to overcome the possible offense of the cross while still asserting it in all of its facility. Müller believes that he has traced the development of Johannine Christology from this Christology of glory through the evangelist's revision of it and on into the apologetic of I John.[21]

It is clear that one of the points of indecision in the present state of Fourth Gospel criticism is the history of the relationship of a theology of glory and a theology of the cross. Were the two combined in a signs-passion source as Fortna and Smith argue? Or was the evangelist responsible for expanding a simpler Christology of the glory of the revealer with the passion? While Müller's community theology is a productive method of theological analysis of the Gospel, it needs to be said that such an effort as his must be premised upon a more precise source theory.

Another more traditional study picks up the theme of the theology of the cross and tries to show that the concept of salvation in the Fourth Gospel is centered on the revelation of the glory of God through his Word, which encompasses the whole of the life and ministry of Jesus. Terence

20. For instance, Urban C. von Wahlde, "A Redactional Technique in the Fourth Gospel," CBQ 38 (1977): 520–33.

21. Ulrich B. Müller, *Die Geschichte der Christologie in der johanneischen Gemeinde*, Stuttgarter Bibelstudien 77 (Stuttgart: Katholisches Bibelwerk, 1975), esp. pp. 69–72. Jürgen Becker has submitted the promising thesis that the dualism of the Fourth Gospel has gone through a four-phase historical development. He contends that this schema could be applied to other Johannine concepts (e.g., eschatology) with fruitfulness. ("Beobachtungen zum Dualismus in Johannesevangelium," ZNW 65 [1974]: 71–87.)

Forestell shows rather impressively that the cross in the Fourth Gospel is not understood as an expiatory sacrifice for sin but is the climax of the process of the revelation of glory. Perceiving Jesus as Word is accepting him as the revelation of God's glory. But Forestell insists that this is not Gnostic, for the revelation is not doctrinal and the cross is an integral part of the revelation.[22] Forestell shows effectively enough the way in which the Gospel explicates the theology of glory even in the death of Jesus; but one must wonder if a tradition analysis might not show that the thought of the Gospel is not quite so neatly unified as Forestell would make it seem. Perhaps the hints of a vicarious and expiatory soteriology in the Gospel (e.g., 1:29) are there because of the evangelist's sources and hence comprise a view not wholly congruent with his own.

A study of Johannine Christology which does not attempt a history-of-tradition approach is the work of Francis J. Moloney.[23] Moloney places each of the Son of Man sayings in the Gospel under the scrutiny of his analysis. He finds that the Son of Man concept is the evangelist's title for the incarnational mode of the Christ and is used to correct mistaken messianic concepts. John has continued the traditional use of this title but blended it with his own understanding (e.g., 3:14–15), where the Son of Man is "lifted up" according to the Johannine understanding of the cross. J. Coppens has done a similar kind of study of the Son of Man sayings in the Gospel and independently comes to some of the same conclusions. Coppens finds that the title emphasizes the humanity of the revealer perhaps in an anti-docetic polemic, but also frees the Johannine Jesus of Davidic, messianic preconceptions. But, unlike Moloney, Coppens stresses the sense in which the Son of Man sayings comprise a distinctive layer of material in the Gospel. He demonstrates the fact that the Son of Man logia are distinctive in style as well as content—they do not, for instance, allude to the Father-Son relationship, even though that is such a dominant theme in the Gospel. He suggests that this stratum of logia came into the Gospel from a tradition, but he will not venture a detailed separation of tradition and redaction. In any case, Coppens believes that the logia have been reworked by the evangelist with the addition of such themes as the glorification after death.[24] Coppen and Moloney together

---

22. Terence Forestell, *The Word of the Cross: Salvation as Revelation in the Fourth Gospel*, AnBib 57 (Rome: Pontifical Biblical Institute, 1974), esp. pp. 191–98.

23. *The Johannine Son of Man* (Rome: Liberia Ateneo Salesian, 1976). See also "The Johannine Son of Man," *BTB* 6 (1976): 177–89, and *Salesianum* 38 (1976): 71–86.

24. Joseph Coppens, "Le Fils de l'homme dans l'évangile johannique," *ETL* 52 (1976): 28–81.

comprise an important expansion of our understanding of the nature of the Son of Man Christology in the Fourth Gospel, and taken together provide us with examples of two kinds of theological study of the Gospel— Moloney working with the Gospel as an integral whole and Coppens attempting to do theology out of tradition analysis. Both approaches have virtue, but tradition analysis promises more success, I believe, than does the method of Moloney.[25]

A fourth vector in Johannine studies today is concerned less with the theology of the evangelist and his community than with *the situation of the community*. J. Louis Martyn has developed the proposition that the Gospel was written out of and for a community locked in controversy with the synagogue.[26] His thesis has been met with widespread agreement and has been further demonstrated by means of a number of independent studies.[27] The last few years of Fourth Gospel criticism have continued for the most part to advance Martyn's proposal.

The most significant recent study concerning the situation of the Johannine community comes from the work of Severino Pancaro. He undertakes a lengthy and detailed investigation of the understanding of Torah in the Fourth Gospel. His conclusions include the confirmation of Martyn's thesis: John reflects a historical conflict between the church and the synagogue. A persistent motif in the Gospel, Pancaro observes, is the discussion of the relationship between the authority of the Law and the authority of Jesus. The authority of the Law is never denied, but the authority of Jesus is made to supersede the Law. John roots his Gospel in the actual antagonism between Jesus himself and the Jews, but his narrative portrays the manner in which that antagonism continued on in the evangelist's own day. His concern is obviously with the defense of the legitimacy of Jesus' messiahship in the face of Jewish attacks. Faithfulness to the Law, Pancaro finds the Gospel asserting, should lead to recognition of Jesus as God's revelation. Those who condemn Jesus violate the Law. "What opposes Jesus (John and his community) to the Jews is a different understanding of the Law; the difference is determined by whether one believes in Jesus

---

25. Other theological studies of the Gospel published within the last few years include the following: Felix Porsch, *Pneuma und Wort: Ein exegetischer Beitrag zur Pneumatologie des Johannesevangeliums* (Frankfurt am M.: J. Knecht, 1974); Michael Lattke, *Einheit im Wort* (Munich: Kösel-Verlag, 1975); Franz Georg Untergassimair, *Im Namen Jesus*, Forschung zur Bibel 13 (Stuttgart: Katholisches Bibelwerk, 1974); and Günter Fischer, *Die Wohnungen: Untersuchungen zu Joh 14, 2f*, Europaische Hochschulschriften 23/38 (Bern: Lang, 1975).

26. *History and Theology in the Fourth Gospel* (New York: Harper & Row, 1968).

27. *Fourth Evangelist*, pp. 149–56.

or not." The Johannine community argued that the Law was valuable as prophecy but now is supplanted by God's revelation in Christ.[28]

Pancaro's study convincingly exhibits the fact that the Fourth Gospel was written in response to the expulsion of Jewish Christians from their synagogues and the condemnation of the Christians as heretics. This action came, as Pancaro points out, from a Judaism struggling to maintain itself in the period following the destruction of the Temple (A.D. 70).[29] His study is a definitive investigation of the concrete situation out of which the Fourth Gospel was written and evinces most forcefully how the conflict with the synagogue has shaped the thought of the Gospel.

Reinhold Leistner's study of anti-Judaism in the Fourth Gospel does not utilize the hypothesis of the church-synagogue conflict, but it demonstrates that the relationship of Christianity and Judaism was a prominent concern for the evangelist.[30] Leistner may all too easily explain away the negative use of the term "the Jews." It would have enhanced his study considerably had he attempted to see the attitude toward the Jews more in the light of the concrete situation of the evangelist and his community. The redactional uses of the expression would therefore become clearer as they do in Pancaro's study.[31]

What seems clear is that current scholarship finds more and more indications that the Gospel was written within a context which involved Christians, Jews, and (probably) Jewish Christians.[32] As scholarship explores this matter the Jewish character of the document becomes more and more transparent.[33]

Another measurable direction in Fourth Gospel criticism might be or-

---

28. *The Law in the Fourth Gospel: The Torah and the Gospel, Moses and Jesus, Judaism and Christianity according to John* (Leiden: E. J. Brill, 1975), pp. 489–533; quotation p. 525.

29. *Ibid.*, pp. 496f. See also "The Relationship of the Church to Israel in the Gospel of John," NTS 21 (1975): 396–405.

30. *Antijudaismus im Johannesevangelium?* Theologie und Wirklichkeit 3 (Bern: Lang, 1974), pp. 142–50.

31. One who does this is Reginald Fuller, "The 'Jews' in the Fourth Gospel," *Dialog* 16 (1977): 31–37.

32. E.g., B. A. Mastin, "A Neglected Feature of the Christology of the Fourth Gospel," NTS 22 (1975–76): 32–51.

33. It is revealing that five introductory books on the Fourth Gospel published in the last two years have all argued for and assumed a generally Jewish setting for the Gospel: Annie Jaubert, *Approaches de l'évangile de Jean* (Paris: Éditions du Seuil, 1976); D. Moody Smith, *John*, Proclamation Commentaries (Philadelphia: Fortress Press, 1976); D. George Vanderlip, *Christianity according to John* (Philadelphia: Westminster Press, 1975); John Painter, *John: Witness and Theologian* (London: SPCK, 1976); and Robert Kysar, *John, the Maverick Gospel* (Atlanta: John Knox Press, 1976). See also C. K. Barrett, *The Gospel of John and Judaism* (Philadelphia: Fortress Press, 1975).

ganized under our fifth vector, *special concerns of the fourth evangelist and his community*. Monographs and articles, of course, have dealt with numerous special aspects of the Gospel of John, but we want here to lift up two areas in which a burst of scholarly energy has been exerted in recent years.

A. One of these special concerns is with the perennial puzzle, the prologue of the Gospel. The question of the source analysis of the prologue still constitutes a storm-center of debate,[34] as does the unity of the passage.[35] But it appears more and more feasible that the prologue is best illuminated in the context of first-century Judaism. Toward that end a number of articles have postulated the Jewish character of this passage. J. S. King sees in the prologue reflections of descriptions of the Torah in rabbinic writings, and claims that verse 17 explicates what is at the heart of the evangelist's intention to the passage.[36] Morna Hooker argues that verses 14–18 must be read in the light of Exodus 34.[37] But Anthony Hanson pushes the connection between the prologue and Exodus 34 still harder to find an actual translation of Exodus 34:6c in the phrase "grace and truth" in verses 14 and 17 of the prologue.[38]

The discussion of the prologue will continue! All that the most recent research demonstrates is (1) the still unsettled question of the sources and the composition of the passage, and (2) the mounting conviction that the prologue is best understood against an Old Testament–Jewish backdrop.

B. Another special concern of the Johannine community most clearly was the person of the beloved disciple. Current research has probed this mysterious figure of the Gospel as unrelentingly as has research in the past.[39] A monograph on 20:1–10 traces the history of the traditions wedded in the passage and their relationship to Lucan and Marcan material. But the author, Robert Mahoney, concludes from his analysis that the beloved disciple is not as central to the message of the evangelist as many have sup-

---

34. David G. Deeks, "The Prologue of St. John's Gospel," *BTB* 6 (1976): 62–78. Contrast L. Paul Trudinger, "The Prologue of John's Gospel: Its Extent, Content, and Intent," *Reformed Theological Review* (Melbourne) 33 (1974): 11–17.

35. Dosithée Atal, *Structure et Signification des cinq premiers versets de l'hymne johannique au logos*, Recherches Africaines de theologie 3 (Paris: Béatrice-Nauwelaerts, 1972), esp. pp. 79f. and 52–54.

36. "The Prologue to the Fourth Gospel: Some Unsolved Problems," *ExpTim* 86 (1974–75): 372–75. Cf. P. Joseph Cahill, "The Johannine *Logos* as Center," *CBQ* 38 (1976): 54–72.

37. "The Johannine Prologue and the Messianic Secret," *NTS* 21 (1974): 40–58.

38. "John I. 14–18 and Exodus XXIV," *NTS* 23 (1976): 90–101. See also Paul S. Minear, " 'We Don't Know Where . . .' John 20:2," *Int* 30 (1976): 125–39.

39. For a discussion of the issues see Cullmann, *The Johannine Circle*, pp. 67–85; and my *Fourth Evangelist*, pp. 86–101.

posed. Except for 13:21–30 and 19:25–27, the beloved disciple is not important for his own sake but is used when the evangelist finds it advantageous to focus on a non-historical (or historically unknown) figure. In the passage under consideration, for instance, Peter is the concrete historical person who is used to notarize the facts of the empty tomb, and the beloved disciple serves as a model of how facts are seen and used to believe. (Thus the empty tomb is made to function as a sign.)[40]

In the final volume of his monumental commentary, Rudolf Schnackenburg devotes an excursus to the question of the beloved disciple. He argues that the disciple was already an authoritative figure in the Johannine community and that the evangelist simply made use of the authority already attributed to him. The disciple, Schnackenburg argues, was the source behind the tradition which the evangelist (not to be identified with the beloved disciple) developed into a Gospel. The disciple was doubtless a historical person, but the evangelist uses him symbolically to make a theological point. He was originally perhaps a leading disciple from Jerusalem who was not a member of the inner circle of the Twelve.[41]

It is likely that Schnackenburg's balanced treatment of the data is nearest the truth. The beloved disciple was probably a figure (who must remain anonymous to us) who was at once the founder of the Johannine community and the originator of the tradition peculiar to that community. Still, we wonder if Mahoney has not made an important point in the fact that the centrality of this figure is often more the result of the curiosity of exegetes than the deliberate intent of the evangelist.

The five vectors in Fourth Gospel criticism give us a glimpse of the general movements of scholarship in recent years. But we must note finally the presence of what might be termed a *counter-vector*. Lest the reader be given the impression that Johannine studies are about to coalesce in perfect harmony, we give attention to an important voice which stands somewhat alone in his message.

The work of Birger Olsoon signals a new type of Fourth Gospel exegesis. His method is essentially that of text-linguistic interpretation. He hopes to find within the text itself criteria for determining how a given passage is to be understood. This method is wholistic in its approach—drastically

---

40. *Two Disciples at the Tomb: The Background and Message of John 20:1–10*, Theologie und Wirklichkeit, Bd. 6 (Frankfurt: Lang, 1974), esp. pp. 302–9. For a discussion of the broad meaning of sign, see A. Feuillet, "Les christophanies pascal du quatriéme évangile sontelles des signes?" *NRT* 7 (1975): 577–92.

41. *Das Johannesevangelium*, pt. 3, pp. 449–63. See also Stephen S. Smalley, "The Sign in John XXI," *NTS* 20 (1974): 275–88.

different, for instance, from the source and redactional criticisms we have sampled. It is premised on the assumption that semantic structure is the decisive feature of language and the clue to meaning. The process involves analyzing the construction of the text and its connections with "an ideal receiver." Then a description of the "text type" (linguistic and literary characteristics) is possible. With this kind of method (which we can here only briefly outline), Olsoon studies both a narrative text (2:1–11) and a dialogue text (4:1–42). He concludes that the texts are deeply influenced by a Jewish environment, are rooted very early in Christian beginnings, and are subject to interpretation as they stand without recourse to their pre-history. "A textual analysis of the type I have here performed is necessary, and is perhaps the best way to find answers to many problems concerning the Fourth Gospel which are not yet solved."[42]

One cannot help but be impressed by Olsoon's efforts to approach the Gospel in this manner, and his work heralds the beginnings of the application of such a method to this Gospel. It must be seen with further examples of such text-linguistic methods, however, whether or not Olsoon's optimism is justified. For now two observations will suffice: First, it seems that this kind of method invariably tends to belabor the obvious, and Olsoon's work is occasionally subject to this kind of criticism. Second, for all of the profession of new methodology, one finds a good deal of traditional exegesis tucked away under the new rubrics of this kind of a study. Nonetheless, the new direction in which this method points may prove most refreshing and enlightening.

Notwithstanding this counterforce, the observer of current Fourth Gospel criticism is able to trace certain broad movements and tendencies. The Fourth Gospel took its origin within a "Christian school" which was related to a marginal and non-normative form of Judaism. It preserved a distinctive tradition all its own (in either oral or written form) which was at the same time related in some way to the synoptic tradition. Out of that tradition the community developed a unique theological perspective amid a struggle with the synagogue. The Johannine community was marked among other characteristics by a special concern with a Logos Christology and with a figure of the past to whom they looked as their founder. In this enigmatic document we have, it appears, a pristine example of community and Gospel.

---

42. Birger Olsoon, *Structure and Meaning in the Fourth Gospel: A Text-Linguistic Analysis of John 2:1–11 and 4:1–42* (Lund: C. W. K. Gleerup, 1974), pp. 1–17, 186–289; quotation, p. 290.

19.

The Presentation
of Jesus in the
Fourth Gospel

D. Moody Smith

It is the genius of the fourth evangelist to have created a Gospel
in which Jesus as the representative of the world above visits and
really lives in this world without depriving it of its verisimilitude
and without depriving life here of its seriousness.

We speak of the presentation of Jesus rather than Johannine Christology.
Obviously, christological teaching is implied, and even uttered, in the
Fourth Gospel; Jesus teaches about himself. But to speak of Christology
is already to put oneself one stage away from the Johannine presentation.
Christology is second-order language about Jesus. John's Gospel is a first-
order presentation of Jesus. It is not without significance that John wrote
a gospel, and thus presented the story of Jesus, and not a theological tract.
He does not talk about Jesus, but purports to describe how Jesus acted
and talked about himself.

JESUS IN JOHN AND IN
THE SYNOPTICS

Because John does this, his work invites comparison with other Gospels,
especially the Synoptics. (Whether by coincidence or not, no surviving
non-canonical gospel extant in its entirety presents a narrative of Jesus'
ministry, although such gospels certainly existed.) In making this comparison one inevitably faces the question of whether John wrote with
knowledge of any or all of the other Gospels which have been canonized.
Yet whether one decides pro or con, and even if he does not decide at all,
he will find the comparisons and contrasts illuminating on both sides.

Jesus has been described as a healing, teaching, and suffering Messiah,[1] and in all four Gospels he appears as a messiah who performs miracles, teaches, and dies. Yet it is not correct to characterize the Jesus of John's Gospel as suffering, nor are his miracles best described as healings. Jesus is certainly designated a teacher in John, yet his teaching is not, and by its nature could not be, understood by his interlocutors. It is a teaching which can, however, be understood by the Christian reader. Although Jesus' suffering is not emphasized in the synoptic passion narratives, the passion predictions describe his death as suffering, and certainly Mark underscores suffering as characteristic of Jesus' ministry. John, on the other hand, does no more than hint that Jesus' death involves him in the suffering which the Synoptics strongly suggest. The differences between the Johannine and synoptic portrayals of Jesus' miracles, teaching, and death are in large measure the differences between John and the Synoptics, and the distinctive features of the former become all the clearer when set in contrast with the latter.

The miracles of the Fourth Gospel are, in contrast to the Synoptics, referred to as signs.[2] Other miracles of Jesus which are not recounted are also called signs in this Gospel (2:23; 20:30). As such they point to Jesus as one sent from God and are acknowledged outside the immediate circle of his disciples (3:2). They have the express function of raising the question of who Jesus is and suggesting an answer. Those who are impressed by his signs do not for that reason only know who Jesus really is (3:2ff.), but they are on the right track. Those who want to reject Jesus are reluctant even to credit the authenticity and actuality of his signs (chap. 9). Faith in the Gospel of John is not simply belief in miracles, whether or not it was that in the source or traditions from which the Johannine miracle stories were drawn. Nevertheless, Jesus' miracles can only be understood as events credited as historical which perform a positive function in the theology of the Fourth Gospel.[3] One can infer from their prominence that the miracle stories are taken up or recounted in the first instance because

---

1. This typology was suggested to, and adopted by, Robert A. Spivey and me by a former teacher, Paul W. Meyer, now of Princeton Theological Seminary. Simple though it is, it nicely and rather fully comprehends the Gospel's portrayal of Jesus (see *Anatomy of the New Testament: A Guide to Its Structure and Meaning* [New York: Macmillan Company, 1974²], pp. 187ff.).

2. Such nomenclature, as applied to miracles, is not entirely foreign to the synoptic Gospels (Mark 8:11–13; Matt. 12:38f.), Acts (2:22), or even the Old Testament (Exod. 4:8f., 17). In the Synoptics, of course, Jesus rejects the desire to see legitimating signs. Precisely such signs are offered in the Fourth Gospel.

3. A view not accepted, or at least not assumed, by Rudolf Bultmann (*The Gospel of John: A Commentary*, trans. G. Beasley-Murray et al. [Philadelphia: Westminster Press, 1971], p. 119 n. 2). Bultmann appears to question whether the historicity of the signs was important to the evangelist.

they aptly put the question of Jesus' identity (and thus create the possibility of genuine faith), not because the author wished to correct their erroneous theology. This use of miracles in John thus differentiates it from the Synoptics, although there is a sense in which the miracle stories of those Gospels perform a similar function. This is especially true of Mark. But what is explicit in John (i.e., the relationship of miracles to faith) is only implicit in Mark. Moreover, Mark more than John sets a question mark over the validity of miracles as propaedeutic to faith. This is especially true if Peter's confession of Jesus' messiahship, which Jesus all but rejects, is seen as the expression of a popular view of Jesus.

Be that as it may, the miracle tradition which John employs is itself quite different from that found elsewhere. It is often pointed out that none of the demon exorcisms common to the Synoptics is found in John. Perhaps even more astonishing is the fact that no Marcan healing narrative has a Johannine parallel, although there are three or four Johannine stories of a similar sort. The one healing story which has a clear synoptic parallel, the ruler's son, is found in Matthew (8:5–13) and Luke (7:1–10) only and is therefore a Q miracle, something of an anomaly. The Johannine miracle stories with clear Marcan parallels are not healings (6:1–15; 6:16–21). Thus one may say that the miracle traditions of Mark and (therefore also of Matthew and Luke), particularly the healings, are not found in John, while the healing miracles of John are also not found in Mark. For that matter, only four miracle stories in John qualify as healings, that is, only a fraction of the number found in Mark or in the Synoptics generally.

Jesus is repeatedly called Rabbi or Teacher in the Fourth Gospel. In fact, "rabbi" is said to mean "teacher" (1:38). Somehow the knowledge that Jesus was a teacher, or that he taught, so prevalent in the Synoptics, is still alive in John. But in John, Jesus' teaching has a very narrow focus. As we have noted, he teaches about himself and that teaching is distinctly Christian. While there may be, and likely are, authentic sayings and parables of Jesus in the Johannine discourses, the content, as well as the style, of his teaching can scarcely be historically authentic. Efforts to explain the Johannine Jesus teaching as essentially authentic historically, whether by invoking the Qumran parallels or not, often end up appealing to well-worn hypotheses of a secret or esoteric teaching found only in John.[4] Such theories, reminiscent of the ancient Gnostics, can scarcely withstand critical scrutiny.

---

4. See, e.g., the proposal of Oscar Cullmann which introduces an element of speculation, or so it seems to me, into the otherwise well-argued presentation of his case (*The Johannine Circle*, trans. J. Bowden [Philadelphia: Westminster Press, 1976]. pp. 93f.).

Quite apart from the christological content and emphasis, which is so dominant in the Gospel of John, one finds there another peculiarity. Aside from his discourses and disputes about himself and his own role, Jesus utters no teaching whatever during his public ministry. Only after he has withdrawn with his disciples, his own, does Jesus offer instruction regard- ing the conduct of life. Even then his instructions lack specificity. Rather, he commands his disciples to love one another as he has loved them (13: 34f.). The character of his love for them, and therefore of the love to which they themselves are enjoined, is spelled out further in John 15:12f. But such specificity as may be found there has to do only with the extent of love—it is to be limitless in its self-giving—not with concrete ways of living and acting in the world. Even the First Epistle of John, which dwells upon the necessity of love, does not elaborate upon the nature of love by referring to exemplary instances of loving acts.[5]

The richness, color, specificity, concreteness, and variety which charac- terize the teaching of Jesus in the synoptic Gospels are by and large absent from John, as is his apparent willingness and intention to teach anyone who would listen the demands and will of God in view of the near advent of his kingdom. We have no parables, no pronouncement stories in John; therefore, we have none of the brief epigrammatic sayings which are so characteristic of the synoptic Jesus. Neither can much of Q or of the didac- tic elements of Mark, M, or L be found. Instead, the Johannine Jesus expounds Christology and argues with his theological opponents, the Jews.

Any suffering of Jesus at his death can at most be imputed to the Fourth Gospel on the basis of other sources. In John, Jesus goes to the cross by his own volition, and by his own decision. He decides when the hour for his departure in death has arrived, or rather he alone knows when the Father has decreed his hour has come. He lays down his own life; no one takes it from him (10:18). In John, Jesus' death is his glorification, not his hu- miliation.[6] No narrative typifies this more than the Johannine account of his arrest (18:1-11). There is no anguish of Jesus just preceding it. Geth- semane is at most alluded to in 12:27. Instead, Jesus seems to direct his own arrest even as later he will direct his own death (19:28-30). Jesus does nothing, and nothing happens to him, by chance; and this is nowhere

---

5. Contrast, for example, James 2. Although the author of James is not using the vocabulary of love, most of his examples would fit the exhortations of I John 4:7-12, 16-21.

6. On this point I agree with the perspective of Ernst Käsemann, without necessarily endorsing his general view of the death of Jesus in John's Gospel and Johannine the- ology (*The Testament of Jesus: A Study of the Gospel in the Light of Chapter 17*, trans. G. Krodel [Philadelphia: Fortress Press, 1968], p. 19).

more evident than in the account of his death, whether in the passion narrative proper or in the many references and allusions to it throughout the Gospel. In his conversation with Pilate at his trial, Jesus explains what is going on, in contrast to the Synoptics where he remains silent throughout. Perhaps it is too much to say that Jesus interrogates Pilate, rather than Pilate interrogating Jesus; yet it is nevertheless clear that Jesus, not Pilate, is really in control of matters. Indeed, Jesus' own fixity of purpose is contrasted, probably quite deliberately, with Pilate's uncertainty.

By way of summary, in John as in the Synoptics Jesus appears as miracleworker and teacher as well as the one destined for death. Yet in contrast with the Synoptics the Jesus of John performs miracles expressly to signify who he is. Such works are not acts of compassion—only a few are healings —nor are they manifestations of the inbreaking eschatological power. The Johannine Jesus teaching is explicitly, and rather narrowly, christological, lacking the diversity and specificity of the Synoptics. Not surprisingly, then, the tragic dimensions of Jesus' death, his own anguish and suffering in the face of it, are largely absent in John. He dies as man is scarcely known to die. If in Mark Jesus utters a cry of dereliction and in Luke a pious prayer, in John Jesus marks the end of his own earthly ministry and work with the imperious pronouncement "It is finished."

It should be possible to account for the obvious and significant differences in this broadly similar portrayal of Jesus, but this is not easy to do, as the history of the discussion of the problem clearly shows. Traditionally, it has been suggested that John knew the other Gospels and intended to deepen or supplement their presentation. Some critical scholarship, working on similar premises regarding the relationship of John to the Synoptics, arrived at the view that John intended not to supplement but to supplant the other Gospels.[7] Subsequently, the assumption that John knew the Synoptics at all was seriously called into question.[8] Certainly it is now no longer possible to assume that John's differences from the Synoptics can be accounted for by recourse to his alleged intention to augment or to

---

7. This is the viewpoint of Hans Windisch who answers, "Ersetzen" (*Johannes und die Synoptiker: Wollte der vierte Evangelist die älterer Evangelien ergänzen oder ersetzen?* UNT 12 [Leipzig: Hinrich, 1926]). It is also the position of E. C. Colwell. who argues that John seeks to allay objections about Jesus among readers offended by aspects of the synoptic portrayal (*John Defends the Gospel* [Chicago: Willett, Clark, & Co., 1936]).

8. Here the seminal work has been *Saint John and the Synoptic Gospels*, a slim volume whose size belies its importance (P. Gardner-Smith [London and New York: Cambridge University Press, 1938]). An impressive array of scholars, including Bultmann, Dodd, and Raymond Brown, has come to share substantially his position. But by no means all agree; C. K. Barrett and Kümmel, among others, remain unconvinced.

alter them. If he knew one or more of them, he did not regard them as authoritative Scripture. They were more or less at the periphery of his consciousness. The shape and character of the Fourth Gospel was apparently determined by other factors.

At this point it is relevant to indicate the hermeneutical issue raised by the question of John's historical relationship to the other Gospels. Whether or not the fourth evangelist wrote with knowledge of the Synoptics, and whatever his intention with respect to them, the church ultimately accepted John's Gospel as a part of the canon of Scripture alongside and in conjunction with the synoptic Gospels. Therefore, the interpretation of the Fourth Gospel in its original purpose and intent is one thing, but the interpretation of that Gospel in its canonical content may be something else. The possibility, suggested by Käsemann, that the Gospel of John was accepted precisely because in the passage of time it was misunderstood cannot be ruled out *a priori*.[9] But if that is the case, is the interpretation of John in the church of necessity the continuation of that misinterpretation? On these terms a positive answer to this question can scarcely be avoided, at least in principle, but the sharpness of the question and the alternative it implies (historical or churchly exegesis) will be mitigated somewhat if it can be shown that the purpose and character of John is a function of historical circumstances different from those of the Synoptics, rather than of a fundamentally antithetical theological insight or intent.

JESUS IN THE JOHANNINE MILIEU

A consideration of the origin of the distinctive Johannine presentation of Jesus is therefore germane to this question. It has frequently been proposed that John relies upon sources, otherwise unknown, which are different from, although not altogether unrelated to, the synoptic Gospels.[10] In all

---

9. It was perhaps canonized "through man's error and God's providence." Cf. *Testament of Jesus*, p. 75.

10. The most imposing and all-encompassing source theory is still that of Bultmann, *The Gospel of John*, *passim*. Cf. my article "The Sources of the Gospel of John: An Assessment of the Present State of the Problem," *NTS* 10 (1963/64): 336–51, and book, *The Composition and Order of the Fourth Gospel: Bultmann's Literary Theory* (New Haven: Yale University Press, 1965). Bultmann discerned *semeia* (sign) and passion sources, among others, in the Gospel. Some more recent source-critical work, while less comprehensive than Bultmann's, is methodologically better grounded. Robert T. Fortna's *The Gospel of Signs: A Reconstruction of the Narrative Source Underlying the Fourth Gospel* is a painstakingly careful and yet bold effort in an area where source criticism is most likely to prove fruitful, i.e., the Johannine narratives (SNTSMS 11 [London and New York: Cambridge University Press, 1970]).

probability he does, but this hypothesis only pushes the question of the Johannine milieu, and the influences shaping the Fourth Gospel, back one step farther. What sort of Christian community, subject to what influences, produced the substance, as well as the present form, of the Gospel of John?

The answer that this book is the product of a community of Christians who had undergone a traumatic exit or expulsion from the synagogue goes a long way toward explaining the distinctive character of the Fourth Gospel, if it does not answer every question about its provenance and purpose.[11] The miracles are signs, if not proofs, of Jesus' messianic dignity, and the discourses and dialogues of the first half of the Gospel concentrate upon the question of Jesus' identity and role. Just such a fixation upon the christological question fits the proposed church-synagogue milieu. That milieu in turn helps explain the eristic character of the first half of the Gospel especially, as well as its intense concentration on Christology. Jesus himself is portrayed as the origin of the dispute between Christians (Christ-confessors) and the synagogue, and his affirmations about himself become the warrant and justification for the Christian community's claims for him.

Doubtless those very claims are, in John, cast in the terminology of the Johannine community's confession. Yet at the same time, that community would insist that the christological claims and confession are rooted in and derive from Jesus himself.[12] (In this John is like each of the other evangelists, but he goes far beyond them in attributing explicit Christology to Jesus.) Whether that position is defensible is a good question, and one scarcely answerable in terms of whether or not Jesus actually said such

---

11. Certainly the leading recent proponent of this position has been J. Louis Martyn, *History and Theology in the Fourth Gospel* (New York: Harper & Row, 1968). The article by Raymond E. Brown included the present volume, which he kindly allowed me to see in typescript, indicates the importance of Martyn's proposals in contemporary scholarship. Before 1966 Brown himself saw the importance of expulsion from the synagogue as an issue in determining the date and provenance of the Fourth Gospel (see his *The Gospel according to John (I–XII)*, AB 29 [Garden City, N.Y.: Doubleday, 1966], pp. lxx–lxxv, lxxxv). Fortna's source theory is, of course, tied to Martyn's overall view of Johannine origins. The "Gospel of Signs" is the first gospel produced by the Christians who eventually gave us the Fourth Gospel. Certainly his source-critical work has not been carried out in isolation from other necessary historical considerations.

12. This insistence is implicit in the narrative gospel form itself. On the significance of this point see my *John*, Proclamation Commentaries (Philadelphia: Fortress Press, 1976), pp. 58–60; cf. pp. 40f., 54–56. Note also the sophisticated discussion of Franz Mussner, *The Historical Jesus in the Gospel of St. John*, trans. W. J. O'Hara (New York: Herder & Herder, 1967).

things. Probably he did not.[13] The real question is whether John's presentation of him in these terms is on any grounds legitimate. Certainly it is not if one is seeking an "objective historical account," whatever that may be. It is understandable and legitimate only from a distinctively Christian perspective, that is, only on the confessional position that Jesus is the Christ. On that basis John's presentation is legitimate and becomes enlightening and suggestive. From any other perspective it is offensive, just as in the Gospel Jesus' claims for himself are offensive to those who do not share the belief of his followers.

That belief, its implicated hopes and uncertainties, becomes transparent in the so-called farewell discourses and final prayer (chaps. 13–17). There the presupposition of a community of his followers surviving more than a generation after his departure, with all the problems attendant upon their perilous situation in the unfriendly world, is plainly evident. It is such a community, with its peculiar traditions and history, which through one of its gifted members has produced the presentation of Jesus found in the Fourth Gospel.

The possible influence of Gnosticism or Qumran upon the Fourth Gospel is certainly not to be discounted.[14] The evangelist and his community were as much influenced by the surrounding culture as any number of other ancient documents one might mention. Yet the similarity of outlook and terminology between John and some Gnostic and Essene writings may be as much a derivative of a similarity of perspective on the community

---

13. The view that he did not is, I believe, essentially correct and compelling, although certainly not universally shared. Cf. the view of Cullmann, *The Johannine Circle*, and the perspective of Leon Morris, *The Gospel according to John: The English Text with Introduction, Exposition, and Notes*, NICNT (Grand Rapids: Wm. B. Eerdmans, 1971), esp. pp. 45ff. Morris also has recourse to the theory of a private, more esoteric teaching found principally in John. Both Morris and Cullmann refer to the work of Riesenfeld and Gerhardsson.

14. Gnosticism and Qumran frequently figure in discussions of Johannine origins as if they necessarily represented mutually exclusive alternatives, although they do not, as Bultmann already saw. In fact, he claimed that the discovery of the Dead Sea Scrolls supported, rather than refuted, his view of the Gnostic antecedents of the Fourth Gospel. See *Theology of the New Testament*, vol. 2, trans. K. Grobel (New York: Scribner's, 1955), p. 13; cf. *Gospel of John*, p. 23 n. 1. A representative collection of essays on John and Qumran is to be found in the book of that title edited by James H. Charlesworth (London: Chapman, 1972). The Gnostic position is not so well represented in the English literature on John, although one may with profit consult, for a judiciously sympathetic but critical presentation, Rudolf Schnackenburg (*The Gospel according to St. John*, trans. Kevin Smyth [New York: Herder & Herder, 1968], I, 135–52, 543–57). A recent statement of the case for the Gnostic origin and, indeed, character of John is Luise Schottroff, *Der Glaubende und die feindliche Welt: Beobachtungen zum gnostischen Dualismus und seiner Bedeutung für Paulus und das Johannesevangelium*, WMANT 37 (Neukirchen-Vluyn: Neukirchener Verlag, 1970).

and outsiders as the expression of an actual direct influence, much less literary relationship. John, Gnostics, and the Essenes shared a similar sectarian
attitude toward themselves and the world. This clear distinction between
those who are in and those who are not, and the history of that distinction,
is as much as anything else characteristic of the Fourth Gospel and determinative of its nature.[15]

JOHN'S UNIQUE METAHISTORICAL
PRESENTATION OF JESUS

The historical circumstances which produced the Johannine presentation
of Jesus are important for understanding it, but they do not really "explain" it, nor can they be substituted for it. John's presentation of Jesus
comes alive in the narrative itself. He is the Jesus of the past who lived
and worked in first-century Palestine among his fellow Jews. His conflicts
with his contemporaries have been overlaid, but not lost, in the portrayal
of him as the origin of his community's struggle with the synagogue.[16] His
miraculous deeds are no longer harbingers of the power of the inbreaking
kingdom of God, or even signs of the eschatological crisis precipitated by
Jesus' ministry, much less deeds of love and mercy, but are signs of Jesus'
messiahship and sonship. Yet in both cases the present role of Jesus and
his followers is understood as based upon the historic work of Jesus of
Nazareth, interpreted and refracted in the community's tradition and in
the Gospel. Moreover, the death of Jesus, portrayed as the work of his
Jewish opponents, was nevertheless a real event. Although John's portrayal
represents a common early Christian tendency to blame "the Jews" for
Jesus' death, at the same time it contains ample evidence pointing in alternative directions.[17]

The Jesus of the Fourth Gospel is also the Jesus of the church's present
and future. He is the source of the Spirit-Paraclete who abides with the

---

15. Cf. Wayne A. Meeks, "The Man from Heaven in Johannine Sectarianism," *JBL*
91 (1972): 44–72.

16. Martyn does not in his two-level theory about the Johannine episodes emphasize
what he calls their *einmalig* dimension, concentrating rather on the later level in which
the church-synagogue dispute is reflected. Without unwarrantedly ascribing to him any
views on the historicity of the incidents recounted, it is fair to say that on his terms
the basic narratives could have been, and presumably were, regarded by the Johannine
Christians as accounts of Jesus' actual deeds.

17. To give some obvious examples: It is only the high priest who decides and
decrees that Jesus must die, when other Jewish leaders are uncertain what to do about
him (11:50); a cohort of (Roman) soldiers participates in Jesus' arrest (18:3); there
is in John no account of a trial and condemnation before the Sanhedrin; although it is
said that Pilate wished to release Jesus, it is finally he who orders him crucified (19:16,
19–22) and takes responsibility for the execution (19:31, 38); finally, (Roman) soldiers crucify Jesus (19:23 *passim*).

church in its witness and especially in its adversity. Even as Jesus is depicted as present in the conflict with the synagogue which produced the
Johannine community, so he is portrayed as the source of unity, stability,
and purpose in the community's continued existence in the world. This
presence of Jesus is not only given in the contemporary Johannine community, that is, contemporary with the author, it is given as an abiding
assurance to the community about its own future: Jesus will continue to
come to, and dwell among, his disciples.

The Spirit or Paraclete as the mode of Jesus' abiding with his disciples
seems to be a felt reality, a presence regarded as given rather than imagined.[18] It is not, in other words, a mere theological idea of the evangelist
or of his community. Exactly how the Spirit-Paraclete makes the presence
of Jesus known and felt in the community is never stated in so many
words. That is, the exact mode of his activity, the phenomenology of his
presence, is not described, although his function is clear enough. Especially,
the emphasis on the Spirit's bringing to recollection and expanding upon
Jesus' own teaching suggests that the Spirit-Paraclete worked through the
leadership or ministry of the Johannine community. This does not necessarily mean that an ordained ministry of the Johannine church adminis-
tered or dispensed the Spirit. Quite possibly the gift of the Spirit, especially
in the functions described, authenticated the leadership of the church. The
leadership of the Johannine church mediates the presence of Jesus to the
congregation through the Spirit. But does the choice of leadership determine who shall possess the Spirit? In all likelihood the other way around;
the intervention and work of the Spirit determined the leadership of the
church. Yet it is clear that the Spirit alone cannot authenticate itself (cf.
I John 4:6). If the Spirit is nothing other than the continuing presence
and revelation of Jesus to his followers, any continuation of that presence
or revelation must bear a positive relation to the historical figure.[19] John's
Jesus is intended to do just that, despite his Christian theological dress.

The conviction that this Jesus, who lived and died a half-century or more
before and in his exalted state returns through the Spirit to abide with his

---

18. On the Spirit-inspired character of Johannine Christianity and the Johannine
community, see George Johnston, *The Spirit-Paraclete in the Gospel of John*, SNTSMS
12 (London and New York: Cambridge University Press, 1970), esp. pp. 127–48; also
Käsemann, *Testament of Jesus*, esp. pp. 36ff.; and Alv Kragerud, *Der Liebingsjünger im
Johannesevangelium: Ein exegetischer Versuch* (Oslo: Osloer Universitätsverlag, 1959),
esp. pp. 93–112.

19. On Jesus and the Paraclete see Raymond E. Brown, "The Paraclete in the
Fourth Gospel," NTS 13 (1966–67): 113–32, esp. 126–32. Cf. also R. Alan Culpepper's interesting observations regarding the parallel functions of the Paraclete and the
beloved disciple, *The Johannine School: An Evaluation of the Johannine-school Hypothesis Based on an Investigation of the Nature of Ancient Schools*, SBLDS 26 (Missoula: Scholars Press, 1975), pp. 267–70.

church, is more than an important historical personage of continuing significance and memory is expressed in the recurring references to his pre-existence, heavenly abode, and descent and ascent to and from the world of men. To say that these "mythological" concepts are exhausted in their meaning by their existential significance, that is, their expression of the importance of Jesus for the believer or the community, may be an unwarranted truncation of their scope. On the other hand, such an assertion is certainly not without foundation. Hazardous as it may be to claim that the evangelist did not take the language of pre-existence and accompanying phenomena literally, it is nevertheless unnecessary to attribute to him the crudest kind of understanding of this constellation of mythological concepts. Surely he shows evidence of some sophistication, whether literary or theological, throughout his Gospel. If an existentialist, or other modern, interpretation of this Johannine language runs the risk of reading too much into the Gospel, or excluding certain dimensions of its meaning, it is not therefore necessarily wrong in principle. The simple, yet mysterious, character of Johannine language invites the reader to inquire about and explore its meaning.

The presentation of Jesus in the Fourth Gospel is multidimensional. He is still the Jewish man of Galilee. But he is also the spiritual presence with, and head of, the community of disciples which we may safely call his church. He has been with the church in its past struggles and will continue with it into the foreseeable future. His nature is, however, never understood until his origin and destiny with God is truly comprehended. He and the Father are one; he goes forth from the Father and returns; not only he, but his followers, will abide with the Father for all eternity. There is no major aspect of this Johannine presentation of Jesus which is absolutely unique or foreign to other strains of early Christianity, even to the synoptic Gospels.[20] What is uniquely Johannine is the way these aspects of, or perspectives on, Jesus are made to coalesce into a single narrative so

---

20. Needless to say, however, John has his unique style, vocabulary, and emphases. John's Gospel is in some significant ways a strange and different book. Yet the main lines of his presentation of Jesus seem to be positively related to, even if they are not derived directly from, the portrayal of him which we find in the Synoptics and in other New Testament writings. The late Sir Edwin C. Hoskyns wrote: "The test that we must in the end apply to the Fourth Gospel, the test by which the Fourth Gospel stands or falls, is whether the Marcan narrative becomes more intelligible after reading the Fourth Gospel, whether the Pauline Epistles become more transparent, or whether the whole material presented to us in the New Testament is breaking up into unrelated fragments" (*The Fourth Gospel*, ed. F. N. Davey [London: Faber & Faber, 1947], p. 133). This test is ultimately theological and cannot finally depend solely upon exegetical conclusions pro or con about literary and historical relationships. It is the question of whether John's presence in the canon makes theological sense.

that each is always present in almost every part of the narrative. For example, in the prologue the reader is reminded of the historical figure as well as the Jesus Christ who is the origin of grace and truth. In the account of his deeds one is similarly aware that the worker of signs is more than a miracle-worker out of the past. In the account of his death one is, on the one hand, made cognizant of the overarching cosmic and historic frame in which that death is overcome, but, on the other, not allowed to forget that it was a real, historic death of a human being.[21] The farewell discourses are words of the exalted one; but he is still recognizably the person whose ministry has just been recounted, and the shadow of his death now looms in the foreground. It is the genius of the fourth evangelist to have created a Gospel in which Jesus as the representative of the world above visits and really lives in this world without depriving it of its verisimilitude and without depriving life here of its seriousness.

A CONCLUDING RESERVATION

Yet the presentation of Jesus in the Fourth Gospel should not be represented as the culmination of a development in the New Testament, or among the Gospels, of such a sort and magnitude as to render all that came before it or stands beside it superfluous. If John Calvin rightly saw in the Fourth Gospel the key to the others, he did not for that reason regard it as rendering the others unnecessary.[22] The uniqueness of the Gospel of John and, indeed, its theological worth, is enhanced when it is placed alongside the other Gospels and seen with them. Apart from the Synoptics the Johannine portrait of Jesus specifically, as distinguished from other characters such as the man born blind, the woman of Samaria, and Nicodemus, loses much of its depth and color. In fact, if we had had no Synoptics, the Johannine portrait of Jesus would doubtless have produced a rather different configuration of Christian belief than has actually emerged historically. Whether or not John should be described as incipiently

---

21. For a balanced presentation of the significance of Jesus' death in John, see J. T. Forestell, *The Word of the Cross: Salvation as Revelation in the Fourth Gospel*, AnBib 57 (Rome: Pontifical Biblical Institute, 1974).

22. ". . . I am accustomed to say that this Gospel is a key to open the door for understanding the rest; for whoever shall understand the power of Christ, as it is here strikingly portrayed, will afterwards read with advantage what the others relate about the Redeemer who was manifested" (John Calvin, *Commentary on the Gospel according to John*, trans. W. Pringle [Edinburgh: Calvin Translation Society, 1847], p. 22).

docetic,[23] whether or not it is in part the product of Gnostic influence, it is nevertheless the case that there is not in that Gospel a depiction of the man Jesus fully capable of standing guard over his genuine humanity. That depiction is present in the synoptic Gospels, whether because of or in spite of the intentions of their authors.

Moreover, the valid spirituality of the Fourth Gospel would have been jeopardized if Jesus' statement that his kingdom is not of this world had been allowed to stand unbalanced by the Synoptics' presentation of the kingdom as a reality breaking into this world. That Johannine statement about the kingdom is not wrong, even by synoptic standards, but standing alone and in the Fourth Gospel it opens wide a door to the temptation to make of Christianity a thoroughly otherworldly religion. In its canonical context, however, the potential thrust of such a statement is balanced, yes, blunted, by other statements about the relationship of God's kingdom (and Christ) to this world. Indeed, such statements do not really contradict the theological intention of the fourth evangelist, who portrays Jesus praying to the Father not to take his followers out of this world, but to protect them from the Evil One.

---

23. Käsemann, *Testament of Jesus,* pp. 26, 66, 70.

20.

Johannine Ecclesiology—
The Community's Origins

RAYMOND E. BROWN, S.S.

> Recent methodology in gospel research is casting light not only
> on church history but also on the growth of theology and faith
> in the first century.

Up to 1965 most of the discussion of Johannine ecclesiology centered
around the failure of the Fourth Gospel to mention the church, or minis-
terial church order, or the institution of the Eucharist and baptism. For
some scholars[1] this silence implied that the evangelist was indifferent to,
ignorant of, or even hostile to such ecclesiastical institutions. Others[2]
probed behind the silence to find implicit ecclesiastical references in the
Gospel which, when combined with explicit references in the Johannine
Epistles, showed John to be deeply concerned with church and sacraments.
In my commentary I tried to steer a middle course between these two
views, although I veered more toward the latter than toward the former. Be
that as it may, one would have to admit that the argument from silence is
quite uncertain and that probably there is little more to be gained from
this approach to Johannine ecclesiology.

A more fruitful approach has been opened up in Johannine scholarship
of the last ten years by attempts to reconstruct the history of the church
of the Fourth Gospel in relation to other forms of Christianity in the first
century. Chronologically and logically this research throws light on three

---

1. I discussed the views of Eduard Schweizer and Rudolf Bultmann in this vein in
The Gospel according to John, AB 29, 29a (Garden City, N.Y.: Doubleday, 1966,
1970), I, cv–cxiv.
2. "John does however show, more clearly than any other evangelist, an awareness of
the existence of the Church" (C. K. Barrett, *The Gospel according to St. John* [Lon-
don: SPCK, 1955]). Oscar Cullmann finds references "in many, even if not all the
narratives, to the sacraments" (*Early Christian Worship*, SBT 10 [London: SCM Press,
1953], p. 117).

phases of Johannine community history: (A) The pre-Gospel era and the origins of the Johannine community (or parts of it) in relation to mid-first-century Jewish and Jewish-Christian groups. (B) At the end of the century, in the Jamnia period when the Gospel was written,[3] the relation of the Johannine community to the synagogues and to other Christian communities. (C) Post-Gospel developments within the community as can be detected from the Johannine Epistles when they are understood as an attempt to deepen or correct theological tendencies which emerged from the Fourth Gospel. Ultimately I hope to develop an overall picture of all three phases, but the space limitations of this essay will force me to confine myself to Phase A, the pre-Gospel phase, which is fundamental for understanding the methodology employed and which supplies an essential basis for discussing the other two phases.[4]

To what extent does the Fourth Gospel tell us about the Johannine community's origins? Wellhausen and Bultmann were the pioneers in insisting that the Gospels tell us primarily about the church situation in which they were written and only secondarily about the situation of Jesus which *prima facie* they describe. I would prefer to rephrase that insight as follows. *Primarily*, the Gospels tell us how an evangelist conceived of and presented Jesus to a Christian community in the last third of the first century, a presentation that indirectly gives us an insight into that community's life at the time when the Gospel was written. *Secondarily*, through source analysis the Gospels reveal something about the history of the evangelist's christological views and, indirectly, something about the community's history earlier in the century, especially if the sources the evangelist used had already been part of the community's heritage. *Thirdly*, the Gospels offer limited means for reconstructing the ministry and message of the historical

---

3. Except for occasional maverick efforts (e.g., that of Bishop John A. T. Robinson to date all the New Testament books before A.D. 70!), there is wide consensus that the Fourth Gospel was written after the destruction of the Temple when the teaching center of Judaism had moved to Jamnia (Jabneh)—largely a Pharisee Judaism and thus no longer so pluralistic as before 70. More precisely the Gospel was written after A.D. 85, the approximate date for the introduction into the synagogues of the reworded Twelfth Benediction (of the *Shemoneh Esreh* or Eighteen Benedictions), called the *Birkat ha-Minim*, involved a curse on heretical deviators, including those who confessed Jesus to be the Messiah. See J. L. Martyn, *History and Theology in the Fourth Gospel* (New York: Harper & Row, 1968).

4. Phase B was discussed in my presidential address to the Society of Biblical Literature in San Francisco in December 1977, entitled "Other Sheep Not of This Fold— The Johannine Perspective on Christian Diversity in the Late First Century," *JBL* 97 (1978): 5–22. Phase C was the subject of the Shaffer Lectures at Yale in February 1978. The three phases have now been reworked and appear as a unified treatment in R. E. Brown, *The Community of the Beloved Disciple* (New York: Paulist Press, 1979).

Jesus. The reader will note the limitation I have placed upon the secondary ecclesiastical information that comes to us from the Gospels—if the recoverable pre-Gospel sources or traditions were formed at an earlier stage in the life of the same community that received the final Gospel, they help us to detect that community's history; but if they were composed outside the community and imported to supplement (or even correct) the community's thought, they may supply very little ecclesiastical information about the community itself. In the instance of the Fourth Gospel, scholars have sometimes assumed that the evangelist used and corrected sources taken from outside the community, indeed, even non-Christian sources. Today, however, the dominant trend presupposes a much closer connection between the detectable pre-Gospel sources/traditions/editions[5] and the Johannine community (or at least factions within that community).

This presupposition has governed several recent attempts to trace pre-Gospel Johannine ecclesiastical history. Let me first survey these attempts as a concrete way to help the reader to understand the approach,[6] and then let me enter into dialogue with them so that the most important church issues can be brought to the surface.

RECENT RECONSTRUCTIONS OF JOHANNINE COMMUNITY HISTORY

The most elaborate reconstruction of Johannine church origins is that of J. L. Martyn,[7] who proclaims as a principle: "The literary history behind the Fourth Gospel reflects to a large degree the history of a single community which maintained over a period of some duration its particular and somewhat peculiar identity." Martyn distinguishes three periods of Johannine community history: Early, Middle, and Late:

---

5. I discussed various theories of pre-Gospel sources and earlier editions that had been proposed in scholarship up to 1966 (*Gospel according to John*, I, xxviii–xxxiv). Developments since then are discussed in Kysar (*The Fourth Evangelist and His Gospel* [Minneapolis: Augsburg Publishing House, 1975], pp. 13–54). All these theories posit pre-Gospel material, so that this article is not dependent on any one theory of sources or editions.

6. Moreover, the most interesting reconstructions of pre-Johannine history, those of J. L. Martyn, whose views will not be readily available to the majority of readers since they are published abroad, and Georg Richter. A full-scale digest in English of Richter's views was recently published (see A. J. Mattill, "Johannine Communities behind the Fourth Gospel: Georg Richter's Analysis," *TS* 38 (1977): 294–315.

7. J. L. Martyn, "Glimpses into the History of the Johannine Community," in *L'Evangile de Jean: Sources, rédaction, théologie*, ed. M. de Jonge, BETL 44 (Gembloux: Duculot, 1977), pp. 149–75. This volume represents the collected papers of the 1975 Colloquium Biblicum Lovaniense (Journées Bibliques).

I. THE EARLY PERIOD. (Before the Jewish revolt until some point in the eighties.) The pre-Gospel formation began with separate homilies, e.g., a homily underlying John 1:35–49 wherein a preacher sought to persuade (fellow) Jews, who had well-formed messianic expectations, to *come* to Jesus and *find* him to be the Messiah. The miracles of Jesus were narrated as signs that he was the Messiah. Success in conversions at first produced relatively little alienation from the Jewish heritage, viz., no debates about the validity of the Torah or about the Gentile mission. The resultant Johannine group consisted of *Christian Jews* who stood "in a relatively untroubled stream of social and theological continuity precisely within the synagogue." One of the preachers in this inner-synagogue messianic group gathered the traditions and homilies about Jesus into a rudimentary written gospel, somewhat similar to the Signs Gospel or Signs Source posited by many scholars. "The possibility that the Beloved Disciple was a historical person who played a role in the Early Period cannot be pursued in the present essay."

II. THE MIDDLE PERIOD. (Presumably the late eighties.) Becoming suspicious of this rapidly growing messianic group, some in the synagogue demanded exegetical proof for what the group proclaimed about Jesus. This led to midrashic debates and to degrees of alignment within the synagogue for and against the group. Two traumas precipitated new developments. The first trauma occurred early in the Middle Period when the synagogue authorities introduced the reworded *Birkat ha-Minim* (curse on the deviators) into the liturgical service in order to be able to identify and eject those who confessed Jesus as the Messiah. Some of the messianic group (and some attracted toward it) turned back to remain safely within the synagogue community. Those who continued in the group now became *Jewish Christians* (no longer Christian Jews), separate and alienated from the synagogue. The second trauma occurred when the synagogue authorities, in order to prevent further defections to the Jewish-Christian group, put on trial and executed some of the Johannine community's evangelists on the charge that they were misleading Jews "into the worship of a second god alongside Adonai" (see John 5:18; 10:33; 16:2). Expulsion and persecution led the Johannine community to new christological formulations; and instead of a simple *heilsgeschichtlich* continuity with Jewish expectations, a dualism of above/below came to the fore. Jesus was now presented as a stranger who had come from above (3:31) and been rejected by "his own people" (1:11). Those who accept him are hated by this world and are not of this world (17:14, 16); they are no longer "Jews" but have become "true Israelites" (1:47) chosen by the stranger from above (15:16). By the judgment of the synagogue itself, they are no longer disciples of Moses but disciples of Jesus (9:28).

III. THE LATE PERIOD. (Not precisely dated by Martyn.) This complex period involved the increasing self-identification of the Johannine community in relation to other Christian groups (and not only in relation to the synagogue). *First*, a relationship to crypto-Christians who remained within the synagogue. The Johannine group argued that one is either from above or from below and that no fence-straddling is possible. The Christian Jews in the synagogue were judged to be unable to maintain a dual allegiance; they were equivalent to the hated "Jews" and were "disciples of Moses, not of Jesus." Moreover the crypto-Christians seemed to have aided the synagogue authorities in their persecution of the Johannine Jewish Christians by informing on them. *Second*, a relationship to other Jewish Christians who had left the synagogue and were scattered by persecution. These were the "other sheep" of 10:16 who would ultimately be joined with the Johannine community into one flock under one Good Shepherd.

When the Gospel was written, at least a quadrilateral situation existed:
1. The synagogue of "the Jews"
2. Crypto-Christians (Christian Jews) within the synagogue
3. Other communities of Jewish Christians who had been expelled from the synagogue
4. The Johannine community of Jewish Christians

By way of comparison with Martyn's reconstruction I would like to digest even more briefly the reconstruction of G. Richter,[8] whose guiding principle is *prima facie* diametrically opposed to Martyn's principle of continuity. Richter is not tracing the history of one community adapting itself to changing circumstances, for he finds in the Fourth Gospel traces of the theological views of four different communities, all of whom worked with and upon an early Johannine *Grundschrift*:

I. MOSAIC-PROPHET CHRISTIANS. Rejecting the idea of a Davidic Messiah, a group of Jews resembling the Ebionites proclaimed Jesus as a prophet-like-Moses. Expelled from the diaspora synagogues in the area of North Palestine, Syria, and the Transjordan, this group produced a *Grundschrift*, a foundational gospel-like work, out of the traditions that were available (including a Signs Source and a non-synoptic passion account).

II. SON OF GOD CHRISTIANS. Part of this Jewish-Christian community developed a higher Christology of Jesus as the pre-existent divine Son of God, a figure who came down from heaven bringing salvation. This Christology caused conflict with other members of the community who retained the earlier Christology of the group. The Son of God Christians split from the Mosaic-prophet Christians and rewrote the *Grundschrift* as a vehicle of their higher Christology.

---

8. "Präsentische und futurische Eschatologie in 4. Evangelium," in *Gegenwart und kommendes Reich: Schülergabe Anton Vögtle zum 65. Geburtstag*, ed. P. Fiedler and D. Zeller (Stuttgart: Katholisches Bibelwerk, 1975), pp. 117–52.

For example, they added the *Logos* hymn of 1:1–13 and the pre-existence state-ments of the Johannine Jesus. The rewriter may be called the evangelist.

III. DOCETIST CHRISTIANS. Some of the Son of God Christians interpreted the evangelist's high Christology in a docetic way: Jesus' divine origins were so stressed that he became a totally divine being whose earthly appearance was only an illusion. The docetist Johannine Christians withdrew from the commu-nities of Group II, as attested in I John 2:19, but continued a missionary activ-ity which produced strife. The Gospel, as it had been revised by the evangelist, served the Johannine docetists as their Gospel, and no new docetic revision was made—only a docetic interpretation.

IV. REVISIONIST CHRISTIANS. A redactor who was decidedly anti-docetic re-wrote the *Grundschrift* by making additions (1:14–18; 19:34–35) and com-posed First John as an apologetic defense of a theology of Jesus as the Son of God come in the flesh. The result was that he and his congregation stood some-where in between the Johannine Christians of Group I and Group II, for in re-jecting the docetism of Group III he had pulled back to a position that was less adventurous than that of the evangelist of Group II.

One might discuss other reconstructions as well,[9] but those of Martyn and Richter are divergent enough to give us an idea of both the method-ology and the span of such reconstructions.

We may profit from considering the points in which they agree,[10] for those would be points commonly found in most modern attempts to analyze Johannine pre-Gospel history. *First*, for both authors a major and basic stage of Johannine Gospel composition took place among Christian Jews of relatively low christological views. Martyn and Richter differ on whether these Christian Jews maintained messianic expectations similar to those which became standard after the seventies (Martyn) or were of a

---

9. Somewhat similar to Richter in maintaining that certain stages in the Gospel resemble the thoughts of the First Epistle of John is J. Becker, "Aufbau, Schichtung und theologiegeschichtlich Stellung des Gebetes in Johannes 17," ZNW 60 (1969): 56–83; and "Die Abschiedsreden Jesu in Johannesevangelium," ZNW 61 (1970): 215–46. He sees in the last discourse the work of three or four different Johannine theologians and a cross section of the theological history of the Johannine community. Oscar Cullmann has the following reconstruction: "We thus arrive at the following line, moving back in time: Johannine community—special Hellenist group in the early community in Jerusalem—Johannine circle of disciples—disciples of the Baptist—hetero-dox marginal Judaism" (*The Johannine Circle*, trans. J. Bowden [Philadelphia: West-minster Press, 1976], p. 87).

10. There is more agreement than first meets the eye, for Richter's last two groups might be considered as post-Gospel and therefore to have come after Martyn's Late Period. (It is in I John that we find opponents who are docetic and a reaction to them. There are no clear anti-docetic passages in the Gospel itself, at least according to the judgment of many commentators.) The real comparison, then, is between Richter's Groups I and II and Martyn's three stages.

peculiarly sectarian outlook[11] such as the (later) Ebionites (Richter). *Second*, both authors see the higher Johannine Christology as a later development in a conflict situation which pitted the holders of this high Christology not only against the synagogue but also against Christian Jews of a lower Christology. For Richter this was a split of two Johannine communities; for Martyn it seems that most of the community of the Early Period became the holders of high Christology in the Middle Period, so that one can speak of a continuity of one community whose Christian opponents were the crypto-Christians within the synagogue.

A DIALOGUE WITH THESE
RECONSTRUCTIONS

Since I am concentrating on what I have called Phase A of Johannine community history, that is, the pre-Gospel era, my dialogue will be primarily with Martyn's reconstruction of the Early and Middle Periods and Richter's reconstruction of Groups I and II.

(A) I agree with Martyn that the Johannine community had its origins among Jews who found that Jesus met their messianic expectations. Martyn finds his key to this in John 1:35–51, where in the first few days of the ministry Andrew, Peter, Philip, and Nathanael come to Jesus and hail him as Rabbi, Messiah, the one written about in the Law and the Prophets, the King of Israel, and the Son of God. Clearly this picture is not historically true to the ministry of Jesus, for the synoptic Gospels show some of these same disciples reaching such a perception about Jesus only with great difficulty and only later in the ministry (or, indeed, after the resurrection). But John's picture may be historically true to the origins of the Johannine community if the disciples named in chapter 1 are characteristic of the first Jews who came to Jesus, and if the titles they give to him echo the way in which such Christian Jews evaluated Jesus. The plausibility of such a picture is confirmed by Acts 2:36 where Peter, as the spokesman of the first followers of Jesus after the resurrection, proclaims Jesus as the Messiah who fulfills the expectations of Israel vocalized in the Law and the Prophets.[12] This means that Johannine origins were not much different

---

11. I am trying to be careful about speaking of pre-70 Judaism in terms of standards or orthodox versus sectarian or heterodox. If we accept the language of Josephus (*Life* 10), the Pharisees, the Sadducees, and the Essenes were all sects, so that there was no standard Judaism until the Pharisees outlasted the others and their theology became orthodoxy.

12. We may compare Luke 24:44: "Everything written about me in the law of Moses and the prophets and the psalms must be fulfilled" and John 1:45: "We have found him of whom Moses in the law and also the prophets wrote."

from what we know of churches which would later associate themselves
with the memory of the Twelve. (Thus, against Richter, I see no need to
posit *at the beginning* a Johannine group of Jews that rejected the Davidic
Messiah, for such a theory contradicts John 1:35–51).

Furthermore, since the disciples of John 1 witness the miraculous sign
at Cana, the first of Jesus' signs, and believe in him (2:11), I have no difficulty with Martyn's suggestion that the first Jews who believed in Jesus
gathered miracle stories and used them in an apologetic way to gain believers. Once again this would mean that Johannine origins were at first
not so startlingly different from the origins of other Christian communities,
for any reconstruction of a signs source must resemble the miracle collection that is posited in pre-Marcan research.[13]

Moving beyond Martyn's reconstruction but not contrary to it,[14] I would
judge it likely that an important component in the Johannine memory of
the Jews who first came to believe in Jesus consisted of followers of John
the Baptist. In other words, I would judge John 1:35–51 to be giving us
community history also in that detail. It is noteworthy that recently D.
Moody Smith has defended Bultmann's association of the signs source
with Christians who had been converted from the following of John the
Baptist and who used it as a missionary tract to convert still more followers of his.[15]

More important, I think we can fill in the lacuna left by Martyn when
he declined to pursue the subject of whether "the Beloved Disciple was a
historical person who played a role in the Early Period." In my judgment
the fact that he was a historical person and a companion of Jesus becomes
all the more obvious in these new approaches to Johannine ecclesiology.
Later in community history when the Johannine Christians were clearly
distinct from groups of Christians who associated themselves with memories of the Twelve (e.g., with the memory of Peter), the claim to possess

---

13. Although I do not accept a source theory in the Bultmannian sense and I doubt
that one can reconstruct the pre-Johannine miracle collection in the exact way in which
Fortna has done, in my AB commentary (I, 195) I maintained, "It is reasonable to
suppose that there were collections of miracles in the corpus of Johannine material that
was edited to give us the Gospel." For pre-Marcan miracle catenae see P. J. Achtemeier,
JBL 89 (1970): 265–91.

14. In another article, Martyn speaks of the author of the source writing to Jews
whom he regards as potential converts and allowing them "to behold a chain of Jews,
expectant like themselves, proceeding to discover the fulfillment of their messianic hope
not in the Baptist, but rather in Jesus of Nazareth" ("We have Found Elijah," in
R. Hamerton-Kelly and Robin Scroggs, eds., *Jews, Greeks, and Christians* [Leiden: E. J.
Brill, 1976], p. 210).

15. "The Milieu of the Johannine Miracle Source," in *Jews, Greeks, and Christians*,
pp. 164–80.

the witness of the beloved disciple enabled the Johannine Christians to defend their peculiar insights in Christology and ecclesiology. The "one-upmanship" of the beloved disciple in relation to Simon Peter in the Fourth Gospel illustrates this. But such a depiction would have been counterproductive if the beloved disciple were a purely imaginative symbol or if he had never been with Jesus, for the community's self-defense would surely have crumbled under such circumstances.[16] Indeed, if I may introduce First John into the discussion, the appeal of that author to eyewitness tradition[17] is needed to correct abuses within the community and to refute those who indiscriminately appeal to the Spirit (I John 4:1). The author of the Epistle was not himself an eyewitness, but his community is one that is aware of its roots in eyewitness tradition—an awareness that supports the thesis that the beloved disciple was part of Jesus' following. This has been perceived by D. Moody Smith:[18] "If the Johannine community which produced the Gospel saw itself in traditional continuity with Jesus, we are in a position to perceive in the 'we' of the prologues of both Gospel and Epistle not the apostolic eyewitness per se, but a community which nevertheless understood itself as heir of a tradition based upon some historical witness to Jesus."

I would further suggest that the Johannine picture becomes more understandable if the beloved disciple, like some of the named disciples of John 1:35-51, had been a disciple of John the Baptist, indeed, perhaps the unnamed disciple of 1:35-40 (a passage which mentions two disciples and identifies one of them as Andrew). Thus the beloved disciple would have had a background similar to that of some prominent members of the Twelve, even as the Johannine community in the first stage of its existence consisted of Christian Jews who shared the messianic outlook which marked the beginnings of communities that would stem from the Twelve.

---

16. I am not claiming that every instance which depicts the beloved disciple is necessarily historical. Rudolf Schnackenburg has argued that the beloved disciple, although a historical companion of Jesus, was "certainly not present" at the Last Supper ("On the Origin of the Fourth Gospel," *Perspective* 11 [1907]: 239f.). I am not so certain, but I admit that John has highlighted him to such a degree that his importance in Gospel scenes goes beyond the importance he would have had in the eyes of an impartial outside observer during the ministry. Of course, for the evangelist this is a matter of perception, not of deception.

17. First John 1:1: "What we have heard, what we have seen with our own eyes, what we looked at and felt with our own hands"; 2:7: "An old commandment that you had from the first."

18. D. Moody Smith, "Johannine Christianity: Some Reflections on Its Character and Delineation," *NTS* 21 (1974-75): 236. The "we" passage from the prologue to the Gospel is 1:14: "And the Word became flesh and made his dwelling among us. And we have seen his glory."

The proposed identification of the beloved disciple has often been debated and rejected on the grounds that elsewhere, when the Fourth Gospel is speaking of the community hero, it clearly identifies him as "the disciple whom Jesus loved,"[19] and no such clarification is found in 1:35–40. The objection loses its force if it is realized that the unnamed disciple of chapter 1 was not *yet* the beloved disciple because at the beginning of the Gospel story he had not yet come to understand Jesus fully—a christological development that would place a distance between him and the other named disciples of chapter 1 and would bring him uniquely close to Jesus. Consonant with the theory that the Gospel is giving us an insight into Johannine ecclesiological growth, I think it no accident that the beloved disciple makes his appearance by name only in "the hour" (13:1) when Jesus, having loved his own, "now showed his love for them to the very end." This does not mean that that disciple was not present during the ministry, but that he achieved his *identity* in a christological context. During his lifetime, whether in the period of Jesus' ministry or in the post-resurrectional period, the beloved disciple lived through the same growth in christological perception that the Johannine community went through, and it was this growth that made it possible for the community to identify him as the one whom Jesus particularly loved.[20]

Parenthetically, I am inclined to change my mind (as Rudolf Schnackenburg also has done) about the likelihood that the beloved disciple was one of the Twelve, namely, John son of Zebedee. In my Anchor Bible commentary I maintained that "the combination of external and internal evidence associating the Fourth Gospel with John son of Zebedee makes this the strongest hypothesis." I now recognize that the external evidence and internal evidence are probably not able to be harmonized. By setting the beloved disciple over against Peter, the Gospel gives the impression that he was an outsider to the group of best-known disciples, a group which would have included John, if we may judge from Acts 3:1; 4:13; 8:14. The external evidence identifying the beloved disciple as John is a further step in a direction, already visible in the New Testament itself, of simplifying all Christian origins by reduction to the twelve apostles. Cullmann, then, may well be right in his long-held theory that we cannot know the name of the

19. See 13:23–26; 19:25–27; 20:2–10; 21:7, 20–23, 24. There is no identification, however, of the "other disciple" of 18:15–16, even though he is probably the beloved disciple; thus, Franz Neirynck, *ETL* 51 (1975): 115–41.

20. "The actual founder of the Johannine community is more likely to be found in the figure of the Beloved Disciple . . . the role of the Beloved Disciple is the key to the character of the community" (R. A. Culpepper, *The Johannine School*, SBLDS 26 [Missoula: Scholars Press, 1975], p. 265).

beloved disciple, even though we can suspect: "He is a former disciple of John the Baptist. He began to follow Jesus in Judaea when *Jesus himself was in close proximity to the Baptist.* He shared the life of his master during Jesus' last stay in Jerusalem. He was known to the high priest. His connection with Jesus was different from that of Peter, the representative of the Twelve."[21]

Now we must ask how the Johannine forefathers, stemming from disciples of John the Baptist who expressed their faith in Jesus under the traditional titles of Jewish expectation, developed into a community with a Christology so high that it provoked suspicion and hatred within the synagogue.

(B) Martyn offers no explicit explanation for the appearance of high Christology in the Middle Period. Richter supposes a conflict between the Johannine Christians of Group I and higher christologians of Group II. I am not satisfied with either of these approaches, and I think that a more precise catalyst must be postulated for the high Johannine Christology. In reference to Martyn's earlier work, Smith[22] observed: "This extension of his thesis suggests connections through a sort of Jewish Christianity with less orthodox forms of Jewish life and thought." Following up on this suggestion, I think evidence can be found in the Gospel itself for the entrance into Johannine Christianity of another group which catalyzed the christological developments. The disciples of John the Baptist from 1:35–51 constitute the main followers of Jesus until 4:4–42, when a large group of Samaritans are converted.[23] This second group of believers is not converted by the first (4:38), and its appreciation of Jesus as "the Savior of the world" (4:42) differs from the standard Old Testament expectations mentioned in chapter 1.[24] The fact that Jesus reconciles his disciples of chapter 1 to the Samaritan converts of chapter 4 (see 4:35–38) means that Richter is not correct in seeing a sharp hostility between the two Johannine groups.

---

21. *The Johannine Circle*, pp. 77f. I remain firmly convinced, however, that Cullmann is wrong in identifying the beloved disciple as the evangelist.

22. "Johannine Christianity," p. 240. See n. 11, above, on the use of "orthodox."

23. Once again we have a picture more true to what happened in church history than to the historical ministry of Jesus, if we can judge from the synoptic evidence. Although Luke 17:11–19 mentions the healing of a Samaritan leper, Jesus does not evangelize the Samaritans (Luke 9:52–53; Matt. 10:5). By not having the Samaritans leave Samaria to follow Jesus, John is sensitive to the fact that the following of Jesus during the ministry did not really include Samaritans.

24. In the Old Testament, Yahweh is the salvation of Israel and of the individual Israelite, but the term "savior" is not associated with the expected king (although in the LXX of Zech. 9:9 "saving" appears). Nowhere else is Jesus called "savior" during the public ministry. The most that one can prove, however, from John 4:4–42 is the use by the Samaritans of a title that is not traditionally messianic; I admit that one cannot prove pre-existence Christology.

Rather the acceptance of the second group by the majority of the first group is probably what brought upon the whole Johannine community the suspicion and hostility of the synagogue leaders. Is it accidental that after the conversion of the Samaritans in chapter 4 the Gospel concentrates on the rejection of Jesus by "the Jews" in light of the charge that he was making himself God's equal (5:18)? The Johannine Jesus (who undergoes the harassment historically suffered by the Johannine community), when he says that he has come forth from God (8:41), is challenged by "the Jews," who exclaim: "Aren't we right, after all, in saying that you are a Samaritan?" (8:48).

Does this imply that the second group which entered Johannine history consisted entirely of Samaritans? I think there are indications that the situation was more complex. When the Samaritans are being converted by Jesus (and not by his first disciples), he affirms a clear Jewish identity: "Salvation is from the Jews" (4:22). He deliberately rejects a distinctive tenet of Samaritan theology, for he denies that God is to be worshiped on Gerizim. At the same time (4:21) he assumes a peculiar attitude toward Jewish cult, for he predicts that God will not be worshiped in Jerusalem either. (This constitutes another difference from what we know of the Christianity proclaimed by the Twelve [and perhaps by the first Johannine Christians], for Acts 2:46 and 3:1 associate the apostles with faithful Temple attendance.) Accepting these indications, one may posit that the second group in Johannine history consisted of Jews of peculiar anti-Temple views[25] who converted Samaritans and picked up some elements of Samaritan thought, including a Christology that was not centered on a Davidic Messiah.[26]

Several trends in modern Johannine exegesis reinforce this thesis. Wayne Meeks,[27] among others, has detected strains in John similar to Samaritan thought; and he argues that the Johannine church has incorporated members, Jewish and Samaritan, who had a high Moses piety. This Moses piety

---

25. While Christology was the main point of dispute between the Johannine Christians and the synagogue, surely a second disagreement centered on the Johannine theology of the replacement of Jewish cult. There are specific texts about Jesus replacing the tabernacle (1:14, with *skēnoun* as a play on *skēnē*) and the Temple (2:19–21; 4:21); and there is an elaborate arrangement in chaps. 5–10 where Jesus speaks on the occasion of the Sabbath, Passover, Tabernacles, and Dedication and in each instance applies to himself the theme of the feast (see Brown, *Gospel according to John*, I, cxli, cxliv).

26. In my judgment Richter attributed to Group I what was the characteristic of Group II.

27. *The Prophet King: Moses Traditions and the Johannine Christology* (Leiden: E. J. Brill, 1967), pp. 318f. See E. D. Freed, "Did John Write His Gospel Partly to Win Samaritan Converts?" *NovT* 12 (1970): 241–56.

has now been shifted over to Jesus (6:32–35; 7:23). It was said that Moses saw God and then came down to reveal to the people what God had said, but John affirms that no one has ever seen God except Jesus who has come down from God to speak of what he heard above (3:13, 31; 5:20; 7:16). Cullmann has argued for "a very close connection, if not a complete identity" between those in John who convert Samaritans by their preaching and the Hellenists described in chapters 6–8 of Acts.[28] Those Jerusalem Hellenists (i.e., Jews who spoke *only* Greek as distinct from Hebrews or Jews who spoke Hebrew or Aramaic) spoke strongly against the Temple (7:48–50); and when they were driven out of Jerusalem, they proclaimed Christ to Samaria. Many of us would not be so certain that one can make this identification as simply as Cullmann does,[29] especially when he seeks to crowd the followers of John the Baptist, Hellenists, Samaritans, and the author of Hebrews under the one umbrella of "Heterodox Judaism." But the evidence of Acts does show that the group which I postulate as entering the Johannine community and serving as a catalyst in the break with the synagogue is not a mere figment of the imagination. And the insistence of Acts (8:1) that the Jewish leaders were especially hostile to the Hellenists, while they tolerated the apostles, corresponds well with my reconstruction. Inevitably the combination of high Christology, opposition to the Temple cult, and Samaritan elements, which were characteristic of the second group that entered the stream of Johannine Christianity,[30] would have made Johannine believers in Jesus particularly obnoxious to more traditional Jews.[31] The *Birkat ha-Minim* probably only formalized a break that had begun at an earlier stage, and for that reason I would judge that some of the developments of Martyn's Middle Period antedated A.D. 85.

---

28. *The Johannine Circle*, p. 43. This book recapitulates almost a lifetime of Cullmann's work on John. We remember that B. W. Bacon wrote of John as *The Gospel of the Hellenists* (New York: Holt, 1933).

29. Reviews of Cullmann by W. Meeks, *JBL* 95 (1976): 304f.; and R. E. Brown, *TS* 38 (1977): 157–59.

30. One would wish to know if this group was also responsible for the high pneumatology of the Fourth Gospel and its picture of the Paraclete. In Acts 6:5, 10 Stephen is "full of the Spirit" and speaks with the Spirit; in Samaria the struggle between Simon Magus and Peter (who completes the work of Philip the Hellenist) concerns the Spirit. But most of the Christian figures in Acts are moved by the Spirit, and it is not possible to show that the Hellenists had a special pneumatology.

31. The hostility between the Jewish leaders and Jesus is sharper in John than in any other Gospel. As Martyn and Meeks have insisted, alienation from the synagogue and the theology of the Johannine group reinforced each other: the theology made the synagogue leaders suspicious; suspicion increased the alienation, and alienation heightened the theological emphases—the Johannine Jesus became the stranger from above. See W. Meeks, "The Man from Heaven in Johannine Sectarianism," *JBL* 91 (1972): 44–72.

(C) While Martyn and Richter call attention to the fact that the basic component in Johannine community history was Jewish,[32] I do not think that either of them does sufficient justice to the presence of Gentiles in that community before the Gospel was written. C. K. Barrett[33] is right when he affirms: "The composition of the book itself took place in a setting which was partly, but only partly, Jewish." The very methodology of reading ecclesiastical history from traces in a description of the ministry of Jesus will inevitably neglect non-conflict situations, for conflicts leave sharper traces. And I would judge with Martyn and others that the type of struggle over admitting Gentiles which marked Pauline history did not occur in Johannine church history, where the admission of Gentiles must have been relatively painless. The Johannine struggle between church and synagogue was over the divinity of Jesus, and the Law entered the picture only as a ramification of the struggle: life-giving terms once applied to the Law (water, light) now apply to Jesus.[34] The group that constituted the second strain in Johannine Christianity (see B above) proclaimed Jesus as "the Savior of the world" (4:42) and promoted a worship in Spirit and truth rather than on Gerizim and in Jerusalem (4:21, 23). Thus Johannine theology was clearly universalist in tendency. Indeed, George MacRae[35] suggests that John may have been uniquely universalist in presenting Jesus in a multiplicity of symbolic garbs, appealing to men and women of all backgrounds, so that they understood that Jesus transcends all ideologies. By hailing Jesus as the stranger from above, Johannine Christians relativized ethnic questions: natural birth does not bring admittance into the kingdom, but begetting from above through water and Spirit (3:3, 5). If "salvation comes from the Jews" (4:22), being a Jew is scarcely a designation to be cherished in the Fourth Gospel. Thus one can see why admission of Gentiles would not have been a matter of conflict in Johannine history.

If the relative silence of the Fourth Gospel does not discount the pres-

---

32. "The history of the Johannine community from its origin through the period of its life in which the Fourth Gospel was written forms to no small extent a chapter in the history of *Jewish* Christianity" (Martyn, "Glimpses," p. 175).

33. *The Gospel of John and Judaism* (Philadelphia: Fortress Press, 1975), p. 19.

34. Important here is the major study by Severino Pancaro (*The Law in the Fourth Gospel: The Torah and the Gospel, Moses and Jesus, Judaism and Christianity according to John* (Leiden: E. J. Brill, 1975), although Pancaro concludes from his study that John is *not* writing for Gentiles.

35. "John's message is that Jesus can be approached in many ways, but he can only be understood on Christian terms, not Jewish or Greek or Gnostic" ("The Fourth Gospel and Religionsgeschichte," *CBQ* 32 [1970]: 24).

ence of Gentiles,[36] are there positive indications that Gentiles had come into the Johannine community, even if in a relatively late period of development? I see a reference to Gentiles in 7:35, where the Jews exclaim to one another, "Where does this fellow intend to go that we won't find him? Surely he isn't going off to the Diaspora of the Greeks [Hellēnōn] to teach the Greeks?" Some interpreters wish to read the genitive as explicative: "the Diaspora which consists of Greeks, that is, Greek-speaking Jews." However, why would the Jerusalem Jews hint that Jesus would find a better and safer hearing among Jews who spoke another language? A more likely suggestion is that he would escape Jewish efforts to destroy him by going among the Gentiles, with the genitive read as one of direction: "the Diaspora among the Greeks." This ironic suggestion (which by the rules of Johannine irony unconsciously predicts what will happen) is that Jesus will become a Jew in the Diaspora living among Gentiles and teaching them successfully—and once again the portrait of the Johannine Jesus is really a portrait of the Johannine community.

Even more important is the passage 12:20–23, where the arrival of "some Greeks" asking to see Jesus is a sign that "the hour" has come— the ministry of signs is over and the hour of glory through cross and resurrection is at hand. That this is symbolic of the coming of the Gentiles to Jesus is strongly suggested by 12:37–43, where the Johannine Jesus reflects on his rejection by those Jews who refused to believe in him despite the signs he had done. He cites Isaiah 6:10, the classical Old Testament passage used in the New Testament to explain the Jewish failure to believe in Jesus and the reason for turning to the Gentiles (Acts 28:26–28; Matt. 13:13–15). The localization of this passage at the end of the public ministry in John may be an indication that when the Johannine community was expelled from the synagogue (see 12:42) it then interpreted the entrance of Gentiles into the community (which had already occurred) as a sign that there was no future for the proclamation of Jesus among "the Jews" who controlled the synagogues and who had rejected him—although the community continued its love/hate dialogue with the crypto-Christians who did not have the courage to leave the synagogues. Increasingly, as "the Diaspora among the Greeks," the community saw its task and destiny "to teach the Greeks."

As I have explained, these observations cover the history of the Johan-

---

36. "There are motifs in the Johannine literature that go beyond the controversy with Judaism" (Smith, "Johannine Christianity," p. 247).

nine community before the Gospel was written. An even richer field of investigation lies in the diagnosis of the alignment of the Christian groups at the period contemporary with the Gospel itself.[37] But even this introductory study suggests that recent methodology in Gospel research means that Acts will no longer be such a solitary source for knowing what happened in the first century of Christianity outside the Pauline churches. New light will be cast not only on church history, but also on the growth of theology and faith, and even on the extent (and need) of inner-Christian "ecumenism" in the first century.

---

37. For this further study, see n. 4.

Contributors

Paul J. Achtemeier, Herbert Worth and Annie H. Jackson Professor of Biblical Interpretation, Union Theological Seminary, Richmond, Va.

Raymond E. Brown, S.S., Auburn Professor of Biblical Studies, Union Theological Seminary, New York, N.Y.

Charles E. Carlston, Norris Professor of New Testament Interpretation, Andover Newton Theological School, Newton Centre, Mass.

Frederick W. Danker, Professor of Exegetical Theology, Christ Seminary— Seminex, St. Louis, Mo.

John R. Donahue, S.J., Professor of New Testament, Jesuit School of Theology, Berkeley, Cal.

Joseph A. Fitzmyer, S.J., Professor of New Testament, Catholic University of America, Washington, D.C.

Lloyd Gaston, Professor of New Testament, Vancouver School of Theology, Vancouver, B.C.

Arland J. Hultgren, Associate Professor of New Testament, Luther-Northwestern Seminaries, St. Paul, Minn.

Howard Clark Kee, Professor of New Testament, Boston University School of Theology, Boston, Mass.

Jack Dean Kingsbury, Associate Professor of New Testament, Union Theological Seminary, Richmond, Va.

Robert Kysar, Co-pastor, Christ's United Lutheran Church, Gordon, Pa.

James P. Martin, Principal, Vancouver School of Theology, Vancouver, B.C.

Ralph P. Martin, Professor of New Testament and Director of Graduate Studies Program, Fuller Theological Seminary, Pasadena, Cal.

Paul S. Minear, Professor of Biblical Theology, Emeritus, Yale University Divinity School, New Haven, Conn.

Robert Morgan, The Faculty of Theology, Linacre College, The University of Oxford, England

Eduard Schweizer, Professor of New Testament Theology and Exegesis, University of Zürich, Switzerland

D. Moody Smith, Professor of New Testament Interpretation, Duke University Divinity School, Durham, N.C.

Charles H. Talbert, Professor of Religion, Wake Forest University, Winston-Salem, N.C.